Emergent Masculinities

NEW AFRICAN HISTORIES

SERIES EDITORS: JEAN ALLMAN, ALLEN ISAACMAN,
AND DEREK R. PETERSON

David William Cohen and E. S. Atieno Odhiambo, *The Risks of Knowledge*
Belinda Bozzoli, *Theatres of Struggle and the End of Apartheid*
Gary Kynoch, *We Are Fighting the World*
Stephanie Newell, *The Forger's Tale*
Jacob A. Tropp, *Natures of Colonial Change*
Jan Bender Shetler, *Imagining Serengeti*
Cheikh Anta Babou, *Fighting the Greater Jihad*
Marc Epprecht, *Heterosexual Africa?*
Marissa J. Moorman, *Intonations*
Karen E. Flint, *Healing Traditions*
Derek R. Peterson and Giacomo Macola, editors, *Recasting the Past*
Moses E. Ochonu, *Colonial Meltdown*
Emily S. Burrill, Richard L. Roberts, and Elizabeth Thornberry, editors, *Domestic Violence and the Law in Colonial and Postcolonial Africa*
Daniel R. Magaziner, *The Law and the Prophets*
Emily Lynn Osborn, *Our New Husbands Are Here*
Robert Trent Vinson, *The Americans Are Coming!*
James R. Brennan, *Taifa*
Benjamin N. Lawrance and Richard L. Roberts, editors, *Trafficking in Slavery's Wake*
David M. Gordon, *Invisible Agents*
Allen F. Isaacman and Barbara S. Isaacman, *Dams, Displacement, and the Delusion of Development*
Stephanie Newell, *The Power to Name*
Gibril R. Cole, *The Krio of West Africa*
Matthew M. Heaton, *Black Skin, White Coats*
Meredith Terretta, *Nation of Outlaws, State of Violence*
Paolo Israel, *In Step with the Times*

Michelle R. Moyd, *Violent Intermediaries*
Abosede A. George, *Making Modern Girls*
Alicia C. Decker, *In Idi Amin's Shadow*
Rachel Jean-Baptiste, *Conjugal Rights*
Shobana Shankar, *Who Shall Enter Paradise?*
Emily S. Burrill, *States of Marriage*
Todd Cleveland, *Diamonds in the Rough*
Carina E. Ray, *Crossing the Color Line*
Sarah Van Beurden, *Authentically African*
Giacomo Macola, *The Gun in Central Africa*
Lynn Schler, *Nation on Board*
Julie MacArthur, *Cartography and the Political Imagination*
Abou B. Bamba, *African Miracle, African Mirage*
Daniel Magaziner, *The Art of Life in South Africa*
Paul Ocobock, *An Uncertain Age*
Keren Weitzberg, *We Do Not Have Borders*
Nuno Domingos, *Football and Colonialism*
Jeffrey S. Ahlman, *Living with Nkrumahism*
Bianca Murillo, *Market Encounters*
Laura Fair, *Reel Pleasures*
Thomas F. McDow, *Buying Time*
Jon Soske, *Internal Frontiers*
Elizabeth W. Giorgis, *Modernist Art in Ethiopia*
Matthew V. Bender, *Water Brings No Harm*
David Morton: *Age of Concrete*
Marissa J. Moorman, *Powerful Frequencies*
Ndubueze L. Mbah, *Emergent Masculinities*
Patricia Hayes and Gary Minkley, editors, *Ambivalent*
Judith A. Byfield, *The Great Upheaval*
Mari K. Webel, *The Politics of Disease Control*
Kara Moskowitz, *Seeing Like a Citizen*

Emergent Masculinities

Gendered Power and Social Change in the Biafran Atlantic Age

Ndubueze L. Mbah

OHIO UNIVERSITY PRESS
ATHENS

Ohio University Press, Athens, Ohio 45701
ohioswallow.com
© 2019 by Ohio University Press
All rights reserved

To obtain permission to quote, reprint, or otherwise reproduce or distribute material from Ohio University Press publications, please contact our rights and permissions department at (740) 593-1154 or (740) 593-4536 (fax).

Printed in the United States of America
Ohio University Press books are printed on acid-free paper ∞ ™

29 28 27 26 25 24 23 22 21 20 19   5 4 3 2 1

Library of Congress Cataloging-in-Publication Data

Names: Mbah, Ndubueze L., 1985- author.
Title: Emergent masculinities : gendered power and social change in the Biafran Atlantic age / Ndubueze L. Mbah.
Description: Athens : Ohio University Press, 2019. | Includes bibliographical references and index.
Identifiers: LCCN 2019028629 | ISBN 9780821423882 (hardcover) | ISBN 9780821423899 (paperback) | ISBN 9780821446850 (pdf)
Subjects: LCSH: Sex role–Nigeria, Eastern–History. | Slave trade–Social aspects–Nigeria, Eastern. | Slave trade–Political aspects–Nigeria, Eastern. | Masculinity–Social aspects–Nigeria, Eastern. | Igbo (African people)–Africa, Eastern–Social life and customs.
Classification: LCC HQ1075.5.N6 M33 2019 | DDC 305.3096694–dc23
LC record available at https://lccn.loc.gov/2019028629

To Janet, Menna, and Adannaya;
And in memory of Ndubueze C. Mbah.

Contents

List of Illustrations ix
Preface and Acknowledgments xi

Introduction 1

Chapter 1 Gendered Kinship, ca. 1480–1850 31
Political and Economic Backgrounds of a Slaving Society

Chapter 2 Military Slaving, ca. 1650–1890 61
The Making of Warrior Masculinities

Chapter 3 Gendered Slavery in the Bight of Biafra, ca. 1750–1890 94
A Transatlantic Perspective

Chapter 4 Gendered Emancipation, ca. 1860–1940 130
New Ogaranya Masculinities

Chapter 5 Revolutionary Masculinities, ca. 1850–1940 158
Female Dissident Sexualities

Conclusion 182

Appendix: Lineage Charts 192
Glossary 197
Notes 201
Bibliography 263
Index 305

Illustrations

MAP

I.1	The Bight of Biafra	xvii

FIGURES

I.1	Ohafia war dance	19
1.1	Ikpirikpe drum	44
2.1	Ohafia war dancer	77
4.1	Missionary residence of Rev. Robert Collins, built ca. 1911	146
4.2	Home of Kalu Uwaoma, built ca. 1916	147
A.1	Chiasara matrilineage	192
A.2	Slave lineage integration I	193
A.3	Slave lineage integration II	193
A.4	Slave lineage integration III	194
A.5	Integration of resident strangers	195
A.6	Unyang Uka	196

Preface and Acknowledgments

This project has evolved from a dissertation on Ohafia-Igbo gendered sociopolitical transformations between 1850 and 1920 into a broader historical ethnography of gendered Atlanticization in the Bight of Biafra and West Africa between 1750 and 1920. I am indebted to the generous support of many people and institutions. Funded by a Wenner-Gren Fieldwork Grant, I conducted much of the original research between 2010 and 2012, including 170 oral interviews with Ohafia-Igbo men and women as well as archival research at the Nigerian National Archives, British National Archives, and National Library of Scotland. *Emergent Masculinities* was conceived amid a vibrant Africanist intellectual community at Michigan State University, where Dr. Peter Alegi directed my general African historiography, Dr. Walter Hawthorne introduced me to a rapidly maturing field of African slavery and Atlantic history, and Dr. James Pritchett guided me through the robust field of African anthropology. This enabled me to situate the Ohafia-Igbo within the scholarship on the south-central African matrilineal belt and to foreground the sociopolitical and ideological conflicts among individuals, and between individuals and structures, as pivotal to gendered social transformations. Most importantly, in addition to very generous graduate mentorship, Dr. Nwando Achebe imparted a rigorous Afro-feminist methodology that enabled me to question prevailing assumptions that patriarchy and egalitarian social norms were timeless features of Igbo culture and history. Thank you Professor Achebe and Professor Folu Ogundimu for providing me a home at MSU. *Daalu!*

The dissertation had revealed the distinctive dual-sex sociopolitical systems of the Ohafia-Igbo, where women developed and maintained relatively more powerful institutions of political rulership, constituted a class of agrarian breadwinners, and were central to the social reproduction of the dominant matrilineage systems until the second half of the nineteenth century. Examining what such a system meant for Ohafia-Igbo men required reconciling diverse gendered local narratives with the literature on female power and authority in West Africa, as well as with the nascent scholarship on African masculinities. The scholarship of Ifi Amadiume, Sandra Greene, Nwando Achebe, Ugo Nwokeji, Emily Osborne, and Stephan Miescher inspired me to explore how the Atlantic slave trade and its repercussions facilitated Biafran male dominance in cash crop productive and exchange economies, Biafran men's mobilization of missionary and colonial institutions, and Biafran women's contestation of marginalization through slaveholding, slave and commodity trading, politicized divination, and the practice of becoming female husbands. It was thus necessary to situate the novel forms of masculinity, femininity, and sexuality that became prominent in the early twentieth century within a *longue durée* perspective that captures the complex traditions of Biafran cross-Atlantic engagements.

In 2013, I began to reconcile the numerous Ohafia-Igbo oral traditions of gendered slave production and slave use during the eighteenth and nineteenth centuries with the transformations in dual-sex sociopolitical systems and shifts in gendered definitions of ethnicity in a multiethnic frontier region. The preliminary result was a chapter in *Gendering Ethnicity in African Women's Lives* (Shetler, 2015), in which I chronicle the competing gendered discourses of Ohafia-Igbo ethnicity, including gender-distinctive memorialization rituals and performative traditions, respectively privileging female-centered matrilineage reproduction and male-centered heroic heritage of warrior masculinity.

In the course of my one-year visiting professorship at Davidson College (2013–2014), I developed a course on comparative slavery systems and immersed myself in Gale's Eighteenth Collections Online. The sources I encountered raised new questions about the Ohafia-Igbo ethnographic evidence. In order to fully historicize the ramifications of slave production for Atlantic and Biafran domestic markets as coterminous with the changes in dual-sex systems and conceptions of masculinity, I expanded *Emergent Masculinities* from 1850 to 1750. This coincided with my relocation to SUNY Buffalo, where I joined the North and South Atlantic graduate faculty. Teaching the North and South Atlantic graduate seminar and having stimulating conversations with colleagues Hal Langfur, Erik Seeman, Jason Young, and Dalia Muller encouraged my reconceptualization of *Emergent Masculinities* as a cis-Atlantic project. Thus, I adapt the concept of Atlanticization to outline the articulations of Biafran and British American cross-Atlantic productive, exchange, and consumption economies, as arenas of gendered sociopolitical differentiation, through the performances of hegemonic masculinities. A generous SUNY Humanities Institute Research Fellowship enabled me to devote the 2016 calendar year to revising the manuscript and helped me share my research with a broader intellectual community through the Humanities Institute Scholars@Hallwalls public lecture and conversation series.

Most critical in the manuscript revision was my transatlantic reevaluation of the Bight of Biafra region's eighteenth- and nineteenth-century gendered slavery systems as pivotal to the emergence of Igbo men in dominant political and economic positions. Such a framing of Biafra's slavery systems considers two questions. First, how did the region's eighteenth-century slave supply to dominant Atlantic markets such as British Jamaica, as evident in the Trans-Atlantic Slave Trade Database, shape local configurations of gendered identities and power? Second, how did the nineteenth-century post-abolition reorientation of slave supply to regional domestic markets consolidate the emergence of men in dominant economic and political positions in Igboland? The evidence reveals that, contrary to accepted knowledge, the Bight of Biafra not only generated predominant numbers of female captives but also retained more enslaved women than enslaved men because of the centrality of women to both patrilineage and matrilineage expansion, the social reincorporation of upwardly mobile male ex-slaves, and the preponderant performances of *ogaranya* oligarchic masculinity through slaving and elite polygyny. These imperatives in turn were predicated on the resilient dual-sex systems of Biafran productive economies and the fluid manipulations of kinship systems. More important, from a transatlantic perspective that privileges how slave production and slave use were designed in gendered terms, the critical distinction between kinship and chattel slavery also conceals an important commonality, namely that the physical and sexual exploitation of enslaved women ensured male ascendancy in the Atlantic world.

I would like to express my profound gratitude to Onwuka Njoku, who introduced me to the Ohafia community, sustained my intellectual curiosity, and clarified my numerous ethnographic questions. I am immensely grateful to my Ohafia research assistants (rather, teachers) Ifeanyi Ukoha, Uduma Uka, and Ndukwe Otta, who unceasingly identified new interviewees and collaborators, perspicaciously debated interpretations of rituals and material culture practices, and gave generously of their time, patience, and hospitality to see this project to fruition. I thank especially the numerous Ohafia women and men whose time, hospitality, and friendship abated my estrangement, and who availed me the personal and family narratives that form the bedrock of this book. *Kaa nu wo!* I am particularly grateful to Kalu Uko for introducing me to the Ohafia *dibia* community and providing rich ethnographic insights into the cross-ethnic gendered and ritual domestications of Atlantic political economies in the Cross River frontier. The vibrant voices of Ohafia-Igbo women, and their tenacious diurnal and biannual political enforcement rituals and practices, afforded indispensable antidotes and alternative perspectives to male-centered narratives, unearthing a much more complex history of gendered Atlanticization. It was especially the *ikpirikpe ndi inyom* (female courts) of Elu, Ebem, Amangwu, and Akanu who taught me that lineages were the major sites of Atlanticization. These women first advanced the argument that enslaved women were pivotal to Ohafia-Igbo agrarian and lineage reproduction, in contrast to the marginality of enslaved men, and they supplied the case studies of female masculinities and dissident sexualities examined in this book. With funding from the SUNY Community Engagement and Public Policy Fellowship and the Wenner-Gren Engaged Anthropology Grant, I was able to return to Ohafia to share my research findings with my collaborators, through video ethnography screenings and community debates across twenty-four villages in 2015. During this revisit, I also conducted twenty-two additional oral interviews, clarified lingering research questions, and photographed important cultural artifacts.

I am thankful for the staff of the Nigerian National Archives at Enugu and Calabar, especially Tony Nwaneri, Mr. Alakwe, and Mr. Ayuk for locating, preserving, and making accessible numerous endangered documents. I thank Robbie Mitchell, Kenneth Dunn, and Alison Metcalfe, special materials manuscript curators at the National Library of Scotland, Edinburgh, for locating the obscure journals and illuminating correspondence of Rev. Robert Collins. I am grateful for the hospitality and accommodation afforded by Chinelo Igbokwe and Bernard Mbah, which made my research at the British National Archives possible. I thank my gracious colleagues at Michigan State University, Davidson College, and SUNY Buffalo who have read drafts of the various chapters of this book and offered constructive feedback, including Cajetan Iheka, Joseph Davey, Hal Langfur, Susan Cahn, Erik Seeman, David Herzberg, and Pat McDevitt. The strain of writing a book was significantly ameliorated by the supportive and collegial environment afforded by the SUNY Buffalo History Department. I especially wish to thank my past chair James Bono and current chair, Victoria Wolcott, for their mentorship. Chapter 3 of this book benefited from the rigorous peer review of the SUNY Buffalo History Department's work-in-progress series. Various parts of this book have been presented at conferences of the African Studies Association in the past four years, as well as at invited campus talks at the University of Illinois at Urbana–Champaign, the Wesleyan University, and Davidson College. Earlier versions of chapters 4 and 5 have been peer-reviewed and published in the *Journal of West African History* (vol. 3, no. 1, spring 2017) and the *Journal of Women's History* (vol. 29, no. 4, winter 2017), respectively. Thought-provoking conversations with Martin Klein and Stephan Miescher encouraged me to examine the regional dynamics of Ohafia-Igbo military slaving and the subjective meanings of Atlanticization for marginal slaves. This book would not have turned out for the better without the support of director Gillian Berchowitz and the rigorous two-stage review process of the Ohio University Press. The painstaking and critical feedback of the series editors Jean Allman, Allen Isaacman, and Derek Peterson, as well as that of two external readers further clarified the book's arguments. An additional grant from the SUNY Buffalo College of Arts and Sciences Julian Park Fund helped complete this book.

 I am grateful for the friendship and support of Fred Smith, Erin and Paul Drucker, Angela and Alex Soriano, Chloé Revuz and Chema Silva, Barbara Bono, Kerry Reynolds, Lakisha Simmons, Tandy Hamilton, Hershini Young, Adam Malka and Jennifer Holland, Yan Liu, Camilo Trumper, Kristin Stapleton and Gregory Epp, Mark Nathan, Sasha Pack, Michael Rembis, Nadine Murshid, Elizabeth Bowen, and Anna Ball. I thank God for the goodwill of the Mbah, Okpalugo, Asoluka, and Baumann families. Most importantly, I am thankful for my beloved wife and best friend, Menna, our daughter Adannaya, my mother Janet, and my siblings, without whose steadfast love this project would lack any fervor. Menna dear, thank you for your patience, for leaving friends and a career in Washington, DC, to join and support me in Buffalo, for the most beautiful gift of Adannaya, for reading multiple chapter drafts of this book, and for making this life so hopeful and cheerful. I dedicate this book to Janet, Menna, and Adannaya, that life might endure for the better.

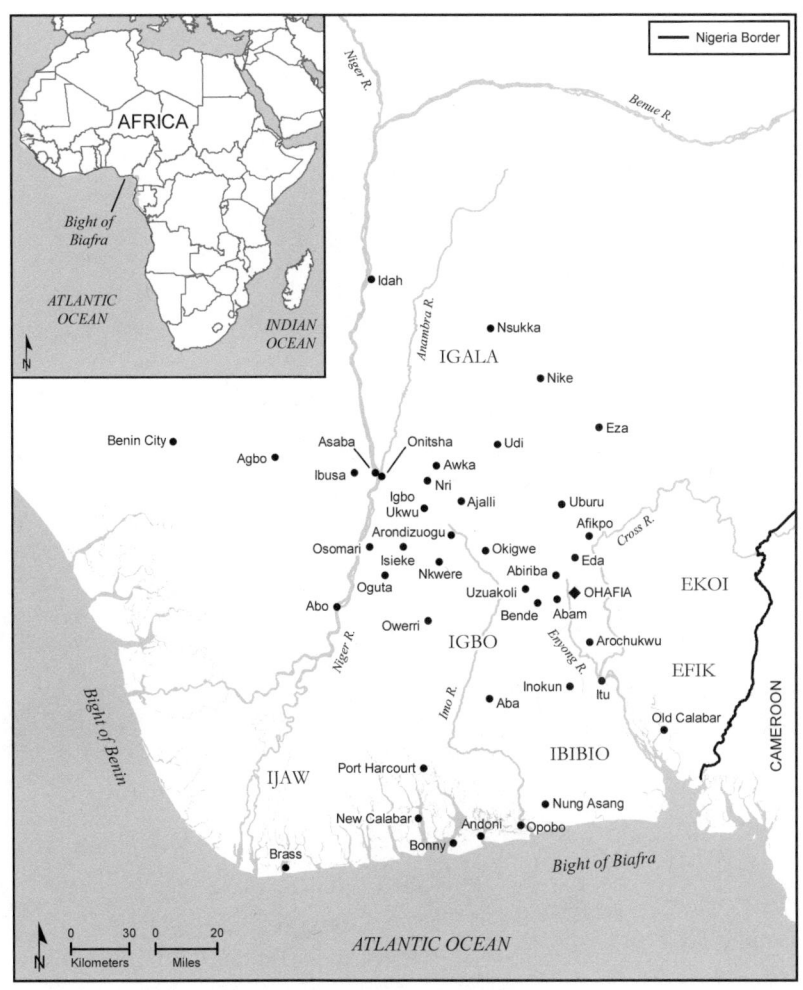

MAP I.1. *The Bight of Biafra. Map by Brian Edward Balsley, GISP*

Introduction

BETWEEN 1750 and 1920, the Igbo peoples of southeastern Nigeria in the historic Bight of Biafra region reconciled their local traditions, gender ideologies, sociopolitical systems, commercial networks, and knowledge systems with the successive Atlantic political economies of the slave trade, "legitimate trade" (or slavery-driven cash crop production), and colonialism in pursuit of individual sociopolitical advancement. The Atlanticization of indigenous political economies (channeling the political and economic forces of the Atlantic world through local institutions) transformed gender identities and regimes, most evident in the emergence of extractive and often violent forms of hegemonic masculinity (*ufiem*).[1] By masculinizing key sociopolitical institutions, Atlanticization enabled men to gradually gain power over women, ushering a shift from precolonial female sociopolitical superiority to male political and economic dominance in the colonial period. The evolving gender regimes, which epitomized hegemonic masculinities, in turn defined how the region participated in Atlantic modes of production and consumption. Lastly, this gendered Atlanticization molded the experiences of Biafra's homeland populations and its diaspora.

More than any other Igbo subethnic group, the Ohafia-Igbo people of the intracoastal Cross River frontier memorialize oral and performative traditions depicting the Bight of Biafra's gendered Atlanticization. Ohafia-Igbo traditions use the dynamic idiom of "cutting a head" (*igbu isi*) to express how African peoples in the region indigenized broad changes in the Atlantic world through shifting local articulations of ufiem. Thus, before the Atlantic slave trade began in force in the 1750s, men accomplished ufiem when they went to war and returned with human head trophies. Retaliatory headhunting had developed among various Bight of Biafra Cross River migrant communities jostling for territory in the seventeenth century. Ufiem evolved from male-centered military practices, the complementary male sphere of a dual-sex political economy within which women were agrarian breadwinners and politically superior. Warrior ufiem did not originally grant men direct economic and political power over women. Rather, it guaranteed adult masculinity, security of wealth and life, and usufruct rights over male individuals who had failed to cut a head (or its equivalent) and were consequently categorized as *ujo* (degendered and socially alienated). The ujo suffered enslavement, dispossession, inability to marry, and public ridicule. Alternative institutions of masculinity such as yam cultivation, *dibia* (divination/spirit mediumship), and secret societies would become subordinate to the hegemony of warrior ufiem. Before the 1750s especially, ufiem was a form of distinction among men, and only possible to the extent that matriliny and complementary feminine power and institutions allowed.

However, in the course of the region's Atlantic slave trade between 1750 and 1840, slave captives came to symbolize "heads" (*isi*) cut by warriors to attain ufiem. Men's dominant role in military slave production vested them with a new form of private wealth, which few women possessed. As women came to constitute the majority of those enslaved for domestic purposes in Igboland, the inherent value of the slave as both a symbolic head and alienable property sowed the seed for the gradual perception of wealth as a masculine achievement, inaugurating men's supersession of women as breadwinners. At the same time, male military slave production introduced new political and religious traditions that reified the preexisting dual-sex sociopolitical system.

From the 1840s, as the "legitimate trade" cohered with and facilitated an expanding domestic and sexual slavery system, seemingly disparate forms of property became equated with prestige heads. These heads that warrior-merchants appropriated to achieve ufiem ranged from yams (*Dioscorea* sp.) to plantations, slaves, wives, guns, kerosene lanterns, fez caps, glass beads, and European textiles. This cadre of emergent male elites used the domestication of violence, especially in the form of female captivity (*ike nwami*), to secure their power over women and other dependents.[2] Ohafia-Igbo society elaborately celebrated men and women rich in cross-Atlantic commodities for having performed hegemonic *ogaranya* (wealth/wealthy person) masculinity. As a new form of ufiem, ogaranya hegemony stemmed from the capacity of wealthy individuals to usurp the political authority of male and female traditional institutions. This revolutionary translation of economic power into patriarchal political advantage set the stage for the indigenization of British colonialism at the turn of the twentieth century.

In many ways, British colonial rule was a patriarchal assault. It replaced indigenous dual-sex political organizations with masculinist political institutions and propagated androcentric religious and education policies that produced modern wage-earning men and domesticated women. Men predominated the nascent colonial ogaranya elite, filling the ranks of warrant chiefs, teachers, pastors, clerks, interpreters, and accountants. In a dramatic reconfiguration of ufiem, academic certificates, modern two-story houses, automobiles, and money came to symbolize heads that conferred ufiem privileges on men. To understand the social workings of colonial state power within African communities, it is less useful to examine colonial state structure and more useful to analyze how African bureaucrats mobilized the colonial state as well as traditional institutions and ideologies to assert their will over others, including preexisting traditional authority holders. Kalu Ezelu (1865–1968), who rose from slavery to warrant chief status, provides a clear picture of this nascent colonial male hegemony. The case studies of Kalu and Udensi Ekea (1820–1890) before him show how Biafra's gender revolution entailed not only the structural marginalization of women but also the emergence of hitherto marginalized males, often ex-slaves, into dominant sociopolitical positions, as well as the subordination of male (and female) elders. Women contested this erosion of power through gender-dissident yam cultivation (deemed a male prerogative), long-distance trade, divination/spirit mediumship, slave ownership, matronship, and the practice of female husbandhood. In so doing, they demonstrated extraordinary wealth and exercised superordinate political power as ogaranya.

Ufiem was a historical motif for domesticating Atlantic political economies, signified through successive heads, through discriminatory and cognitive practices of public dressing (of ufiem) and undressing (of ujo), and through legitimizing social performances (such as the Ohafia war dance), to name a few. Thus, ufiem was generated through performance—what Pierre Bourdieu calls a *habitus*, or what Paulla Ebron describes as "a stylized repetition of acts" (such as military slaving) or discourses (such as the idiom of cutting a head).³ Ohafia men and women transformed existing sociopolitical institutions and adapted new ones such as age-grades, secret societies, unilineal systems, divination guilds, schools, churches, colonial political offices, and wage labor to perform dynamic forms of ufiem during the Atlantic Age. Although hegemonic masculinity entailed power politics, ufiem was neither merely patriarchy nor an exclusively male pursuit. Women helped "make men" (through agrarian production that released male labor) and helped define ufiem (through military rituals, celebration of warriors, and discrimination of ujo). More importantly, Ufiem was a social representation of self-advancement and power over others. These "others" changed over time, from only other local men (before and during the slave trade) to other men and women (during legitimate trade and colonialism). The social meanings of ufiem varied over time depending on the sex, age, religion, and sociopolitical status of the performing individual.

Some women performed ufiem. In the seventeenth and eighteenth centuries, female ufiem performance required going to war or participating in slave raids. In the nineteenth and twentieth centuries, female ufiem meant ogaranya masculinity. Overall, in performing ufiem, women did not become male. Rather, their communities perceived them as superiors over others, including men and women. Society celebrated such ufiem individuals using cognitively masculine material culture and symbols, but the social and political privileges such individuals obtained were not biologically or anatomically male-sex based. Hence, masculinity must be detached from biological sex and studied as a nexus of power politics. Writing a history of ufiem requires bringing the literature on women's sociopolitical power in West Africa into a direct conversation with the nascent field of African masculinity studies. It means that we cannot assume the timeless existence of patriarchy against which women subsequently rebelled. Historicizing ufiem reveals that constructing individual identities for political purposes was an immediate necessity in Atlantic Age West Africa, where the domestication of Atlantic economies transformed the social meanings of boyhood, girlhood, motherhood, fatherhood, sexuality, leisure, work, and domesticity. Sex-distinctive socialization practices, marriage, inheritance, status and wealth symbolization, and social belonging pivoted on changing notions of ufiem among the Ohafia-Igbo.⁴ Men and women of differing economic, religious, and political positions directly and indirectly contributed to these dynamic ufiem conceptions. Slaves and slavers, diviners, hunters, yam farmers, blacksmiths, legitimate traders, rulers, converts, and colonial agents—male and female—espoused ufiem in dynamic, conflicting, subversive, and conciliatory ways. Consequently, individual negotiation of social mobility defined the introduction, adaptation, and gendered uses of sociopolitical institutions in the region.

GENDERED ATLANTICIZATION: SLAVERY AND SOCIAL CHANGE IN WEST AFRICA

The Ohafia-Igbo logic of Atlanticization revises chronological conceptions of gender inequalities in West African history, as well as the dominant understanding of the Atlantic slave trade and European imperialism. Atlanticization illuminates how changes in gender identities and regimes in the Bight of Biafra resulted from the intersection of diverse local and external political economies over a 170-year period. Historian Toby Green best describes the process of Atlanticization as preexisting African cultural and economic "patterns" that helped shape the formation of the Atlantic, while becoming radically transformed, as African communities sought to sustain themselves, build alliances, and restructure their societies. Thus, Africa emerges as a place where Atlantic exchanges produced deep historical transformations that were the result not just of European imposition, but of the internal dynamics of African societies as well.[5] *Emergent Masculinities* centers gender in understanding such internal dynamics and patterns. It demonstrates how a cis-Atlantic perspective of the Bight of Biafra's eighteenth-, nineteenth-, and twentieth-century political economies, especially as evident in transformations in social practice and cultural meaning, improves understandings of African slavery, gender, and kinship.

Atlantic history examines the development of political, economic, sociocultural, and demographic networks and exchanges between the peoples bordering the Atlantic Ocean. *Emergent Masculinities* delineates the gendered permutations of these Atlantic networks and exchanges in one African region. Recently, Africanist scholars have sought to reorient Atlantic history as more than a European invention by centering Africans as active agents in circum-Atlantic, transatlantic, and cis-Atlantic historical frameworks. They emphasize the importance of African culture and systems of knowledge in Atlantic modes of production, exchange, consumption or appropriation, and identity formation. African cultural production was central to contesting European imperial power around the Atlantic rim, and it is pertinent to understanding the emergence of the intellectual world of the modern Atlantic. Hence, Africanists privilege "microhistories" of individuals and local institutions to understand the agency of Africans in articulating larger Atlantic influences within local and diaspora milieus. By placing African and African-descended peoples at the center, Afro-Atlanticists have also sought to extend the thick web of coastal Atlantic Ocean relationships into the West and Central African hinterlands, and beyond the eighteenth and nineteenth centuries into the twentieth century.[6]

These perspectives inform the approaches taken in *Emergent Masculinities*, which traces the early modern development of a social identity—ufiem—that served as a palimpsest of Ohafia-Igbo adaptation to rapid sociopolitical transformation during the Atlantic Age. The various Atlanticized iterations of ufiem were rooted in preexisting historical practices and ideologies. Through dynamic ufiem performances, African women and men diffused Atlantic political economies into domestic, social, and political spheres of life. For example, ufiem performance defined Ohafia-Igbo military slave production between 1750 and 1840, which significantly shaped the gender and age structure of the Bight of Biafra's Atlantic slave trade. In places such as Jamaica, Biafran ufiem practices sustained new sexual slavery practices. And within the Biafra region, ufiem transformed slavery into a predominantly female condition. Ufiem performance inaugurated new consumption practices, especially new sartorial regimes that shaped Biafra's preferences for British-supplied textiles, thereby reinforcing the political economy of eighteenth-century British control of the region's slave traffic. Ufiem performance, which by the nineteenth century mainly manifested in the form of ogaranya masculinity, shaped gendered participation in, and control of, the palm produce trade. It also defined the domestication of twentieth-century colonialism. In effect, this Africanist view of the Atlantic Age demands a theorization of the Atlantic system in cis-Atlantic terms.

Some scholars have come to see gender as a fundamental element of African cultural change during the Atlantic Age, in a process whereby Atlantic and local economies became mutually constitutive.[7]

In his study *Slave Trade and Culture in the Bight of Biafra*, Ugo Nwokeji argues that the Atlantic slave trade shaped the development of Aro culture and social identity, whereas local conceptions of gender structured Biafra's slave trade.[8] Walter Hawthorne has shown that the sex-distinctive character of Balanta sociopolitical institutions, which shaped the gender and age demography of their external slave trade and domestic slave use, defined adaptation to the Atlantic slave trade in Senegambia.[9] Mariana Candido argues that the Atlantic slave trade rewrote African identities in the slaving domains of the Benguela hinterlands in the Central African region, where women were "key historical agents" in the slave trade, and intermediaries and purveyors of knowledge and culture in Portuguese colonial society.[10]

But beyond the slave trade, the impact of the collective Atlantic modes of production, exchange, and consumption (from slavery to colonialism) on shifts in African gender regimes, as well as on changing notions of masculinity and femininity, has received limited attention. For instance, scholars of Igbo history have identified twentieth-century colonialism as the decisive moment when Igbo women's political power and social privileges witnessed unassailable assault as men emerged in dominant positions of sociopolitical power.[11] But, by treating gender-based sociopolitical changes during the era of the Atlantic slave trade and European colonialism as two unrelated historical processes, it has not been possible to generate a holistic picture of the gendered character of sociopolitical change during the Atlantic Age. This requires linking broad changes in gender construction with changes in economic and political power, and collapsing the eighteenth-, nineteenth-, and twentieth-century histories of the Bight of Biafra region into a singular Atlantic Age. The logic for such Atlanticization of the region's history is what John Oriji has called a diachronic approach to African history: accounting for the role of both internal factors such as demographic movements and intergroup relations, and external factors like Atlantic economies to understand sociopolitical transformations in the *longue durée*. Such an approach is critical of the ethnographic present, positing historical change as a result of the interplay between the structural complexity and stratification of African societies on the one hand, and the dynamic politics of individual achievement on the other.[12] It is particularly essential for studying the history of frontier societies, whose commercial and military activities generated zones of cultural exchange, new commercial hubs, demographic displacements, and intraregional diasporas, as well as protean cultural identities.[13]

From a world systems perspective, the economic systems of the Atlantic slave trade (ca. 1750–1840), "legitimate trade" (1840–90), and colonialism (1890–1960) were distinctive mechanisms of African labor and resource mobilization for Euro-American capitalists.[14] From a West African perspective, Atlanticization entailed continuities and ruptures, including sustained engagement with transatlantic markets and metropoles as sources of gendering commodities; expansion of intraregional trade, kinship networks, and military systems in ways that facilitated gendered redistribution of power; and a revolution in gender regimes. Historian Ade Ajayi understood the importance of such a *longue durée* conception of sociopolitical change in West Africa when he argued, "Colonialism must be seen not as a complete departure from the African past, but as one episode in the continuous flow of African history."[15] Recently Emily Osborn concluded, "Research on colonialism that does not adequately explore the precolonial context cannot unearth the full implications of colonial rule or the meanings it acquired for colonial subjects."[16] Represented in Ohafia-Igbo as the "Heroic Age," the Atlantic Age was an era of dynamic mechanisms of production, buttressed by continuities and transformations in gendered personhood. It was an age punctuated with transitions between times when men cut heads in battle, when men captured slaves, which were equated with heads, and when commercial wealth and academic certificates became heads. These ufiem manifestations capture the Atlantic identities and regimes birthed by slavery and its descendant cultural economies in West Africa.

Some scholars argue that the gradual reinforcement of patriarchal authority defined the Atlantic Age, in a process whereby successive political economies built on preexisting male-dominated structures. In a study of household-state relations in the Milo River valley of Guinea-Conakry, Osborn argues that Batê men became steadily more dominant in the political realm between the seventeenth and twentieth centuries. Batê male elites used their households as the building blocks of the state. By exploiting warfare as a mode of statecraft, as well as the commercial networks of the Atlantic slave trade, the wealth patronage of Muslim male merchants, and French colonial chauvinism, Batê male elites increased their power over women.[17] In the same fashion,

Sandra Greene chronicles the cumulative decline in Anlo-Ewe women's rights as a result of Gold Coast regional responses to successive Atlantic political economies.[18] And Edna Bay argues that as the monarchical culture that enabled Dahomean women to exercise choice, influence, and autonomy weakened from the Atlantic slave trade and disappeared after the imposition of French colonial rule, women lost their sociopolitical influence in society.[19]

These scholars affirm that the masculinization of sociopolitical power during the Atlantic Age, whether through consolidation of patriarchy or unprecedented marginalization of women, amounted to a gender transformation in political regimes, economic autonomy, and social identities. Echoing existing scholarship, they emphasize the male-dominated household and lineage as major sites for the domestication of Atlantic political economies of wealth accumulation, and for the oppression of women.[20] They reinforce the need to resituate studies of West African gender and ethnicity formation, political centralization, and expansion of productive economies between the seventeenth and twentieth centuries within a broader Atlantic framework. This framework should focus on ordinary men and women, whose day-to-day experiences amounted to a historical contestation and reinvention of the institutions of production and distribution. However, as the Ohafia-Igbo case shows, gendered Atlanticization also occurred in female-dominated households, matrilineage systems, and dual-sex sociopolitical systems. How did gendered Atlanticization occur differently where women were sociopolitically superior? Moreover, the transformations in West African women's social statuses and identities corresponded to similar upheavals in African masculinities, which has been understudied. What might we learn by examining the historical constructions of masculinities and femininities as mutually constitutive and *longue durée* historical processes predating the twentieth century?

The few studies that have addressed this gap in the history of West African gender formation focus on the colonial period, beginning with an ethnographic baseline of the preexistence of patriarchy, rather than historicize the social production of masculinities and femininities as indeterminate Atlantic Age phenomena beyond twentieth-century colonialism.[21] Thus, Lisa Lindsay and Stephan Miescher's *Men and Masculinities in Modern Africa* examines how African gender relations, constitutive of a patchwork of patriarchies, defined the constructions of masculinities within the contexts of the socioeconomic and cultural transformations of colonial and postcolonial Africa. Similarly, Robert Morrell and Lahoucine Ouzgane's *African Masculinities: Men in Africa from the Late Nineteenth Century to the Present* does not examine precolonial African masculinities, and it focuses largely on southern Africa.[22] In this regard, Ifi Amadiume's *Male Daughters and Female Husbands* is exceptional in arguing that precolonial Nnobi women of southeastern Nigeria used cultural practices of female "husband" and female "son" masculinities to distinguish gender from biological sex, develop gender-complementary dual-sex sociopolitical systems, and eventually resist colonial marginalization.[23] However, *Male Daughters and Female Husbands* does not historicize how men constructed their individual gender identities, or how their gender identities changed over time. There is yet no history of Atlantic Age West African masculinities. Robert Morrell's observation twenty years ago still rings true: "The dominance of men in the public record obscures the fact that little is known about masculinity. Men have been treated in essentialist terms."[24]

Extant scholarship on what has been termed "big man masculinity" illustrates the centrality of gender and the utility of a *longue durée* perspective in obtaining a holistic picture of the social changes that took place in West Africa during the Atlantic Age.[25] Sean Stillwell argues that lineage/kinship formation and the emergence of "big men" were the two formative stages in the evolution of African slavery, especially in noncentralized African societies. Kinship units emerged as distinctive corporate groups among early African communities negotiating land-use rights. Lineages integrated natives and newcomers through real or fictive kinship ties, enabling the expansion of labor. The quest to accumulate wealth-in-people increased conflicts over power and resources, promoting "early political centralization in the form of big men," who "aimed to control more people and resources than anyone else did."[26] The development of big men increased the number of captives available. Once captives were turned into slaves, powerful men had access to the largest numbers of them. According to Martin Klein, "The acquisition of slaves in early societies was one way either big men or descent groups increased their numbers and thus, their power."[27] The acquisition of wealth-in-people informed African participation in the Atlantic trade because lineage chiefs, rulers, and big men acquired more dependents and followers through their access to new trade goods from the Atlantic world.[28]

In his historiography of African slavery, Stillwell further identifies the political ascendancy of big men as instrumental to the abandonment of bilateral kinship and promotion of unilineal forms of descent, in order to provide clearer lines of inheritance and succession. Matrilineal kinship systems ensured that slaves and their descendants belonged only to the matrilineage of a "father" (patriarch), or slave owner, because slave wives and children had no other kinship networks on which to rely. Also, reproduction of patrilineages depended on men acquiring wives or slave wives and producing children and dependents. Within this matrix, "slavery emerged both as a means to address contradictions between the values of accumulation and kinship and as a function of the development of a complex, surplus-producing economy."[29] Slavery permitted the attachment of people to corporate groups who could make none of the claims of free members. Slaves were outsiders, moved into new surroundings, where they were deracinated and overwhelmingly vulnerable.[30] As junior members of kin groups, with fewer rights, slaves enabled big men to expand their rights and claims over people in new ways.

Between 1600 and 1800, the Atlantic "slave trade made African big men that much bigger."[31] Formative kinship practices and big man masculinity became foundational to the transition from low-density slavery (focused on kinship expansion, use of slaves as additional domestic labor units, and securing access to productive resources) to high-density slavery (expansive use of slaves in commercialized productive roles, especially creation of slave-dominated agricultural estates). Most African societies practiced low-density slavery until the abolition of the Atlantic slave trade and expansion of commodity production and legitimate trade, which encouraged high-density slavery by transforming slavery into a central productive institution during the nineteenth century. As this book shows, in the Bight of Biafra, the accumulation politics of ogaranya big men most forcefully shaped these transformations.

In nineteenth-century West Africa, slavery and incorporation continued to be understood through idioms and practices of kinship, and the operative language of power was still grounded in the benefits and inequalities of kinship. However, broader political, social, and economic changes—tied to the expansion of commercialized agriculture and international trade, Muslim and Christian religious influences, and European imperialism—also increasingly shaped slavery and abolition/reincorporation. The big men of this era came in different forms, including *marabouts* that "colonized spirit-lands" and led the peanut revolution in the Gambia, slave-owning merchant-queens and merchant-princes of Biafran coastal states, large-scale slave owners that mediated abolition in southeastern Ghana, Fulani aristocrats of the Sokoto caliphate, Saro evangelists and "male breadwinners" in Yorubaland, "Presbyterian masculinities" of the Gold Coast, colonial male and female warrant chiefs (and a female king) in Igboland, and male migrant laborers and wage earners.[32] In all of these cases, male and female big men consolidated their power by masculinizing specific African means of production and distribution. Largely empowering men and marginalizing women, these sociopolitical changes during the Atlantic Age enabled men, ex-slaves included, to gain political and economic privileges.[33]

UFIEM: A NARRATIVE OF EMERGENT MALE AND FEMALE MASCULINITIES

Emergent Masculinities narrates how Atlanticization enabled men to gradually gain power over women through the masculinization of key institutions during the transition from slavery to colonialism. Before the early nineteenth century, men and women exercised political authority through dual-sex solidarity institutions in Igboland. This book examines how these dual-sex sociopolitical institutions emerged and were sustained. Judith Van Allen and Ifi Amadiume have demonstrated that because the social statuses available to men in patrilineal Igbo societies were greater than those available to women, Igbo women's solidarity politics—assemblies of daughters, assemblies of wives, market associations, and political instruments such as strikes, boycotts, and force—effectively leveraged gender equality and ensured an enduring dual-sex political system.[34] However, unlike the rest of patrilineal Igbo society, Ohafia was matrilineal. How did the constitution and Atlanticization of their dual-sex systems differ from patrilineal Igboland's? How did their transforming dual-sex systems mediate constructions of ufiem?

As chapter 1 demonstrates, ufiem emerged in part as a male response to female dominance. The propensity of Ohafia-Igbo men to fight external wars and undertake long-distance slaving expeditions across Igbo and Ibibio lands during the eighteenth and nineteenth centuries provided a cathartic release from the realities of domestic female sociopolitical dominance.[35] Originally one of the patrilineal Mben groups of seventeenth-century migrants to the Cross River borderland (between the Biafran coast and its hinterland), the Ohafia adopted the matrilineal kinship and inheritance practices of the aboriginal Ekoi and Ibibio. In response to the privations of their bellicose frontier settlement and, subsequently, the demands of regional slaving, the Ohafia developed a mutually constitutive dual-sex economy of female-dominated agriculture and male-centered militarism. Ohafia women's dominance in agrarian food production and distribution through domestic and regional trade enabled them to emerge as breadwinners, mediate the transfer of landed estates, and maintain powerful political institutions. These institutions offered women privileged political, religious, and economic social statuses but also released male labor for military pursuits. Through intermarriages that strengthened kinship ties with matrilineal non-Igbo ethnic communities in the Cross River borderlands, Ohafia women expanded their society's farmlands, made Ohafia into the only matrilineal society in Igboland, and forced male warriors to raid slaves from distant territories beyond their kinship zone. Real and fictive kinship constructions defined the peripheral zones of military slaving to include Ibibioland in the second half of the seventeenth century and the Igbo heartland in the eighteenth century. Women's economic power reinforced matrifocal religious and matriarchal political practices. Between the eighteenth century and the second half of the nineteenth century, the *ikpirikpe* female court under the control of female kings coexisted with the *akpan* male court under the control of male kings. Whereas the female court exercised political jurisdiction over women and men, the male court governed only men. The female court was the most powerful societal political institution. It maintained its superiority through constant public marches, spectacular trials, and ritual ostracism and boycotts, as well as by combining in one institution the powers of a litigant, arbiter, and enforcer. Consequently, lineage reproduction, breadwinner status, political policing, and deification as a matrilineage ancestress became the measure of Ohafia-Igbo hegemonic femininity before the mid-nineteenth century.

Chapter 2 argues that Atlantic slave production furnished men with institutions and sites of sociopolitical authority to counterpoise Ohafia-Igbo women's sociocultural salience. From the mid-eighteenth century, the Atlantic slave trade began to redefine the heroic ethos of ufiem, as captives became equated with heads. The increased role of Ohafia-Igbo warriors in regional slaving within the Biafran hinterland, which was linked to the rise and expansion of the neighboring Aro people, inaugurated a surge in the Bight of Biafra's slave exports beginning in the 1740s. Ohafia-Igbo prominence in military slaving also coincided with Bonny's superseding of Old Calabar as the region's major slave port, as well as an increase in Euro-American demand for slaves from the Bight of Biafra. The Ohafia-Aro slaving dynamic was rooted in fictive kinship practices (*ukwuzi*) and mobilization of secret societies, age-grades, divination guilds, and deities. The economic gains of regional slave production enabled Ohafia-Igbo merchant-warriors to strengthen preexisting institutions of male-centered political authority and introduce new ones such as *okonko* and *ite odo* secret societies. These institutions enabled merchant-warriors to impose their will over vulnerable individuals, including enslaved and adopted persons, dependent women, children, and ujo. Merchant-warriors' new economic gains were manifest in their public displays and practical uses of captives, European textiles, and Dane guns instead of human head trophies, symbolizing a new form of ufiem. This new ufiem edified violent military slaving through popular war dances, secret society celebrations, deification of merchant-warriors, definition of certain social spaces as exclusively masculine, and human sacrifice. In so doing, merchant-warriors counterbalanced the sociocultural superiority of women but did not yet gain political hegemony over them. Subaltern resistance against merchant-warriors' exploitations ranged from mocking the propensity of merchant-warriors to "play with human heads and slaves," to slaves and other vulnerable persons seeking refuge (ukwuzi) within religious shrines. Although deities guaranteed physical protection, they transformed their asylum seekers into spiritual slaves. Hence, military distinction through community defense and slave production defined Ohafia-Igbo hegemonic masculinity before the mid-nineteenth century.[36]

Chapter 3 shows that the economic impact of military slaving in the Bight of Biafra is best understood through a bifocal assessment of (a) its role in empowering ogaranya masculinities during the eighteenth and nineteenth centuries, and (b) the centrality of enslaved women to Biafra's export trade and domestic slavery during the eighteenth and nineteenth centuries. The chapter posits Atlanticization as a critical revision of the female marginality thesis, which assumes that enslaved women were not important in Biafra's slavery systems. The demography of Biafran captives was primarily a product of local gendered practices of production. Ohafia's long-distance, guerrilla-style kidnapping raids and its martial ethos that epitomized cutting off male heads and capturing women and children ensured that most Biafran captives were women and children. For every male, two female slaves were generated. Biafra's 55:45 export ratio of female to male slaves was inverted in other parts of West and Central Africa, such as Upper Guinea with a ratio of 25:75.[37] Euro-American perception of Biafran adult male captives as rebellious and suicidal also encouraged a greater demand for children and women, famed for their reproductive abilities in the Americas.[38] The majority of the Bight of Biafra's slave exports in the eighteenth century went to the British territories of Jamaica and Virginia. Enslaved Igbo women's reproductive lives defined racial slavery in both places.[39] Gwendolyn Hall observed that Virginia planters sought Igbo female slaves for their productive ability.[40] Captain Hugh Crow noted in 1830 that Igbo women were "preferred in the West India colonies for their fidelity and utility as domestic servants, particularly if taken young, as they become the most industrious of any of the tribes taken to the colonies."[41] Biafra's captive demography, American planter demands, and higher male mortality during the middle passage meant that more enslaved women disembarked in Virginia (1716–50) and Jamaica (1776–1807).

Between 1700 and 1750, 57 percent of Africans sent to Virginia originated in the Bight of Biafra. During the 1716–30 and 1741–50 eras, Biafran-Africans constituted 62 and 75 percent respectively, of slave imports in Virginia. More than 60 percent of Biafran captives were "Igbo" whereas "Ibibio" people made up the majority of the rest. Through natural reproduction, the charter generation of Biafran slaves in eighteenth-century Virginia contributed to the source of the internal slave trade in the North American mainland. This entailed the movement of almost a million slaves from the Upper South to the Lower South between 1800 and 1860, double the number of African slaves sent to North America. Their cultural principles, what Douglas Chambers calls "Igboesque creolisms," shaped Virginia's Afro-Creole culture.[42] In Jamaica, British planters received twice as many "Igbo" as any other ethnohistorical group, and possibly four times as many as the number from the Gold Coast. A few scholars have examined the cultural repercussions of the "Igbo" presence in Jamaica. Chambers examines this in the *obeah* (dibia) practice, diet, and language, whereas Laura Smalligan and Michael Mullin excavate the long-lasting Igbo "cultural charter" of individualistic entrepreneurship and *"connu"* or *jonkonnu* (dance form) protest tradition in the urbanizing environment of late eighteenth-century Jamaica.[43] Sasha Turner has recently argued that the "Ebo/Eboe" labels of Biafran female captives in Jamaica provide a window into planter constructions of femininity for the purposes of maintaining slavery: "For the purposes of reproduction, young women identified as Ebo were considered the most fecund, real or imagined," and this informed Jamaican planters' inclination to allow them "every chance of breeding," even forcing them into mating unions.[44]

Chapter 3 uses the relative predominance of enslaved Igbo women in Jamaica's overall slave trade, and the significance of enslaved women to labor, reproduction, and the construction of patriarchy in Jamaica, to reassess the centrality of enslaved women within the Biafran hinterland, where more female slaves than male slaves were retained for domestic agrarian production, commercial accumulation, lineage reproduction, and elite polygyny. This cross-Atlantic feminist conception of gendered slavery acknowledges the distinctions between the racialized chattel slavery of Jamaica and the dynamic kinship slavery of Igboland, but it emphasizes fundamental similarities in sexual uses of enslaved women by, first, redefining what constituted slave work (besides manual labor) to include sex work (slave-wives, concubinage, lineage reproduction) and then theorizing those sexual uses as instrumental to male ascendancy. One of the most important repercussions of the Atlantic slave trade in the Bight of Biafra was the introduction of gender inequality and the exponential increase in the demand for women within domestic economies. The rise in women's productive burdens paralleled a massive increase in male ownership of enslaved women. By the early nineteenth century, Ohafia warrior masculinity had become dependent on ike nwami; the Ohafia matrilineal system encouraged female captivity. Female captives not sold in the Biafran domestic markets at Itu, Asan, Bende, and Uzuakoli were retained within Ohafia as wives and uterine sisters (*nwannediya*) and incorporated through the matrilineages. In her examination of a similar trend among the Kpuawala of Sierra Leone, Mariane Ferme showed that by transforming slaves into kin, matrilineages concealed the legacy of slavery.[45] The increased role of men in reproducing matrilineages thus enabled them to compete with free women, who were traditionally the reproducers of the lineage. This elicited women's discriminatory ritual practices and discourses that sought to distinguish freeborn women from slave-wives. Slaving also enabled merchant-warriors to reinforce patrilineage as a more important method of private property transfer, in the process making father-son relationships unprecedentedly popular. Illustrative case studies of these emergent ogaranya masculinities, people who used the acquisition of slave-wives to masculinize social notions of individual wealth, include Udensi Ekea of Ohafia, Ananaba of Obegu, Okoro Udozuka of Arochukwu, Naomi of Oguta, and Omu Okwei of Ossomari. They demonstrate the widespread importance of enslaved women to Biafra's domestic slavery practices.

Chapter 4 further examines the economic as well as the political consequences of the Atlanticization of the Bight of Biafra's production and exchange systems beginning in the second half of the nineteenth century, arguing that it enabled hitherto marginalized male slaves to achieve unprecedented political and economic power. The nineteenth-century expansion of trade in nonhuman commodities bolstered male-dominated individual appropriation (through leases, rents, and purchases) of land for oil palm and yam plantations. This relatively small increase in the commercialized uses of land through high-density slavery significantly empowered a cadre of ogaranya individuals and inaugurated changes in land tenure. As individual property ownership increased, so did the transmission of property beyond the control of matrilineages. Whereas military slaving had enabled men to leverage sociocultural equality with women, legitimate trade produced male breadwinners, such that the economic gains of men's dominance in long-distance trade increasingly outweighed women's domestic agrarian production. The biography of Kalu Ezelu provides a colorful perspective into these changes. It captures how postabolition emancipation channeled free and captive female labor into domestic production and dispossessed the traditional slave-owning male elite of their wealth-in-slaves, enabling male ex-slaves, who were the first to embrace Christianity, Western education, and colonial collaboration, to emerge as ogaranya. Such ogaranya individuals invested in domestic economies of palm produce production and relied disproportionately on female slaves for sex, for labor, and to produce children. Although legitimate trade enabled some small-scale farmers to participate in the international economic system, male ogaranya individuals, who mobilized the labor of many slaves and dependents, became the leading producers and marketers of palm oil. The 1931 court case *Kalu Idika v. Eme Ado* provides several additional narratives of nineteenth-century ex-slave ogaranya individuals who used slave girls and slave-wives to establish new households, repopulate dwindling matrilineages, and purchase lineage integration and rights to political offices. Ogaranya individuals dramatized their nascent economic power by acquiring slave-wives, erecting modern two-story houses, and adorning themselves with expensive European goods. Following British political enforcement of abolition, emergent ogaranya took action to hold on to their new privileged status and mask slavery: redefining their slaves into dependent kin and domestic servants, transforming slave-wives into concubines, and allying with Christian missions and co-opting British colonial chauvinism to adopt marginalized persons—especially abandoned twins and other outcasts—into their pool of dependents.

Chapter 5 argues that in contrast to male social mobility and consolidation of political authority, the Atlanticization of indigenous political systems through the imposition of the warrant chief system ushered in a decline in women's political power at the turn of the twentieth century. For instance, the ex-slave Kalu Ezelu's ownership of twelve wives, thirty-four concubines, and fifty slaves positioned him to collaborate with the British and become the most powerful political leader in Ohafia-Igbo society, armed with unprecedented authority. Kalu Ezelu exemplifies the ascendancy of other opportunistic ex-slaves like Eme Ado and Okoro Idika in colonial Ohafia. The British reconciled preexisting male indigenous political institutions with the warrant chief system but completely marginalized female institutions. Furthermore, Christian missionary education also functioned to "domesticate" and subordinate women to wage-earning men. Such women would seek to subvert Presbyterian education policies intended to domesticate them into "good Christian wives" for the new African educated male elite.

In the process, they emerged as matrons who created home-run industries that became alternatives to missionary establishments. Most women were, however, alienated from colonial and missionary structures of social mobility. In seeking alternative avenues of wealth accumulation, Ohafia women like Unyang Uka and Otuwe Agwu turned to long-standing practices, including yam cultivation, trade, divination, slave ownership, and female husbandhood, thereby redefining gendered spaces, roles, and opportunities. Women's ogaranya politics simultaneously subverted imperial social engineering and reinforced the social perception of wealth as masculine. Society employed masculine cultural rituals such as war dances and sartorial symbols to celebrate female ogaranya. And the women dramatized their status as did preexisting and contemporary male ogaranya individuals, through the erection of modern two-story houses, redistribution of slaves and dependents to kin, elite polygyny, and displays of Atlantic commodities. They challenged the sexual and gender regulation that underpinned the European colonial repertoire of power, and they contributed to changing practices of ufiem. Their life histories encourage us to reexamine similar cases of rebellious female ascendancy under colonial rule, including the example of the lone female warrant chief and king Ahebi Ugbabe, as a product of the ideological and structural shifts that characterized Atlanticization in the Bight of Biafra.

FIGURE I.1. Ohafia war dance (Historical memory and the Atlantic Archives)

Atlantic history demands methodological pluralism. Focused on the perspectives of diverse historical actors, Atlantic history requires multiple historical modes beyond the European written document. This is both challenging and encouraging for historians of non-Muslim, non-coastal, and noncentralized West African societies where few written sources exist for the pre-twentieth-century period. Because European historical actors were resident on the coasts of West Africa, they left few records of inland societies. This dearth of written sources is reflected in how this book is organized. Chapters 1 and 2 rely heavily on oral traditions of migrations, lineage organizations, military expeditions, merchant-warriors, and political institutions (age-grades and secret societies), combined with analyses of memorializing rituals and material culture.[46] Although oral traditions may be limited in providing specific historical dates and details, they offer culturally situated explanations and patterns of social change. They emphasize intergroup cultural accommodation and distinctive practices, including reciprocal language and religious borrowings, real and fictive kinship and lineage alliances, shifts in unilineal descent systems, migrations, trade, the growth or adaptation of new sociopolitical institutions and practices, and the indigenization of new systems of production.[47] While such oral traditions might center on singular culture heroes or acclaim a heroic group, such as warriors, mercantile diasporas, or a professional caste, they nonetheless preserve local understandings of society-wide social transformations, and the sociopolitical differentiations they engendered.

It is imperative to discuss the makeup of Ohafia traditions and how I use them. There are three major forms of traditions: (1) oral traditions of migration, lineage constitution, and adaptation of political institutions; (2) Ohafia military traditions preserved in the performative war songs; and (3) gendered rituals and memorialization ceremonies. I use these traditions as indigenous historical discourses. The internal dissonance among the traditions reflects distinctions in how men and women recollect the past. These traditions recall the past from common knowledge, but as cumulative interpretations of history, they capture the subjective experiences of groups, such as merchant-warriors, ujo, and women, instead of specific individuals. For instance, the narratives show that all male individuals began life as ujo and had to work their way up to ufiem status. No respondent owned up to an ancestor being an ujo, but everybody could describe the life of an ujo. The narratives also provide explanations of intergroup relations, such as with the Aro and neighboring non-Igbo groups. I conducted 251 audio- and video-recorded oral interview sessions with 192 individuals and groups in twenty-four Ohafia villages between 2010 and 2015. I interviewed male patrilineage elders, female heads of matrilineages, leaders of traditional male and female courts, members of dibia divination guilds and secret societies (okonko, akpan, ite odo), leading performers of the Ohafia war songs and war dance, descendants of renowned male and female warriors and merchants, priests of deities, and local historians. Respondents began by tracing their bilateral descent, and occasionally performing lineage-memorializing libations to ancestors, before offering a generally consistent history of Ohafia migration from the West Niger to Ibeku and to their present location. Then they provided origin traditions of sociopolitical institutions and gave family narratives of ufiem accomplishments, going as far back as they could recall heroic ancestors and their deeds.

Whereas men's historical narratives emphasized Ohafia's military tradition in the contexts of migration, settlement, defensive headhunting, and slaving, my female respondents emphasized the centrality of the matrilineage to women's economic and religious salience, as well as the resilience of their political institution of ikpirikpe. Especially during group interviews with the female courts, women embraced the interviews to project a widely held view that until colonialism, their political institutions were more powerful. They point to persistent political rituals, and they reenact censorious songs and dances, which they still use to "teach men lessons when necessary."[48] Ohafia women's lamentation of the decline of female power is palpable. Women's emphasis on persistent cultural practices encouraged me to examine gender-specific rituals as evidence of self-representation and historical memorialization. Women's rituals such as *uzo iyi* (virginity testing) and *ije akpaka* (ritual declaration of war) are still performed annually. Whereas the former commemorates merchant-warriors' marriage of slave women in the past, the latter reminds society that women had made it possible for men to achieve martial heroism. Other ritual practices including *ibo ezi* (strike and boycott) and *ikpo mgbogho* (social ostracism) are effective political instruments that women continue to use to enforce public morality. During my ten-month continuous residence in Ohafia between 2011 and 2012, I witnessed seven incidents of *ibo ezi* and two incidents of *ikpo mgbogho*. Such women's theaters are only matched by men's war-dance performances at funerals, new-yam festivals, and age-grade retirement ceremonies. These social dramas are often sites for the projection of gendered ethnic and historic visions: how women and men view the past informs the social meanings they bring to present-day cultural performances, and these reenactments, what Jan Vansina called the "practical uses of traditions," are ways for men and women to redefine their history and their place within it.[49] Ohafia women's rituals are simultaneously contemporary enactments of female power and authority as well as gendered memorialization of the past. They center women in Ohafia history, as "culture producers and social actors."[50] These practices elucidate women's vision of Ohafia social identity as matrilineal and culturally oriented toward non-Igbo ethnic communities.

The worldview of Ohafia women constitutes a critical lens for reevaluating masculinist narratives. Ohafia women's rituals encouraged me to ask questions about the precolonial dual-sex political systems. They prompted questions about the meaning of *history* when some male respondents—the same who affirmed that women were breadwinners, owners and transmitters of land, and in control of more effective political institutions than men before colonial rule—also asserted, "our women didn't have much role to play in the history of Ohafia."[51] For men, *history* was preserved in the heroic narratives of Ohafia masculinist military traditions of headhunting and military slaving. For women, the subjective meanings of *history* are enshrouded in how Ohafia became matrilineal, how women determined the dominant kinship affiliation between Ohafia and its multiethnic neighbors, and how the age-grade political system of the bilateral Ibibio enabled Ohafia women to establish powerful female courts, and ancestral matriarchs, whose *ududu* (pot monuments) they continue to consecrate. For Ohafia women, there is a clear link between the decline in the political salience of matrilineages and the emergence of ogaranya men like Kalu. In fact, the female court of Elu Ohafia identified the reign of ex-slave-turned-warrant-chief Kalu (1911–27) as the decisive moment when women's political power declined precipitously. Individuals like Kalu embodied the structural, economic, religious, and political transformations that weakened

Ohafia matrilineages, undermined women's position as breadwinners, and marginalized women's solidary political institutions.

Nonetheless, both men and women privilege lineage narratives as a lens into Ohafia-Igbo Atlanticization, and their narratives suggest that lineages were gendered practices. It was people's practices that constituted lineages, continued to give lineage its meaning, and ushered in significant changes in lineage ideologies over time.[52] In fact, oral traditions posit the political economies of matrilineages and patrilineages as mutually constitutive. According to one such tradition, pioneer Ohafia settlers originally established two matrilineages, Umu-Aka and Umu-Okochi, which they subsequently expanded through patrilineage-centered military slaving and matrilineage-centered acquisition of "foreign" slave-wives.[53] Indigenous wives belonged to different matrilineages but "foreign wives" belonged to a husband's matrilineage. The acquisition of dependents, slave-wives (*aluru alu*), war captives (*ohu ofia*), people bought with money (*ohu mgbere*), pawns, and resident-strangers (*nwa nbina*) therefore was a means that families lacking female children used to integrate women, who sustained matrilineages.[54]

Men also recollect histories through rituals and songs and dances. Ohafia military traditions are preserved in their narrative war songs and war dance, hitherto extensively studied by Chukwuma Azuonye and John McCall.[55] I make use of the fifty war-song narratives collected by Azuonye in the 1970s. He categorized Ohafia war songs into battle songs, invocative war songs, and narrative war songs, and demonstrated that narrative war songs are legitimate historical traditions, in contrast to the first two categories, which allude to historical events and heroic exploits but were primarily used in the military expeditions and rituals of the "heroic age." The narrative war songs were composed by trained oral historians performing in the "conventions of an established bardic tradition" and "historical oratory," comparable to the Mande griot tradition.[56] But whereas the griots emphasized long chronicle and epic poetry, Ohafia-tradition singers emphasized episodic and lyrical narratives.[57] Unlike the griot, Ohafia-tradition singers did not belong to a caste. Yet the Ohafia-tradition singer was "an Orator-Historian." He apprenticed and trained with established tradition singers. His profession is borne out in his name: *onye-oku-aka* (he that evokes the past). His memory as "a tape-recording mechanism" is celebrated. His historical oratory includes subjective commentary on culture and society. He functions as a moralist and a custodian of cultural values. The tradition singer must "sing what Ohafia people as a whole will accept." Thus, singing traditions required participatory audience acclamation and legitimization.[58]

The histories they recollect include traditions about the origins and migrations of founding ancestors and ancestresses and their settlements; the lives and careers of the ancestors in defending and prospering the land; and the origins and significance of customs (such as headhunting and fictive kinship), beliefs (such as ududu veneration), and sociopolitical institutions.[59] The narratives describe Ohafia warriors as headhunters *and* slave catchers.[60] However, Ohafia respondents insist that their ancestors were not slave-dealers like the Aro but rather were contracted to fight various wars across Igboland and Ibibioland, to protect the Aro diaspora and their interests. In the narratives of these wars, Ohafia warriors are represented as heroes in the quest for military glory, whereas their Aro companions are represented as preoccupied with tethering captives. In the narratives, an unexpected hero often emerged, because he had been an ujo, who thus came to achieve ufiem through military distinction.

There are methodological challenges with the narrative war songs. First, the heroic formula of the narratives personifies the collective through singular culture-heroes.[61] The most popular example of this personification is the tradition of Elibe Aja examined in chapter 2, which narrates the mutual violation of fictive kinship between the Ohafia and the Aro as they sought the economic gains of the slave trade.[62] Second, the heroic formula euphemistically masks the unsavory past of military slaving. In the tradition of Amoogu, which chronicles Ohafia wars against the Niike of northern Igboland, the Niike are represented as "the wild cow roaming about in the forest," which Ohafia warriors sought to subdue and tether. Unable to defeat the Niike, Ohafia warriors allied with them to terrorize their neighbors. The narrative shifts emphasis from Ohafia's extensive slave raids in northern Igboland to its mythic relations with the Niike. Third, although they describe Ohafia military slaving, the narratives use various cultural logics to justify them. A prime example is in Ohafia traditions of the Ora Expeditions, which paved the way for the establishment of Aro-Ndi-Izuogu. The traditions justify the destruction of Ora communities and enslavement of its inhabitants with the narrative that Ohafia had a kinship obligation to defend Izuogu (the putative founder of Aro-Ndi-Izuogu), when Ora people dishonored him.[63] Through a chronological reconstruction of Aro-Ndi-Izuogu patrilineages, Nwokeji places the Ohafia destruction of Ora and the establishment of Aro-Ndi-Izuogu around 1700–1740. This tradition captures the strategic importance of the Aro diaspora settlement of Aro-Ndi-Izuogu to the expansion of Biafra's slave trade in the mid-eighteenth century.[64]

The second Ohafia-Igbo male performative tradition is the war dance—a highly masculinized pageantry of military weapons and battle trophies as well as a dance drama in which the lead dancer carries a headdress bearing human skulls. Dressed in leopard caps, eagle feathers, ram's mane, loincloth, leopard skins, and yellow palm frond and carrying machetes and ropes, dancers reenact typical battle scenes and situations, including the march of warriors to battle, field operations, and victorious return from expeditions. Drawing and swinging their machetes, cutting the imaginary head of their enemy and stowing it in the pouches hanging from their waists, and subduing captives and tethering them with ropes, the warrior-dancers bring history alive.[65] In the eighteenth century, warriors who returned from expeditions with human head trophies and captives were celebrated with the war dance. Thus the dance incorporated slaving into the cognitive terrain of "cutting a head." In the nineteenth century, the war dance was performed at the funerals of merchant-warriors and used to celebrate the emergence of male and female ogaranya individuals, equating their wealth with heads. In the twentieth century, the war dance honored Ohafia ufiem, who returned home with evidence of success in trade or academic endeavors, such as automobiles and university diplomas. It is still used to celebrate instances of figuratively cutting a head, such as civil service retirement or election to political office, and is performed at the coronation of male kings to legitimize their assumption of office. Thus the war dance has appended new forms of ufiem to past forms as a comprehensive record of the heroic deeds of ancestors, which the orator-historian incorporates into his lore.[66]

Whereas chapters 1 and 2 thus privilege the above oral traditions, chapters 3, 4, and 5 reconcile African oral histories with European Atlantic archives. Reflecting Atlantic history's predilection for multiple scales of analysis, as well as existing debates in the historiography of slavery in the Bight of Biafra, chapter 3 is a regional and comparative history of the Bight of Biafra's economic transformation as a result of the Atlantic slave trade, as evident in new forms of ufiem. Accordingly, Ohafia case studies are mapped onto broader regional testimonies and amplified with a transatlantic Jamaican lens. I use the Eighteenth Century Collections Online of British parliamentary papers on the Atlantic slave trade and the Trans-Atlantic Slave Trade Database to situate Ohafia regional slaving within the Bight of Biafra–British slave trade. More specifically, I examine how the age and sex demography of Ohafia military slaving preserved in the oral traditions of military expeditions and oral histories of merchant-warriors are reflected in the database and in eighteenth-century testimonies of British slave traders in the Bight of Biafra. This reconciliation provides a rationale for analyzing the Ohafia case in comparative perspective. The documents I collected from archival holdings in Europe and Nigeria in 2012 and 2014–15 are most useful in chapters 4 and 5. Documents found in the British National Archives in Kew, England; the National Library of Scotland; and the Nigerian National Archives in Enugu and Ibadan are valuable in reconstructing the sociopolitical changes in Ohafia and the Bight of Biafra region between the nineteenth and early twentieth centuries. They include correspondence between British consuls, European shipmasters, and Biafran peoples spanning from the 1840s to 1900; reports on Ohafia origins, institutions, and cultural practices generated by British colonial officials between 1900 and 1935; native court cases between 1908 and 1919; correspondence and journals of the Church of Scotland missionaries, who were active in the Ohafia region between the 1890s and 1940s; and the autobiography of ex-slave Kalu Ezelu.

These archival documents provide limited perspectives. The Foreign Office correspondents (FO84 and FO2) focus on commercial interactions between Europeans and African peoples in the coastal communities of Calabar, Bonny, and Opobo. Located 9 miles east of the Cross River, the frontier Ohafia-Igbo were actively engaged in trade up the Cross River to Calabar and Bonny in the eighteenth and nineteenth centuries, because alongside other Cross River peoples, they were suppliers of yams, palm oil, and palm kernel to the coast; and one of the three major Biafran hinterland-coastal trade routes passed through Ohafia.[67] While oral histories are still needed to place Ohafia individuals within these intercoastal trading economies, the Foreign Office records help contextualize the regional systems and implications of Ohafia's changing economic practices. The documents show that the environment in which Africans participated in "legitimate commerce" was one of piracy, bullying, draconian capitalism, British gunboat diplomacy, an unreliable coastal-to-hinterland "trust system," fluctuations in the value and price of European commodities, monetization schemes that forced Africans into losing accrued wealth, and British consulate bigotry. Against this background, we can appreciate that those Africans who attained success in trade and went further to perform ogaranya masculinity did so only with the greatest ingenuity, tenacity of purpose, and agency.

Missionaries left more informative records than traders because their desire to convert Africans made them interested in local cultures; their hostility to traditional religious practices did not prevent them from making detailed descriptions of those "barbarous" customs and traditions. The writings of Mary Slessor, Robert Collins, and A. K. Mincher are consistent with a broader regional tradition of missionary records and shed light on the dialectical spread of Christianity and British imperial influence from Calabar through Ibibio land, to the Cross River Igbo territories of Arochukwu and Ohafia.[68] They capture the impact of Christian missionary evangelism on gendered socialization, indigenous institutions such as dibia, and changes in lineage practices. They document Ohafia social experiences of epidemics (1890s and 1919), the Aro expedition (1901–2), and adaptation of age-grade institutions to modernization schemes (1902–17). Because missionaries intervened in domestic and public disputes, which were often gendered, their journals and letters express the anxieties of Ohafia-Igbo men and women over ongoing sociopolitical transformations. The records and registers of the Ohafia Girls Training School (founded 1922) elucidate the domesticity focus of missionary education for women in contrast to the technical and literary education provided to men.[69]

At the turn of the twentieth century, British colonial officials and ethnographers generated field notes that extensively documented the peoples of southeastern Nigeria, their cultural practices, and the changes occasioned by European rule. As part of the consolidation of colonial rule, colonial officials and missionaries were instructed to collect genealogical records and ethnographic data of the peoples of the

Bight of Biafra. The call was answered with gazetteers, census reports, and annual reports, as well as ethnographies by colonial anthropologists such as Amaury Talbot, Northcote Thomas, G. T. Basden, and C. K. Meek.[70] Some colonial ethnographers represented the region's history as invariable and barbaric, and they espoused a biased view of Igbo peoples as docile and unproductive, particularly women. However, their firsthand accounts of late nineteenth- and early twentieth-century sociopolitical practices remain indispensable. Few colonial anthropologists disagreed with British officials, in principle and in their accounts of the origins and salience of cultural traditions and institutions.[71]

Following the Igbo Women's War of 1929, British colonial officials also began to collect intelligence reports on the sociopolitical organizations and cultural practices of the peoples of southeastern Nigeria. Expressing frustration with the biased tone of the intelligence reports on the Ohafia-Igbo, Ogbu Kalu lamented, "It would appear that the effort to collate reliable data after the Women's Riot failed in this culture zone."[72] Nonetheless, the intelligence reports, annual reports, and court records provide historical and ethnographic descriptions of Ohafia sociopolitical institutions, economic activities, and traditional religious practices as they existed before and during the first three decades of the twentieth century. They contain critical European commentaries on Ohafia kinship systems and residential arrangements, Ohafia military slaving and headhunting, and the activities of exclusively male secret societies. They account for the establishment of colonial courts, the institution of forced labor and taxation, the warrant chief system, and the establishment of Christian missions and schools. The court records indicate a preponderance of gendered disputes, especially between 1908 and 1919, over land and property inheritance, matrilocal versus patrilocal residence, and divorce proceedings. They also show a rise in political leadership disputes among various emergent male ogaranya who sought to use the colonial institutions to translate their economic wealth into political authority.[73]

In order to provide alternative voices to European written records and present the historical experiences of marginalized social groups such as women, Africanists have, since the 1960s, legitimized oral history as a critical practice. Whereas David Henige defines oral history as a methodology by which peoples' traditions and memories of the past are understood as valid historical texts, Paul Thompson insists that "neither oral nor written evidence can be said to be generally superior; it depends on the context."[74] Since the 1990s, some Africanist scholars have insisted that oral testimonies could stand by themselves as authoritative accounts of lived experience, unmediated, and that various forms of oral communication including rumor, gossip, idioms, proverbs, folklore, and jokes are valid historical sources because they evince *how* Africans represent their historical experiences, beyond the framework of colonial institutions.[75] Yet oral histories, like European written records, must be critically evaluated; we must take into consideration the political investments of the narrators and the corroborative evidence of other sources, as well as the valuable subjectivities implicit in oral testimonials. As Ruth Finnegan and Barbara Cooper argue, oral histories, because of their performative nature before participatory audiences, enable us to explore the social production of memory, self, and subjectivity.[76] Doing oral history is a conscious reconciliation of the historian's quest for what really happened based on the assumption that written documents embody objective facts with a patient and tedious exploration of how people understand what has transpired. I examine the oral testimonies about Ohafia male and female husbands, dibias, merchants, slave owners, and colonial agents as subjective African discourses of nineteenth- and twentieth-century experiences of Atlantic political economies. The testimonies are tendentious and teleological because my research collaborators seek to establish the life histories of their ancestors within a positive metanarrative of ufiem accomplishment. Beyond family recollections, however, the stories of such individuals as Eche Iyi-Oke, Udensi Ekea, Agbai Nnate, Aru Otta, Kalu Uwaoma, Nkacha Emetu, Ucha Onum, Sarah Olugu, Grace Anya, Unyang Uka, and Otuwe Agwu, among others, are popularly known and recalled from different perspectives. Moreover, they reflect other known historical actors in the region such as Ananaba, Udozuka, Naomi, Okwei, and Ahebi.

Given the limitations of human memory, and the selective retrospection and conscious masking or silencing of unsavory histories (especially of slavery) implicit in oral testimonies, gendered performative histories are alternative ways of speaking about the past.[77] Similarly, such idioms as "cutting a head" (igbu ishi), "we eat through the mother," and "father's penis scatters, mother's womb gathers" are "word histories" and "artifacts of the past" that make up the language with which people memorialize historical change.[78] Embodying shifting meanings of power, they capture what Fallou Ngom has described as the social, political, and cultural forces that have once shaped or still influence a given community.[79] Such idioms, as E. J. Alagoa has demonstrated, are used to validate historical memories and demonstrate the relevance of accounts of the past to present concerns.[80] And men and women use them differently. Lastly, African archaeologists have come to define material culture as a system of ideas and symbols that express the unspeakable past and convey socially acceptable cognitive meanings.[81] The past and persistent uses and reinterpretations of Ohafia material culture such as ududu (ancestral pots), *nkwa* (sculptural representations), *ikoro* (war drum), war-dance regalia, *jooji* cloth, and dibia commemorative artifacts embody and articulate the dynamic social meanings of ufiem borne out in the life histories examined here. Collectively, these diverse local historical memories give flesh to the Atlantic archives. The centrality of Ohafia worldview as evident in the ufiem concept, and analyses of rituals, idioms, and material culture, in my historical assessment of gendered Atlanticization reflect my preference for an emic rather than an etic interpretation of historical experiences. As various African feminist scholars have shown, respondents' stories and worldviews are theoretical interpretations in themselves, and should be centered in order to make history a collaborative exploration of subjectivities.[82]

1 ～ Gendered Kinship, ca. 1480–1850

Political and Economic Backgrounds of a Slaving Society

BEFORE THE onset of Atlanticization, the Ohafia had developed the key dual-sex sociopolitical institutions as well as the habitus of gendered social mobility that would enable their eventual domestication of the Atlantic slave trade, and its subsequent political economies, within the Bight of Biafra. Most critical to this process was the emergence of matriliny as an organizing force for accumulating wealth and distributing inheritance, mitigating certain types of marital power imbalance, mediating gendered sociopolitical power, and conditioning the performances of masculinity. Matriliny has been defined as a matrifocal system from which men sought cathartic escape. They did so by transforming hunting, warfare, and secret societies into distinct masculine pursuits in order to create idyllic unisexual microcommunities, which enabled older men to exercise control over young men and escape "the inexorable reality of matrilineal descent and female control of the economic basis of survival."[1] However, it appears that late arrival in a bellicose frontier and lack of access to farmlands were immediate and practical reasons for Ohafia-Igbo's forging of a dominant matrilineal kinship system and innovating of a dual-sex political economy of female-dominated agriculture and male-centered militarism. This chapter outlines the resultant female-focused economic subsistence and political policing as fundamental to male militaristic territorial defense and eventual slave production.

In the view of structural-functionalist anthropologists, the Ohafia phenomenon—a matrilineal yet warrior-slaving society—would have been an apparent contradiction. They viewed African matriliny as an unnatural mode of biological and material reproduction because within this system, sons could not inherit alienable property from their fathers, fathers had limited rights of labor requisition from their children, and agnatic kin could not inherit from each other. Thus, the mobilization of male military labor for slave production would be impractical.[2] A secondary view held that individual property ownership was anomalous within matriliny, and thus private property ownership resulted in the breakdown of the matrilineage. Such a system would not support a slave mode of production. Matriliny was doomed with the advance of modern capitalism.[3] Revisionist scholarship later emphasized the plasticity and resilience of matriliny as a norm of strategic resource, including its responsiveness to external stimuli, centrality to female power and authority, and memorialization of descent to resist patriarchy.[4] Wyatt MacGaffey even argued that matriliny developed because of the slave trade in West-Central Africa.[5] The "intellectual war against matriliny," concluded Pauline Peters, was a war against kinship practices of descent, succession, and inheritance sustained by women's agency.[6] Hence, matriliny became redefined as a matrifocal system.[7] This chapter examines how kinship systems defined the dual-sex institutions and gendered parameters of Ohafia's Atlanticization.

Ohafia was one of the pioneer Igbo groups to settle in the middle Cross River between the 1550s and 1650s. Ohafia ancestors, known as Mben, had migrated from the Niger-Benue confluence to Umunede and Owan near Benin before the sixteenth century, but the military expansion of the Benin Kingdom between 1480 and 1517 forced the Mben to migrate first to the western and eastern banks of the Niger River at Aniocha and Andoni and eventually to Ibeku, in the heartland of Igboland, by the end of the sixteenth century. Following military conflicts between the Mben and their Ibeku hosts, the Mben left Ibeku and, attracted by a nascent Atlantic coastal trade, founded the following communities on the Cross River in the early seventeenth century: Abam, Ohafia, Ada, and Abiriba.[8] Ohafia arrival in the region triggered extensive demographic changes among the various ethnic groups in the area.[9] Ohafia migrants displaced most of the aboriginal Ekoi and Ibibio peoples from their territories west of the Cross River, pushing the latter east of the river. This displacement resulted in the emergence of mixed Igbo-Ibibio-Ekoi towns, including Ihe, Ukwa-Igbo, Isu-Igbo, Ikwere, and Arochukwu.[10] The displacements fed into ongoing Efik migrations that resulted in the founding of Old Town (1630s) and Duke Town (1650s) before the expansive growth of the Atlantic slave trade in the late seventeenth century.[11] Many of the displaced non-Igbo peoples viewed the Ohafia as land grabbers, and according to Chukwuma Azuonye, "the young were reminded of their duty to retake all the stolen land or at least render them unsafe for human habitation."[12] Ohafia military defense of newly acquired territories preoccupied male labor until the eve of the slave trade.

The Cross River Igbo, as the Ohafia and their Igbo neighbors have come to be known, mark the eastern limit of Igboland. Comprising twenty-six villages, Ohafia is bounded in the north, west, and south by patrilineal Igbo communities such as Ihechiowa, Ututu, and Arochukwu (south); Abiriba and Abam (west); and Nkporo and Ada (north). Their eastern neighbors are matrilineal and bilateral non-Igbo riverine ethnic communities including the Ibibio (Biakpan, Ikun, Urugbam, and Agbanwan), Annang, Efik, Eket, Qua, Ekoi (Ejagham, Bekwarra, Yako, Biase/Akunakuna, Bahumono, and Mbembe), and Ogoja peoples. Until the 1890s, Ohafia people militarily defended their occupied territories against their eastern neighbors. Before Ohafia arrival, Ibibio, Ekoi, Biase, and Ogoja peoples engaged in headhunting expeditions as a psychological defense mechanism and embarked on raids occasioned by drought, seasonal hunger, and crop failure. In a bid to regain their lost lands, they employed these military methods against the Ohafia. In turn, the Ohafia imitated the war tactics of their hostile neighbors, often taking the battle to the doorsteps of their enemies and successfully taking their heads to deter them from venturing into Ohafia domains. Warrior masculinity came to be defined as "going out into the realm beyond the limits of the familiar Ohafia world . . . confronting the unknown, prevailing against alien forces and conquering them on their own ground. Returning with [a human head trophy] completed the act of [re]incorporation" and marked the passage to full manhood.[13] Hence, various scholars have noted that headhunting developed as a defensive warfare tactic of the intracoastal frontier Cross River ethnic communities.[14]

Ohafia military conflicts with its immediate non-Igbo neighbors over land ownership alienated the latter and provided practical reasons for Ohafia people to maintain ritual kinship contracts (ukwuzi) with their Igbo neighbors.[15] Male preoccupation with territorial expansion and defense strengthened residential patrilineages as major units of male political organization and thereby linked the Ohafia people with the rest of patrilineal Igbo society. However, Ohafia people also adopted the better-organized paramilitary institutions of their matrilineal and bilateral Ibibio and Ekoi neighbors. These borrowed practices included a well-integrated age-grade system with elaborate rites of passage, which ensured a substantial reserve of on-call, battle-ready, able-bodied men; exclusively male secret societies that reinforced the unity of patrilineages; and a village residential layout akin to a military garrison, which perpetuated militant notions of masculinity.[16] These institutions imbued Ohafia with a sociopolitical system more akin to those of its eastern neighbors. Thus, in contrast to most Igbo communities, where the political system was lineage based and age-grades were mostly convivial, the Ohafia political system was based on pyramidal age-grade organizations until colonial rule.[17]

Moreover, Ohafia was geographically isolated, situated on the fringe of Igboland and cut off from most of it by dense forests and narrow, steep-sided valleys until the nineteenth century. This meant that Ohafia remained much more accessible from, and in more constant interaction with, the territories of its alien and hostile neighbors. Through demographic and territorial assimilation, as well as female-centered interethnic marriages that strengthened matrilineal ties across ethnic boundaries, Ohafia aggressively expanded its farmlands and became culturally and politically linked with its matrilineal and bilateral neighbors. Such matrilineal kinship networks ensured that various Ibibio and Ekoi communities occasionally had chiefs of Ohafia maternal descent.[18] Similarly, descendants of Ohafia-origin mothers were occasionally invited from foreign communities to succeed to matrilineal political offices within Ohafia.[19] By appropriating the cluster of norms that constituted matriliny, individuals transcended ethnic boundaries in the Cross River region through marriage and inheritance practices. Whereas the patrilineage gained strength through demographic unity and concentric expansion, the matrilineage gained strength through spatial and demographic diversity, segmentation, and dispersal.[20] As latecomers to their present environment, Ohafia people absorbed the matrilineal inheritance practices of their eastern neighbors. British colonial anthropologists noted the unusual predominance of matrilineal elements among a number of Cross River communities that had been classified as Igbo in 1901. They were uncomfortable describing these societies, including Ohafia, Abam, Afikpo, and Ada, as Igbo since they were not patrilineal, so they called them the "Cross River Igbo."[21] Anthropologist Philip Nsugbe argues in *Ohaffia: A Matrilineal Ibo*, that among the Cross River Igbo, matrilineal principles were strongest in Ohafia, and that matriliny became distinctively definitive to Ohafia ethnicity in the region. This distinguished Ohafia from the rest of Igboland.[22]

The central role that women played in the course of migration and foundation of new settlements fostered religious and political matrifocal ideologies, and came to validate structural principles on which crucial social relations were built. Onwuka Njoku writes, "The Ohafia were a matrilineal people. Residentially, they were patrilocally organized."[23] Such patrilocal settlements were established on lands leased from matrilineages, since land and movable property were passed down through the matrilineages.[24] As Ohafia men were preoccupied with the defense of new territory, women fulfilled the bulk of farmwork and family sustenance, and after so many generations of controlling farmland, women became the sole transmitters of the right of its ownership.[25] Women's control of farmland through the matrilineage, as well as their dominance in agricultural production, emergence as breadwinners, right to inherit their children upon divorce (as opposed to their husbands'), leadership of the matrilineage units, and ritual practices, ensured that they had a central place in maintaining the matrilineage as the dominant lineage ideology in the society. Female ancestor worship memorialized the salvific role of women's material and biological reproduction in a fragile frontier. While descent came to be traced through the matriline and patriline, the patrilineage existed in gross inferiority vis-à-vis the matrilineage. In contrast to patrilineal Igbo societies, within Ohafia, membership within a matrilineage became the parameter of legal citizenship (rights and duties based on social definitions of descent, belongingness, inheritance, succession, and burial).[26]

WE EAT THROUGH THE MOTHER: FEMALE BREADWINNERS, MATRIFOCAL CITIZENSHIP, AND MATRIARCHY

> Women were the breadwinners, and every man, boy and girl depended on the harvests from the farms of the womenfolk.
>
> —Eze Onuoha Uma, *Guidance and Destiny*[27]

Beyond migration and settlement, another way to historicize Ohafia dual-sex sociopolitical institutions is to examine how diverse notions of ufiem became articulated through men's dynamic relationship with women's breadwinner status before 1850. The symbolic figure of the woman in Ohafia traditions of origin as the giver of life, the breadwinner, and the source of community stability and survival became ramified in effective practices including agriculture, trade, property inheritance, marriage and divorce, ownership of children, and ancestor worship. These practices evince the dominant social position of women in pre-1850 Ohafia society. The popular idiom "we eat through the mother" (*anyi eri ala a nne*) expresses the indispensable role of women as premier food producers and distributors, as well as the fact that property was passed down through the mother's line until the twentieth century. Women dominated agricultural production because, besides male preoccupation with warfare, land scarcity in the densely populated region discouraged the large-scale cultivation of yam (*Dioscorea* spp.), a distinct masculine crop in Igboland. Nsugbe describes precolonial Ohafia men as poor farmers, who only cultivated yam as a prestige crop that was not sufficient to provision a family through half the year. Women produced the staple crops (maize, rice, cassava, coco-yam, beans, and vegetables) and carried out the continuous work of weeding the yam farms. British district officer C. J. Mayne observed that agriculture was the basis of subsistence and income generation. Anthropologist John McCall concurs: "The traditional Ohafia economy depended largely on women's agricultural labor," which in addition to day-to-day "market activities formed the basis of subsistence production and consumption."[28]

Women's subsistence helped masculinize yam cultivation. Yam was the only crop cultivated by men, successful warriors were expected to be consummate yam farmers, the ability to grow and keep yams was predicated on distinction in warfare, and ujo were not expected to cultivate yams.[29] The emergence of yam cultivation as a masculine pursuit directly correlated with the dominance of women in agricultural production and subsistence trading. Nsugbe writes that between the months of March and August, known as *unwu* (hunger period), the entire community relied on women for subsistence.[30] Women's responsibility as breadwinners discouraged a reliance on yams, which had a limited yield for subsistence. This breadwinner consciousness is evident in women's embrace of cassava production. Introduced to West Africa in the sixteenth century, cassava was dismissed as animal feed until women perfected its processing and made it a staple, in the process transforming indigenous economies.[31] Unlike cassava, yam was a fragile crop requiring nutrient-rich soil, extensive acreage, and intense labor. British colonial anthropologist G. T. Basden observed, "In comparison with the yield, the production of yam entailed a large acreage, strenuous labor and constant attention during some seven or eight months of the year."[32] Ohafia possessed limited arable land, and military service consumed male labor. According to historian Onwuka Njoku, "[Ohafia] women's farm work kept them busy all year, unlike their menfolk."[33] Thus, assured of female subsistence, men engaged in yam cultivation as a prestigious masculine adventure.[34]

Before, during, and immediately after the era of the Atlantic slave trade, wealth was valued in land, slaves and dependents, regional currencies (such as iron bars and cowries), yam ownership, and later, European commodities. Yam gained value as a rare, unreliable, and ceremonial food item. Various significant transactions involved yams, including bridewealth payment, leasing of farmland, secret society initiation fees, and recompense for property damage. Yam transfer enabled the attainment of adult masculinity. Fathers established their sons as independent men ready for marriage by providing them with their first yam barn and yam seedlings. Indeed, yams were the only movable property fathers could bequeath to sons without challenge from uterine siblings.[35] Warriors distinguished themselves from ujo by dispossessing the latter of their yams. Distinction in yam cultivation facilitated male access to public office.[36] Successful yam farmers performed the rite of *ike oba* (3,000–4,000 yam tubers per annum) as a first step in the performance of yam masculinity.[37] Ike oba was a passport into the prestigious *nnu* society, for which a farmer produced between 7,500 and 10,000 yam tubers per annum and became known as *osuu*. The osuu feasted his community, displayed elaborate wealth, and was celebrated for having accomplished ogaranya masculinity.[38] Membership in nnu society guaranteed a few men decision-making powers in the redistribution of patrilineage farmlands.

Ohafia conceptions of breadwinners before 1850 privileged agrarian women, even though men dominated woodcarving, blacksmithing, and hunting. This was perhaps because Ohafia blacksmiths and woodcarvers never achieved the regional renown of neighboring Nkwere, Abiriba, and Awka craftsmen.[39] Hunting, however, was a major avenue of social mobility and masculine distinction. Successful hunters were celebrated for their ogaranya masculinity and often became political leaders.[40] The display of animal trophies such as leopard and buffalo hides, skulls, horns, and tails legitimated the social identity of leaders as brave, fearless, and wealthy. Elephants yielded tusks used for making bangles worn by men and women of high status, and African and later European demand resulted in the near extinction of elephants by the turn of the twentieth century.[41] Leopard fangs were treasured talismans, and the colorful skin of deer, cobras, and pythons were prized decorations. Until the early nineteenth century, Ohafia environs were a mixture of savanna grassland and tropical rain forest with large groves of big trees. This environment, where bush hogs ravaged farm crops and leopards poached livestock and men, generated a need to subdue the wild. This transformed hunting from a subsistence endeavor into a performance of ufiem.[42] Hunters became celebrated as warriors who protected their communities. Upon killing a leopard, a hunter sent the fangs (believed to cause tuberculosis) to the rulers of his community, presented the hide before the shrine of the gods, distributed the meat to composite patrilineage compounds, and danced with the head before the ikoro war drum of his village. In so doing, he reproduced social solidarity and validated his belongingness as well as the historical order of lineage seniority. Hunting expeditions also served as defensive reconnoitering exercises. Hunters were expected to "conquer the forests, maintain constant community vigilance and retrieve missing citizens."[43]

Although it pertained to social welfare, hunting elevated individualism through youthful apprenticeship and social mobility within the hunters' guild. There were hierarchies of ufiem within the guild. The longevity of experience, mastery of technology, and success in killing big and dangerous animals set seniors apart from juniors. The guild's ritual pot, decorated with the skulls of dangerous animals and presented at public festivals, reinforced the social importance of hunters, provided an avenue for individuals to boast of their accomplishments, and challenged the hegemony of warrior masculinities.[44] Killing a leopard or elephant was a red-letter day in a hunter's life; it was an act of bravery greater than overpowering a human foe.[45] Such a feat often required a gun—a technology that transformed conceptions of hunter masculinity. Guns distinguished senior hunters from juniors because they shaped the type of animal a hunter could kill. Guns came into common use in Ohafia in the 1720s, and by the 1850s, when the percussion cap became popular in the region, guns emerged as the hunter's chief weapon.[46] Arthur Glyn Leonard observed in 1896 that at Akanu Ohafia, "all the way along, the people were armed with flint locks and cap guns." Ohafia obtained European guns through its regional trade on the Cross River and locally manufactured guns from neighboring Abiriba, which consisted "of nothing but blacksmiths, who do all the work in brass and iron for a very great distance around."[47] Despite their seeming prevalence, guns were very expensive, so the individuals who possessed them employed them as symbols of social prestige and ogaranya, especially at social ceremonies.[48] The introduction of a gun culture linked to ogaranya masculinity performance evinced the incorporation of a European commodity into local iconography of gender construction. An Ohafia hunter later likened gun ownership to automobile ownership as expressing the emergence of popular technological symbols of modernity and masculinity in southeastern Nigeria.[49]

Ogaranya masculinity performance through the fringe economies of yam cultivation and hunting did not undermine women's position as breadwinners. And although men dominated the traditional medicine and divination/spirit-mediumship (dibia) profession, dibiahood entailed certain limitations including taboos proscribing farming.[50] The position of women as breadwinners was reinforced by the nature of interregional trade, which was based mostly on the export of food crops from the hinterland to the coastal communities of Bonny and Opobo. The food crops were exchanged for Akwete cloths, Ututu mats, Uburu and Okposi mined salt, Abiriba metal goods, and Efik and Ibibio crafts as well as European commodities until the 1890s. This trade was conducted over an extensive overland route that converged at Abiriba (Abririba-Ada-Afikpo-Uburu, Abiriba-Bende-Uzuakoli, and Abiriba-Isikwato-Ututu) and then went through Ohafia to Arochukwu, Ihechiowa, and Ututu. The hinterland food supplies provisioned coastal trading societies and slave populations destined for the Americas. After abolition, coastal populations continued to increase throughout the first half of the nineteenth century because of incessant slave production, and coastal states produced little food for subsistence. Postabolition palm produce trade, which peaked between the 1820s and 1860s, also increased the number of people involved in producing and marketing palm produce. Various trading societies such as the Aro and Ndoki almost ceased to farm at all. With more labor thus withdrawn from the agricultural sector in the long nineteenth century, greater demand for food developed throughout the Biafran hinterland.[51] Until the 1890s, Ohafia women produced food to meet family needs as well as regional market demands. Oral narratives recall this as a period when men were direly dependent on women for food and income.[52]

As early as the 1820s, palm produce had become Biafra's main export, women providing the bulk of palm produce labor and dominating the local trade in palm produce. Women sold palm oil and kernel in local markets, where male entrepreneurs bulked and transported the produce to Arochukwu, Itu, and Ibibio markets. Thus the regional markets were linked with domestic markets, which women controlled. The female court governed domestic markets, regulated prices, and settled disputes. The court also established and maintained taboos governing male and female participation in the productive economy. It forbade men from participating in the lucrative production and sale of palm oil and kernel. It was not until the 1860s, at the peak of the palm produce trade in the Bight of Biafra, that men were allowed to bulk and sell palm produce to distant markets, but women still maintained a monopoly on its production.[53]

Women's centrality to economic reproduction informed principles of property ownership. Spouses had little or no right over each other's property, and women's economic self-sufficiency was autonomous.[54] In patrilineal Igbo societies, children belonged to their fathers and their patrilineage upon divorce, and first daughters had to become gendered male, by avoiding marriage, in order to retain their father's heritable wealth.[55] In Ohafia, however, all children belonged to their mother upon divorce, and all heritable property of a deceased individual reverted to his or her maternal relatives, since a man and his children belonged to different matrilineages.[56] The only corporate property transferred from father to son was the patrilocal residence. But if such a home was erected on land pledged from a matrilineage, it reverted to that matrilineage. Upon a man's death, his eldest sister took charge of all bequeathed property, including land, farm produce, slaves, and adopted children, which she gradually redistributed to her children and maternal relatives.[57] If the deceased had no brother, his eldest sister inherited his property, and if he had no sibling, his mother became the inheritor.[58] The deceased's children belonged to their mother, who chose to either live alone or remarry; levirate was viewed with horror in Ohafia, in contrast to patrilineal Igbo societies.[59] If the deceased was a married woman, her daughters shared her property including land, slaves, houses, money, farm produce, economic trees, and personal effects. If she was unmarried, her eldest sister inherited. In the absence of a sister, her mother became the inheritor. In all cases, inheritors were maternal relatives. The trustee took responsibility for the deceased's debts and burial expenses, and the deceased's matrilineage presided over the funeral. In effect, all persons and property ultimately belonged to a matrilineage through women. Women constituted an eternal link of successive inheritance, while men could not pass any significant property to their children.[60]

Anthropologist Victor Uchendu's assertion that "an Igbo without patrilineage . . . is an Igbo without citizenship" did not hold true for Ohafia society, where the parameter of citizenship before colonial rule was membership in a matrilineage.[61] The matrifocal definition of citizenship shaped individual rights. Divorce was granted at the wish of either spouse, unlike in patrilineal Igbo societies, where complex bridewealth-repayment procedures made it difficult for women to obtain divorce.[62] Because women were productive and reproductive resources safeguarded by matrilineages, the divorce rate in Ohafia was very high. To curtail prostitution and ensure socioeconomic support for aged women, every four years widows and unmarried women had an opportunity to choose a man as a husband, and any man thus chosen obligatorily accepted.[63]

Whereas the death of a man represented a relative increase in the redistributive resources of his matrilineage, the death of a woman constituted a grave loss in persons (including children) and property, which would have accrued to the matrilineage. Thus, Njoku writes, "it was considered a calamitous circumstance if a matrilineage was faced with the possible extinction of its femalefolk."[64] Nsugbe concurs, "Daughters were highly prized in Ohaffia," such that households purchased and married women from neighboring patrilineal Igbo societies and incorporated them and their descendants as members of matrilineages.[65] Marrying wives and purchasing female slaves were mechanisms through which male and female husbands and wealthy individuals ensured the continuity of dwindling matrilineages.[66] Such a wife or female slave was designated as a "husband's sister" (nwannediya) and symbolized the wealth and affluence of the incorporating matrilineage. They were occasionally satirized by indigenous wives as "expensive property" and "slaves" of the matrilineage, through gossip, rumor, verbal aspersions, and rituals—mechanisms that women used to shape discourses of legitimate citizenship.[67] This was in contrast to anthropologist Simon Ottenberg's observation in the case of the neighboring Afikpo, where "there was no device of bringing an outside female into the descent group as a fictional relative to produce children for a dying matrilineage."[68] Through marriage practices, women also positioned themselves as the sole mechanism through which individuals from neighboring Ibibio and Ekoi societies attained Ohafia citizenship, since it was an individual's belonging to a wife and mother that ensured citizenship.[69] This matrifocal conception of citizenship was regarded by anthropologists as exotic, deviant, and unstable because they failed to see the matrilineage, as opposed to the nuclear family, as the primary social unit, for while patrilineal endogamy was allowed in Ohafia, matrilineages were strictly exogamous.[70]

The reconstitution of lineages in the ancestral world was also matrifocal. Even though male and female ancestors were worshipped, matrilineal ancestor veneration through the raising of pot monuments (ududu) was dominant. As Ifi Amadiume observed, Igbo individuals created their own gods and goddesses in terms of their own gender relations.[71] According to Uchendu, the dead were a part of the Igbo social world, the principle of seniority makes the ancestors the heads of the lineages, and there is constant interaction between the human and spirit world.[72] Through libations, prayers, and sacrifice, the dead were venerated as ancestors. But ancestor deification was selective and earned. For males, deification (*idoru nna*) was reserved for those who accomplished ufiem by "cutting a head" in their lifetime. Men who did not receive the honor of deification were believed to constitute restless spirits, stuck between the world of the living and the dead, and attracted shame and derision to their descendants. The ududu of male ancestors were arranged in a chronological order in the patrilineage meeting halls (*obu*), where they received periodic libations. Male ududu emphasized individual accomplishments, and their representation as cult objects was confined to specific patrilineage segments, as opposed to the village-group.[73] Deceased women, on the other hand, had ududu raised in their honor within their matrilineages—a practice that began with village-founding female ancestors in the sixteenth century and continued with greater diversification into the late twentieth century. Female ududu attainment was predicated on achieving breadwinner status and begetting a daughter, if necessary, by purchasing female slaves or becoming a female husband. The oldest woman in a matrilineage functioned as its spiritual head, who kept and ministered to the ududu of the female ancestors. She chronologically arranged the ududu in her home, emphasizing an unbroken chain of matrilineage matriarchs.[74] Amadiume has noted the exceptional "ritual superiority of the female" in Ohafia, in contrast to patrilineal Igboland.[75]

Nsugbe writes that the female ududu "evoked stronger and deeper emotions of loyalty than their male counterparts."[76] Unlike the male ududu, which were not under the care of any particular priest and suffered from exposure and neglect, the female ududu were "fed" daily with prestige food items by the matrilineage matriarch, who offered sacrifices on behalf of the entire matrilineage community, within and outside Ohafia. This matriarchal ududu appeasement ensured good harvest. It was accompanied by an annual ritual called the "Uduma festival" (*omume iri Uduma*) in which husbands gave gifts to their wives to appease them. Husbands weaved beautiful baskets and filled them with yams and luxurious textiles, as well as a hoe, which they presented to their wives in commemoration of women's status as breadwinners.

Whereas the hoe was an iconic male tool in patrilineal Igbo societies, it was a woman's tool in Ohafia and reflected women's position as "those who feed the community" (*nde n'aku nde ife nri*). During this ceremony, men, women, and children from various communities trooped to the home of their matrilineal matriarch to worship female ancestors, pray for the new agricultural year, and offer thanksgiving for good life and harvest. Ohafia people attest, "the matrilineage matriarch's home was like a church in the days of old."[77] Unlike the male ududu, confined to patrilineage segments, the female ududu enjoyed intervillage and interethnic religious loyalty. They were not stationary like the male ududu because they moved to the homes of successive matrilineal matriarchs. Because matrilineage members were resident in practically every village, and in neighboring communities, matrilineage ududu enjoyed religious veneration beyond segmentary patrilineage units. While matrilineage members were dispersed, their allegiance to both the living head of the group and the sacred pots of their ancestresses afforded them a formidable cohesion, which inspired the idiom "father's penis scatters; mother's womb gathers."[78] In this way, matrilineages and their matriarchs symbolized societal well-being and solidarity.

FIGURE 1.1. Ikpirikpe drum

GENDERED POLITICAL ORGANIZATION AND POLITICAL POLICING

> Women's power is as old as the community, and as established as female parturition.... Women are the owners of the community. We are possessors of power who hold onto our power.
>
> —Nnenna Emeri[79]

Ohafia's dominant matrilineage system provided the basis for profound mother-centered and profeminist ideologies and principles. These not only reinforced matrifocal conceptions of social identity and translated into female dominance in the pre-1850 agro-based economy; they also informed the adoption of forceful mechanisms to uphold female political power and authority, defend women's rights, and govern moral precepts. The matrifocal conception of citizenship and the high sociocultural value placed on women defined the society's moral order. Political power is best understood in this case as the exercise of coercive influence based on the threat or use of sanctions and rituals, control over public morality and communal values, and control of the distribution of material resources. Through the age-grade system, Ohafia women maintained one of the most powerful formal political institutions in southeastern Nigeria, employing political strategies that were more effective than their male counterparts until colonial rule. This is significant given that several authors have erroneously dismissed Ohafia women as historically invisible and docile, inferior and subordinate to men, until the salvific influences of Christianity and Western education.[80] Such views, which were originally espoused by colonial anthropologists, have also been perpetuated in scholarship on other parts of Igboland.[81] In fact, I argue the exact opposite: as chapter 5 will show, Christianity and Western education grossly undermined female power and authority and helped place men in dominant positions of power.

The precolonial Ohafia political system was sex-differentiated as an organization of parallel gender institutions: a dual-sex system in which each gender managed its own affairs, each with its own kinship institutions, secret societies, and title societies. The age-grades were gender inclusive until a certain age (the *uke ji ogo* stage), when male and female members separated to form distinct political organizations: the all-male akpan and the all-female ikpirikpe. These constituted the male and female courts respectively under a male king and a female king.[82] Colonial records cloud this political differentiation. In his 1934 report on Ohafia, district officer C. J. Mayne presented the precolonial Ohafia political system as axiomatically male. Then, under the subtitle "Ethnological," where he discussed land tenure, he cursorily noted the existence of the female king, who settled "petty disputes between women in matters touching land and other small matters between females."[83] Mayne never indicated that the female king was part of any formal political administrative and judicial system. In his proposal for the future administration of Ohafia under colonial rule, he argued that "the Clan Council membership consist of the [male king] of each village, the [male patrilineage] family heads and senior men of the AKPAN of each village."[84] Similarly, colonial annual reports on the region focus almost exclusively on European and African men.[85] Recovering women's voices, therefore, has entailed extensive oral interviews, as well as documentation of rituals and political enforcement strategies that evidence self-representation, gendered memories, and the practical uses of traditions.[86]

Adapted from neighboring matrilineal societies, the age-grade, which involved elaborate initiation rituals, became the foundation of Ohafia political administration by the end of the eighteenth century.[87] It was central to the mobilization of male warriors, women's exercise of sociopolitical power, and gendered socialization. It also served as a social welfare and self-help developmental agency. It has been described as "the matrix of socialization, resource mobilization, self-actualization and community development."[88] The age-grade was used to differentiate seniors from juniors "irrespective of sex."[89] Boys and girls within a three-year bracket were grouped into the same age-grade, and this grouping was repeated every three years for each new set of three-year-olds.[90] The gendered distinction of girls from boys began informally through play; anthropologist Robert Rattray noted that young children were daily "undergoing unconscious instruction, mostly perhaps by a process of imitation of their elders."[91] This culminated in a boy's performance of *igba nnunu* (to shoot and kill a hummingbird using a bow and arrow) and a girl's performance of *ino nhiha* (menstruation seclusion).[92] The former introduced a boy into the world of men, and the latter enabled a girl to attain womanhood. In the latter, girls learned a secret dance form called *ojo-ojo*, which inculcated the virtues of chastity, reproductive sexuality, hard work, and group solidarity. This differed from the boys' hummingbird dance, which emphasized agility in warfare and initiation into male secret societies.[93] They both laid the foundation for the dual-sex political system.

From informal associations (up to eighteen years old), the age-grades earned formal recognition (eighteen to thirty-six years old) and later (thirty-six to forty-five years old) became gendered political organizations.[94] An age-grade earned political leadership of the female ikpirikpe and male akpan governments by fulfilling a significant community project such as constructing a new bridge or market and having its female members feed the entire community. As the ruling age-grade (*uke n'ogo*), they served in daily governance as political leaders, judges, and orators, responsible for the peace of the community.[95] One local historian Onwuka Oti defined them as "the pulse, the active, the taxable and the major productive cream of the society."[96] Njoku described the male members as "the arrow-head of community defense," the seasoned war leaders "so dreaded throughout most of southeastern Nigeria."[97] The female members regulated communal peace by superintending over the ethical and legal conducts of men and women, married and unmarried, and constituted the major productive resources in the agro-based economy.[98] At about fifty-five to sixty years old, members of the ikpirikpe and akpan retired from active community service through an elaborate ceremony (*igba uche*). To attain retirement, they fulfilled a mandatory community project such as building a town hall, constructing a major road or market, or providing recreational facilities. Since the 1900s, such projects have included provision of pipe-borne water, school buildings, maternity homes, and electricity.[99] Upon retirement, they became elders (*nde-ichin*), which Azuonye has described as "the supreme goal of life," when the individual was looked upon as a "living ancestor."[100] Elders were the ultimate repositories of customary and historical traditions, only serving as expert witnesses in the male and female courts to resolve intractable social conflicts.[101]

It is imperative to outline the power limits of the male court in order to appreciate the authority of the female court. Members of the akpan and male representatives of patrilineage compounds constituted a men's court or assembly (*amali*), headed by the male king (*ezie-ogo*). In consultation with the women's court, the amali set the annual farming and festive calendar. It made rules governing relations with neighboring villages. As a judicial body, it settled disputes that defied resolution within patrilineage compounds. The amali sometimes summoned a meeting of all freeborn male adults to deliberate on grave matters such as an untraced murder, the threat of external attack, mobilization for external attack, or an epidemic. At such ad hoc assemblies, any person, irrespective of age, could sway public opinion.[102] The akpan served as a police organ of the amali. As Mayne observed, before colonial warrant chiefs emerged in 1910, the akpan investigated all matters both criminal and civil, arranged for the appearance of litigants and witnesses, and carried out the decisions of the men's court.[103] Its major means of law enforcement was the imposition of fines, often paid in brass rod currency.[104] As Njoku noted, during fine impositions, members of the akpan "walked in a single file, speechless and no person dare[d] to cross their way."[105] Akpan arrested offenders in their homes. Upon the akpan members' arrival, the offender paid a "summons fee." Refusal to comply constituted a calamitous offense that incriminated the offender as well as all male members of his compound. The latter often pressured the offender into appeasing akpan. Otherwise, akpan then seized the offender's property and any property of significant value in the vicinity. In the latter case, the owners of the seized property forced the offender to meet the akpan members' demands, which were often severe.[106] The akpan reinforced its authority through its hideous and frightful masquerade secret society. The masquerade symbolized the emergence of ancestors in corporeal form.[107]

The men's court had no jurisdiction over women. Its political prerogatives emphasized defending the community and regulating intergroup relations within and outside Ohafia. Its level of organization depended on the size of the community and the personal influence of its leader. The ezie-ogo wielded considerable moral power as the custodian of the sacred symbols of the community's ancestors, as well as the communal land of the patrilineages. But the power of the office was often a reflection of the man occupying it. Nsugbe noted that the ezie-ogo of Amaekpu, one of the largest Ohafia towns in the nineteenth century, was "kept out of village politics. . . . He did not openly participate in the running of the affairs of his own village; he did not attend meetings and therefore did not preside over them; nor did he undertake any ritual duties. He was greatly respected but not regarded in any sense as a sacred functionary."[108] Mayne similarly observed that before colonial rule, the ezie-ogo's authority "amounted to that of a figure-head. He had no actual control over any outside village in any matter," he "had no autocratic power whatsoever in his village," and "he had also no autocratic power even in his own family." His position gave him "only the right to announce the decisions of his Village Council."[109] Azuonye affirms that the ezie-ogo's function was, "interestingly, limited to the management of relations" between one village and another.[110] No uniform rule of succession existed for the selection of the ezie-ogo. Personal distinction rather than seniority determined selection, and wealth and influence sometimes governed a choice.[111]

The female court exercised more political power in the society, over and above men, until colonial rule. Njoku writes, "In fact, ikpirikpe [was] much sterner and stricter in exacting fines and commanding obedience than its male counterpart."[112] While akpan's primary duty was law enforcement, ikpirikpe was both legislator and enforcer of its own laws.[113] Whereas the male court had no jurisdiction over women, the female court exercised its power and authority over both men and women. Derived from the age-grade and led by a female king, ikpirikpe functioned as a formal political institution. Ikpirikpe contradicts Nina Mba's assertion that while precolonial Igbo women largely controlled their own world, they lacked direct influence over communal politics and were not allowed formal direct participation in making decisions.[114] The influence of ikpirikpe over communal politics was not informal and indirect, but formal and direct. It refutes Caroline Ifeka-Moller's conclusion that in eastern Nigeria, what is ethnographically known as the formal political system was by custom allocated to men, and that women's sociopolitical institutions were merely nominal instances of female autonomy.[115] It also challenges Annie Lebeuf's argument that in kinship-based societies, women rose to formal leadership positions only through religious practices and inheritance from fathers.[116]

The Ohafia political system was the age-grade system writ large, and the makeup of the female court distinguished it from women's political organizations in patrilineal Igbo societies. The female court comprised ikpirikpe women, who were simultaneously wives and daughters, and thus combined the powers of the "assembly of wives" and "assembly of daughters," similar to those that existed in Igbo societies. The former has been described as a police force, a supreme court of appeal, a rotating credit union, the custodian of religious morality, the preserver of market peace, and a welfare organization. The latter has been characterized as the regulator of husbands' treatment of their wives, a self-help group, and a lower court where cases involving women were initially brought. But in all cases, they have been portrayed as ad hoc in nature.[117] But in Ohafia, unlike in the rest of Igboland, these female assemblies were not ad hoc and did not exist independent of and in conflict with each other: endogamous marriage practices within Ohafia patrilineages, which were considered an abomination in other Igbo societies, ensured the existence of women who were simultaneously wives and daughters.[118] This wife-cum-daughter duo social status of Ohafia women shaped their conceptions of legitimate citizenship. The female king earned the right to govern the female court by being both daughter and wife of a royal patrilineage. Ohafia was the only Igbo women's assembly with a female king.

The concept of a female king (a woman who is king over women) as distinct from a male king (a man who is king over men) emphasized the autonomy of the female sphere. Thus, Amadiume translated the Ohafia title *ezie-nwami* as "female king" instead of "queen."[119] The latter refers to a female sovereign or monarch as well as the wife or consort of a king. The ezie-nwami's right to rulership did not derive from her being the wife of a king; indeed, her husband could never be king. She was installed as a king in a complex ritual known as *isuyi nzu isi*.[120] In an interview with ikpirikpe of Elu Ohafia, Uche Kalu Ebi asserted, "In Ohafia, women managed their affairs. The *ezie-nwoke* [male king] ruled over the men, and *ezie anyi* [our king], who is ezie-nwami, ruled over the women. . . . Since the days of old, women's rulership in this Ohafia have been stronger than the men's."[121] The ezie-nwami is, in a sense, comparable to the *omu* in Onitsha, Asaba, Osommari, Ilah, and other Ika-Igbo areas, who, Basden observed, "[was] installed with regal ceremony, for the rites include[d] symbolic crowning . . . on similar lines to the coronation ceremonies observed when installing a king. After this ceremony, [she was] known and saluted as 'Omu' (Queen). It was merely a courtesy title, for the 'Omu' [was] never the wife of a king."[122] Indeed, the market was the domain of Ohafia women, serving as a venue for trade, socialization, gossip, and political mobilization. But the female king differed significantly from the *omu* because unlike the latter, most of the ezie-nwami's powers were exercised not over the regulation of trade and the market but rather over all sociopolitical spheres of the society involving women.[123] Ezie-nwami also differed from Ahebi Ugbabe, studied by Achebe, who had to transform herself into a "man" to become king in a society with no kings.[124]

The Ohafia female king, writes Nsugbe, "combined the secular function of presiding over meetings and speaking for the female court, with the ritual one of initiating the planting of crops."[125] She governed the setting of the annual calendar and maintained taboos that forbade men from participating in certain economic ventures.[126] She governed all political organization of women. Her home was a palace and court where the female council held meetings and heard cases. She occasionally summoned all adult women and young girls to initiate a decision-enforcement strategy.[127] The female king articulated her authority with the ikpiripke drum: the instrument of legislation and law enforcement. By placing the drum in the home of an offender, the female court invoked its power to impose fines, ostracize an individual, or in severe cases, boycott a compound or community. The drum summoned both men and women to the village square to hear ikpirikpe pronouncements and coerced both men and women into social responsibility for the rulings of the female court.[128] Ohafia women assign various names to the drum that characterize the authority of the female king, including ancestral mother, oracular truth establisher, the vagina that consumes the wealth of others, the sneaky troublemaker, and the terror of men.[129] The drum evoked the sacredness of the female body, the violation of which attracted grave penalties.[130] By legislating against sexual abuse, abortion, and male marital infidelity, ikpirikpe fiercely defended the moral integrity of women, female virginity, chastity in marriage, and motherhood.[131] As Mayne observed, adultery was considered a serious crime in Ohafia, but while the male culprit could face punitive enslavement, "nothing was done to the woman."[132] Nwokeji cites one such example: "Among [Sigmund] Koelle's respondents was one Okon (or John Thomas, as they called him in Sierra Leone) from the Igbo warrior community of Ohafia, northwest of Arochukwu, who was sold at Bonny for adultery in about 1820."[133] Contrary to Nwokeji's interpretation, however, it was Ohafia's dual-sex political differentiation rather than the status of the individual as lower class that determined punitive enslavement. Besides the regulation of marriage, sexuality, divorce, and female rites of passage, ikpirikpe was solely responsible for administering all cases involving both men and women.[134] Men observed rules of "no entry" during ikpirikpe meetings unless invited for a hearing. The secret nature of ikpirikpe consultations elevated its aura and promoted public anxiety.

Through their offices, Ohafia female kings forged cross-ethnic sisterhood alliances across village groups in the region, which enabled women to effectively implement boycotts against men in order to coerce compliance with their political decisions. "Home desertion" (ibo ezi) involved the female folk of one village deserting their homes in protest and seeking refuge in other villages or in neighboring communities in the care of the local female king. Njoku has described it as women "voting with their feet," concurring that the effectiveness of this strategy rested primarily with the fact that women controlled food production, preparation, and distribution.[135] Several scholars have argued that the right to order strikes by all women was the most powerful political strategy employed by precolonial Igbo women.[136] The concentration of both human and material resources of the female members of one village in caring for women from another village often proved unbearable for male members of both communities, resulting in the appeasement of women. The choice of a destination for ibo ezi was political. Women's decision to seek refuge in a rival community was a public defamation of their men; it emphasized men's inability to live up to their social responsibilities, and sometimes inspired male military aggression against the host community. Women's choice of a distant community was often calculated to attract notoriety, public empathy, and participatory condemnation of men (*igba mkpu*).[137] Ibo ezi sometimes entailed the female court of one Ohafia village summoning the women of the remaining twenty-five villages to constitute a pressure group against men.[138] Women's desertion of homes and "children, except suckling babies," en masse was deployed against the male courts over the setting of the annual calendar and warring against neighboring communities until the late nineteenth century. It was used against colonial labor mobilization and colonial courts in the first three decades of the twentieth century, and it continues to date in spite of modern systems of law. It thus speaks to the effectiveness of female group solidarity.[139]

Ikpirikpe enforcement strategies differed from precolonial Igbo women's protests, which have been presented as economic and political responses to male sociopolitical domination that expressed "a shared consciousness of being a disadvantaged sex."[140] According to Achebe, such protests in northern Igboland included strikes, boycotts, sit-ins or sleep-ins, force, nudity, and sitting on a man.[141] The Ohafia female courts used physical force and rituals to enforce their rule, against the background of female economic and political domination. Indeed, rituals were, as the French sociologist Georges Balandier noted, "instruments of political action just as much as rulers and bureaucracy."[142] Through rituals, the female courts regulated male conduct of warfare. As Nnenna Uma Eke of the Akanu female court attested, "In this our land, before men could go to war, there was a traditional rite which women must perform. We call it ije akpaka [ritual declaration of war]. If women did not perform ije akpaka, men could not go to war."[143] After men returned from battle, women performed a ritual cleansing before warriors were readmitted as legitimate members of society. Women's refusal to perform ije akpaka illegitimated and often undermined a planned warfare.[144] As an established formal practice, ije akpaka differed from Igbo women's other informal protests against men's engagement in warfare.[145]

Through rituals of excommunication and reincorporation, women established themselves as guardians of public morality and definers of Ohafia-Igbo ethnic citizenship. In an interview with the female court of Akanu Village, Ohafia, Nnenna Emeri stated: "If men violated the laws upheld by women, they were held to severe punishments. . . . If a man abused his wife in relation to her sexuality, once women learned of it, the women's court went and showed him that there was a power above him. . . . And once they came in, if the man was not cooperating, they may put him down and urinate upon him!"[146] As noted earlier, the matrifocal principles of citizenship, inheritance, and political succession encouraged an intense preservation of women's civil rights.[147] Urinating upon men manifested what Judith Van Allen has described as "sitting on a man" and what Shirley Ardener has described as African women's "sexual insult" upon men, employed to enforce women's political decisions.[148] The ability of women to punish men as individuals and as a group distinguished ikpirikpe as more than a protest organization (like the Igbo women's assembly); it was a formal political entity that constantly governed social mores.

Urinating upon men was part of a larger mechanism known as ikpo mgbogho (to desecrate, ostracize, and pronounce an individual socially dead) and typified women's show of power and authority.[149] During ikpo mgbogho, women danced through the community chanting derogatory songs against the offender, tore down the offender's home, filled his compound with garbage (domestic refuse, animal and human feces, grasses, and tree branches), stripped him naked, and paraded him around the community in a dance of shame. Ohafia women applied ikpo mgbogho against men (and sometimes women) in all cases that threatened the moral integrity of women, including abortion, divorce, and refusal to comply with ikpirikpe directives.[150] Mayne observed that "such automatic punishments, without any formal trial, where the offender was caught flagrante delicto" were never enacted by the men's court.[151] These punishments were often followed by a cleansing ritual (*iyi ose*) of the repentant accursed individual by the womenfolk, which involved yet another level of social degradation and rebirth, after which the individual could be readmitted as a legitimate member of society.[152] As a "nostalgic genre" through which the meaning of past male misbehavior became reinterpreted, iyi ose dramatized the futility of defying female power and authority, and it was often imposed upon men.[153] The cleansing ritual involved a dramatic reconfiguration of Ohafia society's moral imagination, for by focusing on the human body as the locus of personhood and the material manifestation of self, the ritual positioned women as the definers of the metanarrative of right and wrong and the conditions under which an ostracized individual was reintroduced as a legitimate member of society.[154] Through rituals of excommunication and reincorporation, women controlled the social perception of individuals and reinforced women's power to define Ohafia-Igbo citizenship.

The intersection of political power and the power to define ethnic citizenship in Ohafia women's rituals is further manifest in two biannual rites: *idighi omara* (the land purification rite) and uzo iyi (virginity testing). Both were distinguished by significant age-role inversions, where virgin girls assumed the role of a public supreme court of critical opinion, primarily against the male elders of the society. Here, ritual ceremonies were transformed into political platforms for registering dissent and bringing to public ridicule male elders who had committed social ills in secret, even in the privacy of their homes, in order to restore moral purity in the society.[155] During idighi omara, women were deemed sacred and husbands honored wives with gun salutes as homage for being breadwinners and maintaining public morality.[156] Uzo iyi was an eight-day ritual that began with girls' rites of passage into womanhood and "becoming as men" through wrestling bouts, virginity testing to ensure fertility, and elderly women's instruction of the successful candidates in the secret scandals of male society. Afterwards, the girls assumed the oracular persona of the Ekidi goddess, and mounting a podium in the village square, exposed and condemned wife abusers, bribe takers, and other male offenders.[157] Ikpirikpe utilized these ceremonies to check the moral conducts of men. Moreover, during these rituals, Ohafia women sang songs that discriminated against nonindigenous Igbo and Ibibio wives as foreigners and slaves of matrilineages, disqualifying their daughters from partaking in the rituals and thereby simultaneously questioning and reinforcing matrilineage-based citizenship incorporation. Lastly, these rituals locate the female body as a site of great moral anxiety and a site for the negotiation of various forms of identity, including the lineage seniority of settlement, slave or freeborn status, Ohafia citizenship or foreign origin, aboriginal or visitor status, childhood or womanhood, sexual purity or sexual defilement, and membership in a just social system or a corrupt moral order. The ritual songs emphasize women as breadwinners and equate motherhood with community survival.[158]

THE FEMINIST CONCEPTION OF OHAFIA MILITARY TRADITIONS

Female-focused economic subsistence and political policing was fundamental to male militaristic territorial defense and eventual slave production. Beyond plausible male escapism from a female-controlled society, women's agrarian production released male labor for territorial defense in the years following settlement, and by the eighteenth century, male military energies would be channeled toward long-distance slave raids and Aro-contracted territorial conquests. By the mid-eighteenth century, Ohafia's ritual kinship contracts and matrilineal kinship networks defined the geographic safe zone within which military slaving was deemed illegitimate, and women's policing through ije akpaka shaped the direction of Ohafia military engagements.

When men decided to embark on warfare, they informed women. At midnight the day before men went to war, all adult women assembled in the village square, led by a young woman who would become the "expeditionary war leader" (*ochi agha*). The expeditionary war leader dressed up as a male warrior; she tied a men's loincloth (*onugwe*), she did not cover her breasts (just like men), and she donned a "leopard cap" (*okpu agu*) with eagle feathers. On her head, she carried a large farm basin, which the women filled with species of every local plant seedling, as well as a hoe (Ohafia woman's farm tool) and a machete (Ohafia man's farm tool and weapon of war). The female expeditionary war leader symbolized two personas: a male warrior and a female breadwinner, and both identities were fundamental to communal survival.

The rest of the women went naked—they tied a wrapper cloth but beneath they were naked. Their bodies decorated with sacred white clay (*nzu*), which signified ritual purity, they formed a circle around the female expeditionary war leader so that the two sets of adult male age-grades who accompanied them from a distance as guards on this ritual expedition would not behold her. Singing and dancing, the women marched to a river, where they performed a ritual bath, offered their farm basin and its content as sacrifice, and prayed for the successful military expedition of the male warriors. At the end of this rite, all the women reapplied white clay on their bodies, donned their leopard caps, and tied loincloths, signifying their ritual rebirth as warriors and their sanction of warfare. The communal wooden war drum (*ikoro*) announced the women's return. At dawn, male warriors then embarked on warfare.

Anthropologist John Wood has argued in the case of the nomadic camel-herding Gabra of East Africa (where men become women) that indigenous logic of gendered power and agency become evident in the juxtaposition, symbolic reversals, and interrelation of opposites.[159] This is manifest in the ije akpaka, where all adult women in the community ritually became men. The female war leader was concealed from the vision of men because of her persona's ambiguity. On the one hand, she symbolized ujo (a man in the skin of a woman; a queer social aberration) that men must overcome in order to attain warrior masculinity (*ikperikpeogu*). On the other hand, she symbolized the reproductive power of women—their ability to give birth to male warriors.[160] The women's ritual was also a script for the ideal conduct of warfare, namely that all warriors fight as a unit (symbolized in unified singing and dancing), successfully cut a head (symbolized in their rebirth as ufiem), and return home before the war drum to be celebrated.

Besides teaching men how to fight, women were indispensable in the life cycle of male warriors, including boyhood socialization, preparation for warfare, postbattle purification, and celebration of warrior masculinity. According to Nnenna Emeri, "It was a woman that made the public announcement of her husband's accomplishment," by inciting ululation and dancing from the women of her community.[161] Women went to the village square with their symbol of authority, the ikpirikpe drum, to welcome back and legitimize successful warriors as ufiem. Having shed human blood, the warrior was considered defiled and would undergo ritual purification before being readmitted into society, and before reentering his home. When a wife or mother applied the sacred white clay on her husband or son, she enacted the first step in his ritual reincorporation into the community. After the white clay application, the wife/mother, accompanied by fellow women and the warrior's age-grade members, led the warrior to his residential compound, where a goat was slaughtered in his honor and his body was cleansed with the sacrificial blood in the presence of the lineage ancestral deities. The mother/wife next offered the warrior a calabash of water with which he washed his face, legs, and hands. Having cleansed himself thus, he threw the calabash on the ground, breaking it into pieces. Then the warrior presented himself before the *kamalu* deity of his patrilineage with a cock sacrifice. The priest of the deity ritually blessed him and welcomed him back with strokes of white clay on both feet. The warrior thereafter was confined to seclusion for eight days, to complete the purification.[162] Since murder was a heinous crime, the reincorporation ritual reconciled the moral contradiction of celebrating a successful warrior: it celebrated the sanctity of human life by having the warrior undergo a tenuous purification rite, thereby reminding all that warrior masculinity was motivated not by bloodlust but by honor.[163] Njoku argues that the ritual "demonstrates the sacredness with which Ohafia people, even in those times of uncouth valour, held human life."[164]

Even the Ohafia war dance (*iri aha*), the society's hallmark cultural tradition, is popularly traced to a woman from Ebem Ohafia called Nne Ugoenyi (or Ocha Aruodo). During the historical period of Ohafia migration and settlement in the Cross River region, Ugoenyi lost two of her sons in battle and consequently vowed to protect her third son, Egbelenwa, by forbidding his participation in any war. Throughout

Egbelenwa's childhood, Ugoenyi prevented him from playing with other boys and often dressed him up as a girl. However, when he came of age, Egbelenwa followed his age-mates to battle without his mother's awareness. He was successful and returned not only with a human head but with live captives as well. The entire community rejoiced at Egbelenwa's successful return, bearing him high over their shoulders. Upon learning of her son's return, Ugoenyi dressed him up as an exceptional warrior and killed many goats and chickens, providing an elaborate feast. She commissioned some male members of her community to commemorate her son's feat with a special dance, and the war dance has been performed ever since. The men subsequently assembled three human heads in a basket, representing heads they had cut from Benin, Umunede, and Ajakata Ibeku (the three major successive settlements of the Ohafia-Mben before their arrival in their present location). This basket was known as *oyaya*, and the war dancers carried it on their heads when they danced.[165]

Women were instrumental in the social distinction of ufiem and ujo, and some women performed warrior masculinity. Several Ohafia traditions account that some women embarked on warfare in the seventeenth and eighteenth centuries to put an end to their husbands' ujo status. Nne Mbgafo and Unyang Olugu were such women, whom Azuonye describes as "man-like female warriors, who surprised their generations by taking up arms and marching to battle, fighting even more ferociously than men."[166] Mgbafo lost her first husband at Arochukwu and came to Ohafia to find a new husband. Before setting out on her quest for a husband, she went to a market and bought a war cap, a Dane gun, and a sharpened machete. She dressed up like a warrior. Her search led her to Akanu Ohafia, where she met a man named Uduma and took him for a husband. Later, when Uduma went to war at Atatum in Ibibioland and was killed, Mgbafo set out to find him. She took her husband's hunting gun, machete, *jooji* cloth, and war cap. When she found her husband slain in the battlefield, Mgbafo became so upset that she overpowered an Ibibio warrior and sacrificed him on her husband's grave. The inability of Uduma to successfully return from battle defined him as ujo. Nne Mgbafo sought to change his status, posthumously. She is remembered in oral traditions as "she that was her husband's heart," "she that did things like her father," "woman that behaved like a man," and "great leopard."[167]

Similarly, in the oral tradition of Unyang Olugu, her husband is described as an ujo from whom "the penal-yam-for-cowardice" was exacted.[168] Ohafia oral historian and current lead singer of Ohafia war songs Kalu Oki described Unyang Olugu's husband as a "weak man" (*onye ngolongo*).[169] In order to put an end to her husband's ujo status, Unyang Olugu went to war against the people of Nkalu (the original inhabitants of neighboring present-day Afikpo), who were engaged in mutual hostilities (abductions, raids, and headhunting) with the Ohafia in the mid-eighteenth century.[170] In the ensuing battle, Unyang Olugu killed five Nkalu men, assembled their heads (which she dressed in leopard caps) in a long basket, presented them to her husband, and escorted him before the village war drum in order to establish him as ufiem. However, when the ikoro began to praise her husband, Unyang Olugu insisted, "They should not chant praises to him. Rather let them chant praises to Unyang Olugu, killer-that-gave-the-honor-to-her-husband; she-that-kills-and-packs-in-long-baskets; woman that won heads in battle."[171]

The present chapter has outlined the social, economic, and political contexts of female power and authority from the period of Ohafia migration and settlement to the mid-nineteenth-century peak period of postabolition legitimate trade. The broad chronological framework provides a *longue durée* ethnographic baseline against which subsequent sociopolitical changes took place through the articulation of local institutions with Atlantic political economies. This chapter suggests that the matrifocal systems that defined hegemonic femininity also shaped the military traditions and intergroup relations that would later underpin regional slaving. As apparent in the traditions of Nne Mgbafo and Unyang Olugu as well as the women's rituals of war declaration and reincorporation of male warriors, male-centered militarism was a gendered practice because it was a complementary side of a dual-sex political economy, which women facilitated. Ohafia-Igbo women's lineage systems and gendered sociopolitical institutions, especially the preeminent role of women in the local agrarian economy and their political policing, made it possible for men to principally engage in military activities. One cannot conceive Biafran Atlanticization without understanding the ways that African societies in the region organized themselves, the institutions that enabled them to participate in Atlantic slave production, and the lineage and gender ideologies that defined their modes of Atlantic engagement. Whereas chapter 1 provides the feminist perspective of Ohafia's institutional foundations, chapter 2 advances male-centered narratives of Atlanticization and their impact on the dual-sex sociopolitical systems and practices of hegemonic masculinity. The traditions of Nne Mgbafo, Unyang Olugu, and several others analyzed in chapter 2 will elucidate the transformation of male militarism from territorial defense to slave production, as well as the centrality of militarism to changing conceptions of masculinity in the seventeenth and nineteenth centuries.

2 ◈ Military Slaving, ca. 1650–1890

The Making of Warrior Masculinities

WHY DID the Ohafia-Igbo aggressively expand their military operations in the eighteenth and nineteenth centuries? What commercial and cultural frameworks enabled them to participate in the Bight of Biafra's slavery system? How does a historical assessment of Ohafia militarism improve our understanding of Biafra's slave production in the era of the Atlantic slave trade? What were the immediate and long-term ramifications of their militarism? In particular, how did military slave production *gender* social identities and social institutions? By answering these questions, this chapter demonstrates that the Atlantic slave trade introduced a new cultural logic of hegemonic masculinity, which juxtaposed nascent male power to the preexisting female sociocultural superiority, thereby reinforcing the dual-sex sociopolitical system. New male sociopolitical institutions such as *okonko* and *ite odo* confraternities, established to advance slaving, would offer competing alternatives to female-centered religious and lineage traditions, and popularize violent notions of masculine respectability. One legacy of military slaving was the social vision of Ohafia as a heroic (and macho) Igbo society.[1] This was in juxtaposition to conceptualizing the society as a matrilineal (and matriarchal) Ibo people.[2] The latter emphasizes those tenacious female-centered sociopolitical institutions like ikpirikpe, and rituals and practices such as uzo-iyi (virginity testing), ije akpaka (ritual declaration of war), ibo ezi (strike and boycott), ikpo mgbogho (social ostracism), and ududu (matriarchal religion), which had centered women in the memorialization of Ohafia historical identity. The former, however, references a different set of historical traditions and metanarratives about male-exclusive secret societies and military institutions, as well as the Ohafia war dance and war songs, which venerated a heroic age of manliness. This chapter situates such military traditions within the broader scholarship on slaving in the Bight of Biafra to show how the Ohafia mobilized new sociopolitical institutions and regional alliances, and transformed preexisting ones, in order to generate captives from the Igbo and Ibibio hinterlands and exploit rapidly expanding markets during the eighteenth and nineteenth centuries. In the process of Atlantic slaving, warriors came to define the dominant stereotype of masculinity in the region. The performance of warrior masculinity became social performance of power over others through capture, enslavement, dispossession, and differential social mobility. Warriors dramatized their social power through monopolistic displays of certain cross-Atlantic commodities acquired through slave supply.

From the perspective of the Ohafia-Igbo, warfare was a major source of captives from the Bight of Biafra, and it was an institutionalized historical practice. There was a notable shift in the objectives and modalities of warfare, from a seventeenth-century political economy of headhunting to pacify a bellicose frontier settlement, to an eighteenth- and nineteenth-century era of concerted slaving to meet regional and overseas demand. Before the Atlantic slave trade, human head trophies obtained in territorial battles served as evidence of military distinction, ensuring social, economic, and political privileges for warriors who defended their communities. But during the Atlantic slave trade, captives ensured even more direct socioeconomic power for warriors. As shown in chapter 1, seventeenth-century warfare, distinguished by its emphasis on headhunting, focused against eastern Ibibio, Annang, Efik, Eket, Qua, Ekoi, and Ogoja neighbors. These were the wars that generated the oral traditions of brazen female warriors like Unyang Olugu, Nne Mgbafo, and Nne Ugoenyi. Historian and specialist on Ohafia war songs Chukwuma Azuonye suggests that the memorialization of female warriors in the war songs alludes to the "state of constant warfare" between the Ohafia and their "non-Igbo" neighbors: conflicts were so incessant that women, usually nonfighters, distinguished themselves in battle. Azuonye insists that these Ohafia wars against Ibibio and Ogoja peoples were "a struggle for survival." Yet he acknowledges that beyond the boundary Ibibio communities of Agbawan, Ikun, and Biakpan, Ohafia warriors ventured as far as Biase and Ekoi territories to take men, women, and children captive. Most of these captives were sold into the Atlantic trade, either through the Aro or directly to the Efik of Old Calabar, in exchange for European goods such as guns, textiles, and animal traps, as well as Efik masquerade outfits.[3] Historian David Northrup further writes that the Ohafia allied with the Odoro Ikpe clan of the Ibibio and raided other Ibibio communities for slaves, whom they sold to the Aro. And they also supplied slaves to the Ikpa and the Enyong on the Cross River.[4] This was possible because the Uduma River linked Ohafia with Arochukwu, Itu, Ikpe, and Ikot Eto, while the Enyong River and the Cross River linked Ohafia with the Ekoi, Obubra, Efik, and Calabar peoples.[5] The Aro and the Efik are identified in the war songs by the trade goods they supplied in exchange for Ohafia's captives, namely *nde-ekpu-okara* (dealers-in-cloths), *nde-ekpu-ole* (dealers-in-silver), and *nde-ebu-anwuru-ebu-akawa* (dealers-in-tobacco-and-saltpeter). And both are personified as the primary dealers-in-slaves (*nde-ekpe-ohu*).[6] Nwokeji has analyzed how changing volumes of slave supplies from the Bight of Biafra simulated shifting frontiers of slave production in the region's hinterland. Between 1651 and 1690, when the eastern Cross River region constituted the frontier of Ohafia warfare, there was a 16 percent increase in Biafra captives, most obtained from the riverine Ibibio communities.[7]

According to historian John Oriji, by the eighteenth century, however, Ohafia military practices had become an essential arm of a vast regional trading network facilitated by the Aro.[8] Nwokeji demonstrates that this expansion was a response to the increasing demand for African captives, incentivized by the expansion of the American plantation complex between 1700 and 1740.[9] Ohafia elder Nna Agbai Ndukwe explains the resulting Ohafia-Aro slaving dynamic:

> Aro people revered Ohafia people and always came to us for aid in battles. Our soldiers were provided by the age-grades, and every man was expected to go to war and bring back a human head. When the Aro came to Ohafia for military aid, Ohafia would go to war, preoccupied with obtaining heads, while the Aro would be busy looting property and pillaging people. This was how Ohafia fought in Ibibio, Ugep, Ogoja, Okigwe, and so forth . . . Ohafia people participated in the slave traffic, and sold slaves as well, even though it was the Aro that principally traded in slaves. Some Aro traders even came to Ohafia to buy

captives.... The Aro came with silver, cloth, guns, tobacco, alcohol.... When Aro people purchased captives from us, they took them to Calabar. There is a river called Eze-Iyi Aku in Abiriba, where Ohafia people also took their captives to sell. The Eze-Iyi River was a point of no return; every slave that got on a boat there went to Calabar. Aro people usually came at night to meet our elders. They brought yards of cloths, alcohol, palm wine, and ram, to seek ukwuzi, asking, "Please come and lead us to a foreign land." Ohafia did not seek to establish how exactly this foreign land had offended the Aro. As far as our fathers were concerned, war was an opportunity for self-distinction. Our warriors would go and start killing, while the Aro would be busy pillaging and looting, and sometimes establishing colonies, such as Aro Ndi-Izuogu, Aro Ujari, and so on. Ohafia warriors, on the other hand, were after the human head; and they were eager to return home in order to celebrate it [the head] before the ikoro [war drum].[10]

Nna Agbai raises two important questions that shed light on the eighteenth-century transformation of Ohafia military practices. First, were Ohafia warriors headhunters or slavers? Military distinction, epitomized in headhunting, was cardinal to respectable manhood (ufiem) in Ohafia society, in contrast to many West African societies where astute oratory, mastery of proverbs, and title taking constituted ufiem performance.[11] Njoku writes that in precolonial Ohafia society, "A man of intelligence and uncommon power of speech was admired and respected. But if he could not match his words with deeds, his prestige was compromised.... The proficient farmer, the master-wrestler, and the proficient hunter were heroes.... But this genre of heroism stood no comparison with military heroism."[12] Indeed, the exaltation of militarism in Ohafia cultural traditions and social differentiation has led several scholars to the conclusion that the Ohafia had no knowledge of alternative civil pursuits and were bloodthirsty headhunters and mercenaries, who accepted every war.[13] This perspective overlooks the changes in Ohafia's modes of warfare and ignores the diverse roles of women as traders and food producers in Ohafia's dual-sex economy. The military heroism narrative, which the legacy of headhunting substantiates, also serves to distance the Ohafia from the odium of slaving.

Thus, various Ohafia respondents were quick to blame the Aro for slaving, whereas the Ohafia warriors are remembered as noble warriors. According to Olua Iro Kalu, "It was the Aro that customarily contracted the Ohafia for head cutting. While the Ohafia were cutting heads, the Aro would be busy looting the property and capturing slaves for sale."[14] Similarly, Chief K. K. Owen asserts, "When the Aro came to us for ukwuzi, our warriors would go and fight for them. Our fathers were interested in cutting a head in order to be able to *answer a man*. The Ohafia man who goes to war is preoccupied with bravery, and obtaining a human head to put in his bag. But while the war is going on, the Aro would be plundering the people, carrying off their goods, and kidnapping people."[15] Others like Kalu Oki adamantly insisted, "The Ohafia did not trade in slaves. It was the Aro. What the Ohafia did was that as warriors they fought a lot of wars. The Ohafia were warriors and the Aro came to them for aid. While the Ohafia fought, and killed the enemies, the Aro would be busy carrying away property, and taking people captives."[16] To many Ohafia respondents, historical perspective was at stake. Although warriors may have generated captives, the raison d'être for warfare was heroic man making, not slaving. Thus, Kalu Oki, who steadfastly denounced the notion of Ohafia military slaving, also stated that his great-grandfather Nna Iyi-Oke Echi (1790–1870) went to various wars with ropes and took numerous captives, which evidenced his military prowess and distinguished him as a powerful ufiem.[17]

There was not always a neat distinction between "headhunting," slave production, defense, punitive expedition, pacification, protection, and honor in the military activities of Ohafia. Some Ohafia battles were interventionist attempts to restore law and order in troubled areas, to safeguard major trade routes in the Biafra hinterland, or, upon invitation, to defend militarily weaker communities from their more powerful neighbors. In most of these instances, warriors cut heads and took captives. Several Ohafia men who performed ikperikpeogu (warrior masculinity) in the eighteenth and nineteenth centuries are memorialized in oral traditions as *ochi-udo-eje-ogu* (he-that-went-to-war-with-a-rope). The rope was used to tether slaves, not human heads.[18] Historian Martin Klein observed that warriors often fought for selfish reasons when he pointed out that slave-producing warriors of the Western Sudan did not always act as expected, for they could unmake rulers in order to strengthen their own positions.[19] In much the same way, Ohafia warriors took captives for material gains. Richard Roberts has also observed that what may have been a political decision to wage war on the part of a group often became an economic or social one for warriors. Even though warriors engaged in warfare in the interest of contractual parties, they retained their own agenda, and continuous warfare became the result of the warriors' need to reproduce their sociopolitical relevance and privileges.[20] Ethnographic evidence suggests that the "heads" that warriors sought changed over time. They were not always human heads, but rather idioms for expressing the symbolic achievement of superiority or ufiem, which indeed manifested itself in material social differentiation.

Chief Kalu Awa Kalu explains:

> The ikoro [war drum] and iri aha [war dance] constitute the respect and honor accorded those who had cut a head in battle. Many of my grandfather's age-mates fought in Nnewi and Nneato [1860s], and were called *o-chi-udo-eje-ogu* [those-that-went-to-war-with-ropes]. When they returned with captives, the war drum broke out for them, and the war dance was performed for them, because they cut a head. After the white people came with Christianity and Western education [post-1900], when an Ohafia man went abroad to study and, upon his return, brought back a school certificate and money, he was said to have cut a head. Even some people who became ogaranya from trading or working in the colonial service also returned with a lot of money or an expensive vehicle. The person would go to the elders bearing gifts, and the elders would say that even though he did not cut a head with a machete, he had actually cut a head, one that is visible and materialistic *[O gbughi nke mma; mana o gbuu nke a fu anya]*. So the war drum and war dance would be performed in his honor. Today, if an individual provides the finance for the construction of motor roads for the community, which was something customarily assigned to an entire age-grade, the war drum and war dance are performed in his honor. Men who built modern duplexes had the war drum beat for them, because they performed the feat of "brave man," of "one who performed bravery." It is as though wealth replaced heads.[21]

In this sense, anthropologist John McCall echoed the historical genealogy of "heads" narrated by Kalu Awa when he wrote that in Ohafia, "the academic certificate and the Mercedes Benz [have become] 'heads' that when brought home, established the passage to full manhood."[22]

In the eighteenth and nineteenth centuries, besides being honored with the war drum and war dance, Ohafia warriors who "cut a head" were also distinguished in public by wearing the rare and expensive red *jooji* cloth.[23] Originally produced in India until the late nineteenth century, when large quantities were imported into Biafra from Manchester, the jooji cloth was a major commodity that the Ohafia obtained from the Aro in exchange for their military services and captive supply. Jooji gained popularity among African royal families in the Gold Coast, Calabar, and Opobo as a status symbol. Ohafia people incorporated jooji as a social marker of ufiem attainment. In this sense, the jooji practice was an example of what historian Robert DuPlessis has described as an Atlantic sartorial regime, which involved dynamic and syncretic appropriation of Atlantic objects to refashion, supplant, or sustain norms; signal inclusion and exclusion; impose circumscribed ascendancy; and symbolize gender, ethnicity, occupation, and class.[24] Warriors complemented the jooji cloth with a red-and-white-striped leopard cap (okpu agu) decorated with red tail feathers of parrot and eagle plumes, as well as a ram's mane worn over the left arm. Men who failed to distinguish themselves in battle were forbidden to wear jooji and disdained as ujo: "women in the skin of men." This meant that they were deemed a social aberration because they embodied cowardice and were neither male warriors nor female breadwinners. If the ujo wore jooji in public, he was stripped of his dress. Ujo were socially ostracized and excluded from age-grade activities and secret societies. In effect, they were denied a voice in the political administration of their society. They were subjected to all forms of humiliating insults. Children taunted them in public. Their ufiem-accomplished age-mates often dispossessed them of their property, especially domestic animals and yams, referenced in the war songs as the "penal-yam/goat-for-cowardice." The ujo were not allowed to take yam titles, and they were sometimes sold to the Aro as slaves for various offenses. It was difficult for the ujo to marry because they lacked honor. Thus, they hardly achieved adult masculinity, which marriage signified. The ujo were considered to be adolescents.

If they married, their wives were obliged to dress in mourning attire and wear short hair. Freedom, social incorporation, and the security of life and property were forlorn to the ujo.²⁵ To overcome ujo status and achieve social integration, Ohafia men *hunted heads* through slaving and military services to the Aro.²⁶

A 1901 British colonial correspondence corroborates the nature of the Ohafia-Aro slaving dynamic described by Nna Agbai and others. According to British High Commissioner Ralph Moore, in the course of the last quarter of the nineteenth century,

> several attacks by the Inokuns . . . the several Aro tribes [against] the Ibibios [were reported by] representative chiefs [from] Old Calabar, Degema, Bonny, Opobo, Okrika, New Calabar, and Brass. . . . Natives *seized by organized slave raiding and sold in slave markets* . . . are obtained in the East of the Niger principally from the Aro tribe, *portions of which are engaged more or less in continuous slave raiding*, while one branch of the tribe — the Inokuns — are the business people engaged principally in the slave dealing. . . . The *raiding sections of the tribe* are the Ohafia-Abams, Ekpaffias [Ahoada] and Baribas [Abiriba]. The four sections may regard themselves as separate tribes forming a portion of the Ibo nation, but they are undoubtedly closely connected and work together in all transactions, fighting, slaving, trading, & c. . . . In May [1899], the Inokuns brought down the [Ohafia-Abam], and under a false pretext concerning the non observance of Juju rites on the killing of a dangerous leopard, attacked and raided the Ibibios and Kwas, killing large numbers, *in one case wiping out a whole village, and carrying off all they could seize to sell as slaves*. This raid occurred on the S.E. border of the Aro country, and the natives seized will no doubt be sold on the Western and Northern borders.²⁷ [emphasis added]

Moore's report confirms the resilience of the slaving dynamic in which Ohafia warriors (the portion "engaged more or less in continuous slave raiding") attacked communities in the Biafra hinterland to enable the Aro (the portion "engaged principally in slave dealing") to loot property and seize captives. Moore also sheds light on the second question raised by Agbai: the nature of the relationship between the

Ohafia and the Aro. Moore deemed the Cross River Igbo communities of Ohafia, Abam, Abiriba, and Arochukwu to be branches of a "tribe," intimately connected by slave production. The language that the Ohafia use to characterize this intimate relationship is *ukwuzi*, a system whereby a more powerful deity, individual, or group offered protection to another individual or group of persons in return for favors or services. Thus, in an ukwuzi between a man and a woman, usually a widow, the man provided shelter and protection in exchange for household reproduction. Slaves and sometimes criminals sought ukwuzi with powerful deities. Weak or socially marginal individuals sought ukwuzi with powerful patrons, and land and other property could be secured through ukwuzi with a superior body.[28] Regionally renowned for its military prowess, Ohafia provided ukwuzi to neighbors such as Abam, with which it shared putative kinship; Abiriba, in exchange for metal weapons; and Arochukwu and its diasporas (Arondizuogu, Bende, Uzuakoli, Ujari, and Ndieni), in exchange for European trade goods and access to regional slave fairs.[29] According to Nwokeji, the Aro contracted protectionism and negotiated for fighters from Ohafia "utilizing blood and marriage bonds."[30] The Ohafia did not fight for direct territorial and political hegemony over other groups, but they were responsible for Aro conquest and establishment of diaspora settlements at Ndieni, Ujari, Ndikelionwu, Arondizuogu, and Otanchara.[31] Anthropologist G. I. Jones observed, "the Aro were not warriors but an organization of traders."[32] Historian David Northrup writes that they were "the god men of trade" who lacked a "military force" and so formed alliances "based upon equality" with strategic groups.[33] Nwokeji notes, "Before the mid-nineteenth century, the Aro had been averse to directly partaking in martial activities. In fact, they had taken pride in not being warriors themselves."[34] Oriji adds, "The Aro, during the slave trade, took advantage of the burning zeal of [Ohafia] youths to attain the Ufiem status . . . the Aro gave gifts to [Ohafia] chiefs and entered into blood covenants . . . the chiefs then summoned the Ujo in their various communities to join the Aro in their invasion."[35] The combination of shared ancestry, blood covenants, intermarriages, and mutual protection ensured kinship (real or fictive) among the Cross River Igbo groups and provided a foundation for collaborative slaving ventures.

However, it is only in light of eighteenth-century developments in Biafra's regional slaving systems that we can make sense of Nna Agbai's seemingly contradictory statements: that the Ohafia went to war "preoccupied with obtaining heads" but that they "participated in the slave traffic, and they sold slaves as well." Azuonye writes, "The spread of the warlike activities of the Ohafia people to other parts of Igbo country, in the 18th and 19th centuries, was accelerated by their contacts with the Aro."[36] Nwokeji specifies that between 1700 and 1740, the Aro established their principal settlements (Arondizuogu and Ndieni) in the Nri-Awka region of central Igboland with the aid of Ohafia military. During this period, the Aro duly contracted the Ohafia army in the ukwuzi tradition by presenting "items of kola" including two rams sacrificed to the Ohafia war god (Ikwan Di Orie), as well as alcohol and kola nut.[37] The Izuogu expeditions were major military undertakings for the Ohafia, and therefore "each of the twenty-[six] village-groups contribute[d] a 'battalion' of *abuo-adighi-ya-na-nnu-abo*, i.e. 'two short of four hundred times two,' or 798 men."[38] That sums up to 20,748 soldiers. We have no way to ascertain that this number of warriors actually participated, but the outcome suggests a massive military force. Ohafia's wars in Izuogu resulted in "the most spectacular . . . destruction of Ora . . . one of the severest acts of violence committed during the Atlantic slave trade era . . . the massacre of the . . . entire population [in which] the territory was plundered and completely laid waste." Perhaps it was because Izuogu's mother originated from Ohafia matrilineal society that they responded in such massive numbers on Izuogu's behalf, thereby increasing Chief Izuogu's influence over various conquered communities.[39] And Ohafia continued to supply Izuogu's people (Ndi-Izuogu) with captives. When the neighboring Uruala challenged Ndi-Izuogu, Ohafia warriors slaughtered their able-bodied men and guaranteed Aro hegemony in the area. Izuogu served as a springboard for further Ohafia military raids in the Okigwe area. The warriors destroyed many Isu towns including Uzi, Umuagwo, and Umuakuru, yielding a large number of captives, which made Arondizuogu the major source of slaves for the fairs in Bende. In effect, Ohafia in the first half of the eighteenth century enabled so-called Aro proliferation, prosperity, and expansion, actualized through conquest, marriage, enslavement, and aggressive incorporation.[40]

Then between 1750 and 1850, Aro "merchant-warlords negotiated of their own accord for fighters from Cross River Igbo communities" and expanded Aro influence into southern and northern Igboland.

During this period, alliances with Ohafia warriors were made "through the agency of Aro freelancing private enterprise," which made violence a key feature of Aro expansionist strategy.[41] Instead of the customary "items of kola," Ohafia warriors began to demand "consultation fees" in war caps, textiles, guns, tobacco, and liquor. And warrior bands began to harass regional routes and engage in kidnapping.[42] This commercialization of the Ohafia-Aro ukwuzi is memorialized in the oral tradition of Elibe Aja, one of the most popular war-song narratives. Elibe Aja personified the self-sacrificing valor of Ohafia warriors, who customarily fought for the Aro in return for minimal material gains. According to this tradition, when Aro chiefs presented the usual "items of kola" to Ohafia elders and requested their military aid, Ohafia lineages rebuffed Aro pleas and accused the Aro of kidnapping and selling off their countrymen lost in battle during the "Ora war" in utter disregard of ukwuzi. Ohafia elders demanded "to be given four hundred pieces of *okpogho* [iron bars], given a box of *okara* [jooji cloth], given a box of shirts . . . a box of wine, [and] forest-guns." It was only after the Aro presented these items that Elibe Aja (personifying Ohafia warriors) "went with the people of Aro to their territory." But afterward, Ohafia warrior bands began to harass Aro trade routes and fringe settlements. Thus, Elibe Aja transformed himself into the "terror of the silver-peddlers," "the terror of them that trade in salt-petre," and the "terror of Nde-Aba-Ahaba [Aro diaspora]."[43]

In this way, the oral tradition of Elibe Aja alludes to how the Ohafia may have adapted to the economic opportunities presented by the slave trade. In particular, it sheds light on how the ujo, fed up with their marginality, embraced banditry and violated ukwuzi to ensure their survival and escape the control of fastidious elders. Ohafia military organization had been based on the *uke* age-grade sociopolitical system. Warriors were recruited from *obon* and *akang* secret societies and organized into age-grade regiments. Adapted from the Ibibio during the seventeenth century, akang and obon have been described as guerrilla military training institutions for Ohafia warriors. Because membership in obon and akang was compulsory for patrilineage sons, the societies provided older men a means of social control over younger men. By mastering the societies' secret language and symbols, warriors built camaraderie, and membership became foundational to military distinction and social mobility. But by the eighteenth century, it was the elders who gained the most from Aro "consultation fees." Denied membership in secret societies, some ujo engaged in robbery and kidnapping along trade routes for economic sustenance. Such crimes were often cited for the punitive enslavement of ujo.[44] Historians Walter Hawthorne and Robert Baum have observed similar transformations among the Balanta of the Guinea Coast and the Esulalu Diola of Senegambia, respectively, where young men, frustrated by the control of elders and anxious to acquire titles, guns, cloth, and wives, resorted to kidnapping of mostly women and children, which was deemed to be an illegitimate form of slaving because it often violated kinship bonds and honor codes.[45] Although some warriors may have violated conceptions of "legitimate war," Njoku, Isichei, Azuonye, Oriji, and Northrup argue that the entire Ohafia military was not mercenaries kept and controlled by the Aro.[46] According to Azuonye, "The Ohafia were rather an independent group in full control of their fighting forces and free to offer or withhold their services as they saw fit."[47] Northrup affirms that the Aro were able to safeguard their territories from Ohafia military attacks because of ukwuzi, but the Aro "did not control [Ohafia] activities elsewhere."[48] In other words, when Ohafia warriors received payments for their services, they did so freely and independently.

The oral tradition of Elibe Aja signals a major shift in the ethics of Ohafia military practices as a result of the Atlantic slave trade, which increased the intensity, geography, and trauma of military raids. According to Ohafia veteran lead-singer of the war songs Kalu Oki, the tradition marked a transition from "a period when men went to war with baskets" to "a period when men went to war with pouches and ropes."[49] The shift meant that warriors defied the heroic ethic of cutting the heads of conquered foes in battle by enslaving communities. The specific age-grades involved in this transformation of martial ethos are memorialized in oral traditions through nicknaming such as *Omere ndi ata mgbamgba* (the victimizer of Upper Imo River communities), *Okpoduru Ora* (those that annihilated Ora community), *Omekashiri Igbo Ohu* (the slavers of central Igboland), and *Omekashiri Agbaja* (enslavers of Agbaja in northern Igboland). It is difficult to assign specific dates to these oral traditions, but allegorically, going to war with baskets to bring back human head trophies is often represented—especially in the war dance—as having deterred military assaults from Ohafia's pugnacious eastern neighbors, and thus places that custom within the pre-1740 incessant Ibibio Wars. From the mid-eighteenth century, however, the dramatic increase in the volume of Biafra's slave trade encouraged independent warriors to act illegitimately. Warriors cut male heads in battle but also tethered captives, mostly women and children, with ropes.[50] Oriji writes that Ohafia militarism became more widespread as the demand for slaves increased in the Bight of Biafra during the eighteenth century. From the 1740s, Ohafia military activities became increasingly oriented toward northern Igboland, where ecological deterioration combined with high population density intensified political rivalries, land disputes, and family feuds. Consequently, wealthy and powerful men, who could afford "consultation fees," allied themselves with Ohafia warriors to fight local wars, raid nearby communities for slaves, and strengthen their political power. In this way, Ohafia warriors invaded Nteje, Afikpo, Uburu, and Agbaja in the second half of the eighteenth century. The Nteje War in particular is popularly recalled as "one of the most futile wars Ohafia had ever encountered," because the long trek was dreary and very few warriors returned to tell (or dance) their tales before the village war drums. The battle against Agbaja is said to have raged fiercely for four days, and Ohafia warriors only emerged victorious at great cost of lives. Some warriors settled at Abboh and allied with the Niike, the major slave traders of the Udi-Nsukka axis, and raided Opi, Ukehe, and other towns for slaves. Ohafia raids in the north became more destructive as they competed for supremacy with Onoja Oboni, the Igala slave trader.[51]

Further evidence of the eighteenth-century shift in the frontier of Ohafia military activities from Ibibioland to Igboland comes from a cluster of documented regional responses to Ohafia slave raids. In southern Igboland, Ohafia mercenary activity for economic gains caused the Igbere to flee their Oroni homeland and reorganize their military institutions. According to Oriji, Ohafia-Abam invasion of the Umuajuju of Okporo Ahaba resulted in the enslavement of many of the inhabitants, the dislocation of numerous survivors (who founded four new settlements), and the institution of new protector deities and taboos. Their attacks on Ohia-Ukwu of the Ngboko-Ohanze led to a "massacre" and "enslavement" of the inhabitants and precipitated the most massive population movement in the region. Throughout Igboland, Ohafia-Abam raids aroused a new sense of military alertness.

Women went to farms and markets in groups accompanied by armed guards, the use of emergency-signal war drums proliferated, and new war gods and military institutions promoted a heroic martial ethos.[52] In northern Igboland, Nwando Achebe chronicles how the Nsukka region established protector deities in response to incessant Ohafia-Nkanu raids.[53] According to Arua, Njoku, Isichei, and Richard Henderson, many Igbo communities reorganized their sociopolitical and territorial systems in the nineteenth century in response to Ohafia raids. This included the expansion of military and political operations through the formation of confederacies. Isuochi and Nneato towns in Okigwe merged into the Isumisu confederacy. The Amakwan and Umuchu confederacies emerged in the Awka region.[54] The king of Nri formed the Amakom confederation (Awka, Nibo, Nise, Amawobia, Ugwuoba, Enugu-Agidi, Ebenebe, Ukpo, and Amansi) to militarily check Ohafia raids.[55] Communities such as Enugu Ezike and Enugu-Ukwu resorted to poisoning their waters, wine, and food. Awka communities surrounded their compounds with high walls, watchtowers, and firing loopholes. Ohuhu people built trenches around their homes, and many in the regions that would become Anambra and Enugu resorted to hilltop settlements with poor soils.[56]

The increased violence of military slaving no doubt had to do with the guerrilla mode and extensive geography of warfare, which also encouraged warriors to act arbitrarily. Because ukwuzi established a real and fictive kinship zone between Ohafia and their immediate neighbors, headhunting and slave-raiding expeditions were delimited to distant marginal communities and territories beyond the zone. Thus, the military/slaving zone comprised densely populated Ibiobioland, south-central Igboland where Aro expansionism incentivized Ohafia militarism, and northern Igboland, where semi-savannah-induced territorial struggles proved conducive to Ohafia guerrilla military tactics.[57] It took warriors several weeks to reach their destinations, and their return was made dangerous by reprisal attacks and ransom kidnapping.[58] Some lost their way and settled on the periphery of Aro communities. Consequently, a number of Ohafia settlements emerged in various parts of Igboland, such as Orofia in Abagana, Uduma Achara in Awgu, Lohum in Uzuakoli, and Ohambele in Ndokiland.[59] Long-distance expeditions made warriors less accountable to elders and may have encouraged ambitious warriors to hire out their services as mercenaries or to violate ukwuzi safe zones, take captives they could use to ransom themselves, and meet more immediate economic needs.[60]

From the mid-nineteenth century, when the external slave trade effectively ended, the Bight of Biafra's trading economy entered a terminal crisis and Aro merchants hired Ohafia warriors as mercenaries, "fueling a state of instability rarely witnessed even during the long centuries of the overseas slave trade."[61] The restructuring of local economies and markets from slave trade to palm oil trade had created intense land disputes and civil strife, buttressed by a new discriminatory language of landlords and strangers.[62] Heightened intergroup conflict increased the demand for military services. Thus, in central Igboland, communities like Nnewi contracted Ohafia warriors to attack and displace their Awka-Etiti neighbors. Ohafia warriors intervened in the civil war among the different sections of Nnewi between the 1860s and 1890s, in the process raiding neighboring towns like Nnobi and Oraifite for slaves. The Obosi enlisted Ohafia warriors to invade Onitsha people in the 1870s, just as the Awkuzu deployed Ohafia warriors in the 1890s to raid Nteje, Igbariam, and Aguleri. Communities such as Eror and Ukpati were nearly destroyed in the 1880s. During this latter period, Ohafia warriors charged "consultation fees" in British pounds, war caps, textiles, guns, tobacco, iron bars, and liquor.[63]

Ohafia's extensive regional militarism does not fit into Paul Lovejoy's framework, which subsumes noncentralized African societies into a category of "random enslavement" that did not affect population density.[64] This implies that in noncentralized African societies, warfare was not a major source of captives. British Commissioner Moore defined slaves generated by Ohafia warriors as "natives seized by organized slave raiding and sold in slave markets." The consequences of Ohafia raids were devastating. Nwokeji provides another late eighteenth-century example: Ohafia raids in Enugu displaced the inhabitants and enabled the Aro to establish their colonies of Ndienu and Ujalli, and Ohafia invasion of Otanchara resulted in the enslavement of most of the population.[65] Oriji argues that incessant military raids created a vicious cycle of fear, insecurity, famine, and poverty, which led impoverished parents to pawn themselves or their children. Since a majority of about 1.34 million Igbo people shipped to the New World were young people (fourteen to thirty years old) and children (fourteen years old on average), generated mostly through raids and kidnapping, the economic and demographic impacts of population loss were far reaching.[66] As a result of the shifting frontiers of military slaving from Ibibioland (1650–1700) to central Igboland (1700–1750) and then to southern and northern Igboland (1750–1890), Biafra's captive supply increased by 61 percent, well above the expansion rate of the overall African slave trade.[67] After reviewing Andreas Oldendorp's 1777 diary account of modes of enslavement of Biafra-African captives enslaved in the Caribbean islands and Sigmund Koelle's report on Biafra-African resettled ex-slaves in 1850s Sierra Leone, Nwokeji concludes,

> The overwhelming majority of captives [in both sources] were enslaved through warfare and kidnapping. . . . Without question, therefore, warfare was an important source of captives. . . . Wars remained an important source of captives until the end of the overseas slave trade in the mid-nineteenth century, according to the accounts of contemporary British visitors and African missionaries. . . . When we account for [the] large number of captives involved in warfare, war captives may account for a greater share of the sample than the nominal figures suggest.[68]

Isichei and Oriji also contend that warfare and kidnapping accounted for 60 percent of slaves sold in the Igbo hinterland, whereas only 20 percent were obtained through the judicial process of political deportation and 20 percent through outright purchase.[69] Whereas captives acquired through sale due to economic necessity and pawning were mostly retained as household slaves, those generated through warfare, kidnapping, and judicial processes often ended up as market slaves and were likely exported. Of these categories, mostly adult men constituted captives enslaved for dissidence and criminality (political deportees), whereas mostly women and children were generated through kidnapping and warfare. The Bight of Biafra generated mostly women and children, which fits with the region's military mode. From his interactions with slaves embarked from Bonny, sea surgeon William James, a master in the British Royal Navy who made three voyages from Bonny and Old Calabar between 1764 and 1771, attested that military captivity and kidnapping in the Bight of Biafra generated mostly female slaves and children.[70] Even though Koelle's account of the modes of enslavement of Biafran captives resettled in Sierra Leone was derived mostly from male slaves (without accounting for women and children that warfare and kidnapping mostly generated), his report still showed that war captives made up the largest category (34 percent) followed by kidnapped victims (30 percent).[71]

And the distinction often made between kidnapping and warfare may be an artificial one. Olatunji Ojo has argued that raids—operationally

FIGURE 2.1. Ohafia war dancer

small wars lasting shorter periods—embraced tactics used in major wars such as sieges, which could last a few weeks to several months and cut enemies off from their sources of food, water, and arms. Raids also involved arson and the poisoning of water reservoirs, both of which forced noncombatants—mostly women and children—to flee, making them more likely to fall into enemy hands as kidnapped victims.[72] Eighteenth-century Igbo captive Olaudah Equiano did not make such a sharp distinction of his own captivity when he wrote about assailants or kidnappers: "they sometimes took [advantage of parents' absence] to *attack* and carry off as many as they could *seize*. [emphasis added]"[73] Oldendorp's account shows a similar overlap between military invasions and "slave chasers' robberies," highlighting that warfare produced "many others" and unspecified numbers of "children."[74] Ohafia's guerrilla-style military slaving, which involved warriors setting towns on fire, killing adult men and taking their heads, and tying people up with ropes—mostly women and children—as they fled from flames, facilitated military enslavement through kidnapping. Thus, kidnapping was often indistinguishable from slave raids. Sea surgeon Alexander Falconbridge and his assistant James Arnold insisted that when it came to Biafra, "prisoners of war" included by definition captives acquired in kidnapping expeditions.[75] Their views were echoed by Captain Hall, who made several voyages from the Biafran port of Bonny and reported that Biafran slaves were mostly "war captives" and "kidnapped victims taken in raids."[76] Such raids might appear random, but they were underpinned by a historical tradition of military heroism, secret societies, age-grade systems, and regional alliances, as well as a transatlantic market for captives.

THE SOCIOCULTURAL LEGACY OF MILITARY SLAVING AND WARRIORS' HEGEMONY

The commercialization of the Ohafia military apparatus, or its transformation into a slaving system, reshaped local conceptions of masculine honor and social prestige and was accompanied by the domestication of two new sociopolitical institutions: okonko and ite odo. The former enabled warriors to become active economic actors in Biafra's regional slave trade, and the latter facilitated the social acceptance of slaving by celebrating the most fearful perpetrators of martial violence and representing slaves as "heads" cut by warriors to achieve ufiem status. Both okonko and ite odo redefined the economic and social basis of status differentiation among men.

Nwokeji suggests that the okonko confraternity either diffused into the Cross River Igbo communities from the Akpa or emerged along with the trust system in Calabar during the seventeenth century. Then, in the early eighteenth century, it crystallized in the forest region of the Bight of Biafra (the Cross River region and southern Igboland) when the Atlantic slave trade was already underway.[77] Ohafia oral traditions trace okonko's origin to their borderland Efik neighbors.[78] As a secret society that cut across Ibibio, Efik, Ekoi, and southern Igbo territories, okonko became the most important institution that ensured the safety of traders, because it guaranteed members legal immunity against robbery and enslavement. To ensure the safety of members, okonko established safe houses along major trade routes, imposed jural sanctions against offenders, and employed the secret language of *nsibidi*—a repertoire of bodily, gestural, and written signs that enabled peoples from different language groups to communicate intelligibly and establish their status as okonko members.[79] In Old Calabar, where it plausibly originated, okonko (*ekpe* or *egbo*) was used to regulate both trade and political life, it was the supreme judicial authority, and it was gender inclusive.[80] In some Igbo societies such as Amuzo-Ihe, okonko similarly admitted both men and women. In Ngwaland, women were not admitted into okonko, and the society served as the most powerful administrative organ.[81] In Ngwaland, okonko members arbitrated disputes associated with feuds, divorce, and inheritance; policed trade networks; collected debts; enforced commercial contracts; used masquerades to terrorize offenders and destroy their property; sold offenders into slavery; and weakened the power of traditional authority holders.[82] In many parts of Igboland, observed British colonial officer J. G. C. Allen, okonko members "began to take over many duties which hitherto had been regarded as the prerogative of the village council."[83] However, in Ohafia, okonko or ekpe excluded women and lacked society-wide political authority, beyond protecting the interests of its own members. The exclusion of women afforded men another institution of ufiem performance but reinforced the autonomy of female political institutions, thereby limiting okonko members from realizing political sovereignty over the entire society, unlike in Calabar and Ngwaland. Indeed, the political roles that okonko served in Old Calabar were fulfilled in Ohafia by the ikpirikpe and akpan dual-sex institutions. Ottenberg similarly observed in the case of Afikpo that the holders of the senior secret-society titles were powerful only to the extent of "reinforcing the authority structure of the village" and performing ritual and prestige functions.[84]

It is plausible, therefore, that in matrilineal and bilateral societies, okonko attained limited authority, while in patrilineal societies, okonko reinforced patriarchal authority structures. In Ohafia, okonko accentuated preexisting class differences among men by enabling powerful warriors to become economic actors at an unprecedented scale. Initiation into okonko was cost-prohibitive, so not many men could become members. The few that did were often veteran warriors who had acquired wealth through slaving and enjoyed high social status and regional political clout.[85] They became part of a widespread regional trade monopoly spearheaded by the Aro. Through okonko membership, Ohafia merchant-warriors could march their slaves to the four-day slave fairs at Bende and Uzuakoli using an extensive overland route that converged at Abiriba (Abiriba-Ada-Afikpo-Uburu; Abiriba-Bende-Uzuakoli; and Abiriba-Isikwato-Ututu), then went through Ohafia to Arochukwu, Ihechiowa, and Ututu.[86] These new plutocrats (*ogaranya okonko*) embraced the hierarchies of titles within the confraternity to usurp economic power. By wearing special insignia, members distinguished ranked grades and determined the allocation of authority. They set up toll stations on major trade routes, collected expensive fees from prospective members (ranging from two bottles of gin and a goat to several goats, £10, and 1,600 manilas), and held secret meetings and extravagant entertainments, even though they lacked legislative or judicial powers over the rest of the community.[87] By bringing the wealthiest group of men together, okonko prevented rivalry among powerful men and ensured the thorough exploitation of enslaved, weak, immigrant, and other marginal persons. It offered protection to the elite through religious rites, mystery, and secrecy, which elicited fear among free society and entrenched economic inequalities. Because okonko had its own courts in many communities, it protected its members by inflicting harsh punishments against people who threatened, harmed, or stole from members. Okonko membership provided creditors with a powerful legal institution that forced debtors to make payments and enabled creditors to enslave their debtors, redefining pawnship parameters.

Because okonko enabled a specialized political class of powerful men to exact tribute and labor, engage in "political manipulation," and victimize vulnerable individuals through enslavement, Nwokeji has questioned "that much-vaunted Igbo egalitarian norm."[88]

However, the impact of okonko was more socioeconomic than political. Simulating the Biafran incorporative social kinship slavery system, okonko allowed slaves who amassed wealth to purchase membership and thus secure some legal immunity. The society admitted slaves to its lower and middle grades until the mid-nineteenth century, after which slaves could be admitted to any grade. Nonetheless, it vested more power in the wealthiest male members of the society, a category that excluded most slaves and the poor. Moreover, since a man could not gain membership in the society before his father, poor fathers were ensured higher social status within the society than their wealthy sons, who customarily purchased membership for their fathers before they themselves could gain entry. Thus, while wealth was important, age and seniority also shaped the politics of okonko masculinity. But within the overall Ohafia ufiem system, age was not a prime factor for social differentiation. This may partly explain the limited political authority that okonko exerted in the dual-sex sociopolitical system. This interpretation is buttressed by the fact that the contemporary ite odo society valued military heroism and wealth far above age in its masculine social hierarchy. It was not until the British colonial introduction of the Native Court system in 1907, when okonko was co-opted into colonial structures, that Native Court members, who were often okonko men, became the primary political authorities in the region, often ruling favorably upon members' petitions.[89] This later transformation in gendered distribution of political power is examined in chapter 5.

Unlike the region-wide institution of okonko, the ite odo confraternity was a homegrown and localized Ohafia masculine sociopolitical organization. There is no documentation of its exact origins, but oral traditions situate it most prominently within the period of the Atlantic slave trade, oral histories offer vivid descriptions of its practices, and extant colonial reports confirm its nineteenth-century survival. Ite odo derived its name from a clay pot, about 40 gallons in volume, that was covered with human skulls. This pot was a cult object that served as a totem of the most accomplished warriors. One such warrior was Uma Ukwu Ukpai, son of Ukpai Ezema and grandson of Ezema Atita (putative leader of the Ohafia-Mben founding settlers). Genealogical descent from the period of Ohafia settlement would place Uma Ukpai's existence in the early eighteenth century, when he founded the village of Asaga. He is memorialized as a man of extraordinary endowments: a prodigious hunter, military tactician, and invincible warrior. He first lived at Eziama with his father, until a leopard began to terrorize their settlement. Uma Ukpai killed the leopard and set up his home on the spot (Nde Ufere), which became the nucleus (Eziukwu) of the new Asaga village. He drove out the earlier inhabitants, including Umunkwo, Obom, and Umuezichi Ebule, and expanded Asaga. To commemorate his victories, he was honored with one of the earliest Ohafia war dance performances. Other warriors who achieved great victories in battle began to visit Uma Ukpai to mime their brave deeds and gain honor. Thus, the ite odo society was born. Upon his death, Uma Ukpai was transformed into a deity of wide repute known as Uma Ukwu (the Great Uma). The resulting Omoukwu or Obu Nkwa shrine (which survives as a national monument) later became a protective deity that offered ukwuzi protection to marginalized peoples and slaves during the nineteenth century.[90]

Ite odo was instrumental to the valorization of warrior masculinity. It was similar to the documented *ese-ike* institution among the Ngwa people in that it comprised the most distinguished warlords who had achieved spectacular acts of bravery.[91] Such acts included being the first among peers to cut a head, single-handedly destroying an enemy fighting force, or participating in multiple raids and returning unscathed with a head and captives. Men of this caliber were hailed as *ogbusua* (first to cut a head), *olua oha* (conqueror of a community), *oji isi eke oba* (he that displayed human heads/subjects as a farmer displayed yams), *omere isi kpara ndu* (he that returned from war with a human head and live captives), and *okere ndi ife* (he that returned with tethered folks).[92] Ohafia elder Egbe Abba described ite odo members as "the inner core of the ufiem social class, revered by all."[93] They regulated the conferment of ufiem status on warriors. By the 1830s, most Ohafia villages possessed an ite odo society.[94] British officer Mayne indicated that during the nineteenth century, warriors trooped to the homes of ite odo elders to pay homage and present the heads they had cut in battle in order to gain prestige.[95] This "warrior's boast" was a continuation of the heroism mime that began in the time of Uma Ukpai. It was a public dance performance that announced the emergence of a new ufiem in society. According to elder Ndukwe Otta, "the dance of ite odo was not a formal entertainment, but rather, an occasional performance of *ndi ikike* [warlord] masculinity, which was more violent, because ite odo members unpredictably swung their machetes up and down, demonstrating their greatest conquests and headhunts."[96] Nna Agbai was aged about ninety-five years during my fieldwork. He recalled that his late father led the ite odo in Elu Ohafia between 1880 and 1920:

> In my father's time [1860s–1940s], he used to strip the jooji cloth away from the waists of his age-mates and tie them around my mother's waist! These were his peers that had not been able to cut human heads. *Ajaa*! He was a great warrior. He terrorized the peoples of Nteje and Aguleri [1890s]. My father's ite odo . . . he was well known for that huge pot that ndi ikike carried; they danced bare-chested, and if you encountered them you would be overtaken by fear. They wore only their jooji cloth, armed with their machete. People watched ite odo members in action from a distance. Their performance sometimes got so charged that it was no longer safe for people to come out of their houses.[97]

Nna Agbai's father, Agbai Nnate, was a leader of the ite odo society (*ezie-ite-odo*), and as such, he housed the pot monument in his home. Ndukwe Otta's father, Aru Otta (ca. 1878–1958), also served as ezie-ite-odo of Ebem Ohafia in the 1920s. During ite odo public performances, in the course of annual new yam festivals, the pot of skulls was filled with palm wine, and Nnate and Otta carried the pot on their heads, rocking it back and forth, and sideways, in a counterclockwise motion, accompanied by other warlords. Thus they marched to patrilineage compounds in their communities to pay homage to elderly ufiem, who acknowledged the homage with gifts of wine poured into the pot. As the pot filled up, ite odo members drank it down, always keeping the pot half-full. As Ndukwe Otta narrated, "They filled tall cups for men to drink and as the men drank, the senior ite odo members hit the top of their heads with their machetes until the cups were drained. This was to show that ite odo members were invincible."[98] From patrilineage compounds, they marched to the village square, where, as Njoku writes, their arrival was "announced with ikoro beat and the sound of *opu ike*, the trumpet of bravery."⁹⁹ The ikoro was a "talking drum," and "real men" understood its language. During the new yam festivals, as people arrived at the village square, the ikoro master of ceremonies welcomed the community by drumming praise beats for the ufiem and insolent beats for the ujo. Otta stated:

> When the ikoro saw one wearing jooji, it would ask, "Which people have you killed to provide skulls for your hearth?" ["*Gu o gburu ole ndu were uko turu isi?*"] If you failed to understand the ikoro or ignored it, it would then insult you, saying, "There goes an empty and weak male! He is no man!" ["*O di ogologolo pu!*"] If you understood the ikoro, you would instantly perform your warrior's boast. My father would always tell me what the ikoro was saying. Sometimes, he would be lying down at home, listening to the beats of ikoro, and he would laugh and say the ikoro was insulting so and so person. When he went to the village square, the ikoro hailed him as "the terror of the shoe-wearers" [*O-mere-ndi-a-duyi-mweyi-okpa!*], which refers to his campaign against Nnewi [1890s]; "the terror of Ibibio peoples" [*O-mere-ndi-ata-mgba-mgba!*]; and "the head that carries the pot of the braves" [*Ishi-e-bu-ite-ndi-una!*]. Because my father accomplished ufiem, when I danced with my age-mates, I would often boast, "I was born by a real man!"¹⁰⁰

The legacies of ite odo militarism were evident in the Ohafia landscape: in the architectural layout of villages, and the location and gendered uses of artifacts such as the ikoro, obu, and patrilineage shrines. Nsugbe's 1960 description of Ohafia village architecture is similar to Mayne's nineteenth-century record: "From the air, each village would be seen to consist of very low [houses], strung out in unbroken rows as if from an instinctive urge of self defense against a danger that was once real and constant . . . a protective response to a turbulent frontier environment. . . . Compounds are structured [such] that each presents the appearance of a . . . military garrison."¹⁰¹ The ikoro, a large wooden slit-drum 9 feet in length, 5 feet in height, and 10 feet in circumference, occupied the village square, and its primary function was to distinguish the ufiem from the ujo. Upon a warrior's return from battle, he attended an elaborate ceremony where he displayed the head and slaves he had acquired and "saluted" the ikoro through vigorous miming of his heroic deeds (*ibiri ikoro*) and gallant boasting of his prowess (*iba mba*). Saluting the ikoro and performing the warrior's boast were nineteenth-century mundane practices that entrenched the social perception of warriors as the most powerful group of men in society. Male age-grades took turns keeping vigilance over the ikoro because it represented the "military strength of a community"—a reference to the arduous labor involved in its creation, its ritual function as a protective medicine, its role in summoning men to war, and its symbol as a platform where warriors presented the heads and captives they had acquired in battle.[102]

At the periphery of every village square was the obu, which symbolized the inception of the public sphere. The obu was a male domain, a major site for the organization of warfare, and a platform for ite odo performances. Its wall decor and murals embodied various ancient masculinities—warriors, hunters, diviners (dibias), and wrestlers. The masculinization of the obu was in direct structural opposition to the absence of matrilineage residential compounds, and its site facilitated a public sector of male visibility. In front of Anaga-patrilineage obu in Elu Ohafia is a deity called *egbo*, which contains arrows said to be more than two hundred years old. Until the 1930s, it was customary for warriors who passed the Anaga obu to shoot an arrow into the egbo in demonstration of their ufiem social status. The egbo was a medicine believed to protect the community, and it gained its power through warriors' spectacular performances of archery skills. Constant archery performance reinforced the social perception of Anaga obu as a male space.[103] The subsequent preservation of patrilineage ududu within obu structures, as a result of British colonial government transformation of Ohafia obu houses into monuments at the turn of the twentieth century, was a contrast to Christian male converts' destruction of matrilineage ududu housed in the homes of matriarchs. Such contrary outcomes have reinforced the masculinist social vision of Ohafia history as a chronicle of male martial heroism. Moreover, women were forbidden to pass through the patrilineage shrines unless they were virgins.

Collectively, the obu, ikoro, and patrilineage shrines were male cultural symbols that characterized the public space as a masculine geography. They structured the masculinist perception of Ohafia's gender system as one comprising omnipresent male warriors and invisible female farmers. However, when we consider the contemporary female court's public marches and spectacles of public morality policing, especially in village squares (chapter 1), the public space is effectively transformed into a contested domain of gendered status performance. Little wonder the ite odo society consciously constructed its social power. At public gatherings, members barricaded themselves from public view. Only warriors who had cut a head were allowed in their midst, to behold the pot and what was inside. An admixture of societal dissonance against the rising social power of warriors and a desire to name what was inside the pot generated rumors that human heads were inside the pot of skulls—a rumor that ite odo members ironically did not stifle but rather encouraged to bolster their aura.[104] This rumor laid a foundation for the myth of ite odo cannibalism espoused by British colonial officers and Christian missionaries in the late nineteenth century. Thus, Mayne asserted in his intelligence report on Ohafia that "slaves were eaten by their respective owners and his relatives" at the funeral of ite odo members.[105] G. I. Jones purported that Cross River Igbo warriors not only took the head of their enemy as a trophy but also removed as much as they could of the body to sell as meat in the local markets.[106] The Church of Scotland Mission (CSM) celebrated the 1901 British expedition against the Aro as a triumph over the "barbarous" and "savage" Aro and their bloodthirsty, "cannibalistic" Ohafia and Abam allies.[107] And Frank Ashcroft, board chairman of the United Free Church of Scotland Foreign Mission at Edinburgh, described the Ohafia as "head-hunters and cannibals" in his subsequent 1921 tour of the Calabar Mission District.[108] Colonial anthropologists such as Partridge, Leonard, and Basden perpetuated these impressions.[109]

Neither Mayne, Jones, Ashcroft, Leonard, Patridge, nor Basden ever witnessed cannibalism in the region. Rather, they observed indiscriminate uses of human skulls by ite odo members. Leonard for instance observed, "At Akanu [Ohafia] the Ju Ju, which was composed of an array of human skulls stacked on a wooden stool, looked, to say the least of it, a grim and gruesome spectacle."[110] Basden equally writes of the practice of using human skulls as protective medicines placed over farmland to scare away potential intruders.[111] Njoku argues emphatically, "Cannibalism had no place in the headhunting calculations of Ohafia people."[112] Until the Aro expedition of 1901, European missionaries and British officers did not gain access to the Cross River Igbo territories, and the CSM, which was the most active in the region, remained a coastal church, with minimal influence in the middle Cross River. CSM missionaries stationed at Calabar, Unwana, Akunakuna, Okoyong, and Umon had no firsthand knowledge of the Igbo territories west of the Cross River, and their rumors of cannibalism and human sacrifice encouraged the British colonial government to open up the region and make it safe for missionary work.[113] The British preemptively deployed one of the two columns of the Aro expeditionary forces through Ohafia in 1901 because of the Ohafia's reputation as headhunters and Aro mercenaries. Even after conquest, British officials Captain Mowatt, Mr. Weir, and Mr. L. T. Chubb continued to represent the Ohafia as bloodthirsty headhunters who had to be closely supervised.[114] The discourse of punishing cannibalistic headhunters was mobilized in 1906 to sack Asaga, one of the Ohafia villages, which refused to submit to colonial control.[115]

The cannibalism censure of ite odo members was inspired by the fear and aura that they evoked in nonmembers, as well as their exclusivism and social privileges. The criticism through rumor questioned why they "played" with human heads by literally dancing with them. Indeed, warriors made extensive use of human heads. In order to establish a new home after marriage, warriors buried human heads in the foundation of their houses and under patrilineage compound shrines such as *kamalu*, *fijoku*, and *onu-agba*. The preponderance of human heads surrounding warriors generated the deprecatory discourse of cannibalism. It was in this sense that historian Luise White argues that rumors of vampirism in colonial East and Central Africa were social constructions, genres, and mediums through which people articulated and contested differential power dynamics in intergroup relations, especially in violent situations.[116] Indeed, human heads and slaves occupied a singular symbolic plane in the Ohafia worldview of ufiem accomplishment, undergirded by a common economic rationale. To illustrate, James Sweet shows that head cutting and slave production were two sides of a coin in Dahomey. When English slaver William Snelgrave approached the king's gates at Allada, he saw "two large Stages, on which were heaped a great number of dead Men's Heads, that afforded no pleasing sight or smell." The heads had once belonged to four thousand Huedas. Dahomean soldiers received two hundred cowries for each enemy head they returned. Of the 1,800 captives brought to Dahomey from Ouidah the next day, many were sacrificed in the same manner as the Huedas in gratitude to God for victory over Oiudah. The rest were retained for domestic use and for sale to European merchants.[117] Ohafia's military traditions did not differ much from Dahomey's. The display of human heads dramatized the power of a conquering state and its warriors, and this valorization of martial masculinity fostered the taking of captives, who became merchandise, laborers, and lineage reproducers. Hence, Ohafia warriors went to war with pouches and ropes.

Until the twentieth century, the burial of ite odo members was an occasion to dramatize their eminent position in society. Otta recollects that during the burial of his father in 1958,

> the warriors confiscated all the palm wine in the community.[118] During the entire one-week period in which my father died, the warriors owned the land. . . . They fasted and avoided sexual contact with women. . . . On the day of burial, they marched the length and breadth of Ohafia, singing and dancing. Their eyes were bloodshot; they wore loincloth; they were armed with machetes, which they clapped as they danced, and they had guns, which they shot into the air. I saw them dance, until they reached our home. During their march, they cut down and killed various things in their path, including trees and animals. In the olden days, this was the time that they would have killed slaves, in those days when they required another human being to bury the warrior. Once they reached our home, they started performing . . . I don't know what to call it, because they were under influence of possession. I saw them running on the rooftop, then removing the roof, digging a grave in the middle of my father's living room [obi], and erecting a bamboo pole in the grave. From the rooftop, they threw down a pot of undiluted palm wine into the grave, and we heard the warriors roar, *whoa!* That was the first stage. . . . They returned and performed various acrobatics, poured wine into the pot of skulls, and drank from it. . . . They covered the grave and took out the bamboo pole, leaving a hole, which led into my father's mouth.[119]

Njoku corroborates Otta when he writes that in the precolonial period, "at death," ite odo members were "immolated with human heads and live captives."[120] Mayne also noted that the warrior was dressed with jooji cloth, leopard cap, and eagle's feather and buried inside his house with human heads and slaves killed to serve him in the afterlife.[121] Burying the warrior within his home ensured that he maintained a daily connection with the living through food and drink offerings, put into the hole in the grave. This heroic burial was a prerequisite for the deification ritual known as *idoru nna* (to lay a father to rest), which transformed warriors into revered ancestors and deities. It entailed the raising of a pot monument (ududu) in the warrior's honor within the patrilineage obu, where it received periodic libations.[122] Apart from warriors, matrilineage matriarchs were the only category of people that received ududu veneration. Ite odo was in effect creating an ancillary religious cult for men, thereby reinforcing the dual-sex sociopolitical system. Juxtaposed to its female counterpart, male attainment of ancestral honor strengthened patrilineage units, in contrast to the segmentation and dispersal of matrilineages. The ritual of idoru nna was actualized with a special warrior dance known as *okerenkwa*. Njoku describes it as "the highest heroic honor that could be bestowed on a dead man in Ohafia."[123] Uka writes, "Happy was the man entitled to don the eagle's plume and the red tail feathers of the parrot in token of his prowess in battle. In life he enjoyed special privileges, and in death was accorded the dignity of a warrior's funeral with the special dance known as okerenkwa."[124] The deceased's son purchased the services of a great warrior to perform the okerenkwa, which was accompanied by gunshots and the clashing of swords. The okerenkwa warrior was considered a man not "because he has a penis; but because he had accomplished the requirements of manhood in Ohafia: he went to war and returned with a head and captives."[125]

Men that did not receive idoru nna were believed to be stranded between the worlds of the living and the dead. As anthropologist Victor Uchendu observed, for the Igbo, life on earth was a link in the chain of status hierarchy, which culminated in the achievement of ancestral honor. Those who died unaccomplished suffered frustration in the spirit land because they remained "boys" in both the human and spiritual worlds.[126] Chinua Achebe demonstrates that while age was respected in Igbo society and was important to gender construction, achievement was revered.[127] Only men that achieved ufiem received the honor of idoru nna, irrespective of age. Azuonye writes that in contrast to ujo, who represented repugnant and ancestral boyhood, warriors who accomplished ufiem constituted the "highest rank in the hierarchy of spirits of the dead, and are known as *arunshi* (i.e. 'ancestral' as opposed to ordinary spirits)."[128] Moreover, the names and acts of valor of ite odo members became edifying songs in the repertory of the traditional heroic war songs and war dance performances. Posthumous deification, ududu veneration, and incorporation into the heroic war songs were the ultimate aspirations of Ohafia male individuals in the era of the Atlantic slave trade and constituted, in David Eltis's words, "the cultural parameters within which economic decisions [including slaving] were made."[129]

MERCHANT-WARRIOR MASCULINITY AND SPIRITUAL SLAVERY

The equation of slaves with heads was manifest in the increasing use of male child slaves for human sacrifice in the Bight of Biafra.[130] In eighteenth-century Ohafia, warriors were buried with human heads; in the nineteenth century, merchant-warriors and other individuals who accomplished ogaranya masculinity were buried with male slaves.[131] As late as 1901, Richard Morrisey, the commissioner of the Cross River Division, reported that in the Igbo and Ibibio communities on both sides of the Cross River, at the death of a wealthy man, sometimes one hundred young boys were sacrificed, and no attempts were made to conceal such acts.[132] Although Morrisey's report must have exaggerated the scale of human sacrifice, putting a stop to human sacrifice at the burial of ogaranya individuals was a major justification for British military campaigns between 1905 and 1907 in Afikpo, Arochukwu, and Owerri during the Bende-Onitsha hinterland expedition.[133] The heightened rate of human sacrifice in the region was a result of the surplus of slaves on the domestic markets during the postabolition era, in addition to the depressed prices of male slaves and the performance of ogaranya masculinity. Elizabeth Isichei and Raphael Njoku attribute this to "ogaranya syndrome" bred by the slave trade and obsession with foreign goods, which produced arrogant and lawless political patrons, rogue barons, and absolute patriarchs.[134] Ogaranya was anchored on the ideology of "wealth-in-people," such that control over labor and human bodies through slavery and elite polygyny became an essential basis of socioeconomic differentiation.[135] Ogaranya found expression in the ownership of slaves, possession of wives and concubines, and burial of deceased elites with male slaves.

Various scholars have argued that the best way to understand the impact of the transatlantic slave trade on African societies is to look at its "permutations," "repercussions," and the "quality of the population left behind."[136] In altering the degree and mode of exploitation of slaves and their labor, ogaranya masculinity transformed indigenous slave systems. The high rate of inhumane uses of slaves in Igbo society due to ogaranya practices in the nineteenth century produced a new class of spiritual slaves. Many slaves escaped human sacrifice at the burial of ogaranya individuals by running to and seeking ukwuzi protection from Omoukwu, the shrine of Ohafia's ancestral deity, Uma Ukpai. The effectiveness of *obu nkwa* protection (which stemmed partly from merchant-warriors' adoration of the founder of the ite odo society) and the corruption of indigenous judiciary systems, which increasingly disposed political dissenters and minor offenders by condemning them to slavery, encouraged vulnerable individuals to seek protection from the deity. This corruption of judiciary systems was facilitated by the emergence of ogaranya individuals who usurped the power of preexisting authority holders and established competing institutions of arbitration such as okonko. Those who sought refuge at the Omoukwu shrine became "children of the deity" and "automatically saved." However, "securing the protection of a deity" stigmatized such individuals as *osu* (spiritual slaves and outcasts).[137]

Uchendu describes an osu as a cult slave who has been dedicated to a deity and whose descendants automatically become osu. He argues that the practice was most prevalent in the Owerri-Okigwi region and was linked to powerful protector deities. The osu's main public duty was to offer sacrifices on behalf of their masters and to tend the shrines of their deity. Unlike bought slaves and pawns, the osu were not exploited economically. Like other free Igbo people, they farmed on their own account and held property, but their social, cultural, and economic achievements were undervalued by society. Excluded from mainstream Igbo institutions in spite of their impressive wealth, they formed a compartmentalized and parallel subaltern social structure.[138] The

Ohafia term *osu* refers to an individual who voluntarily sought a deity's protection. This differed from sacrificial dedication of individuals to a deity, which, as Achebe argues in the case of Northern Igboland, involved giving women in marriage to a deity in order to help repopulate communities decimated by incessant slave raids. Unlike osu refugees, these people enjoyed enormous legal immunity and social power.[139] In addition to distinguishing osu from dedicated individuals, the Ohafia also used the term *ibemike* to describe a class of outcasts who were not slaves but who became socially ostracized because they had committed heinous crimes such as murder. Thus, the osu were a specific category of people who transitioned from ephemeral (in)human slavery to permanent spiritual slavery because they resisted ogaranya malpractices. A remarkable difference in the Ohafia osu/ibemike system was the fact that whereas male osu/ibemike descendants were not allowed to intermarry with the rest of the free population, the female descendants were exempt from this social inhibition because they were important to the reproduction of matrilineages. As a result, over time, it became difficult to identify and discriminate against osu/ibemike descendants. This reinforces the idea that matriliny as an institution of kinship incorporation concealed some of the legacies of slavery.

"Atlanticization" effectively describes the intercourse between the Atlantic slave trade and the deep gendered sociocultural transformations that took place in Ohafia-Igbo society in the eighteenth and nineteenth centuries. When one reconciles the feminist conceptions of Ohafia military traditions in chapter 1 with the male-centered narratives examined in this chapter, it becomes apparent that intraregional differences in lineage practices defined the dominant modes of slave production, and the demography of captives from the Bight of Biafra. Kinship practices conditioned the geography of military slaving, the domestication of new masculine secret societies, and male competitive practices of sociocultural salience. Furthermore, the expansion of the Atlantic slave trade in the first half of the eighteenth century transformed Ohafia military practices into a major arm of the Bight of Biafra's slaving network. To explain this process, this chapter examines the motives behind African participation in the Atlantic slave trade. The motivations were grounded in social practices of ufiem. The impetus for warriors to go to war may have been to obtain human head trophies, but warriors inadvertently generated captives, whom the Aro redistributed as market slaves (*ohu mgbere*). Through the exclusively male societies of okonko and ite odo, war captives also came to be seen as heads that conferred ufiem privileges. This was a process whereby the new economic role of warriors as slave producers enabled them to exercise control over local uses of Atlantic commodities like jooji cloth. This empowered warriors to deny nonwarriors a voice in masculine political institutions, effectively defining the ujo as resident strangers. Being ujo was a liminal male condition, which could be overcome through military distinction and slave production. It differed from male slavery because although male slaves could eventually be absorbed within kinship systems, the era of the Atlantic slave trade and its associated ufiem practices meant that most male slaves ended up in the markets, in the graves of deceased ogaranya individuals, or as spiritual slaves. The sociocultural power of warriors became enshrined in religious rituals, material-culture practices, and memorialization of heroic traditions. The practices of okonko, ite odo, and idoru nna were cultural legacies of the Atlantic slave trade that reshaped ideologies of personhood, social space, and sacred traditions in Ohafia society. The economic ramifications of military slaving and gendered uses of slaves are examined in chapter 3. Notably, neither the rising cultural nor economic prominence of men would effectively undermine those powerful female-solidarity institutions and matrifocal religious principles examined in chapter 1. Rather, they laid a solid foundation for the eventual shift in gendered sociopolitical power between 1850 and 1920. These later radical processes will be examined in chapters 4 and 5.

3. Gendered Slavery in the Bight of Biafra, ca. 1750–1890

A Transatlantic Perspective

FOCUSING ON the economic ramifications of military slaving and the gendered uses of slaves, this chapter argues that the articulation of Ohafia-Igbo kinship systems with the Atlantic slave trade and legitimate trade was pivotal to widespread mobilization of female productive and reproductive labor and male economic hegemony. Examining the Atlantic slave trade and its successor legitimate trade as interlocked gendered systems of production reveals how Atlanticization catalyzed economic shifts in gendered power within Biafra.

It was not until the second half of the eighteenth century that the Bight of Biafra emerged as the single largest source of captives for the British slave trade. The most important destination for Biafran captives during this period (1776–1807) was Jamaica. Roughly 51 percent (600,248) of the 1,164,819 slaves who embarked from Biafra between 1750 and 1850 ended up in the British Caribbean. Of these, 43 percent (257,438) embarked for Jamaica.[1] Whereas the Bight of Biafra and the Gold Coast had respectively accounted for 22 percent (144,008) and 32 percent (207,963) of the 646,439 slaves that disembarked in Jamaica between 1651 and 1775, between 1776 and 1808, the Bight of Biafra furnished 43.1 percent (177,529) of the total 411,900 Jamaican captive imports and the Gold Coast accounted for 23.8 percent (98,032).

After abolition, however (1820s–1880s), Biafra's captive exportation gradually declined as internal demand for slaves and thus captive production expanded to meet a new European demand for cash crops. Accordingly, the Ohafia-Igbo intensified their military slave production. Overall, the age and sex demography of slaves generated, retained, and exported during the eighteenth and nineteenth centuries reflected the demands of local and external reproductive economies. This chapter demonstrates that those reproductive economies were transatlantic and gendered, enabling us to understand the transformations in gendered power within the Bight of Biafra. More specifically, by reevaluating Biafra's slave trade and domestic slavery through the lens of the region's intercourse with Jamaica, this chapter argues that women were central to Biafra's slavery practices and the enslavement of women became foundational to male ascendancy in the nineteenth century.

Slavery affected the migrating population and altered conditions of the homeland.[2] As people, goods, and ideas circulated in ever wider and deeper flows among the pan-Atlantic continents, changes in one corner of that "vast inland sea" had repercussions in others.[3] Movement and exchange characterized Atlantic perimeter dialogues.[4] Ohafia-Igbo people's engagements with Atlantic slavery shaped this inland African society but also contributed to changes elsewhere, capturing how the Bight of Biafra's slavery was a transatlantic conversation. As shown in the previous chapter, Ohafia military slaving generated mostly women and children as opposed to adult men. The demography of slave production had significant implications for both African and American Atlantic littorals.

First, the unusually high proportion of women in the Bight of Biafra's captive exports shaped slavery practices in the Caribbean, particularly in Jamaica. The experiences of these enslaved *Ebo/Eboe* women in Jamaica have significantly shaped our understanding of West Indian chattel slavery. The relevant sources, examined later in this chapter, emphasize that white male sexual predation, as well as "womb practices" often associated with Ebo/Eboe slaves, characterized slaves' diurnal lives in an environment where "labor and reproduction" underscored the rigors of sugar slavery.[5] They demonstrate that in eighteenth-century Jamaica, gender was as important as race in defining social relationships, and white male patriarchal authority was premised on the power of slave owners to satisfy their desires "unbounded."[6]

Second, slavery within Biafra relied on the dynamic uses of women as wives, mothers, units of slave relineagization, resources of male slaves' social mobility, and as labor and political units of predominantly ogaranya-accomplished individuals. The role of the slave trade in reshaping gender and power within Biafra illustrates what Diana Paton and Pamela Scully have described as the "Atlanticization" of people who never themselves crossed the Atlantic.[7] The role of Biafra's slave production in shaping Jamaican slavery encourages a cis-Atlantic reassessment of Biafra's slavery practices. What does African kinship slavery look like from a cross-Atlantic perspective, and how did it shape local dynamics of gendered power in the Bight of Biafra?

FEMALE MARGINALITY? THE QUESTION OF LABOR VALUE, MILITARISM, AND SEX

In Nwokeji's assessment of how the Bight of Biafra's "constructions of gender roles" shaped the "age and sex structure of the Atlantic slave trade," he concludes that "the institution of female slavery was marginal."[8] The impression of women's marginality in Biafran slavery and its impact has been premised on the demographic fact that although most people forced to leave Biafran ports were male, the proportion of women who entered the transatlantic slave trade was higher in the Bight of Biafra than in any other coastal region of Africa. The explanation of this gender ratio purports that it existed because first, the female-oriented trans-Saharan market did not permeate the forest belt of Biafra, because the Igbo revered and refused to supply kola nut, a major Saharan commodity. Therefore, the Sahara did not become an outlet for Biafra's enslaved women.[9] Second, the female marginality argument purports that because of the "Igbo reverence for yam," which relied principally on male labor for mound making, women were not major players in Igbo agriculture. And "because women did not primarily work yam and were not acknowledged as important in its production," Biafra's leaders "were more willing to countenance the forced migration of females." Therefore, the Bight of Biafra exported more adult women slaves: "Yam production was partly the reason for the relatively high female ratio of captives leaving the region."[10] Third, Nwokeji argues that female domestic slavery was marginal because women did not establish lineages.[11]

Whereas the Sahara/kola nut thesis transforms two nonfactors in Biafran slavery practices into major factors of Biafra's slave production and export demography, the assumptions about women's marginal roles in agricultural production and lineage establishment do not accord with the Ohafia case, where women were agrarian breadwinners and pillars of the lineage. Moreover, comparable historical findings in northern, central, and southern regions of Igboland show that women were central to societal economic reproduction because they constituted the primary labor pool of agrarian production in the precolonial period. Indeed, women's subsistence production of root crops and vegetables enabled men to cultivate yams as a niche cultural prestige crop. And women's laborious weeding during eight months of the year ensured the survival of the yam crop.[12] Likewise, Audrey Smedley has demonstrated that women played critical roles in the reproduction of patrilineage units and ideologies in southeastern Nigeria, and that men primarily relied on women for their own economic reproduction.[13] As this chapter shows, in patrilineal and matrilineal Igbo societies, women were central to lineage expansion.

Neither examining "the age and sex structure" of the slave trade nor reifying cultural practices can provide a full picture of the institutional practice of slavery in the Bight of Biafra. To understand how Biafran constructions of gender shaped the institutional practice of slavery, this chapter pays attention to slave production but also examines how changing constructions of masculinity shaped the uses of slaves and the meanings of slavery in Igboland. Attentive to property, power, and differential social mobility, the chapter reaches an opposite conclusion: far from being marginal, Igbo women slaves were critical to practices of social domestic slavery in the Bight of Biafra and were prominent in the region's transatlantic slave trade, as well as West Indian chattel slavery. They fulfilled the most versatile conception of slavery as the "exercise of commodity rights-in-persons," enabling men, including ex-slaves, to emerge as breadwinners, landowners, and arbiters of more powerful political institutions. Furthermore, the chapter argues that to evaluate the *impact* of Biafran gender constructions on Atlantic slavery, beyond slave-production mechanisms and gendered slave uses, we need to look at both embarkation and disembarkation volumes of Biafran captives in order to get a transatlantic view of how Igbo women slaves shaped the institutional practice of slavery. Such a transatlantic perspective reveals that in both Biafran and Jamaican regions, Igbo women were vital to slavery practices.

In 1790, the British Parliament established a committee on the slave trade. It observed that "the number of male slaves exported annually from the coast of Africa exceeded generally the number of females" and inquired into the cause. The committee heard testimonies from the Company of Merchants Trading to Africa as well as thirty captains and sea surgeons. They attested that males predominated because African polygamy encouraged retention of women and because men were of less value in Africa and more valuable in the West Indies. Women were more valuable in Africa because of their labor in the fields and their varied domestic services. Captain Healey, who traded slaves in Bonny, the Bight of Biafra's principal port in the second half of the eighteenth century, observed that whereas in the rest of Atlantic Africa, males fetched £5–£10 more than females, an Angola or Igbo female slave fetched as much as a male. Angola and Igbo female slaves were considered "good" and above "ordinary" and were in high demand. Bonny traders "customarily" brought "prime males" to slave ships to "exchange for an ordinary or indifferent female, or for small boys and girls, from five to ten years of age."

Captains Matthews, Dalzell, and Norris testified that though European traders were faced with a greater demand for males, they purchased every available slave, and in Bonny, they gave "a superior price for women," although in the West Indies, where comparable numbers of women and men often disembarked, women cost forty shillings less than men.[14] Whereas in the rest of Atlantic Africa, traders easily obtained two-thirds males and one-third females, in the Bight of Biafra, which supplied the overwhelming majority of female captives in Atlantic Africa, adult women were sometimes scarce. According to Bristol captains Miles, Anderson, and Baillie, "It was difficult to procure female slaves from the Eboe country because rich and powerful natives [ogaranya]" kept women for domestic services. It was *"the custom of the country for women to work in the field* [emphasis added]." In contrast, in the Gambia, according to Captain Wilson, there was no difficulty in procuring female slaves.[15] Indeed, the Atlantic slave trade intensified gender inequality and increased the demand for women in Biafra's domestic economies.[16] Women became more important to agrarian and lineage production because they constituted the majority of the locally enslaved population. Yet as shown below, Biafra's slave-production mechanisms and differential gender mortality also ensured that the numbers of captive women that disembarked in Jamaica roughly equaled the numbers of captive men.

Military slave production significantly shaped the gender and age demography of Biafran captives and was coterminous with the preeminent role of women in agriculture and other forms of domestic reproduction. The instantaneity of slave raiding did not allow captors to discriminate among captives based on the importance of their sex to Biafra's yam cultivation or based on the trade route of captives' disposition postcaptivity (whether trans-Saharan or transatlantic). Warriors had immediate concerns such as ease of capture and transportation. In his 1790 testimony to the British Parliament on the slave trade, sailor Isaac Parker reported that in the 1760s, he was invited to go on a slave raid in the Biafran hinterland, during which raiders "seized men, women, and children promiscuously."[17] Audra Diptee suggests that the capture of women and children in disproportionate numbers during raids was no doubt because they were more vulnerable and more likely to be overpowered by enslavers.[18] Ohafia war-song lyrics and oral traditions that speak about slave captivity emphasize that brave warriors easily "tied up" female captives *but* made sure that they also cut male heads in battle. Indeed, the long distances that warriors had to travel with captives incentivized female and child captivity (see chapter 2).

Another factor that may have shaped slaving warriors' sex and age preferences for captives was a synchronous impression of their domestic *and* export value. In this latter regard, military slaving popularized a masculinist ethos of female captivity among Biafra's premier warriors because, on the one hand, Igbo dual-sex socioeconomic and kinship systems centered women in domestic mechanisms of reproduction, and on the other hand, European planter preferences for slaves from the Bight of Biafra did not discriminate against female captives. In fact, Jamaican planters, it has been argued, were more willing to purchase young African women, particularly "Eboe Cargoe" from the port of Bonny, and quite reluctant to import adult African men into the island during the second half of the eighteenth century.[19]

In both Jamaica and the Bight of Biafra, there was a considerable increase in the importance of female slavery that corresponded with an expansion in regional commercialized agriculture and an attempt to co-opt enslaved women's wombs as instruments of economic and social reproduction. In Jamaica, this occurred in the last three decades of the Atlantic slave trade (1776–1807), following the cessation of the Maroon Wars and the onset of the Haitian Revolution, both of which facilitated the establishment of new sugar and coffee plantations in the western and northern frontier regions. In the Bight of Biafra, the centrality of enslaved women to commercialized agriculture and kinship practices became most pronounced in the postabolition nineteenth century, when domestic slavery exponentially expanded to meet growing European demands for palm produce. Jamaica's eighteenth-century slave trade reflects the prominence of Biafran female captive demography as much as Biafra's nineteenth-century domestic slavery systems emphasized the centrality of female slavery. A gendered perspective of Biafra's modes of slave production suggests that military slaving and women's centrality to agrarian production and lineage reproduction guaranteed more women and children within Biafra's enslaved population, as well as the retention of more female slaves than male slaves within Biafra.

The female marginality thesis does not fully provide the gendered historical context of slaves' experiences. For instance, in addition to physical labor and childbirth, enslaved women were also coerced into sex work. According to Campbell, Miers and Miller, "Sex is a powerful tool, emotionally as well as physically."[20] Enslaved women's sexual exploitation is often subsumed within the discourse of elite polygyny and kinship incorporation, and the tendency to efface enslaved women's sexual functions within "concubinage" has aptly been criticized as the "harem assumption."[21] Theorizing sex as a nexus of coerced labor, gendered definitions of property, and exploitative constructions of hegemonic masculinity juxtaposes the context of enslaved Igbo women's experiences in Jamaica with the role of ogaranya masculinity in transforming the gendered uses of enslaved women and girls. Jamaican planters used sex to increase their labor force, incentivize overseers, and demonstrate forceful control over slaves' bodies.[22] In Igboland, ogaranya masculinities exploited enslaved women as sexual, labor, and political units and popularized slave traffic in girl-wives. In both cases, the intimate positions of "work" open to female slaves presented them with more system-definitive modes of resistance than the overt physical options privileged by male slaves. In Jamaica, enslaved women employed "womb strategies" against a racialized chattel slavery system.[23] Self-manumission occasionally meant economic autonomy for enslaved women, but in most cases, enslaved women's position as mothers, as well as their familial ties, often led them to embrace accommodation. Similarly, female slaves in the Biafra region sacrificed socioeconomic autonomy to gain kinship incorporation. It was easier for male slaves in Biafra to achieve socioeconomic autonomy through skilled labor in traditional institutions such as blacksmithing and divination.

In both Caribbean and West African regions, the predominantly male ownership and control over enslaved women's reproductive bodies and productive labor defined the slavery system and shaped the experience of most slaves. Unlike the enslaved in diaspora, slaves in the Bight of Biafra did not form a distinct racialized stratum or class apart, and they were used in a great variety of capacities other than units of labor. Yet, in both Jamaica and Igboland, women slaves were used in critical gender-distinctive ways that underscored labor value and sexuality. In Jamaica, they worked as cash crop and food producers, hucksters, midwives, and nurses, as well as mistresses and mothers, who reproduced racialized plantation systems and mediated the transmission of servile and rebellious cultures. Slaves from the Bight of Biafra especially, who constituted the majority (43.1 percent of 411,884) of the slaves who embarked on the African coast for Jamaica between 1776 and 1808, left the most lasting impact on the region's creole charter generation.[24] Similarly, in the Bight of Biafra, women were the heart of social slavery, and their sexuality, wombs, and physical labor became resources of gender differential social mobility for men, including ex-slaves. In Jamaica and the Bight of Biafra, the conception of slavery as gendered structural power and wealth accumulation, and the importance of sex and motherhood practices, centered women in regional slavery systems.

A comparative perspective that foregrounds gender shows that the categorical distinction often made between chattel and "benign" kinship slavery conceals an important commonality, namely that the physical and sexual exploitation of enslaved women ensured male ascendancy in the Atlantic world, irrespective of race. From both temporal (origin and destination) and structural standpoints, Jamaica and the Bight of Biafra mutually refract the importance of female slavery during the Atlantic Age. As the principal destination for the majority of Biafran captives in the second half of the eighteenth century, Jamaica captures the relative transatlantic significance of the Bight of Biafra during this period. It accentuates the implications of British slave traders' debates about the economic value of African slaves in terms of their age and sex that were specific to the Bight of Biafra's domestic slavery practices and embarkation and disembarkation volumes. And comparatively, it illuminates how the Bight of Biafra's "(re)productive relations of slavery were conceived and designed in gendered terms."[25] Thus, it serves as an ideal reference for positioning the Bight of Biafra within a cis-Atlantic framework.

BIAFRA, JAMAICA, AND THE GENDERED DYNAMICS OF ATLANTIC SLAVING

Previous transatlantic assessments of how the Bight of Biafra's slavery shaped Atlantic slavery systems and creolization have focused on the ethnogenesis debate. Philip Morgan and David Northrup have criticized the use of ethnological labels to identify West and Central African peoples in the New World as a "tribal approach" that vitiates the syncretism of creole cultural forms.[26] Conversely, Douglass Chambers and Michael Gomez argue that failing to provide a sense of African cultural origins leaves impressions of African slaves as little more than ciphers, and constitutes an erasure of African historical experiences and categories of knowledge.[27]

Liverpool captain Hugh Crow, who made thirteen voyages to West Africa as a slave trader between 1790 and 1807, principally to the Biafran port of Bonny, emphasized in his memoir that the captives he embarked socioethnically differentiated themselves according to spatial occupation of the slave ship, ethnodistinctive scarifications and sartorial practices, and middle passage spiritual and dietary survival, maintaining social bonds after disembarkation in Jamaica.[28] When Oldendorp interviewed "Eboe" slaves in the Caribbean, he observed that they worked with ethnicity daily in making sense of traditions such as birth, circumcision, caste, and funeral rites, in a multiethnic African slave community.[29] Thomas Thistlewood's diary is riddled with observations that the "Negroes of each Nation" organized "Negro Diversions" of music and worship "by themselves." Whether slaves were ethnically Igbo in provenance or embraced an "Eboe" identity in Jamaica based on conscious affiliation, ethnicity defined slaves' social relations. But more importantly, this chapter embraces a gender-focused assessment that captures the importance of African origins and the process of adaptation in the New World, as well as the centrality of enslaved women's reproductive capacities to the social reproduction of racial and kinship slavery systems in Jamaica and Igboland respectively. Gender was at the root of Biafra's regional slavery and transatlantic slave trade to

Jamaica, and as Jennifer Morgan observed, it constituted power relationships through which slave owners and those they enslaved defined, understood, and adjusted the parameters of New World racial and chattel slavery.[30]

As shown in chapter 2, in contrast to Ohafia slave raids, which generated mostly women and children, other Biafran means of slave production such as criminal convictions generated adult men. The transatlantic slave trade database reflects the importance of Ohafia military slave production in distinguishing Biafra's captive demography. During the seventeenth century, males predominated the proportion of captive exports from all other Atlantic African regions, but in the Bight of Biafra, females constituted about 51 percent. And, whereas the combined eighteenth-century female proportion of other African regions was 32.6 percent, the Bight of Biafra's was about 44 percent. The decline in the volume of female captives embarked from Biafra in the late eighteenth century does not account for the fact that greater numbers of enslaved women than men were retained locally. Thus, the demography of captive exports did not reflect the demography of slaves produced. Also, although adult women and men remained more numerous than girls and boys in the rest of Atlantic Africa, within the Bight of Biafra, beginning in 1700, the population of boys doubled, and girls outnumbered adult women six to one, thereby bolstering the overall female captive demography. In effect, unlike the rest of Atlantic Africa, the Bight of Biafra witnessed an exceptionally high supply of women and children.

Ohafia ethnographic evidence reinforces the database and Company of Merchants' testimonials. Kalu Oki is a lead singer of the war song narrative, and he reckons his lineage even better. His great-grandfather Nna Iyi-Oke Echi lived sometime between 1790 and 1870, and his grandfather Eche Iyi Oke died in the 1920s, aged about eighty-five years. Oki narrates:

> Nna Iyi-Oke Echi begot Eche Iyi-Oke. Eche Iyi-Oke behaved exactly like Nna. He and many of his age-mates were called *o chi udo eje ogu* (he-who-went-to-war-with-ropes). He fought in many battles including Ukpati [1880s] and Nteje [1891]. When he went to war, he took his ropes and tied them around his waist. After cutting a male warrior's head, he took several captives and

tethered them to his rope, and upon reaching home, the village broke out in celebration. . . . Most of his captives were women. Some gave birth to children for him. His descendants are still in Okon today. . . . He was a great yam farmer, and owned plantations. When he brought home his slaves, he sent them to his farms as laborers. Many of his slaves worked in the farms. . . . He sold some of his slaves at Itu.[31]

Kalu Oki's attestation is consistent with the views of numerous Ohafia research collaborators, who viewed eighteenth-century military slaving through the lens of nineteenth-century military slaving practices. For them, these tactics of slave production were continuous. American market preferences did not transform slaving mechanisms. Rather, conceptions of heroic ufiem and imperatives of long-distance warfare shaped captive demography. Like his son, Nna Iyi-Oke Echi would have generated mostly female captives, at an earlier period when most captives would have been channeled into the Atlantic slave trade. As shown in chapter 2, most eighteenth-century captives were not taken back to Ohafia, but delivered to Aro middlemen.

Igor Kopytoff and Suzanne Miers observed that slavery in Africa was rooted in the need for wives and children, the wish to enlarge one's kin group, and the desire to have clients, servants, and retainers, because "political power rested with those who could command a large number of kinsmen and dependents."[32] This was the predominant definition of ogaranya masculinity in Igboland. The tendency to take women captive, in lieu of men, was popular among warriors, who not only relied on women for food provisioning and household reproduction but also increasingly represented *ike nwami* (capturing/possessing women) as the signifier of ogaranya masculinity. This woman-possession ideology of ufiem through slavery made economic sense. It was more expensive to purchase female slaves than to marry wives because of differential degrees of labor requisition from wives and slaves.[33] Whereas young slave women cost one-and-a-half times the average bride price, young male slaves cost two-thirds the price of slave girls. Payments were made in items such as cloth, gunpowder, guns, and machetes.[34] Warriors circumvented the exorbitant cost of female slaves through female captivity.

According to Claire Robertson and Martin Klein, the predominance of women among the enslaved in Africa stemmed primarily from the domestic and agricultural productive labor of women, and secondarily from their biological reproductive function and utility for expanding the number of people within kinship systems.³⁵ African "social slavery" emphasized a heavy domestic demand for people, which was only partially a demand for units of labor and largely a demand for social and political units. Women, much more than men, fulfilled this multiuse conception of slavery as the acquisition of a "bundle of 'commodity rights' in a person," as opposed to the notion of slavery as the singular commoditization of labor.³⁶

The correlation between the prominence of women in Biafra's captive population and the predominance of Igbo women in Jamaica's demography of African captive arrivals over time is striking. Nearly half of the slave exports from Biafra in the seventeenth and eighteenth centuries were women, and most of them ended up in the British Caribbean.³⁷ In contrast to Cuba and Brazil, Anglo-American regions received larger shares of African female slaves.³⁸ Besides the gendered character of the modes of Biafran hinterland slave production, what other factors may have accounted for the export of relatively high volumes of Igbo female slaves to Jamaica?

A reinterpretation of slave ships' demographic classification and gender-differentiated mortality is imperative. British slave traders often distinguished between men and women, men-boys and women-girls, and boys and girls based on arbitrary height estimations of adolescence. For instance, in 1793, the ship *Jupiter* embarked at Bonny with "110 men, 88 women, 29 men/boys, 32 women/girls, 33 boys, and 50 girls."³⁹ Its actual female cargo totaled 170, and male, 172. Although more male captives overall embarked from the Bight of Biafra, more female captives sometimes disembarked in the West Indies because of greater male mortality during the middle passage. Predominant captive male mortality partly explains why on most eighteenth-century Jamaican plantations, there were relatively equal numbers of men and women.⁴⁰

The entire system of hinterland–coastal–middle passage commodification of captives contributed to this gendered mortality difference. Slaves from Igboland traveled an average of 20–25 miles a day for two months and exchanged multiple hands before reaching the major regional markets. According to James Penny, who commanded eleven voyages from the African coast (the majority from Bonny to Jamaica), Bonny and Calabar traders, who were "expert at reckoning and talking the languages of their own country and those of the Europeans," went upriver about 80 miles to the inland marts to purchase these slaves. The slaves were bought with the manufactures from Biafra, as well as goods from India and European spirits, brass pans, guns, and copper manilas. The traders returned to the coast once every fortnight with their purchased slaves. Twenty or thirty canoes, each carrying thirty to forty slaves, returned from each trading expedition.[41] The executors of Hugh Crow's memoir wrote in 1830 that boats from Bonny returned from the interior with "1500 or 2000 slaves, who are sold to the Europeans the evening after their arrival, and taken on board the ships."[42] As Falconbridge attested, "They [brought the slaves] in a miserable condition from the fairs, half-starved, and exposed to the wet, in boats, with hardly any covering." Male slaves were especially tied and pinioned in the canoes, submerged in water. On their landing, slaves were taken to the traders' houses, where they were oiled, fed, and prepared for sale. European captains and surgeons went ashore to examine and purchase them. Captives not sold because of age or debility were sometimes killed. Purchased slaves were taken to the ship, forty or fifty at a time, generally in the evening. Some tried to jump off the canoes but were recovered and punished. Aboard the slave ships, men were put into bars for the duration of embarkation and the middle passage. Children and women were not chained.[43]

According to James Frazer, who spent twenty years in the African slave trade mostly in Bonny, Angola slaves were "peaceable," but slaves from Bonny were "viciously suicidal" and so kept under "stricter confinement." They were more reluctant to leave the coast and were "of the opinion that white men intended to eat them."[44] In 1777, Frazer commanded the *Valiant* from Calabar. This was his last voyage to Jamaica. The mortality on the coast, during the middle passage, in Kingston harbor (which received 62.3–86.6 percent of slave shipments to Jamaica from 1751 to 1808), and on shore before sale exceeded one hundred. Because of their reputation as rebellious and suicidal, "Eboe" male slaves aboard the *Valiant* were "chained two and two with leg-irons and handcuffs" below deck, unlike women.[45] "Eboe" slave men "had not so much room as a man in his coffin." Their confinement was so injurious that they went to sleep in good health only to be found dead in the morning.[46] According to Falconbridge, "Eboe" slaves' "peevishness, perverseness, and obstinacy" counteracted most entreaties, leading to severe punishments, including burning with hot coals. "Eboe" male slaves often escaped through the gun-port gratings and jumped into shark-infested waters. Many committed suicide.

Writing from Old Calabar in late August 1790, Captain William Blake of the slave ship *Pearl* reported that he had "buried 13 women & girls, 56 men & Boys [and] Sixteen White people," because Surgeon I. P. Degreaves was unfamiliar with African "disorders." By October, the captive death count had risen to 113. The ship surgeon Degreaves attributed the mortality rate to the purchase of unhealthy slaves, bad yams that brought on the "flux," and lack of meat and protein. The heavy food requirements of the slave trade often caused food rationing among slaves. Given that on average, men burned more calories than women because of greater body weight and muscular build, it is possible that enslaved men succumbed to debilitating hunger and malnutrition much more than women did. Another reason might be the greater disposition among male slaves to mutiny. Blake reported that the *Pearl* left Calabar with "only" 474 captives, as 282 died before they even began the journey across the Atlantic, and 3 drowned in an attempted "mutiny with the men slaves."[47]

Falconbridge made two voyages from Bonny. The first, aboard the *Alexander*, carried 380 slaves to Granada, and more than 100 slaves died, about 90 percent of them male. The second voyage, aboard the *Emilia*, carried 420 slaves to Jamaica, and 40 slaves, mostly male, died of fevers and dysentery.[48] James Penny commanded about eleven voyages from Bonny to Jamaica. He observed that Biafran slaves, in particular males, were subject to the greatest mortality in contrast to Gold Coast, Whydah, and Windward Coast slaves.[49] Robert Morris commanded five voyages carrying 400–500 slaves between 1769 and 1777. He also testified that Bonny and Calabar male slaves suffered the greatest mortality rate, much more than Whydah and the Gold Coast.[50] In May 1788, Navy surgeon Isaac Wilson sailed in the *Elizabeth* (John Smith commanding) from Bonny to Jamaica, with three other ships. As soon as "Eboe" slaves were boarded, many of them jumped overboard. Upon recovery, they were chained by the ankles to the boat and whipped over and over. The first ship lost 155 of 602 slaves, the second lost 200 of 450 slaves, the third lost 73 of 466 slaves, and the fourth lost 158 of 546 slaves. Wilson testified that overall, the ships lost two or more males to one female.[51] Indeed, there is a consistent picture of greater male mortality in the transatlantic crossing from Biafran ports.

Another transatlantic logic for the prominence of Igbo women in Jamaica has to do with the Biafran port of Bonny, from which most of the female "Eboe" slaves embarked. There was a preference for slaves from Bonny over the other two Biafran ports of Old Calabar and New Calabar; Bonny slaves were perceived as "Eboe," although slaves at the three ports derived from the same hinterland and included people of Igbo and Ibibio ethnicities.[52] In another letter written from Old Calabar, after waiting on the coast for several weeks, Blake lamented that Old Calabar was a "disagreeable sickly place" and that to keep the ship on the coast much longer "would be destroying everything," as there would be much "expense of provisions, [and daily] burying [of] slaves."[53] Diptee provides a detailed account of the *African Queen*, which spent eight months in Old Calabar, during which two successive ship captains, nine European crew members, and more than forty-one African captives died. Similar examples show that British ships sometimes waited in Old Calabar sixteen months, making minimal purchases. Diptee concludes, "In general, the enslaved from Old Calabar were *not* favored among Jamaican planters and required a brisk market." In contrast, captives purchased at the other Biafran ports, New Calabar and Bonny, could be sold with relative ease to the Jamaican plantocracy."[54] Jamaican planters specifically requested young slaves of "Eboe Cargoe" from Bonny, as they were "the sort most run upon" in Jamaica. Slaves from Old Calabar sold in Jamaica for £28–£30, but those from Bonny were purchased for about £25 and sold at an average of £60–£62:10 per head in the West Indies.

Planters' preferences reflected the regional shift in the organization of Biafran hinterland slaving networks and the volume of slave supply to Biafra's ports in the second half of the eighteenth century, when Bonny surpassed Old Calabar and became the busiest port in the Bight of Biafra, and in Atlantic Africa north of the equator. Between 1776 and 1808, Bonny exported about 56 percent of all captives transported from the Bight of Biafra, whereas Old Calabar and New Calabar accounted for 17 percent and 12 percent, respectively. Jamaica, the largest single destination for captives from this region, received 46 percent of the enslaved.[55] Whereas trade expanded dramatically and embarkation rate peaked at Bonny, at Old Calabar, rivalry between

Liverpool and Bristol merchants drove up prices, exorbitant custom duties discouraged trade, and the shortage of captives necessitated longer wait periods for slave ships and increased mortality. Bonny enjoyed an advantageous location and regional alliances that reinforced more efficient links with the hinterland where the majority of export captives originated from. Bonny's regional linkages, argues Nwokeji, enabled the Aro to more quickly move captives to that port, and sell them at higher prices. Slaves sold at Bonny were styled as "Eboe" to distinguish them from rebellious "Calabar" captives.[56] Thus the term "Eboe" designated a port of origin, Bonny, much more than the Igbo ethnicity.[57] The slaves sold at Bonny included both Igbo and Ibibio captives. But of the two principal ethnicities in the Bight of Biafra, the Igbo constituted about 68 percent and the Ibibio 25 percent of captive exports from the ports of Calabar and Bonny in the eighteenth and nineteenth centuries.[58] Because Ohafia military slaving took place in Igbo and Ibibio hinterlands, they complicate a scholarly quest for a distinct "Igbo" ethnicity in the New World based on Biafran embarkation ports.[59] As has been argued, the circumstances of African enslavement (like demography-definitive guerrilla captivity) could be more important in understanding New World identities of Atlantic Africans than their assumed ethnolinguistic provenance.[60]

The third consideration is that Jamaican planters demonstrated a notable preference for women from the "Eboe" country. Jamaican planters understood that African conditions, rather than New World planters' choices, defined the demography of slave captives, and that in the late eighteenth century, adult males were always heavily taxed higher than adult females on the island; and planters and merchants, wary of importing large numbers of African men in the shadow of the Haitian Revolution, often specifically requested for African women and young people of both sexes as opposed to adult men. According to Diptee, Simon Taylor, one of the wealthiest Jamaican planters, observed in 1805 that in a "proper assortment" of enslaved Africans none should be "above 18 years old or below 12" and the "more women and boys and girls the better." Jamaican merchant James Rolland believed that slave traders should "avoid grown men, as much as possible & let the majority be young women, with girls & boys in proportion." And Jamaican planter Bryan Edwards insisted on "a greater restriction against importing adult males," because of their propensity for rebellion. In

Jamaica, women, children, and youths could be readily sold for better prices, whereas a proportion of adult males imported into Jamaica were precisely destined for reexport to Cuba. The Jamaican plantocracy believed that women (especially "females who have not borne children") and young people were best suited for establishing a permanent and self-reproducing enslaved labor force. Besides sex or age, or "assorted cargo," Jamaican planter preference also emphasized good condition and tolerable health of slaves. One solution was minimal time spent on the African coast and a speedy voyage.[61] The Biafra port of Bonny fulfilled these conditions of sex and age captive demography as well as timely departures much more than any other African slave-trading port.[62]

The demography of the Bight of Biafra's gendered slave production and shipboard mortality is reflected in Jamaica's disembarkation ratios. Higher proportions of women arrived in Jamaica from the Bight of Biafra than from the Gold Coast, even during Jamaica's formative first century (1650–1750), when Gold Coast Africans dominated the Jamaican slave population. Whereas 38.6 percent (49,521) of 128,293 enslaved Africans from the Gold Coast in Jamaica were female, 50.5 percent (38,400) of the 76,040 captives from the Bight of Biafra were female. Between 1750 and 1807, when the Bight of Biafra accounted for the dominant 43 percent (256,859) of total Jamaican slave imports, its regional proportion of adult women slaves was 108,500 in contrast to Gold Coast's 67,000.[63] Most Biafran slaves arriving in Jamaica in the second half of the eighteenth century embarked at Bonny, the port that exported primarily "Eboe" slaves. Between 1775 and 1800, Bonny exported 68,000 slaves to Jamaica, compared to 16,500 from Old Calabar and 8,000 from New Calabar.

From 1751, abolitionism in Britain, the disruptions of the American War of Independence, and the French and Haitian Revolutions gave Jamaican planters the incentive to create a self-sustaining slave population. Planters began purchasing more women and children. Between 1751 and 1775, women and children accounted for 60 percent of all slaves shipped to Jamaica. Most were Igbo. Between 1776 and 1808, 58,585 adult women and 15,978 young girls from the Bight of Biafra arrived in Jamaica. Comparatively, 28,429 adult women and 4,902 young girls arrived from the Gold Coast. West-Central Africa followed with 22,218 adult women and 4,597 young girls. In effect, the volume of female captive arrivals from the Bight of Biafra was double that from comparative regions. The dominance of Biafran captives in the British slave trade during this period meant that among those captives purchased for sale in Jamaica, more than twice as many women and children left this region than other African export regions. And Biafran girls outnumbered the combined number of girls from all other regions.[64]

FEMALE SLAVERY WITHIN IGBOLAND AND JAMAICA: THE NEED FOR A TRANSATLANTIC PERSPECTIVE

The subjects of sex and reproduction are important in understanding slavery in both Jamaica and Igboland, and they position women as central to social conceptions of slavery. In view of the post-1750 preponderance of Biafran captives among British Caribbean African slaves, David Eltis and David Richardson observe, "The opportunities for family formation and the perpetuation of language and culture were likely stronger [there] than elsewhere in the Americas."[65] Enslaved women's importance to Biafra-homeland kinship practices placed women in a special position to reconstitute family life within the Jamaican slave sector. The 1750–1807 period, during which Biafran women constituted the majority of new African arrivals in Jamaica, coincided with a shift in the pace of reproduction and creolization. In the period before 1750, the proportion of Jamaican slaves born in Africa was about 89.4 percent. Between 1750 and 1807, however, the percentage of Jamaican slaves born in Africa decreased to 45 percent, and plantation survival increasingly depended on natural reproduction. Whereas brutal work regimes, gender imbalances, and diseases had generated low survival and birth rates and impeded family formation in Jamaica between 1650 and 1750, the subsequent 1751–1807 era, marked by a considerable boost in the enslaved female population, ushered in stable family formation, settled plantation life, and a creolized population.[66] Although the British Caribbean is not known for natural reproduction, compared to North America, this change in Jamaica was significant.

Jamaican planters always hoped that African slave women would help them maintain their slave populations, and they represented enslaved women's fecundity and fertility practices as critical to the viability of sugar plantation slavery, even when such representations did not make sense. The relative degree of the masters' control over enslaved women's wombs came to shape the slavery system.[67] Until abolition in 1807, Caribbean planters necessarily purchased adult Africans because relying on enslaved women's natural reproduction proved too risky for stable sugar plantations. Yet pro-natalist policies offered overseers a £3 bounty for each slave child born under their authority, exempted any enslaved woman who had six children alive from field labor, and provided lying-in-house facilities and elderly women slave nurses and midwives. For instance, Alexander Willock owned several sugar plantations between 1745 and 1781. His slave holding was at first made up of Africans (not creoles), and he increased their population by birth in an environment where "breeding had been more profitable than buying, one Creole being worth 3 Africans." Willock exempted pregnant slaves from hard labor, provided lying-in rooms and attendants, and gave midwives a dollar for each child that lived nine days. When in 1779 an epidemic killed fifty of his five hundred slaves, mostly women on two plantations, which amounted to a £4,500 loss, Willock turned to slave importation but never regained the original stature of his estates. This forced his retirement from sugar slavery in 1781.[68]

"Considered the most fertile of all Africans imported via the slave trade," writes Sasha Turner, "Ebo women were singled out for close inspection by buyers interested in their childbearing histories." Turner reviews the following evidence from Jamaican planters. According to Nathaniel Phillips, an absentee owner of two sugar estates, "Eboe is the country to buy women off to breed." In 1800, Phillips instructed his local attorney, Thomas Barritt, to allocate all monies owed to his property for buying new "Negroes when good ones come in [and] if Eboes take 20 women." Barritt accordingly procured "14 New Negroes," including "6 young women [and] 5 women girls," whom he deemed "all fine people, the best kind of Eboes." Similarly, Simon Taylor reported to his absentee employer, Chaloner Arcedekne, that he "bought the 10 wenches [Arcedekne] required. [He] sent 5 to Golden Grove and 5 to Blanchelors Hall. . . . They are Eboes which we think are the best breeding people." Taylor sought for his "Ebo women" to breed, intending "for every man [slave] to have his wife." Taylor reflected a widespread practice whereby Jamaican planters attempted to pair newly arrived "Eboe" slave women with Coromantee slave men. "Eboe" women supposedly had domestic tendencies that tamed the more unruly and unsettled Gold Coast male slaves. In return, the more enterprising and mentally resilient Coromantee men mitigated the suicidal tendencies in "Eboe" women.

Planters' breeding efforts manifested more as "cunning manipulation, wherein planters strategized their purchases and interfered in the sexual relations of the enslaved." "Eboe" women were popularly advertised in Jamaica. One advertisement in the 1790 *Daily Advertiser* read, "For Sale On Tuesday 4th January 303 Choice Young Ebo From New Calabar." Jamaican planters determined pro-natal reforms based on their perceptions of how ethnicity shaped captive women's reproductive capacities. Jamaican proprietors' convictions about "Eboe" women's fecundity came from "their years of perceiving these as having more children than other ethnic groups." According to Jamaican estate doctor David Collins, Igbo and Ibibio women were "hardy" and capable of a variety of labor, and thus "are superior to any other and very little inferior to men." "Ebo women" concludes Turner, "had larger, more stable families and communities because they were generally more attached to the land, their children, and their spouses. A higher number of fugitive women with children and families were listed as Ebo, because they 'placed their lives in peril to keep their families intact.' Additionally, Ebo women were arguably more prolific because they formed sexual relationships with males outside their ethnic grouping."[69]

Jamaican planters' attempt to use enslaved women as reproductive units paralleled ogaranya slavery practices in Igboland. In both regions, captive women were increasingly viewed as mother-workers in the late eighteenth and early nineteenth century. The acquisition of enslaved women and control over their labor and wombs was one of the fastest and most secure means of social reconstitution, even for Igbo male ex-slaves, who achieved relineagization and kinship incorporation through wealth acquisition and marriage.[70] Such was the case with Ekea Udensi of Ohafia, who was born around 1820. He was initiated into the dibia guild as a boy, and quickly gained popularity as an efficient medicine man not only in Ohafia but also in neighboring communities such as Arochukwu and Abam. His uncles, jealous of his rapid prosperity at an early age, sold him into slavery to Chief Agbomina Agbo of Opobo, a wealthy merchant, whom Ekea served as a domestic servant. However, Ekea would medicinally enable one of Chief Agbo's wives, who battled with infertility, to become pregnant and have a son. In appreciation, his master made him head of his household slaves and his chief physician, in charge of the health of Agbo and his wives, children, and slaves. Over time, Agbo granted Ekea freedom and adopted him as a son. However, incorporation into his foreign master's lineage was not sufficient for Ekea. Sometime in the 1840s, Ekea decided to embark on a medicine pilgrimage (*ije ogwu*) to his ancestral shrine (*okpogho elu*) in Okon, Ohafia. Chief Agbo furnished him with trade goods and five female slaves, two of whom he made "wives."

Returning to Ohafia dressed in khaki shorts and shoes, and armed with new wealth in European commodities, including a kerosene lantern that he proudly paraded around his village, Ekea became a legendary ogaranya, with a social capacity to usurp the political power of both male and female traditional authority holders. Slave ownership constituted ogaranya performance because it was a mark of social and economic advancement and an outward expression of wealth and position that enabled ogaranya to manipulate social mores, enslave debtors, and strong-arm political opponents through membership in secret societies like okonko, ite odo, and dibia. Prevailing notions of ogaranya masculinity defined slavery in the Bight of Biafra, which pivoted on dynamic uses of marginalized persons as sexual, labor, and political units. Thus, Ekea would go on to "take possession of" (*kere*) twenty-two captive "slave-wives" and also acquire numerous male and female slaves, who worked his yam and palm plantations, which encompassed over 50 hectares of land by 1880. Through the labor of his slaves, Ekea established a thriving palm produce and salt trade between the Ohafia hinterland communities of Okon and Okagwe and the riverine commercial centers of Calabar and Opobo.[71]

The exclusively male dibia guild practice was the backbone of Ekea's ascendancy. His mastery of riverine and hinterland languages and healing systems enhanced his mystical reputation and set him apart from local competitors. His social power and wealth as a dibia placed him in an advantageous position to provide protection to vulnerable populations, including widows, orphans, and slaves, who sought his patronage. Through the "adoption" of marginal persons, including women who produced children, Ekea is said to have built a village of dependents. He is renowned as one of the most prominent Ohafia dibias. His legacy placed wealth-in-people and commodities at the center of dibia masculinity. Thus, Njoku argues, "because of the wide demand for their services, traditional medical practitioners, especially the renowned ones, were among the wealthiest members of Ohafia society."[72] More importantly, Ekea's case was symptomatic of a broader male-dominated system of slave ownership in the Bight of Biafra, in which women's unfreedom became central to male ascendancy.

Remarkably, Trevor Burnard in his examination of the life of Thomas Thistlewood, the son of a poor English yeoman farmer, who left England to flourish in Jamaica as a planter and slave owner, argues that Thistlewood exemplifies how the exploitation of slaves, in gendered and sexual ways, was central to the construction of white maleness in eighteenth-century Jamaica. Indeed, most disconcertingly, we are introduced to "Ebo" enslaved women in Jamaica through the recurrent picture of their experiences of sexual predation at the hands of white male slaveowners. This is ancillary to another imagery of enslaved "Ebo" women in Jamaica: their "womb practices." There is an implicit correlation between these two imageries, which bring into sharp relief the transatlantic repercussions of Ohafia-Igbo gendered slave production and Biafra's demography of captive exports to Jamaica in the second half of the eighteenth century.

In his categorization of the 89 slaves at the Egypt plantation in Westmoreland Parish, where he became an overseer in 1751, Thistlewood lists 31 "men," 29 "women," 6 "boys," 8 "girls," 8 "male children," and 6 "female children." None of the male slaves were identified by their African origins or African/Creole status. Of the 29 women, Thistlewood designated 6 "Ebo," 2 "Nago,"[73] 1 "Congo," 1 "Mandingo," and 4 "Creole," while 15 had no origin designations. Of the 9 "girls," Thistlewood identified 4 "Ebo" and 1 "Creole," while 4 had no origin designations. Of the 6 "female children," he noted 1 "Congo" while the rest had no origin designations. African slaves newly arrived in Jamaica occupied an alien social and cultural position, accentuated by their dressing, hairstyle, "country marks", filed teeth, accents, limited English proficiency, and skin color, which distinguished them from Creoles.[74] Thus, it would have been relatively easy for Thistlewood to identify any additional creole slaves.[75] Hence, we may assume that the rest of the female slaves were African born. Since these identifications reflect Thistlewood's *intimate interests* (his obsession with female slaves is palpable from his diary accounts), it is possible that his predominant identification of "Ebo" female slaves (10 out of the 15 African born identified by ethnic region) reflected the differences in the regional percentages (and, thus, numerical and cultural presence) of African female captives in Jamaica. It was, after all, a period when the proportion of female captives from Biafra was more than double that of the Gold Coast and West-Central Africa, the other leading suppliers of African captives to Jamaica.[76]

Thistlewood's diary is a litany of his sexual abuse of female slaves under his charge. Coerced sex punctuated the daily works that female slaves carried out, including holing and dunging for cane; clearing fields; cane cutting and stripping; boiling sugar, rum, and molasses; picking cotton; building bridges and houses; making ropes; constructing collars for and herding cattle; gathering wood and fish; and going to markets to sell some of these products. Thistlewood incessantly molested "Ebo" slave women and girls. He chronicles raping the "Ebo" slave girl Ellin, "by the morass side [on the ground] toward the little plantain walk," while he was infected with gonorrhea. Upon recovery, he turned his attention to the "Ebo" slave woman Abigail, who ran away four times from the plantation between September and November 1751 in order to escape Thistlewood's assaults. The "Ebo" slave woman Maggie joined Abigail in her flight, as did the "Ebo" slave woman Chrishea. If adult "Ebo" slave women escaped Thistlewood's sexual predation through flight, female child slaves did not. By December, Thistlewood began terrorizing the "Ebo" female child slave Jenny, assaulting her three times in one night, and cohabiting with and raping her for the next two years (January 1751 to December 1753). He occasionally "took" other female slaves, but Jenny was his object of infatuation. He gave her presents, took them away when she displeased him, and returned them when he was appeased. At nights, he was with Jenny; in the days, he was "taking" the Congo female child slave Susannah, the creole slave woman Big Mimber, and the "Ebo" slave woman Belinda.[77]

The case studies of Ekea and Thistlewood demonstrate important similarities in female-slavery-focused constructions of hegemonic masculinities, as well as stark differences in degrees of violent coercion within Biafran and Jamaican slavery systems. The relative conditions of enslaved "Eboe"/Igbo women within the respective slavery systems in turn shaped enslaved women's modes of accommodation and resistance to slavery in both Jamaica and Igboland. Chattel property, violent coercion, lifetime servitude, and inheritance of the slave condition from an enslaved mother distinguished Jamaican slavery from slavery in Igboland.[78] If Biafra's domestic slavery is conceived through the lens of chattel slavery, one could say that women were "marginal," because their easier kinship incorporation did not suit chattel slavery's ideal of permanent alienation. However, as a number of scholars have indicated, African social slavery is best understood in the larger context where people were an important and much-wanted resource. Because political and social power rested with those who could command a large number of kinsmen and dependents, whether clients, followers, or slaves, slavery entailed manipulating the concept of rights-in-people to increase the number of people under one's control.

Therefore, kinship incorporation shaped the way that enslaved women negotiated slavery. Both freeborn people and slaves were equally the property of lineages, and both could be alienated to meet necessary obligations. But slaves were more alienable because they were strangers to the corporate group, and their marginality entailed an ambiguous lack of corporate bond. Long residence, often over multiple generations, made slave descendants more integral members of the community. Whereas female slaves accelerated the pace of incorporation through marriage with freeborn people, male slaves seldom did so through the arduous establishment of autonomous means of social reproduction, wealth acquisition, initiation into exclusive sociopolitical institutions, and marriage. Unlike fatherhood, motherhood mitigated the servile status of slave parent and offspring. Slaves born in a master's household ranked higher than bought slaves, and among bought slaves, there were distinctions among old, new, and slaves-in-transit. Whereas new slaves, who had not achieved incorporation, could be used for human sacrifice, slaves-in-transit had no attachment to the master's household. Male slaves were the majority of slaves-in-transit, particularly during the Atlantic trade, when the volume of slaves-in-transit surpassed the number retained for domestic use. The incorporation of slaves as labor and political units, especially through the transformation of female slaves into "wives," defined domestic slavery. And new slaves were incorporated through matricentric units of the household, which became the working, cooking, and eating units for affiliated slaves.[79]

The fact that it was more expensive to purchase female slaves (due to high demand and greater labor utility) than to marry wives raises critical questions about the presumed "impracticality" of keeping women slaves in Igboland.[80] Among the matrilineal Ohafia, women's position as breadwinners and their centrality to lineage production and property expansion encouraged the acquisition of female slaves and their incorporation as wives and sisters. According to Ebem Ohafia oral traditions, during the eighteenth and nineteenth centuries, matrilineages relied on a practice of free women and men "taking possession of" slave-wives to sustain and expand their corporate lineages; immolate, deify, and replace deceased matriarchs; and determine the allocation of political leadership.[81] Enslaved women were preferred over enslaved men and free wives because it was easier to incorporate enslaved women as uterine sisters (nwannediya) of a local matrilineage. Enslaved men lacked the corporeal ability (wombs) and social malleability to reproduce matrilineages, and free wives reckoned a natal matrilineage elsewhere. Deracinated female slaves did not have legitimate preexisting matrilineages, however, so they constituted the majority of Ohafia domestic slaveholding. Through the practice of female husbandhood, female slaveholding, and biannual political rituals of ethnic citizenship, freeborn Ohafia-Igbo women both contributed to and contested mechanisms of slave-wives' incorporation in their society. On the one hand, Ohafia women married wives and "adopted" female slaves to save dwindling matrilineages and perform ogaranya masculinity. And on the other hand, women used songs, public ridicule, and virginity-testing rituals to discriminate against slave-wives as liminal aliens who lacked local matrilineal kinship and, hence, ethnic citizenship.[82]

Beyond Ohafia, the neighboring patrilineal Aro sustained and expanded their hinterland diaspora settlements by acquiring and incorporating slave-wives. Indeed, among the Aro, the importance of women to lineage constitution "left fewer females for the Atlantic traffic" and accounted for the late eighteenth-century decline in the proportion of women leaving the Bight of Biafra. The Aro expanded their settlements through incorporation (*mmuba*). They acquired enslaved women as "wives" and absorbed more females than males from central Igboland. Beginning in 1775, more adult women and young boys were retained within Biafra, whereas more young girls and adult men were sent to the overseas traffic, because women and boys were "instruments of the lineage." Women procreated, and boys founded new patrilineages to accomplish Aro "big compound" ideals.[83] Thus, enslaved women's wombs became critical.

Biafra's slavery system relied on women and afforded enslaved women greater avenues of kinship incorporation, but it limited their socioeconomic autonomy and mobility. This encouraged an increase in the retention of enslaved adult women within the region over the course of the eighteenth and nineteenth centuries. Of the total departures from Biafra between 1650 and 1700, 51 percent were female and, of that number, 46 percent were adult women. But the proportion of female slaves exported from Biafra increasingly declined over the course of the eighteenth and nineteenth centuries: from 44 percent between 1750 and 1800 to 35.3 percent between 1800 and 1850, of which only 15 percent were adult women. The significant nineteenth-century decline especially was due to the postabolition increase in the local demand for enslaved Igbo women's services.[84] Throughout the nineteenth century, the prices for female slaves continuously rose higher than the prices for adult male slaves in domestic markets such as Itu and Asan, frequented by Ohafia merchant-warriors.[85] The captivity, enslavement, and gifting of women became popular practices of differential social mobility. It is plausible that this woman-possession ideology (*ike nwami*) was reinforced by the observed high incidence of divorce (*ikpe kupu m aka*) in the early nineteenth century, when freeborn women increasingly revolted against male exploitation of their labor.[86] By 1890, female captivity, elite polygyny, and sexual slavery had skewed the adult-female-to-adult-male ratio to five to two in Ohafia.[87] Throughout southeastern Nigeria, female Igbo slaves became popularly used as wives, surrogate mothers, mistresses, petty traders, and domestic servants, with minimal opportunities for social mobility.[88]

Whereas Igbo slave women in Biafra negotiated bondage through incorporation as wives and mothers, "Eboe" women in Jamaica negotiated bondage with abortions, infanticide, and rebellious motherhood. While maternity facilitated incorporation in Igboland, in Jamaica, children posed challenges to enslaved "Eboe" women attempting to escape slavery, such as Coobah (Molia), who was fifteen years old when she arrived in Jamaica in 1761 and birthed a deceased mixed-race daughter named Sylvia five years later. Between 1770 and 1774, Coobah was "openly defiant and even reckless" in her disobedience of Thistlewood, running away at least fourteen times and surviving through theft of vegetables, "rice, beans, calabashes, & c." until Thistlewood sold and shipped her off to Savannah, Georgia.[89] Moreover, having children did not permanently change a slave's economic situation or decrease her physical workload in the long term. Pregnancies and miscarriages benighted enslaved women. The "Ebo" slave women Little Mimba and Mirtilla became very ill in February 1752 and "miscarried." Thistlewood recorded 153 pregnancies over thirty-seven years, resulting in 121 live births. As Diana Paton deduced, the thirty-two miscarriages and abortions "must be an underestimate, since Thistlewood would not have known about all pregnancies." At least fifty-one of these children—more than one in three—died before the age of seven. Only fifteen definitely reached the age of seven.[90]

Given that women in their prime childbearing years spent 88 percent of their working time in the "great gangs" tasked with strenuous cane holing, planting sugar, and harvesting it, and additionally survived inadequate nutrition, those "Eboe" women who raised children under chattel slavery developed rebellious means of reconstituting their humanity and social bonds. Motherhood gained some "Eboe" women access to additional provision grounds and housing spots, at least in the case of Taylor's Golden Grove plantation. Pregnancy also afforded enslaved women in Jamaica access to other mechanisms of rebellion. They nursed their children for two to four years, in spite of planters' punitive discouragement, whereas enslaved women in North America breastfed their infants no longer than a year. Longer lactation served as a means of contraception either through the physical suppression of fertility in the mother or through the social impact of constant nurturing of infants and unavailability to men like Thistlewood.[91]

However, children presented masters the means to elicit compliance from slave mothers through the threat of separation.[92] "Eboe" women therefore negotiated the demands of slavery through extended birth spacing, "dirt eating" (consumption of clay to stop menstruation), ingestion of contraceptive herbs and abortifacients such as okra and aloe, and infanticide.[93] Planters condemned "Eboe" slave women for widespread practices of self-abortion, and singled out "Eboe" *obeah* (dibia) men for assisting women with abortion.[94] In the decades following abolition, the reproductive rate for African-born slave women declined to half that of creole slave women. Verene Shepherd argues that Afro-Jamaican slave women, realizing the planters' need after 1807 to reproduce the slave population, "sought to free their previously enchained wombs, refusing to bear children who would, themselves, be enslaved."[95] The notion that enslaved women practiced abortion as political rebellion—what Orlando Patterson calls "gynecological revolt" and Shepherd styles a "petticoat rebellion"—attributes overt political agency to slaves.[96] Yet cultural practices like abortion, infanticide, prolonged lactation, consumption of baked clay, and postnatal abstinence taboos stemmed from enslaved women's African backgrounds and were brought to Jamaica through the transatlantic slave trade.[97]

The responses of recently arrived "Eboe" slaves like Coobah, Abigail, Belinda, Margie, Violet, and Chrishea, who endured Thistlewood's sexual predation, pregnancy, miscarriage, and loss of children, were partly informed by Igbo cultural expectations of female slavery, in which motherhood was supposed to ameliorate slave status, not compound enslaved women's plights.[98] They reflect how the large numbers of female captives that made up 43 percent of Biafra's slave exports between 1776 and 1808 "put an African stamp" on Jamaica. They were part of a process of "intense Africanization" of Jamaican culture in the last decades of slavery.[99] European commentators saw this "Africanization" specifically in terms of African women's corruption of white female virtue, and in terms of "scheming black Jezebels" that created an environment where "so little restraint is laid on passions," thereby luring white men of "every rank" into "goatish embrace" and away from "lawful bliss derived from matrimonial, mutual love."[100] The visibility of "Eboe" women, "Africanization," white male sexual predation, and "womb practices" became mutually constitutive processes that defined Jamaican slave society. These realities encourage a reassessment of Biafra's kinship slavery in terms of sex and reproduction.

FEMALE SLAVERY, OGARANYA, AND SOCIAL REPRODUCTION IN NINETEENTH-CENTURY BIAFRA

The correlation between ogaranya hegemony and female slavery underscores the notion that slavery facilitated gender inequality. The abolition of the Atlantic slave trade in 1807 and the shift to legitimate commerce increased the volume of the domestic slave trade in nineteenth-century Biafran region. Even the number of slaves (eleven thousand) shipped annually from the region, which had declined during 1801–1811, nearly doubled by 1826. In spite of the presence of a British naval squadron, illicit slave exports, particularly to Brazil and Cuba, persisted. It was not until the 1840s that Biafra's external slave trade ended. As Adiele Afigbo points out, the trade in palm produce (used in manufacturing lubricants, candles, soaps, margarine, cooking fats, and cattle feeds) with which the British hoped to replace the slave trade largely depended on domestic slave labor.[101] The re-increase in the volume of slave exports paralleled the increase in the volume of palm oil exports from 3,000 to 8,000 tons between 1819 and 1829, and from 13,600 to over 40,000 tons between 1839 and 1860. This burgeoning cash crop production relied on an equally increasing volume of domestic slavery, which was primarily female oriented.[102]

As Oriji demonstrates, whereas the nineteenth-century external slave trade featured mostly men, the domestic slave trade victimized mostly women and children. Female Igbo slaves became more expensive because of the growing demand for their labor services. As the leading producers of palm oil and kernel in the Biafran hinterland, the Igbo supplied about 85 percent and 75 percent of all palm oil exports from the continent in the late 1820s and 1840s, respectively. Although legitimate commerce enabled small-scale farmers and common people to participate in the international economic system, it intensified social stratification in Igbo society, leading to the rise of wealthy and powerful male and female ogaranya, who exploited slave labor to reproduce their wealth and undermine preexisting authority holders. The ecological and social problems that the commercialization of palm produce generated, including soil depletion and food shortages, adversely affected small-scale farmers (reliant on a family unit of production), who faced poverty and hunger. Large-scale producers and leading traders, who had more land and labor, easily adapted to the economic crisis of food production.[103]

Women played major roles in the production, bulking, transportation, and marketing of palm produce. They transported the palm fruits from the forests to their residence, where they shredded the nuts from their clusters, boiled and pounded them, and expressed the oil, with minimal assistance from their husbands. Assisted by their children, women set about the tedious task of cracking the outer casing of the palm kernel, ensuring that the nuts were not damaged. It took about four hundred cracked nuts to generate 1 pound of palm kernel. Three hundred pounds of palm fruit (twenty-five to thirty clusters) are required to produce a 36-pound tin of semihard oil, and the labor required is about three to five person-days per tin. The average headload of oil a person could carry was about 5 gallons (40–50 pounds). Hinterland traders walked long distances to the riverine communities to market their palm produce. As late as 1916, when roads had been constructed to ease transportation, a 44-mile journey (Aba to Opobo) lasted six to seven days, and a 70-mile journey (Umuahia to Opobo) lasted twenty days. Because the exchange centers were far from the primary producers, women traveled in groups with a few men, who provided them with security. Some of the men were husbands or slaves. Women were paid with iron bars, cowries, salt, stockfish, and other imported goods. In most patrilineal Igbo societies, women kept the proceeds from palm kernel for themselves and gave the lion's share of palm oil proceeds to their husbands, who "owned" the palm trees. Through polygyny and slavery, ogaranya individuals expanded their household labor, particularly the number of women, and were thus able to produce palm oil and kernel in commercial quantities.

Oriji cites the example of Ananaba of Obegu, who exploited the labors of his over two hundred wives, as well as slaves, to become the "king of the Ngwa" in 1895.[104] Nwokeji likewise proffers the story of a mid-nineteenth-century Arondizuogu merchant-warrior, Okoro Udozuka, who also relied on "female possession" to reproduce his lineage and society at large. Udozuka exploited his matrilineage home in the Nri-Awka region to acquire slaves and his patrilineage home in Arondizuogu to dispose of these slaves. "Besides his numerous children by an army of wives, Udozuka was able through the institution of slavery to build a miniature empire for himself. His subjects numbered more than 200 and contributed so much to the increased population of Ndiakunwata." Through his dependents, Udozuka forged new trade links in the region. The measure of his affluence came to be based on the number of slaves, wives, and dependents he had, as well as the success of the dependents in trade and acquisition of people. This was true of many Aro men.[105] It can be argued that Udozuka performed ogaranya masculinity. Numerous Aro men retained enslaved women rather than export them because of enslaved women's versatile use. Because women's centrality to the labor-intensive production of palm oil reinforced the local demand on women's labor, many Aro men turned to polygyny and the acquisition of slave-wives. Men acquired women "not because of the abundance of women, but because men needed women's labor and reproductive resources."[106] In other words, through the sexual enslavement of women and the commoditization of wombs, ogaranya individuals built up their power. Similar stories punctuate the nineteenth-century history of Igboland.

Widespread insecurity, transport handicaps, and lack of access to labor and credit impeded free women's large-scale exploitation of regional trade. But a few elite women, mostly wives of leading male authority holders and credit brokers, exploited the system of kin-dependency slavery to secure credit facilities from coastal middlemen, acquire female slaves as itinerant merchant-agents, and deploy the labor of large numbers of slaves to become among the wealthiest and most powerful people in their communities. Naomi of Oguta and Omu Okwei of Ossomari are frequently cited examples. The former married a rich slave dealer, joined her husband in selling slaves, and after 1840, switched to the palm produce trade. Her retinue of slave girls constituted the cornerstone of her retail business empire. Like her male ogaranya contemporaries, Naomi established a large compound as the head of a kin group, surrounded by the homes of her female slaves, her sons, and her sons' wives. Like the wealthy men of Oguta, Naomi sat on a wooden chair in her house, "sipping neat whisky as men did."[107]

Omu Okwei, the wealthiest and most powerful female merchant on the Lower Niger involved in legitimate commerce, capitalized on her royal heritage to marry a prominent brass trader and later king of Nembe, Joseph Alagoa, which enhanced her business connections with European firms. In 1895, Okwei remarried and settled at Onitsha with her second husband, Peter Opene of Aboh, and became an agent of the Niger Trading Company—one of the major firms that purchased palm produce and marketed imported goods. Okwei acquired girls (mostly "adopted" children), brought them up, and gave them out as mistresses to influential African and European businessmen in order to secure trading monopolies. Her mistresses were expected to come back to her household when the traders left Nigeria. Any children the women begot during their association with the traders reverted to Okwei as property. With her wealth, Okwei invested in money lending, real estate, and transportation, and by 1935, she was crowned the Omu (Queen Mother) of Ossomari.[108] Such Igbo women who acquired wealth-in-slaves and performed ogaranya were perceived as masculine.

Much like Ekea, Ananaba, and Udozuka, Naomi and Okwei exploited the ogaranya habitus of slavery, including sexual slavery (forcing enslaved girls into sex work), to obtain superior sociopolitical authority in their communities. But these female ogaranya were rare exceptions. Although it was possible for a male ex-slave like Ekea to attain ogaranya status through the masculine dibia guild, such rapid social mobility was virtually impossible for female ex-slaves until the twentieth century, when, as Nwando Achebe shows, somebody like ex-female slave Ahebi Ugbabe could exploit colonial collaboration to become a lone warrant chief and king. Therefore, what is pertinent is that although ogaranya masculinity would take new forms at the end of the nineteenth century, it was forged in the fire of Igbo gendered slavery practices.

The foregoing examples of female-centered lineage and economic reproduction underscore the centrality of gender to local slavery. The gendered character of domestic kinship slavery was manifest even in the uses of child slaves. Slave boys grew to become farmers, fishermen, hunters, herders, canoe paddlers, porters, and soldiers, whereas girls took to cooking, porterage, childcare, dyeing, and hawking. Child slaves were generated through warfare, raids, banditry, debts, kidnapping, treachery, crime, ritual sanctions, and birth. In Igboland, high population density—one of the highest in Africa—had led to intensive cultivation, land infertility and scarcity, and incessant conflict. Kidnappers took advantage of political instability to attack and capture mostly children and women, and displaced farmers resorted to banditry and child pawning. It was common for children to be pawned as debt security. They remained with and served the creditor until the debt was paid. Labor extracted from the pawn was the interest on the loan. Given that pawning contracts usually had no payment deadlines, creditors could enforce payment at any time, often by *panyaring* (seizure of pawn), which meant the permanent enslavement or alienation of the child pawn. At times, debtors had no intention of repaying, so they gave girls as collateral in the hope that the creditor would take pawned girls in lieu of payment. Pawned girls constituted a pool of future slave-wives and sex slaves, and young girls made up the great majority of people pawned.[109] A girl could marry her master, offering opportunities that a slave boy could not. Men sought slave girls for marriage, thereby avoiding the huge bridal fees for freeborn girls. Indeed, girls were often pawned in the idiom of marriage. The trade in slave-wives became more popular in the second half of the nineteenth century when the cost of female slaves was nearly twice that of male slaves in the domestic markets at Itu, Asan, Bende, and Uzuakoli.[110] Because pawning thrived on calamity, it reduced the cost of child slaves, who were attractive because of their ease of exploitation, labor versatility, ease of adoption, and utility in redressing childlessness, as well as the social prestige they conferred on their owners. In the postabolition period especially, child slavery enabled the transgression of antislavery legislation when bonded children passed as "adopted" dependents.[111]

SLAVERY, OGARANYA MASCULINITY, AND THE GENDERED TRANSFORMATION OF PROPERTY PRACTICES

The new wealth that ogaranya slave owners generated from cash crop trading enabled them to expand individual land ownership and foster gendered transformations in property practices. Whereas individuals had previously negotiated access to land through kinship networks, leases, pledges, and rent, by the mid-nineteenth century, wealthy individuals established liens through the provision of variable forms of wealth such as yams and slaves.[112] Such land became "controlled by the individual and all matters in connection with pledging or renting was for him [or her] to decide."[113] Predominantly male slave retainers secured large tracts of land from matrilineages and established oil palm, kola nut, raffia palm, and yam plantations, such that large-scale individual land owning complemented communal land ownership. The new land-tenure practice was cash crop driven, reliant on female slave labor, and male dominated.[114]

As individual ownership increased, so did the transmission of property beyond the control of matrilineages. In addition to yam seedlings and residential compounds, wealthy fathers (often slave owners) began to apportion farmland and slaves to their sons (as opposed to their sister's son), in spite of their matrikin. This property transfer was, as a rule, transacted in the presence of the son's matrikin; otherwise the son lost his claims upon his father's death. Slave ownership in particular engendered a shift in property practices because sons, as apprentices and partners to their fathers, established considerable stake in family slaving ventures and increasingly asserted usufructuary rights-in-slaves. This was against traditional matrilineage units' entitlement to the labor of matrikin and their dependents including slaves. Matrilineage entitlement had been predicated on their assumed responsibility for the welfare of matrikin including bride-price payment, provision of apprenticeship fees and subscriptions for initiation into secret societies, debt payments, and fulfillment of burial rites.

In enabling their sons to attain adult masculinity and become owners of land and slaves, fathers gained respect as ufiem.[115] Elder Arunsi Kalu averred, "Masculinity is the individual prowess of every man. A father who trained his son instead of abandoning the responsibility to matrilineage, helped him to marry a wife, established a home for him and secured him a farmland; that father attained ufiem."[116] First, establishing a home was considered essential to adult masculinity because a man who lived in the home of his wife's family (uxorilocal residence) upon marriage was perceived as ujo. Second, establishing a home was predicated on marriage. According to elder Olua Iro, "Proper marriage was an elaborate and expensive rite of passage into full manhood."[117] As was the case in Ovamboland studied by Meredith McKittrick, fathers who married wives for their sons gained control over their sons' labor-time and loyalty.[118]

Mayne noted that Ohafia bride price consisted of rare and expensive brass rods known as *okpogho*, which were mainly acquired in exchange for slave supply.[119] By the nineteenth century, the term *okpogho* had come to represent all forms of wealth including wealth-in-slaves, and okpogho-possessing individuals came to be known as ogaranya.[120] Sons of slave-owning ogaranya demonstrated their love for their fathers in two ways. First, they popularized a practice of burying their deceased fathers (often with male slaves) on land the deceased had privately purchased, thereby transforming such land from matrilineage property into patrilineage compounds, which they then inherited, as opposed to the matrilineage units. Second, they built new houses for their fathers, thereby performing ogaranya masculinity themselves. In so doing, they became known as *enyi nnaya* (father's friend).[121] The upsurge of the enyi nnaya phenomenon in the nineteenth century threatened matrilineage rights-in-people and rights-in-land, inaugurating a significant change in lineage ideology and conceptions of fatherhood. Indeed, it can be argued that male-dominated slave ownership enabled fathers to become breadwinners, who fulfilled social obligations to their sons, and also introduced new property practices that threatened women's position as primary transmitters of land in society.

～

Atlanticization, conceived here as a transatlantic definition of gendered captive demography and slave use, challenges the female marginality thesis by reframing the gendered repercussions of Ohafia-Igbo slavery practices within the broader context of Biafra's eighteenth-century transatlantic slave trade with Jamaica and Biafra's nineteenth-century domestic slavery. Illustrating the significance of enslaved Igbo women to Biafran reproductive economies, Atlanticization privileges slave-production mechanisms and slave use over cultural determinism. It demonstrates that the Bight of Biafra's transatlantic and domestic slavery *gendered* bodies, social identities, and sociopolitical practices. It highlights the broader significance of Ohafia-Igbo military slave production, and regional conceptions of gender. In addition to notions of masculinity, other factors including embarkation volumes, shipboard mortality, and disembarkation volumes reflected the gender differences that recast the significance of enslaved Biafran women in analyses of the region's contribution to domestic and New World slavery.

Reading Biafra's ethnographic and archival evidence through the lens of the region's intercourse with Jamaica underscores the importance of enslaved women and enables a reevaluation of kinship slavery. In Jamaica, "Eboe" women slaves' reproductive lives, sexuality, and versatile labor contributed to the stature of sugar plantations and reproduced violent white hegemonic masculinity. Similarly, in the Bight of Biafra, the violence of slave production and the sexual and labor exploitation of enslaved women by ogaranya individuals like Ekea and Okwei reproduced the socioeconomic hegemony of slave owners. Juxtaposing female slavery in Jamaica and Igboland highlights the agency of Atlantic masculinities in transforming gendered slavery practices. Acknowledging the role of enslaved women's productive and reproductive labor reveals that denying women freedom and inhibiting their social mobility was pivotal to male ascendancy, including that of male slaves.

Ogaranya was the prominent representation of nascent patriarchy in eighteenth and nineteenth century Igboland because it enabled slave-owning men to manipulate social mores and exploit vulnerable individuals. Ogaranya was so masculinist that women who acquired slaves and approximated ogaranya status were socially conceived as masculine. The next chapter examines ogaranya in the context of gendered emancipation and British colonialism.

4 ⌇ Gendered Emancipation, ca. 1860–1940

New Ogaranya Masculinities

As THE culmination of Atlanticization, slave emancipation reconstituted the categories "man" and "woman" throughout the modern Atlantic world, reflecting the gendered construction that enslaved peoples carried with them, the masculinization of emancipation through militarized creation of imperial and revolutionary state structures, and the gendered ambivalence of abolitionist discourses and unfree labor practices.[1] Claire Robertson and Martin Klein have argued that colonial-era emancipation of slaves in West Africa favored men because of the following: women slaves were more likely to have been assimilated within their owners' lineages; women slaves had more difficulty than men in acquiring the money needed to achieve self-emancipation; and free and slave women were more likely to be involved in labor-intensive unskilled occupations than men, while colonialism drew more men into skilled or wage labor.[2]

In *Things Fall Apart*, Chinua Achebe portrays as coterminous processes the disarming of traditional elites signified by Okonkwo's exile to Mbanta, and the social mobility of disenfranchised cult slaves and ujo through Christian conversion and colonial collaboration. Achebe depicts a context in which colonial onslaught uncovers and radically transforms the moral and legal dispensations in which African slavery existed, and alludes to the gendered political economy of nineteenth-century slave emancipation.[3] Between 1850 and 1900, most Igbo slaves who attained freedom and social mobility through colonial and missionary structures were male. They were the first to convert to Christianity, enroll in schools, accept wage labor, offer colonial collaboration, and assert British subjecthood. Some of them became warrant chiefs, armed with unprecedented executive and judicial powers. Their social ascendancy enabled them to undermine the authority of preexisting senior masculinities.[4] Thus, colonial emancipation facilitated the economic and political subjugation of women and the emergence of hitherto marginalized men into positions of power in the Bight of Biafra.[5] It is why Nwando Achebe argues that Ahebi Ugbabe, the only female warrant chief in colonial Igboland, sought to "become a man" in order to gain social mobility out of slavery and perform warrant chieftaincy and kingship masculinity.[6] Masculinity is a cardinal prism in illustrating the distinctive emergence of male slaves into privileged economic and political positions. It enables us to write a history of the ujo, those Atlanticized to the margins of society, who nonetheless transformed society.

Like Ahebi, who escaped spiritual slavery, collaborated with the British to become a warrant chief, and usurped the power of male elders in northern Igboland, Kalu Uwaoma (1865–1968) is representative of the broad structural shifts and inverse class and gender formation that characterized emancipation. His social mobility from slave to slaver, warrant chief, Presbyterian elder, and British knight between 1865 and 1940 provides a subaltern view of age- and gender-distinctive enslavement and attainment of freedom in the Bight of Biafra. In securing freedom without legal manumission, Kalu harnessed the muscles of emerging colonialism, Western education, and Christian modernity, as well as local configurations of power and masculinity. This chapter restores Kalu to historical memory by drawing attention to his autobiography, one of two known personal narratives of pre-twentieth-century Igbo-Africans. Kalu's biography was an argument against reenslavement, a social projection of his newfound freedom, and a rebellious manipulation of ogaranya masculinity, which signaled the further masculinization of wealth and the emergence of men as arbiters of more powerful political institutions.

The Atlanticization processes (industrial legitimate trade, Christianity, and colonialism) that brought about the end of slavery also transformed the norm of ogaranya masculinity in Igboland. Indeed, ogaranya was a historical habitus that informed slaves' freedom politics. As chapter 3 has shown, slave ownership had constituted ogaranya performance because it was the outward expression of wealth (social distinction and economic advancement) and political power.

Emancipation threatened to impoverish slave-owning freeborn males and relegate traditional authority holders to positions of insignificance.[7] Therefore, slaves seeking freedom had to reckon with the inhibitive hegemony of aristocratic slaveholders. Such slaves had to forge alternative avenues of ogaranya performance to gain prestige and secure their freedom. For Ahebi, the accumulation of wealth in goods and wives was a mechanism to attain respectability and community membership and leadership. Likewise, the major thread in Kalu's autobiography is how his ogaranya performance facilitated social reintegration and ensured against reenslavement. By converting alienated twins and their mothers into "dependents" and "concubines," Kalu synchronized local and transatlantic articulations of moral paternalism to perform ogaranya. Like his maternal grandfather Ekea Udensi, Kalu mobilized the dibia institution and elite polygyny to overcome slavery, but he also capitalized on colonialism and Christianity, which created new possibilities for enslaved men to achieve unprecedented mobility and challenge existing norms of masculinity. This intergenerational revolution in gendered power also characterized emancipation in Northern Namibia and French West Africa.[8]

Kalu's life history invites a gendered reframing of the literature on slave emancipation in West Africa. Several scholars have pointed out that African slaves and slave owners ought to be centered in studies of slave emancipation in West Africa, to capture the complex modes of liberation and the development of postemancipation means of existence, the local and imperial ideologies that shaped slavery and abolition, and the transformative role of emancipation. Local gender ideologies, and adaptations to changing Atlantic economies in the postabolition era, informed the particular ways that slaves in West Africa engaged with opportunities presented by religion and imperialism. These scholars argue that in the Gold Coast and Senegal, following abolition, the labor of female slaves was primarily channeled into domestic servitude, while many male slaves rose to a class of waged laborers. This laid the groundwork for a new class of wealthy male elite who built their political and economic power on the labor of predominantly female slaves.[9] Raphael Njoku described these nouveaux riches, who rose to prominence in the new economic order birthed by abolition in the Bight of Biafra, as ogaranya.[10]

The role of *gender* in slave emancipation in West Africa has received limited attention, and most research has focused on women's experiences.[11] In her exceptional essay on postemancipation slavery in Accra, Claire Robertson notes that male slaves had greater capital-oriented opportunities to achieve emancipation than female slaves. Whereas the former gained access to wage labor through missionary education, the latter were retained in domestic services. While the demand for young female slaves increased, that for boys decreased. As enslaved girls got older, they became sexual partners to male members of the household. Though some women achieved manumission through marriage and merchant capitalism, full assimilation proved futile because of patriarchal expropriation of women's capital. Women who sought manumission through British officers were often denied rights to children and kinship. Robertson concludes that free womanhood was a lower status than male slavery, for while the latter could be overcome, the former was a permanent subjugated condition fashioned during emancipation.[12]

Trevor Getz's graphic biography of slave emancipation in nineteenth-century Gold Coast, *Abina and the Important Men*, clarifies that although the British criminalized slavery within the protectorate in 1874, British administrators permitted slavery through paternalistic conceptions of property and dependence, as well as transatlantic imposition of New World legal conceptions of chattel slavery, "will," "consent," and transactional "contract" on West African domestic slavery practices. Like Kalu, Gold Coast slave owners popularized female and child slavery by claiming that such slaves as Abina were wives and dependents, and in so doing, they mobilized British paternalism to circumvent abolition. The British were not invested in eliminating slavery because the wealth and stability of their emerging colonies relied on their economic and political alliance with leading local men, who maintained large numbers of enslaved women and children. Convinced that West African slavery was "not that bad" and more akin to a parent-child relationship, British administrators did not enforce the 1874 law that made it possible for any slave to liberate himself or herself through British courts. Getz concludes, "After 1875, more and more children, especially girls, were enslaved outside the colony and protectorate, and brought to serve as slaves."[13] The British were not unlike the French in Senegal, who undermined enslaved women's exploitation of new courts to secure manumission between 1905 and 1910 by arguing that manumission increased the instability of African families and by forcing runaway slave-wives to return to their husbands.[14]

A growing scholarship on the modern Atlantic shows that slave emancipation everywhere took gendered forms. Diana Paton and Pamela Scully observed, "Emancipation both drew on existing ideas about the meaning of manhood and womanhood, about the content of the categories 'man' and 'woman,' and contributed to new ideologies and practices of gender."[15] In the Americas, state-sponsored emancipation intruded on the domestic privacy of households, restructuring relationships between men and women by centering men's entitlement to leadership of a family in postemancipation societies, while the exclusion of women from public spaces became integral to the process of creating modern civic nations.

Enslaved men and women negotiated emancipation differently. In her study of gendered emancipation in the French Caribbean, Sue Peabody argues that marriage and military service, respectively, were distinctive options open to female and male slaves to gain freedom.[16] Whereas marriage shaped dynamic patterns of female emancipation in French West Africa, the centrality of military service to male slaves' freedom politics is the subject of a growing scholarship.[17] Christopher Brown argues that "as a form of labor, military service . . . was highly gendered. In its demographic proportions the practice represents the inverse of sexual slavery, for which women were acquired in disproportionate numbers."[18] European governments armed African male slaves to establish their colonial authority.[19] Kalu's ascendancy out of slavery began with his military service to the British West African Frontier Force (WAFF).

Yet male slaves' social mobility beyond initial emancipation involved complex negotiations. Taiwo Osinubi writes, "Slavery in Africa was a complex system of labor use, of the exercise of rights in persons, and of exploitation and coercion, tempered by negotiation and accommodation."[20] Don Ohadike argues that in Igboland, "female ex-slaves fared better than their male counterparts" because "once women were married to freeborn men, they sooner or later lost the stigma usually attached to slave origin."[21] Igbo male ex-slaves like Kalu spent their entire life battling against the disempowering stigma of slavery. His significance lies primarily in how slaves negotiated freedom in postabolition Bight of Biafra, and how a freed person secured protection against reenslavement, by mobilizing cross-Atlantic colonial and missionary social capital, fused innovatively with indigenous notions of masculinity. His case contributes to the scholarship that posits gender as central to slave emancipation—how slaves' strategies of emancipation constituted "the very apparatus of production whereby the sexes themselves [were] established."[22] The political economy of his enslavement elucidates the emergence of ogaranya masculinities that transformed the mode of slave labor exploitation through practices of human sacrifice, elite polygyny, concubinage, and the gendered uses of slave labor in plantation agriculture and trade. Kalu recast these ogaranya practices in his social projection of freedom and quest for reintegration in his Ohafia homeland, after escaping slavery on the Biafran coast.

"THE AUTOBIOGRAPHY OF MR. EKE KALU, OHAFFIA'S WELL-HONORED SON"

"My biography had taken up thirty pages of 'The City' Writing Pad—all on God's care and guidance over me," penned Kalu at the end of his autobiography in 1937.[23] Kalu's biography differed from most African slave narratives of the nineteenth and twentieth centuries, which were produced through missionary amanuenses.[24] Its tone simulated what Sandra Green has described as a post–American Civil War captivity-and-conversion slave-narrative genre. Kalu portrays his flight from slavery in terms reminiscent of St. Paul's miraculous escape from captivity: in the course of his prayers, Kalu purportedly had a vision of "a white thing covering the whole house when [his] watchers were fast asleep." He also saw "sparks of fire and instantly [his] chains began to slacken."[25] In this regard, his autobiography was an expression of Christian faith, which informed his cynical account of his manipulation of Ohafia social mores. Kalu further portrays himself as a visionary, who led his people out of regressive superstition and into Western modernity. He parodies slavery and the religious institution of dibia; he defines himself as an icon of Presbyterian masculinity, distinct from the "illiterate" and "heathen" local populace.[26]

The autobiography was central to his maneuvering to maintain freedom and reintegrate as a legitimate member of society. The *Nigerian*

Field journal in which he published his biography aimed to remedy the concern that "one seldom saw articles in the *London Field* about Nigeria and West Africa."²⁷ Hence, Kalu was addressing a British colonial audience. Following the publication, the British government, under the auspices of Governor Sir Bernard Bourdillion (1935–43), issued Kalu a certificate of honor and "knighthood" in the name of His Majesty King George VI (1936–52).²⁸ British recognition brought the ex-slave great prestige and legitimacy within his natal community, at a time when he faced an imminent danger of social ostracism. Kalu's performance of ogaranya through the accumulation of wealth-in-commodities and wealth-in-people had protected him from the danger of slipping back into slavery. Yet his ascendancy through courting the support of British colonial authorities and Scottish missionaries had entailed deliberately violating certain cultural taboos related to twins and their mothers, undermining preexisting political authorities, and abusing his power to tax and requisition. Against this background, the autobiography symbolized a literary rebellion against Ohafia male elders, and it affords clarity into his consciousness and resistance.

Kalu's autobiography provides a rare insight into African gender conceptualization, practice, and subjectivity in an era of rapid social change. It comprises captivity and ascendancy narratives. The first begins with his birth, alienation, kidnapping, and enslavement and ends with his miraculous escape and return to his homeland. This captivity narrative shows how Atlantic and internal slaving transformed ogaranya into a capitalist masculinity, which constructed male slavery as social emasculation, as well as how colonial emancipation afforded slaves new possibilities for social mobility. Kalu's ascendancy narrative illustrates how in redefining himself out of an enslaved past, he performed ogaranya masculinity by strategically using Christianity and colonialism, which conflicted with local norms. His relationship with British officers, and his lordship over local authorities, was an elaboration of big man masculinity.²⁹

The self-laudatory tone of Kalu's autobiography required my factual collaboration. I integrated British colonial and Scottish missionary archives, with photographic documentation and validation of place names, and sixty-five oral interviews with Ohafia men and women.

The disparities between oral accounts and Kalu's recollection of the exact circumstances of his kidnapping and enslavement call to mind Anne Bailey and Marianne Ferme's observations that silence, secrecy, and deliberate forgetting constitute coping mechanisms against the traumatic memory of slavery.[30] Kalu fails to mention that his kidnapper, Nsi Oji, was in fact his maternal uncle. On their part, Ohafia narrators are quick to adduce a moral logic for Kalu's enslavement: he was a stubborn and unproductive child, who often wandered the village unattended, and created much anxiety for his mother. Kalu's portrayal of Nsi Oji as a stranger indicates psychological distancing from a painful memory and alludes to other silences. He depicts his experience of slavery in Bonny and Opobo as benign, emphasizing his triumphs and hushing his ordeals. Oral narratives help amplify the significance of his experiences, and written sources help clarify the time-place contexts of his enslavement. However, corroborative accounts of Kalu's exploits to achieve ogaranya and social reintegration are numerous. *Mgbe ochichi Nna Kalu* (in the reign of Master Kalu) has become a popular indigenous time marker that speaks to changing conceptions of ogaranya masculinity in the early twentieth century.

Hence, I provide a double reading of Kalu's autobiography, as both a construct and a historical source. First, it is a deliberate attempt to fashion a prestigious image of a self-made man. Second, it is a rich firsthand account of the complex mechanisms of enslavement, not just in the Igbo hinterland but also in the coastal communities of Bonny and Opobo. Besides Olaudah Equiano's narrative, Kalu's is the only detailed firsthand account of the capture and transportation of slaves from the Igbo interior to the coast. Indeed, Kalu's autobiography has primarily been employed by Akuma Njoku to retrace slave-trade material-culture objects and routes in the Biafran landscape.[31] However, since Kalu's life was embedded in complex social processes including slavery, legitimate trade, colonial rule, and Christianization, restoring him to historical memory requires centering his life in the transition from slavery to colonialism. Historicizing an African individual like Kalu, who did not merely appropriate unfiltered European ideologies of modernity but also functioned as a palimpsest that fused new and old worldviews, constitutes what John Cooper has described as critical postcolonial biography.[32]

THE CAPTIVITY NARRATIVE

Around 1860, Nwangbo Okoro, Kalu's mother, left her home and husband in Elu Ohafia and sought refuge in Amaekpu Ohafia when her brother accidentally killed a man with stray bullet shrapnel at a funeral. Ohafia customary law required a penitent exile of such a killer and his extended family to appease Ala, the earth goddess. At Amaekpu, Nwangbo, daughter of famed dibia Ekea Udensi, fell in love with Kalu Ugwoke, a distinguished dibia, who had fled Arochukwu to escape punitive judiciary slavery. By 1865, she returned home to her husband pregnant with Kalu. Kalu's adoptive father posed a constant threat to his life. Kalu writes, "He resolved to kill me through thick and thin. . . . My mother would not tolerate this, and so she wanted me to leave home to escape this impending danger."[33] In order to save Kalu from his abusive stepfather, Nwangbo apprenticed him to his uncle Nsi Oji, a local blacksmith.

In 1877, Nsi Oji ran away with Kalu, accompanied by Okwara Isinku, Kalu Akata, and Otusi, fellow blacksmiths. Carrying young Kalu on their backs, the group passed through Abiriba, Uzuakoli, Ohuhu, Aba Ngwa, Obegu, and Nkpuru to Akwete, where they spent a year providing blacksmithing services. Leaving the Igbo hinterland, they spent another year in the adjoining Cross River communities trading metal wares. There, Isinku fell into captive slavery. The group retreated to the home of an Nkwere chief. It was at Nkwere that Nsi Oji entered a contract with Chief Ogbonnaya of Bonny to sell an Ibibio slave. Nsi suffered a great loss in the transaction. The Ibibio slave was the shared property of Chief Akara Oja of Bonny and Chief Mini Epelle of Opobo. Nsi salvaged his debt by pawning Kalu to both chiefs.

Ojo has rightly observed that kidnappers sometimes belonged to the same community as their victims, and children often fell prey because they trusted adults as protectors or mentors.[34] Kidnapping and pawning of children were the most common and persistent forms of slavery in southeastern Nigeria throughout the late nineteenth and early twentieth century.[35] Since pawns could not be legally sold into slavery or transferred to a third party without the permission of the debtor, Kalu's status as a debt slave may have ensured against his permanent alienation on the coast. However, various contemporary cases suggest that when payment was not forthcoming or when a pawn proved stubborn or unproductive, creditors often seized pawns as slaves—a practice known as *panyaring*—and such panyar slaves were often sold.³⁶ Thus, for Kalu, pawnship must have been a frightening state of uncertainty and dislocation.

As a debt slave in the coastal trading entrepôt of Bonny, Kalu labored for a five-year period as a skilled blacksmith and canoe crew member, transporting palm produce and slaves between Ogoni, Opobo, and Bonny on his master's behalf. Akara Oja made Kalu the keeper of his keys, and Kalu became a Christian convert and learned to speak English, which proved decisive for his eventual social mobility. Around 1884, Kalu was transported in a canoe through Ogoni to Chief Epelle at Opobo, where he quickly rose to become the overseer of Epelle's house slaves and conducted trade between Opobo and the Igbo hinterland. He established a slave and palm produce bulking enterprise at the inland market of Ikeka-Orie and settled disputes among Epelle's traders at Opobo and abroad between 1884 and 1885. Kalu's success endeared him to Epelle, who encouraged him to enroll in a Presbyterian mission school at Opobo.

During his three years of service to Epelle, Kalu was loaned to King Jaja of Opobo, where between 1885 and 1887 he rose to become "one of the most trusted servants of Jaja."³⁷ Kalu left the service of Jaja after 1887, when the British, under the auspices of Consul Henry Johnston, kidnapped Jaja and exiled him to St. Vincent. Kalu took advantage of Jaja's exile to bolster his economic status. By 1890, exploiting the social capital and good graces of his former master, Epelle, he had become an independent palm produce trader in Bonny and Opobo.

The seeming ease with which Kalu was transferred from one master to another suggests that interpersonal relations undergirded the fluid slave-transaction system of the Biafran coast. Slave owners loaned out and contracted the labor of their slaves periodically, affording skilled slaves, often male, greater exposure to the coastal-hinterland trading system, with its attendant opportunities for social mobility. It also seems that the greater the autonomy or trust that masters granted slaves, in terms of traveling longer distances and farther from the master to conduct business, the greater the likelihood of a slave's social integration within a master's household.

In 1899, writes Kalu, "I was recalled to Opobo [by Epelle] to follow in the Eket War . . . when the [British] government asked all the chiefs to send gun carriers. . . . We subdued Ibeno, Emene, and other places on our way to Eket. There I had this scar on my right hand."[38] The Eket War was celebrated in London and Scotland as a Pax Britannica victory over African barbarism.[39] Kalu articulated his military service as grounds for his status as a British subject. This suggests that he might have been familiar with the popular practice of contemporary Biafran coastal ex-slaves, who asserted British subjecthood to legitimate their immunity against reenslavement and their freedom to participate in postabolition palm produce export trade.[40]

Returning home to Ohafia preoccupied Kalu in the 1890s. Roberts and Miers rightly observed that the transition from slave to free status was always a complex and continuing process of negotiation, struggle, and adjustment. Freed slaves had three options: they could leave their former owners and move away, they could remain near them but sever ties, or they could remain in their former owners' households and renegotiate the terms of their relations. None of these options guaranteed complete autonomy, and the danger of reenslavement was constant.[41] Upon returning to Opobo from the war, Kalu learned that Epelle had panyared and sold Nsi Oji to "Nembe people" for failing to pay his debt. Nsi Oji soon escaped from the Nembe and fled to Ohafia, but in the interim, Kalu was free from Nsi Oji. He sought out dibias from Ohafia, who had come to the coast to render itinerant medical services. He secured Epelle's support to depart for Ohafia in the company of dibia Ukoha Nnake. However, Ukoha suddenly died and Kalu had to wait another year until he found another dibia, Orie Obosso, to lead him back home.

His choice of a dibia was strategic. The dibia was a spirit-medium and diviner, healer, exorcist, rainmaker, and producer of protective medicines, who was feared and revered by all. Uchendu writes that because of the Igbo respect for dibia, a fact reflected in the great immunity they enjoyed in the precolonial period, members of the dibia fraternity were among the most traveled Igbo in the nineteenth century. They were able to establish pan-Igbo solidarity, even in the days when travel was dangerous.[42] The high incidence of slave raids, head-hunting, and robbery rendered roads unsafe for travel, and predisposed ex-slaves to reenslavement.[43]

On the homeward journey, Obosso deceived Kalu, seized his property, and delivered him to Aro slavers at Okporoenyi, Bende. Kalu recounts:

> I was assured that I would be sold and not killed, and so was bound hand and foot and taken to Amanangwu at Arochukwu, where one Ochi Abuto came and offered to buy me. I was locked up in one Okoroafo Ukpabi's house along with three Oru people and two from Ibibio, victims from the Long Juju. I was chained with my hands to neck.... Upon information that one Ifere Mbo was seeking for some body to buy for his mother's funeral, Obosso, Okoronkwo, Ipotomo, Ezuma Ukpabi and Ufere Imaga took me to Ameke Ututu to sell me to Ifere Mbo. After the customary entertainments by Ifere, he began to bid several prices—£4, £5, etc. I told him that he would die like his mother if he bought me. With other threats from me, Ifere was obliged to let me go back to Arochukwu. On our way to Aro, I asked permission to attend to my bowels, and was given in charge of Ufere. Then Ufere told me that [Ifere] who wanted to buy me was my [biological] father's friend. When we reached Aro, I was bound and I kept praying to God as before.

Kalu next describes his prison escape. While praying, his chains began to slacken:

> Those on my hands and feet became loose, and by means of raffia strings, I loosened the one on my neck. By this time, Obosso and the rest of the people were fast asleep while Ukpabi was still in Itu. Packing the chains aside, I escaped.... My course brought me before a crowd of people playing at Obon [masquerade parade]. When my pursuers came to the crowd, they began to ask, "Where is he?" ... I joined them and began to ask the same questions. I then fled to the latrine, taking a road that led from Ibom to Abagwu. With the chains on my head, I swam across the Uku Ibom [River]. Reaching Abuma Ututu I saw four watchmen each with a gun. I passed in their midst [undetected].... In the evening, I went back to Ifere Mbo and identified myself as his friend Kalu Uwaoma's son.... On oath, I promised to give £60 if I would be taken to Ohafia.[44] We set out, and passing through Okpo Ihe and Achara Ihe we came to Abia Ohafia at midnight. We left Abia and came to Akanu, and from there to Ndi Anya Orie and to Ndi Okala.... When we came to

Nkpogolo Ebem, I began to recognize where we were.... My people did not know me again from Adam.... Even my mother did not make me out after 29 years' stay at Bonny. I then began to identify myself as her true son and she then knew me again. Now was the time for great rejoicing.[45]

Did Kalu's "father's friend" Ifere help miraculously loosen Kalu's chains and subsequently lead him to Ohafia for an exorbitant fee of £60? We may never know the historicity of said miracle, but it is clear that Kalu's familiarity with persons and the hinterland environment was critical in his escape from Aro captivity. We need to situate Kalu's captivity within the political economy of male slavery in the Bight of Biafra. In Ohafia, where a military ethos of masculinity prevailed until the nineteenth century, male slavery constituted social commoditization and emasculation, such that male slaves like Kalu were classified as ujo, and juxtaposed to ufiem. As shown in chapter 2, ufiem status was ensured by economic autonomy, including the possession of ujo as property. In the second half of the nineteenth century, when the sale prices of female slaves nearly doubled the market value of male slaves in the Cross River Division markets, male slaves like Kalu nonetheless symbolized prestige "heads" acquired by warriors to achieve ufiem.[46] But also, because other material forms of wealth including the labor that slaves provided reinforced ogaranya masculinity, male slaves like Kalu were central to the commoditization that defined late nineteenth-century capitalism in the Bight of Biafra.

The ufiem/ogaranya and ujo distinction shaped Kalu's conception of his enslavement and the terms of his subsequent social mobility. It is noteworthy that Kalu carefully avoided the word "slave" in describing himself during his pawnship to Akara Oja, Mini Epelle, and Jaja until his account of his reenslavement by the Aro. On the coast, Kalu probably viewed himself as a "boy-boy" (domestic servant) and apprentice, albeit forced against his will to labor for alien masters of a different ethnicity. He may have understood his pawnship as an impermanent condition with the possibility of future freedom. His masters certainly tasked him with leadership responsibilities, and he exhibited considerable autonomy in conducting trade and settling disputes within a fluid slave-owning environment. As Randy Sparks has observed, the growth of the slave trade in Biafran coastal societies increased the power of ogaranya individuals, who amassed larger retinues of slaves at the expense of traditional rulers. The result was that many freemen who did not prosper from the trade became poor and were little better off than slaves, while slaves who prospered gained the social prestige of ogaranya.[47] Kalu was one such ascendant slave, who lived in trading towns as opposed to being employed in countryside plantations. His economic autonomy shortly after his freedom typified the fluid social mobility of 1890s Biafran coastal states.[48] Ogaranya reflected the rise of an elite male culture that incorporated Atlantic capitalism into indigenous textures of gender construction.[49]

Kalu's maleness, Epelle's support, and British colonial interests combined to enable Kalu to overcome ujo status on the coast. Whereas male slaves like Kalu were employed as carriers and trading staff, which afforded opportunities for social mobility, most female slaves became domestic servants, plantation laborers, wives, and concubines.[50] Female slaves also lacked access to colonial military service. In asserting freedom through trade and military service, Kalu circumvented one local alternative to "freedom," namely, social ostracism as an osu (cult slave). Against this background, the prospect of being used as burial good by Ifere in the hinterland was a horrendous ordeal that must have made Kalu realize that his new situation was indeed slavery: he had become an ujo, to be appropriated by ogaranya individuals in performance of ufiem. Thus, £60, the cost of three male slaves, was a relatively minimal cost for his freedom.

THE ASCENDANCY NARRATIVE: OGARANYA MASCULINITY AS FREEDOM PERFORMANCE

While Kalu escaped slavery on the Biafran coast, he had yet to prove himself as ufiem to Ohafia people. Overcoming the emasculation and alienating stigma of slavery through ogaranya performance is the focus of his ascendancy narrative. Kalu's quest for freedom from slavery and reenslavement led him to draw on local representations of wealth and power in the form of ogaranya masculinity, by exploiting the nascent colonial administrative and European missionary apparatuses. In spite of his professed identity as a Christian convert, Kalu's first major act upon his return to Ohafia in 1900 was to purchase membership in the dibia guild, in effect becoming a virtuoso bastion of Ohafia traditional religion. Dibiahood imbued Kalu with immunity against reenslavement.

His membership in the dibia guild enabled him to requisition the property he had lost during his Aro captivity from Obosso. As a dibia, between 1900 and 1905, he embarked on divination and healing missions to various Cross River communities, where he acquired significant wealth and became "famed as a great native doctor."[51] During one of his trips to Calabar in 1901, Kalu learned of the proposed British Aro expedition. Since Ohafia lay on the major route to Arochukwu, Kalu rushed back home to forewarn his people, counseling Ohafia elders to welcome the British and allow them free passage.[52] Upon the arrival of the British WAFF to Ohafia in late 1901, Kalu raised a white flag to signal peace and, relying on his English proficiency, assured the British of their safety. Kalu served as an interpreter during peace negotiations with British officers James Watt, Captain Mowatt, and Mr. Weir. By mobilizing the community to provision the soldiers with food, he secured a friendship with the British.[53]

When Kalu was captured at Bende, he had protested his reenslavement as illegitimate, arguing that it was a breach of a long-standing mutual contract (ukwuzi) that existed between Arochukwu and Ohafia whereby members of both societies could not enslave each other.[54] In what seems like an act of willful revenge against the Aro in 1901, Kalu volunteered to lead the WAFF column to Arochukwu, which was razed to the ground in ten days.[55] This expedition, which was based on the ill-informed British notion of Aro political hegemony over the Biafran hinterland, destabilized the two-hundred-year-long commercial dominance of the Aro in the region. Indeed, the Aro expedition marks a turning point in the history of British colonization of southeastern Nigeria. Until the Aro expedition, British colonial exploits were restricted to the Biafran coast, and European missionaries did not gain access to the Cross River frontier Igbo territories. The Church of Scotland Mission, which was the most active in the region, remained a Calabar church, with minimal influence in the middle Cross River.[56] The expedition paved way for the spread of British colonial rule, accompanied by a dramatic decrease in the incidence of warfare, headhunting, and militant slave production. It also consolidated the reorientation from an agrarian to a commercial economy, which forced many to seek alternative avenues of social mobility.[57]

The warfare against the Aro was an advancement of Kalu's freedom politics. His role in the Aro expedition established him as a local hero who had gone to battle and cut a head. He writes, "My exertions gained me honor amongst Ohaffia people. They therefore passed a law to the effect that I was to be the adviser to the bulk of Ohaffia people."[58] Kalu's elevation to the status of community adviser, an intermediary between British colonial officers and Ohafia, enabled him to play two major roles that transformed him from a vulnerable ex-slave into a community leader. Kalu championed the expulsion of two corrupt Native Court officers from Ohafia and engineered the establishment of the Church of Scotland Mission in his community.

During the British occupation of Ohafia (1901–2), the village of Ebem had put up a militant resistance, in spite of Kalu's counsel. As a result, Ebem was sacked.[59] In order to keep Ebem permanently pacified, the British established a Native Court at Ebem between 1905 and 1907, with jurisdiction over Ohafia and neighboring communities.[60] Mr. Vincent, of Sierra Leonean origin, was appointed clerk of the Ebem Native Court, and Mr. Cobham, a Calabar man, was made a court messenger. Vincent and Cobham were harsh, unscrupulous, and morally bankrupt, and they imposed a reign of terror on Ohafia people.[61] In dealing with the corrupt Native Court officers, the Ohafia community turned to their adviser, Kalu, who pioneered litigation against Vincent.[62] The officers were tried at Bende Native Court, convicted, and imprisoned for three months with hard labor for using unnecessary brutality, ill-treating the natives, obtaining money under false pretenses, and unscrupulously using the authority of the court for personal aggrandizement.[63] Kalu writes that he then "lectured [Ohafia elders] on the necessity of educating their children by establishing and supporting schools."[64] He sent an application to the United Church of Scotland for a missionary to come to Ohafia and set up a school and church. British colonial officer G. I. Jones noted that the peoples of Bende district welcomed missionaries because they believed that "if the young men of [their] village were educated, that is, could speak or write English, they could obtain the same superior employment as [court clerks and messengers, who were seen as] favoured Africans."[65] Kalu led a delegation to Reverend Rankin at Arochukwu, agreeing that if Rankin kept Vincent away, Ohafia would accept a missionary and support the opening of schools.[66] Thus, Reverend Robert Collins was sent to Ohafia in 1901.

FIGURE 4.1. Missionary residence of Rev. Robert Collins, built ca. 1911

Under Kalu's auspices, a residence was erected for the Scottish missionary, and a new church was completed in 1924.[67] The house of Rev. Collins continues to serve as the official residence of Presbyterian ministers in Ohafia. It was prefabricated in Scotland, shipped to Calabar, canoed to Ohafia, and erected by European masons and African laborers.[68] Even though the residence and church were a result of four years of monthly contributions of six pence and one shilling by all adult Ohafia men and women, Ohafia people portray them as a legacy of Kalu's ogaranya masculinity performance. In addition to mobilizing local support for these projects, he made the most substantial financial contribution. Kalu paid the salaries of schoolteachers appointed by the mission when the community was unable to afford the money.[69] He also built the first personal modern multiroomed story-house in Ohafia in 1916, covered with corrugated iron roof and filled with numerous European manufactures. The house, which was launched by the British district officer C. J. Mayne, rivaled the mission residence. Jones noted that the British considered such houses "permanent buildings." They were so cost-prohibitive that the British discontinued the provision of such houses to colonial officers between 1904 and 1906.[70]

FIGURE 4.2. Home of Kalu Uwaoma, built ca. 1916

Kalu captures how the dramatization of cosmopolitan habits through conspicuous consumption and embodied modernity had spread from the coast to the hinterland by the late nineteenth and early twentieth centuries. As early as the seventeenth century, Richard Watts writes that coastal Old Calabar slave-owning male elites used European-style storied housing and clothing in addition to elite polygyny to distinguish their class and gender hegemony.[71] In the mid-eighteenth century, Grandy King George of Old Calabar distinguished his elite status by learning to speak English and adopting many aspects of English culture, primarily by building multiroomed story houses and filling them with European fashions. In his letter to an English captain, Grandy King George demanded the following in exchange for his slave supplies: glass tankards, hats, tea kettles, utensils, iron bars, a coat with a lace, and razors.[72] Old Calabar chief Antera Duke documented in his diary in November 1785 that Efik traders deemed such houses and European fashions fundamental to hegemonic masculinity because they reinforced an elite slave-owning and trading monopoly, polygyny, and belongingness in ekpe society, as well as enabling the elite to entertain English captains at Christmas and New Year dinners.[73]

As the writings of Edward Bold, James Holman, Richard Francis Burton, Hugh Crow, Hope Masterton Waddell, and Hugh Goldie make clear, these practices continued through the postabolition nineteenth century. Bold emphasizes elite West African men's demands for Manchester cloth and silk, gunpowder, guns, tobacco, and smoking pipes as both a reflection and reinforcement of their sociopolitical hegemony. Holman, Crow, Waddell, and Goldie show that cross-Atlantic sartorial practices were central to class distinctions in Old Calabar, and Duke Ephraim and King Eyo, as well as various Efik elite men, dramatized their wealth and sociopolitical hegemony through their large "English houses" and the numerous manufactured goods contained within. This social prestige reinforced their control of the ekpe society and their ability to hold numerous slaves and upward of sixty wives. King Eyo Honesty's "Calabar costume" consisted of "a few yards of broad fancy coloured silk round his loins, descending to the ankles," complemented with strings of ornamental beads on his neck and arms. King Eyamba wore "several yards of Manchester cloth around his waist" and often hosted Europeans to Sunday dinners. In 1850, Old Calabar male elites passed an ekpe law forbidding anyone below the rank of "gentleman" from wearing long shirts and morning gowns. In Bonny, elite men similarly distinctively wore flannel shirts made of cotton in addition to their waistcloths. Burton describes how wealthy men in Bonny used silk pocket handkerchiefs attached to their sword scabbards, as well as "Africanised models of the Swiss cottage" with multiple rooms, filled with European manufactured goods, especially cloth, to distinguish their sociopolitical status. Such wealth performance enabled leading Bonny traders to acquire as many as fifty wives.[74] These wives, as Crow noted, "generally provide[d] in a great measure for their own subsistence, and contribute[d] to that of their husband," through farming, weaving, hat making, and trading.[75]

These descriptions emphasize the intermeshing of diverse cross-Atlantic material cultures of housing, dressing, entertainment, and social comportment with local African sociopolitical practices including trading, marriage, slaving, rulership, and gender and class distinction. By the second half of the nineteenth century, these ogaranya practices had taken hold among the Niger-Igbo communities and the middle Cross River intracoastal communities. Writing about the former in the 1830s, Macgregor Laird and R. A. K. Oldfield emphasized that Igbo Niger River traders used European "soldier's jackets," plaid stockings, plaid sashes, scarlet coats, and trousers to distinguish their status as "the better class," which in turn reinforced elite men's (as opposed to women's) control of "the traffic in slaves, cloth, and ivory."[76] Commenting on the Cross River peoples in 1886, Scottish missionary Mary Slessor noted, "The peoples . . . are becoming quite civilized and decent. They are getting houses of a better stamp, they have candles and paraffin lamps, clocks, pictures, etc. and have begun to wear hats and boots and nice things."[77] However, contrary to Slessor's imperialist vision of gradual African attainment of civilization through the adoption of European fashions, which suggests that Africans merely domesticated European modernities, ogaranya hegemonic masculinity is better understood as African articulation of indigenous gender ideologies with cross-Atlantic commoditization. The instrumentality of adopting "European fashions" (themselves products of coerced African labor, European capital, and American/African land resources) was not evident in achieving a greater civilization, but rather in creating a narrow social vocabulary of class- and gender-based social ascendancy. This enabled particular individuals with demonstrated monopolistic access to new forms of wealth and its redistribution to determine local configurations of power. In building houses for himself and a Scottish missionary in "European fashion," Kalu was, therefore, replicating the Biafran coastal vernacular of Atlanticization within a hinterland landscape.

As he rose to leadership stature among his people, Kalu gained further upliftment from the British administration. He was appointed the first warrant chief of Ohafia in 1910.[78] As a warrant chief, Kalu sat on the Native Court council to hear cases, but his reputation as a competent negotiator and ogaranya-accomplished individual led communities and individuals to bring cases to his compound.[79] The district officer, James Watt, invited Kalu to settle a land dispute between the Ohafia village of Ebem and the neighboring Cross River–Igbo town of Ozu-Abam in 1912, and Rev. Collins regularly enlisted Kalu's services in the settlement of marital and intervillage disputes.[80] Kalu acquired wealth serving as a warrant chief. In addition to sitting fees and monthly salaries, warrant chiefs received remuneration from litigants, to serve as their attorneys and spokesmen, when the bench retired to consult on their verdict.[81]

But the stigma of slavery shadowed Kalu. In 1914, he writes, Dibia Obosso "came once more on the scene," suing him for a purported financial debt; as a result he was imprisoned at Akwete. Again, Kalu enlisted the support of his former master, Chief Epelle, to gain quittance.[82] It is plausible that Obosso and Epelle were members of the region-wide okonko society, whose members enjoyed considerable economic and political clout in the various nascent colonial Native Courts of 1900–1929, and their ogaranya influences possibly shaped Kalu's struggle to transcend slavery. As Kalu reveals, to effectively overcome the vulnerable stigma of slavery, he intensified his ogaranya-status pursuit. His consequent wealth in money, people, land, and material objects of "European fashion" symbolized, within an Ohafia gendered context, the heads that he had cut to accomplish ufiem. By 1916, he owned more than fifty slaves, had married twelve wives, and had numerous concubines and children, who worked on his various plantations, processed and purchased palm produce for him, and traded such produce at the Itu market on the Cross River.[83] By the mid-1920s, Kalu owned one-quarter of the land in Elu Village, which he had acquired through purchase, inheritance, pledges for loans, and supervision of colonial projects such as road construction and the dredging of rivers.[84]

Kalu viewed his extensive wealth-in-people as a symbol of his ogaranya status, and he consciously worked to expand his household. He was baptized as a Presbyterian in 1918 and became an elder of the Church of Scotland Mission (CSM) in 1919. When the CSM insisted that Kalu should divorce all but one of his wives, so that he may fully embrace his new status as an icon of Presbyterian masculinity, he left the CSM. He then invited the Salvation Army Mission to establish a church and school in his expansive compound and switched over to the Church of Christ, where he was made an elder in 1920.[85] By that singular move, Kalu drew more than half the CSM membership away from the mission. This forced the CSM to reinstate him as an elder, allowing him to keep all his wives, with the proviso that he officially wed one of them, who had been trained in Victorian domesticity by Scottish missionary Miss Arnault at Arochukwu.[86] Kalu would exploit his position as a Presbyterian elder to adopt numerous abandoned twin children and take ostracized twin mothers into his household as wives and concubines.[87] Clearly, he saw churches as critical ogaranya resources.

Kalu's manipulation of social mores, his self-aggrandizement, and his impish delight at fooling people is emphasized in his autobiography, positioning his subjective discourse as a continuation of his conscious rebellion against Ohafia senior masculinities. His frank account of his exploitative behavior is corroborated by oral accounts. Upon returning to Ohafia in 1900, Kalu stole animals sacrificed to local deities, and from these, he established a livestock farm and raised money to purchase promotion in the dibia guild.[88] His initial social mobility within the dibia guild was accomplished through cosmological manipulation. He confessed that Ohafia people had consulted him as a dibia to forecast the day that the WAFF column would depart Ohafia. Having obtained the relevant information from Captain Mowatt, Kalu made "incantations" and declared the day of the WAFF departure. When the WAFF "actually left [on] that day, [his] fame as a prophet became very much."[89] Similarly, as the "most influential British agent in the northeastern part of the Bende district," Kalu extorted unsanctioned gifts and taxes from Ohafia villages by parading an albino who impersonated a European officer.[90] The district commissioner (DC), Mr. Hives, noted that it was common to find such "blackmailing" impostors who paraded men disguised in police uniforms and who held judiciary courts of their own from one community to another, extorting exorbitant court fees.[91]

Indeed, for Kalu, ogaranya masculinity entailed playing with colonial institutions and eliciting fear from the populace. The DC of Bende, Major W. A. C. Cockburn, observed in 1910 that because the valleyed Ebem Native Court was difficult to access during the rainy season, British officers were unable to visit it regularly, and thus the warrant chiefs emerged as the principal authorities in Ohafia, doing as they pleased.[92] According to Ohafia elders, after Kalu's appointment as warrant chief, because he was the only person that understood and spoke English fluently, he often misinformed the people that the DC had demanded contributions of goats and yams from them. After stockpiling these contributions for a period of time, Kalu then embarked on a tribute trip to the DC at Bende or Nkporo. Usually carried on a hammock, like British colonial officers of his time, Kalu was accompanied by young men who served as porters. Upon his return, Kalu sometimes informed Ohafia people that the DC was displeased with the quantity of their contributions and was preparing for an invasion. The twenty-six villages would then make further contributions and send them to Kalu's home.[93] Through these practices, Kalu constructed his political power over indigenous political authorities. Hence, Isichei argues that ogaranya individuals usurped the power of local authorities during colonial rule.[94]

While Kalu's political career transcended and outshone other warrant chiefs', Mayne noted that these men also exercised political power beyond the capacity of preexisting indigenous authorities.[95] Whereas traditional rulers "had no autocratic power whatsoever in [their] village," the colonial system vested executive power "in one man known as the Warrant Chief."[96] Njoku writes, "The administrative system based on the native courts and warrant chiefs raped the foundations of the Ohafia traditional system of government . . . [and] concentrated legislative, judicial and executive powers on the warrant chief."[97] Mayne continues:

> The arrival of the British who, forthwith proceeded unknowingly to sap the foundations of the only conceivable mode of government the people knew [was] viewed with extreme disfavour. . . . The people had not intended their representative, who was of no "locus standi" to be an intermediary between the British and themselves. It was their impression that he was required to appease the anger of the "Whiteman" and the irony of the situation was only comprehended when it was too late and the representative had not only usurped the position of the indigenous figureheads but had virtually made himself their ruler. This representative better known as the "Warrant Chief" has been the link between the people and the Government.[98]

Mayne may well have been writing about Warrant Chief Kalu, who soon transformed himself from a warrant chief of Elu Village into a de facto ruler of the Ohafia people. In 1927, Chubb wrote that the entire Ohafia "people are splendidly ruled by Chief Kalu-Ezelu. The Chief's hereditary right to occupy the post is open to question as he is of mixed Aro blood but he is one of the few outstanding chiefs in the Division and it is hoped will be of great assistance to the Local Administration."[99] The introduction of direct taxation in 1927–28 was an opportunity that Kalu exploited to secure British legitimation of his incipient authority over the entire Ohafia region.[100] He proved himself a competent tax collector and came to be seen as "a loyal servant of the Government."[101] Kalu was responsible for about 85 percent of the total taxes collected in Bende Division in 1928. He summoned to the Ebem Native Court adult men who failed to pay taxes, "and as a result of this action, the balance was collected immediately."[102]

Kalu represented a broader region-wide social transformation in gender and class structure in the Bight of Biafra. Like Kalu, who led the British to Aro, two other Ohafia-Igbo emancipated slaves on the coast, Uduma Uwara of Ebem and Nnanna Uka (a.k.a. Atiyonu) of Amangwu, led the British expedition to Ohafia before Kalu intervened with his white flag. Both were rewarded with warrant chief appointments. Mazi Uche Ibe became the warrant chief of Okon Ohafia in 1913 after serving as a houseboy of missionary Mary Slessor and as a court messenger at Old Calabar. When he established a school in Okon in 1916, he was celebrated as ogaranya/ufiem.[103] In neighboring Arochukwu, the Native Court (1902–28) was established with arbitrarily chosen representatives from each of the nineteen villages. As British officer H. F. Matthews observed, these representatives were not "the real chiefs"; they constituted "an artificial judicial body" having no sanction in native eyes "but force as represented by the D.O. [district officer] and the Police." The new court members became the district officers' medium of communication to the villages, and thus they became the "new aristocracy" based "on no principles understood by the native mind." Whereas "the old aristocracy in Aro had been a well-defined body of free-born individuals enjoying the privileges [of] a hereditary caste system" and ruled by fiat, "the new court members had no tradition behind them, were often slave-born," and took advantage of their new position.[104] Local disillusionment with the arbitrary rule of the emergent ogaranya colonial agents in Arochukwu came to a head in 1922, when the *amadi* (freeborn) effectively challenged the right of persons of slave origin to serve as members of the Native Court.[105]

Kalu faced a similar communal resistance against his burgeoning hegemony. As Mayne observed, Ohafia people viewed the warrant chiefs' usurpation of power with disfavor. He also noted that the indigenous system of administration "still functioned to a considerable extent."[106] In his quest for social mobility, political power, and ogaranya status, Kalu had committed an abomination (*nso ala*) by adopting twins and cohabiting with ostracized twin mothers.[107] According to Kalu, "All Ohafia chiefs consulted against me for my care over these outcast women ... charging me vehemently with nursing up twin children ... torturing people and practicing slavery."[108] Fed up with Kalu's revolution, the Ohafia council of male elders brought the following charges against him before the DO of Bende: he was violating customs through social contacts with twin mothers; he extorted money from people under false pretenses; he refused to give back land held on pledge even after the owners tried to redeem the pledge; he appropriated individual land under the pretext of engineering colonial projects; he tortured vulnerable people; he owned slaves and engaged in slave trading in spite of abolition; he had murdered some Ohafia people; and lastly, he was not eligible to become the ruler of Ohafia because his father was from Arochukwu and he was a slave.[109]

Ohafia elders presented human skulls to the DO of Bende as evidence that Kalu had committed murder, and further exhumed a body from the forest and bargained with one of Kalu's "concubine-wives" to testify that he had killed the individual.[110] Fearing that he would not get a favorable trial at Bende, Kalu, without consulting the DO, transferred his case to a higher court administered by his friend, Mr. Watt at Owerri. Kalu's subversion of the DO's authority left the officer chagrined, but as Kalu writes, he apologized to the former and informed the DO that "the Government was trying to reward [his] good deeds with death," and that the DO was biased against him. Watt ruled that Ohafia elders had made the allegations out of jealousy. Kalu returned to Ohafia "only to find [his] compound [demolished], [his] servants all scattered with [his] money."[111]

The rebellion of Ohafia senior masculinities against Kalu's legitimacy and freedom performance was short lived, but it shows how the lingering stigma of slavery constituted a social weapon against nascent junior masculinities. It equally highlights the limits of ogaranya masculinity, attesting that in African colonial situations, there were multiple hegemonic masculinities, each exercising situational valence.[112] In his study of Malian ex-soldiers of World War II France, Gregory Mann observed that ex-slaves' social reintegration entailed both subversion of and reconciliation with traditional norms of hegemonic gerontocratic masculinity, since soldier masculinity resonated with the legacy of slavery.[113] Achebe also points out that when female warrant chief Ahebi transcended ogaranya masculinity and sought to realize full manhood by producing a masquerade, Nsukka-Igbo male elders, with British colonial support, seized the masquerade and unraveled her prestige beyond recovery.

But Kalu, unlike Ahebi, was able to reestablish his social prestige through colonial bureaucracy. The contrast elucidates how postslavery social reintegration through hegemonic masculinity performance was mediated by gender-biased colonialism. Kalu exploited his personal relations with British officers to secure construction contracts. He often went on fishing trips with British district officers Mowatt and Weir, and he undertook hunting with Watt.[114] Thus, Weir contracted the construction of Ohafia-Abiriba and Ohafia-Arochukwu roads, the native dispensary, and the native post office to Kalu in the 1930s, which enabled him to become the wealthiest individual in Ohafia.[115] Kalu was appointed the overseer of the Bende Native Court prisons in the 1940s, and he retired as a wealthy commercial farmer.[116] Contrary to Ahebi's experience, Kalu's machismo and chauvinistic camaraderie with British male political officers constituted a patchwork of Afro-European patriarchies that mediated his sociopolitical revival.

Nonetheless, Kalu's process of social rebirth was fastidious. The subsections of his biography detailing his exploits to regain social acceptance include the titles "Once More Settled," "Eke the Road Maker," "Eke the Building Contractor," and "A Step Further on Trade in the District."[117] Kalu demonstrated that ogaranya performance entailed the social legitimation of economic and political power. He reflects Uchendu's description of a "big man" among the Igbo, as a man who commands prestige, respect, and obedience, because he "helps others to get up."[118] From 1930, he began to purchase lorries to transport goods and people between Ohafia and various markets in the region. He called his lorries "community vehicles" and contrasted them with the "pleasure cars" of European colonial and medical officers because his lorries enabled the upliftment of Ohafia people.[119] This same logic informed his dredging and transformation of the Uduma River into a major riverine artery of trade between Ohafia and the coastal states, his philanthropic payment of Presbyterian teachers' salaries, his opening of public water pumps in landlocked villages, and his establishment of a trading station of the United African Company in his compound by 1943. His monopoly of regional commercial transportation and transatlantic-commodity and material-wealth redistribution centered him in popular understandings of changing ogaranya-masculinity politics in his society.[120]

In the twilight of colonial rule, some Ohafia people, seeking to reclaim land that Kalu had seized from them, sued him in the 1950s. He remained partly scorned and partly revered until his death in 1968, but he successfully eluded the abasement of reenslavement and the vulnerability that defined economic dependence and ujo status, as well as the stigma of social ostracism. Kalu concluded, "patience is what can make a man what he is."[121] His invocation of patience hearkened back to fastidious elders' and established warriors' control over slaving-era mechanisms of ufiem attainment, but it also articulated the lengthy negotiation between indigenous notions of masculinity and European imperial-cum-missionary ideologies of modern personhood.

༄

We need to focus on gender to get a full picture of emancipation in West Africa. Kalu's life elucidates how a new powerful masculinity emerged with the changes that brought about the end of slavery. His mobility out of slavery highlights the new political and economic opportunities open to male slaves but unavailable to free women. It was only in the context of the late nineteenth-century social transformations that male slaves like Kalu profusely accomplished the ogaranya masculinity that ensured against reenslavement or permanent ujo status. The life history of this one individual provides a metanarrative on slavery dynamics and emancipation, colonial order and power, and tradition and adaptation in the context of gender, mobility, and social reordering. Avoiding the tyranny of possible reenslavement, Kalu positioned himself both in the shifting world of the indigenous, through guild-membership, slavery, polygamy, and ogaranya, as well as in the emerging world of Christianity, Western education, and colonial service, as a warrant chief. Kalu's life draws our attention to the context in which men gained the upper hand in the first two decades of the colonial presence as men were favored by the Europeans to become Christian converts, go to school, and serve in various positions as colonial agents, while women were restricted to domestic spheres. This was the culmination of Biafran gendered Atlanticization.

Kalu's freedom politics reshape conceptions of African slavery, resistance, and the role of cross-Atlantic influences in social change in the Bight of Biafra. He exemplifies that African slaves achieved freedom and social reintegration beyond the facilities of kinship, in his case by marshaling the moral economies of the Biafran coast, the Ohafia-Igbo, British colonists, and Scottish missionaries. His resistance to slavery and its lingering stigma involved an individualized reimagination of community—a skillful manipulation of African and European social worlds to garner massive economic and political power.[122] His life shows that individual slaves exhibited conscious resistance even in the absence of overt collective revolutionary class-consciousness.[123] Kalu was emblematic of the cross-Atlantic commoditization and neocapitalist redefinition of hegemonic masculinity in the late nineteenth-century Bight of Biafra. His life history enables an African-centered conception of Atlantic influences over the *longue durée*, by showing the dialectics of slavery, legitimate commerce, colonialism, and Christianity in individual social transformations in the Bight of Biafra. His autobiography makes possible the reconstruction of the shifty subjectivity of an African individual in an era of rapid social change.

The next chapter shifts attention to the contradictory ways in which women, who were relatively marginalized from the control mechanisms of Biafran Atlanticization, simultaneously resisted sociopolitical disempowerment and reinforced masculinist conceptions of ogaranya.

5 ～ Revolutionary Masculinities, ca. 1850–1940
Female Dissident Sexualities

THIS CHAPTER examines women's responses to gendered Atlanticization. Colonialism, Christianity, and Western education alienated women from the dominant resources of social mobility, which reinforced the masculinization of wealth in early twentieth-century Igboland. Beyond that liminal moment in 1929 when Igbo women collectively mobilized traditional strategies of "sitting on a man" to mount the largest grassroots movement against British colonialism, how did women, especially as individuals, adapt to changing practices of gendered access, sexuality, and power in the Bight of Biafra? How might the few case studies of the social mobility of individual Igbo women such as Naomi, Okwei, and Ahebi during the nineteenth and twentieth centuries be framed to dialogue with the broader gendered social transformations that the scholarship on African masculinities and Atlanticization has revealed? By performing ogaranya masculinity through trade, divination, and matronship, Ohafia women expanded the ideological scope of gender hegemony beyond colonial patriarchal structures. The case studies of two Ohafia women, Unyang Uka and Otuwe Agwu, who performed ogaranya masculinity and dissident sexuality of *oke-nwami*[1] (masculine female husband), bridge a gap in gender theory in African studies by reconciling the literature on West African women's power and authority with the nascent field of African masculinity studies. They show that women's sociopolitical power paralleled the shifting constructions of masculinity in West Africa. Igbo women's masculinity performances simultaneously elided and reinforced changing notions of gendered power.

In the Ohafia village of Asaga, colonial anthropologist G. I. Jones likened a 1906-built shrine he saw in one family compound in the 1930s to an "African Madame Tussaud's." In fact, Jones was describing the Omoukwu or Obu Nkwa shrine of the ite odo founder discussed in chapter 2. The obu had burnt down and was rebuilt in 1906. Among the carved wooden figures newly housed within the shrine, Jones noted various hegemonic male and female ogaranya—people who embodied wealth-power masculinity through the accumulation of wealth-in-commodities and wealth-in-people. These wooden figures were displayed in a masculine meetinghouse (obu). The inclusion of women in sculptures and murals in obu houses reflected women's invasion of masculine spheres of social mobility under colonial rule.[2] Jones writes:

> It [the obu] houses no less than 22 male and female figures, the majority the life size or over. Rather like an African "Madame Tussaud's," the figures stand on pedestals along the walls and front verandah—a warrior in an Amaseri war cap with a fighting matchet in one hand and a head in the other, a warrior in a trillby hat with a dane gun standing on the head of another enemy.... A court messenger, a rich woman with ivory anklets, a young girl with brass rods on her legs, a woman with a [basket]. ... Standing beside the figure of the seated woman ... is the figure of a man bound hand and foot, said to be the [ujo] husband of the woman.[3]

As has been made clear, the head is a pervasive symbol; its presence confers authority, its attainment denotes honor, and its commemoration reaffirms identity. Whereas the head held by the warrior with a machete signified human heads cut by Ohafia warriors in defense of their newly settled territories in the seventeenth century, the head held by the warrior with a Dane gun symbolized slaves that Ohafia warriors generated in the course of the Atlantic slave trade, which were equated with figurative heads acquired to attain ufiem. In the nineteenth century, individuals who acquired wealth through trade—effectively achieving ogaranya status—were said to have cut heads. Women like Unyang Uka and Otuwe Agwu, whose "brass rods," "ivory anklets,"

Female Dissident Sexualities ∽ 159

and market baskets symbolized revolutionary new heads or material wealth and breadwinner status, featured prominently in the transformative politics of ogaranya, alongside individuals like warrant chief Kalu Ezelu, represented by the figure of the court messenger. Like Kalu, these women eclipsed and subjugated preexisting warrior and gerontocratic masculinities.

The "African Madame Tussaud's" representation of gender hegemony reached beyond the Ohafia-Igbo environment, reflecting a coastal-hinterland phenomenon. In the course of their 1832 "Niger Expedition," Macgregor Laird and R. A. K. Oldfield provide various descriptions of similar female ogaranya in the Bight of Biafra. Laird describes a "fat woman" in the Niger-Igbo territories, someone like Omu Okwei, who informed Laird that she owned more than two hundred slaves who collected palm oil and grew yams for her. Upon visiting her home, Laird found that she owned several canoes, which she used to trade slaves and palm oil up the river to Brass and Bonny. Upon visiting Laird, she brought his crew gifts of palm wine and bananas to consolidate their trading arrangement. Laird's "fat friend" wore a straw hat 5 feet in diameter, necklaces, brass bracelets, and ivory leglets.[4] Numerous other "such superior class of women" wearing large anklets of ivory that were so heavy that "they are almost unable to walk" and "several bracelets of brass around [their] wrist[s]; an infallible mark of [their] being person[s] of considerable consequence" featured in Laird's descriptions. These included descriptions of councilors and wives of the Obi [King] of Onitsha, independent traders wearing "half European dress," and "landladies" who owned a "large family" and provided "very clean" accommodations to Laird's expeditionary crew.[5] Later in 1854, William Balfour Baikie provided similar descriptions of female ogaranya of the Niger-Igbo territories, noting that ivory was in such high demand because "all women who [could] afford it, [wore] ponderous ivory anklets" and were buried with the anklets. Such women acted "as big-man" of their villages, "meaning thereby the principal official[s]."[6] The performances of ogaranya by Uka and Agwu in Ohafia mimic these descriptions.

Like the "African Madame Tussaud's," this chapter lays bare the sociopolitical processes that shaped emergent masculinities in the first two decades of the twentieth century, as well as their roles in the changing constructions of gender through ogaranya performance. Igbo men emerged as clear breadwinners and politically dominant only between 1900 and 1920 because of Western education, colonial wage labor, and Christian leadership, and the processes of sociopolitical power masculinization were simultaneously resisted and reinforced by women in their quest for social mobility.[7] Because most ogaranya were male, wealth was perceived as a masculine characteristic. Styled as court clerks, warrant chiefs, interpreters, teachers, and accountants, male ogaranya individuals performed their social power by usurping the judicial prerogatives of traditional political authorities. They acquired a large number of human dependents through slavery and elite polygyny, erected modern houses, and adorned themselves with expensive European goods. This nascent male privilege contrasted with the immediate precolonial dual-sex system in which women enjoyed political and economic autonomy.[8]

Failing to see the political roles and power of Igbo women, male British colonial administrators made no effort to ensure women's participation in the modern institutions they fostered beginning in 1900. Ignoring the diffuse and dual-sex political power structures in Igboland, British administrative reform created composite Native Court Areas that violated the autonomy of villages, and it appointed male warrant chiefs, who asserted arbitrary powers over women and traditional authorities. Women suffered particularly under the arbitrary rule of warrant chiefs, who extorted agricultural products and livestock from women and seized young girls as wives without fulfilling marital obligations, in a fashion reminiscent of *ike nwami* (female captivity) during the Atlantic slave trade era. Colonial political reforms forced women to become dependent on men. Christian missionaries reinforced the marginalization of women by entrenching a misogynistic Victorian ideology of female domesticity and male political visibility. Women had less access to Western education, which became the new prerequisite for economic and political leadership. When girls gained access to schools, they received domestic training as subservient wives, mothers, and helpmates, erroneously conceived as lacking the mental ability to handle the so-called masculine subjects of science, business, and politics.[9] Some Western-educated Igbo women overcame the handicap of "good Christian wives" by forging autonomous entrepreneurships as tailors, chefs, and teachers, becoming known as "matrons."

Unlike matrons confined to monogamous Christian marriages and constricted by patriarchal missionary institutions, most Ohafia women exploited traditional and Western institutions in sexually and gender-transgressive ways in a bid to achieve social mobility and perform ogaranya masculinity. Women's stylistic performance of ogaranya masculinity, by building modern houses, acquiring slaves, marrying wives, and adorning themselves in local and cross-Atlantic ogaranya commodities, reinforced the local perception of wealth as masculine. Therefore, ogaranya does not lend itself to a simple narrative of the marginalization and subsequent rebellion of African women under colonial rule, which the Igbo Women's War typifies.

My conceptualization builds upon revisionist studies on West African women, which challenge the assumption of a preexisting patriarchy against which women rebelled, and emphasize rather the need to separate gender from biological sex.[10] Since Ifi Amadiume argued that the flexibility of the Igbo gender system mediated its "dual-sex" social organization, such that women were able to occupy and perform male roles, and vice versa, various scholars have demonstrated how West African women utilized precolonial institutions to resist marginalization under colonial rule through fluid gender performances.[11] Advancing this scholarship, ogaranya challenges the equation of masculinity with patriarchy, and the misrepresentation of masculinity as an articulation of how "real men" should act and represent themselves.[12] Uncoupling masculinity from maleness and patriarchy enables us to see that women were innovators of novel forms of dissident hegemonic masculinity, especially against colonial patriarchy.

The ogaranya masculinity performances of Unyang Uka and Otuwe Agwu demonstrate that female masculinity flourished in both heterosexual and homosocial environments. Their life histories complicate the notion of female masculinity as women who feel themselves to be more masculine than feminine, the notion of masculinity without men. Whereas the self-representations of Unyang Uka, who sought to become a man through elite polygyny and cross-dressing, elicit the former image, Otuwe Agwu does not fit into the mold because she became a dibia (medicine "man"), oke-nwami (masculine woman and female husband), and ogaranya, not because of a desire to "become a man" but rather as a means to become a matrilineage matriarch and revered ancestor—the ultimate manifestation of Ohafia hegemonic femininity. In a particularly illuminating article titled "The Portrait of a Brave Woman," anthropologist McCall provides the subjective life history of another Ohafia woman, Nne Uko, who, like Unyang Uka, transformed herself into a man, by marrying two wives, constantly dressing as a man, joining exclusively male secret societies, participating with men in the war dance, and performing ogaranya masculinity in the mid-twentieth century.[13] Both Unyang Uka and Nne Uko employed the art of bodily presentation and the symbolic potential of clothing to equate themselves with Ohafia warrior masculinities of the precolonial period. Nne Uko further attests that women drew on traditional gender ideologies in their society to perform subversive ogaranya during the colonial period. She amassed wealth through farming and performed the masculinity of yam cultivation (*igwa nnu*), like many other Ohafia women.[14] In addition, like Otuwe Agwu and many other Ohafia women who performed hegemonic masculinity in order to fulfill hegemonic femininity, Nne Uko realized full womanhood by means other than biological motherhood, and her position as female husband (oke-nwami) was as much a feminine as a masculine prerogative.

However, McCall is not right when he argues that women's ogaranya performance during the colonial period did not constitute a cathartic release from male domination. Certainly, in the pre-1850 period when Ohafia women were agrarian breadwinners and possessed a more powerful political institution than men, women's performances of hegemonic masculinity through warfare and yam cultivation did not constitute a revolution against patriarchy, since no such patriarchy existed then. However, a process of wealth masculinization began with male-dominated slave production in the eighteenth century, crystalized in the mid-nineteenth-century period of postabolition slavery and emancipation, and was catalyzed by colonial encroachment and missionary evangelism. The expression of rebellious female power and authority took the form of ogaranya masculinity. Women's ogaranya performance became both an economic and political endeavor that constituted a social expression of power over men and women.

What were the prevailing ideologies of gender and sexuality that Unyang Uka and Otuwe negotiated? In both European archives and published literature, the voices of Ohafia women are silenced. In the course of an eighteen-month ethnographic study and 180 oral interviews with the Ohafia between 2010 and 2013, I was struck by women's consciousness of precolonial female power, and their eagerness to comment on this historical awareness. Old women often transformed the interview sessions into public performances, reenacting women's tactics of shaming or "making war" on men. They danced and mocked men, emphasizing women's power to "teach men lessons when necessary." It was while members of Ohafia female courts were narrating instances of female power that the stories of Unyang Uka and Otuwe Agwu emerged. Both were equated with male political rulers and ogaranya of the early twentieth century. The full picture of these women's lives could only emerge, however, when situated within broader social processes—legitimate trade, Christianity, and colonialism. As Theodore Jun Yoo points out, the life-history method involves both an account of individual life as well as a reconstruction of the individual's social world.[15] In Penny Russell's words, this entails unearthing the historical "domestic, social, political, and cultural contexts" of identity formation.[16] Both women are remembered for their nonconformity to imperial-Christian gender norms and their superiority over men. Thus, the present-day male king of Amangwu Ohafia stated: "She [Unyang Uka] did things which even men could not do."[17] As for Otuwe Agwu, members of the Ebem female court said, "she performed masculine bravado."[18] My research collaborators framed these women's lives in terms of gender transgression, but the content of their revolutionary ogaranya entailed the dissident sexuality of oke-nwami within a prescriptive colonial-cum-missionary environment.

Indeed, the life histories of Unyang Uka and Otuwe Agwu contrast the sexual and gender regulation that underpinned the European colonial repertoire of power. As various scholars have observed, the social articulation of colonial dominion was manifest in the reconfiguration of indigenous family structure and the erection of a mostly male bureaucratic elite, who regulated sexuality through control of reproduction and kinship.[19] In Ohafia, the Presbyterian Church promoted the conjugal family as the primary kinship unit, in contrast to the traditional matrilineage units, by enthroning monogamy, virilocal residency, "paternal responsibility" (i.e., heteropatriarchy), and male breadwinners. As a cultural production that represents the appropriation of the human body by an ideological discourse, sexuality and its governance undergirded Presbyterian conceptions of femininity and masculinity.[20]

Presbyterian masculinity entailed a reordering of the iconography and social practices of masculinity through monogamy, wage labor, Western education, and Christianity, which undermined preexisting forms such as warrior and senior (gerontocratic) masculinities. Presbyterian conceptions of masculinity produced a Christian church led by male elders, who were rewarded with "good Christian wives." Presbyterian femininity was the transformation of autonomous Igbo women into domestic "good Christian wives," "matrons," and "ladies." Kristin Mann has described matronship or ladyship as a colonial hegemonic femininity, represented by educated, Christian, and married elite women who performed the domesticity of the "good housewife." Presbyterian femininity encouraged women to be "first wives and mothers, responsible for the all-important task of civilizing home and family life." Presbyterian femininity was based on the social reproduction of the husband as breadwinner, and the wife as the subservient domestic.[21]

By refusing to conform to prevailing notions of Presbyterian femininity, women like Unyang Uka and Otuwe Agwu realized what Henriette Gunkel describes as the "subversive potential of . . . female masculinity" to disrupt heteropatriarchal ideologies and practices.[22] Situated on the margins of the imperial-Christian gender regime, such women nonetheless played a primary role in redefining hegemonic conceptions of masculinity through ogaranya wealth politics. From the perspective of the Presbyterian Church, these women enacted dissident sexuality. By marrying fellow women, they refused to conform to heteromonogamy. Whereas Presbyterian sexuality reproduced male hegemony, female husbandhood reproduced superior women's dominance over junior women and men. Whereas marriage was mobilized for monogamous reproduction in the former, in the latter, marriage served to proliferate the power of the oke-nwami.

The nonconformist performance of oke-nwami was made possible by what David Halperin has called a sociosexual system—the theory that sexual-object choices were determined not by typology of anatomical sexes (male vs. female), but rather by the social articulation of power (superordinate vs. subordinate).[23] The precolonial Ohafia sociosexual system had been based on matrilineal conceptions of citizenship. The primary basis of social identification and reproduction was the matrilineage. Within this system, matriliny (as opposed to patriliny) was the primary denominator of kinship. Maternal uncles (as opposed to biological fathers) fulfilled the social obligation of fatherhood. Ohafia oke-nwami often married wives from neighboring patrilineal societies. Lacking a matrilineage within Ohafia, such wives were incorporated into the oke-nwami's matrilineage as kin (nwannediya). Such incorporation ensured that the children did not belong to two different matrilineages, in effect two different "mothers."

By performing ogaranya masculinity in the early twentieth century, women gained the capital to marry other women. By populating their matrilineages with wives and offspring, oke-nwami mobilized the traditional sociosexual system to secure legal rights over their children, thereby positioning biological fathers as sperm donors lacking lineage claims over such children.[24] Oke-nwami thus fulfilled the prerequisite of becoming matrilineage matriarchs. By marrying wives, using such wives to procreate in order to achieve matriarchy, and distributing wives to their male matrikin to gain ogaranya prestige, oke-nwami enacted the power of their superordinate sexuality over subordinate bodies, male and female. These women force us to think of sexuality as power politics beyond physical sex acts. Yet their dual role as wives and husbands elicits the probing of sex and desire, as does their articulation of embodied modernity through ogaranya capitalism, construction of modern houses that reconfigured intimate social spaces, and invasive politicization of desire through kinship.

In his study of "the great process of transforming sex and desire into discourse," Michel Foucault acknowledged varying forms of discourses: spoken, written, and performative. The life histories of Ohafia-Igbo women who performed ogaranya masculinity capture what Foucault has described as the "everyday bit of theatre," which defines the "polymorphous techniques of power" that produce "manifold sexualities." The desire to control and the ability to evade surveillance undergirded the power politics of sexuality. British colonial administrators, Presbyterian missionaries, Igbo male church elders, and female ogaranya masculinities participated in generating a multiplicity of discourses on sexuality through a "whole series of mechanisms operating in different institutions."[25] Alongside the missionary discourses used to foster Presbyterian sexuality, Ohafia women's ogaranya masculinity performances elucidate how sexualities were contested and produced through the power to control others' bodies. The hegemony of Presbyterian teachings and misogynistic colonial policies positioned Unyang Uka and Otuwe Agwu as transgressive of prescriptive sexuality. Contrasting them with contemporary women, who espoused Presbyterian femininity, further illuminates their lives.

MALE BREADWINNERS AND "GOOD CHRISTIAN WIVES"

The aforementioned renowned British expedition against the Aro (1901–2), who had maintained a 150-year trading monopoly in the Igbo hinterland and resisted European commercial and political incursion from the coast, opened up the Cross River Igbo hinterland to formal colonization and Christian missionary evangelism.[26] As various European missions struggled for territory in the Bight of Biafra, the British colonial government defined, in 1905, separate spheres of missionary influence. This granted the Church of Scotland Mission (CSM) monopolistic control over the Ohafia region.[27] African conversion to Christianity became a medium for warding off British military interventions, gaining access to Western education, and resisting the oppression of European and African colonial agents.[28] The Scottish missionaries viewed the Cross River region as a pestilential district and forged a policy to develop a native agency of select educated African men to propagate Christianity under European supervision.[29] Ohafia's massive response to Christianity was largely informed by the agency of local ministers and desire for Western education, the passport to colonial wage labor.[30]

However, what is most significant about the evangelism of the CSM is that it was an all-male affair from the beginning. The CSM administration enthroned Ohafia men in leadership positions, and the latter came to see the mission as an avenue to sociopolitical power over women and non-Christians. The Ohafia mission district consisted of a hierarchy of emergent masculinities. At the top were the resident European missionary, Robert Collins, and his wife, Elizabeth. Church historian Geoffrey Johnston observed that Rev. Collins "functioned like a typical Ohafia elder. The successful missionary had to be a successful chief, one who was skilled at settling disputes, and who had influence in the right quarters."[31] Rev. Collins was subordinate only to the British district officer, and he worked conscientiously to fashion Ohafia boys into Presbyterian masculinities: most Ohafia men who emerged as schoolteachers and ministers between 1916 and 1920 apprenticed as the Collinses' houseboys between 1911 and 1915.[32]

Below Rev. Collins functioned a number of certified teachers of coastal Efik origin, who managed the central mission school and supervised several semitrained hinterland Ohafia teachers in the surrounding twenty-six villages. Most of the local teachers had finished standard VI (US grade twelve) but could not afford to proceed to the Hope Waddell Training Institute at Calabar for teacher training. These native teachers also doubled as itinerant preachers and personal interpreters (English and Igbo) for Rev. Collins, who preached in Efik, the language of coastal Calabar, where the CSM established its first mission in 1846.[33] Indeed, many Ohafia men systematically graduated from being teachers to becoming ordained ministers between 1916 and 1920.[34] These teacher-ministers, who were pioneers of educated Christian converts' elitism in the Cross River region of Igboland, have aptly been described by Johnston as "emergent aristocrats."[35] They were largely responsible for the mission work of the CSM and enjoyed a robust local prestige as Presbyterian masculinities: they were the first class of Ohafia people to own bicycles, wear European-tailored suits, and build modern houses in demonstration of their ogaranya status.[36] Their opinions became paramount in the affairs of their local communities, and they emerged as role models to ambitious young men, who violated age-old traditions in pursuit of ogaranya masculinity and its associated modernity.[37]

Above the teacher-minister class of Presbyterian masculinities were the ordained church elders. Rev. Collins chose educated men of influence, especially those of ogaranya status, to become church elders so that their influence would attract people to church.[38] Elderhood was the final reward for educated Christians who accomplished Presbyterian masculinity. Elder Agwu Kalu stated: "There were no female elders in the church. It was only men. The Presbyterian Church was a man's world. It was very masculinist. It was not until the 1970s that we started having female elders little by little. It used to be an all-male affair."[39] Elders were placed in charge of congregations and worked directly under Rev. Collins's supervision.[40]

Johnston writes, "In Ohafia . . . the elders took a more prominent part in the affairs of the church than they did in Ibibio country [Calabar]."[41] Although they were few, the church elders had a lot of power. By 1930, about 40 percent of the total population were Christian converts, including more than seven hundred communicants, and the social laws regulating the life of these Christian converts were governed by twenty church elders in 1924.[42] The elders were responsible for managing the congregations and the affairs of the whole parish. Their major business in session was settling marriage cases and disciplining sexual offenders—duties hitherto fulfilled by the traditional female court. It was the elders who upheld the church mandate on monogamy as a requisite for true Presbyterian masculine identity. They often denied women's divorce petitions, in contrast to the freedom enjoyed by women in the precolonial period. They also settled land disputes and decided whether litigants could proceed to the Native Court—duties hitherto fulfilled by the traditional village assembly. Moreover, the elders sometimes constituted a diocesan court, including Rev. Collins, teachers, and ministers, in which Collins assumed the position of a bishop, leader, judge, and dispenser of sacraments; this system remained intact until the 1930s.[43]

The social principles introduced by Christianity, including condemnation of divorce, matrilineage inheritance, postnuptial uxorilocal residence, divination, ancestor worship, secret societies, age-grade activities, polygamy, and new yam festivals, undermined indigenous avenues of social distinction.[44] As a result, many Ohafia people channeled their energies from the military defense of their villages, post-abolition slave production for Bight of Biafran domestic markets, and agriculture to Western education, leadership in the Christian missions, and colonial service—opportunities that women were denied.[45] Thus, Christianity and Western education facilitated the subversion of both male and female indigenous political systems, enabling male educated Christian converts and church elders to usurp the political prerogatives of preexisting institutions. British officer C. J. Mayne observed in 1931:

> The indigenous rulers, now, once again [in addition to the warrant chiefs] behold a menace that threatens danger to them, namely, the expansion of Christianity. They perceive that whereas in the past, their position was not challenged by reason of their extensive knowledge of the laws and customs of their forefathers that now this is insufficient, for with civilisation, education has come, which is represented in their villages by the

Christian element [converts], who no longer are content to listen to the voice of age.[46]

Christianity undermined women's political authority. It transferred their duties, including arbitration and intervention in divorce and the regulation of social mores, to male Christian church elders.[47] Women lamented the destruction of matrilineage female deities (ududu) by zealous male Christian converts; in contrast, the British colonial government preserved patrilineage deities as museum artifacts. In the immediate precolonial period, matrilineage matriarchs were at the helm of traditional religious worship. Ohafia people say that "the matrilineage matriarch's home was like a church before the white men came."[48] Christianity effectively undermined this matrifocal religious corpus by placing male church elders at the center of spiritual life. Whereas women were breadwinners in the agro-based economy of the precolonial period, missionary education enabled men to emerge as breadwinners in the colonial wage-labor economy while marginalizing women from lucrative ventures.[49] Women made financial and labor contributions to the erection of new schools and churches. However, as elder Ukpai Ndukwe stated, "there is no record attesting that a girl was among the intakes into any of the schools opened by the missionaries between 1911 and 1921."[50] Until 1928, female education was outside the objectives of missionaries and colonial officers.[51]

The creation of an elite cadre of Christian male elders and teachers went hand in hand with that of an underpaid labor force including the majority of the population. Whereas the colonial government dismissed African teacher-ministers as duplicitous and illiterate men of undesirable character that needed to be closely supervised, the CSM regarded Africans as a simple-minded people who lacked the capacity for literary education.[52] The result of this bigoted ideology was a policy of industrial education for Africans (carpentry, brickmaking, tailoring, printing, and baking).[53] Thus, key jobs such as district administration, medical services, and school management were reserved for Europeans, whereas African men became ill-trained teachers, preachers, catechists, interpreters, and clerks who assisted Europeans.[54] The first indigenous Ohafia headmaster emerged only in 1928.[55] Nonetheless, mission education enabled many men to become entrepreneurs (masons, carpenters, tailors, and printers) and educated elites (teachers, preachers, ministers, clerks, policemen, and railway workers) between 1916 and 1920.[56] These men announced their new social status by marrying "good Christian wives."[57] Between 1917 and 1922, such wives were trained at Slessor Memorial School, Arochukwu, by Scottish female missionaries Mrs. Arnot, Susan McKennell, and Marion Gilmour. McKennell and Arnot believed that training girls for marriage was of paramount importance.[58]

There was no interest in creating a cadre of African women teachers even with the opening of new schools for girls. In 1922, the Ohafia Girls' School (OGS) was established, administered by Scottish missionaries Miss Marion Gilmore, Mrs. J. D. Moffat, Miss Barclay, Miss Reid, Mrs. McLachlan, and Miss Flemming.[59] Its goal, according to Ukpai, was to train "good Christian wives for the new Ohafia educated elite."[60] The OGS was a boarding school that combined Christian education and domestic science. Young Ohafia women were trained in Bible reading, cooking, weaving, dressmaking, personal hygiene, gardening, soap making, and palm oil processing. Literary education for girls began only in the mid-1940s.[61]

The 15 percent of the Ohafia adult female population trained at OGS between 1922 and 1930 would quickly redefine themselves as matrons, challenge the limits of their education, and inspire a new generation of women who would subvert the incipient gender hierarchies of their society. Matronship was a new class created by Cross River Igbo women between 1930 and 1950. Some of the renowned first-generation Ohafia matrons include Miss Nkacha Emetu, Miss Ucha Onum, Mrs. Sarah Olugu, and Mrs. Grace Anya. These women began their careers by supervising the domestic science training of OGS students. As OGS matrons or substitute mothers, they enjoyed social capital as mediators between male suitors and the prospective brides under their tutelage. Through practical experience, rather than literary instruction, they became sufficiently skilled to serve as substitute teachers during the absence of their European counterparts. After retiring from OGS, these pioneer matrons set up tailoring and domestic science schools in their homes, thereby creating competitive informal economies on the fringes of colonial missionary institutions. Finally, some matrons paid their way through standard VI and obtained teaching certificates so that they could teach in regular colonial missionary schools in the region.[62] Nonetheless, these matrons were domesticated

Female Dissident Sexualities ⇋ 171

wives and mothers, confined to monogamous unions, and their espousal of Presbyterian femininity reinforced their husbands' prestige as individuals who fulfilled Presbyterian masculinity.

THE REVOLUTIONARY MASCULINITY AND DISSIDENT SEXUALITY OF UNYANG UKA AND OTUWE AGWU

Most Ohafia women, thus increasingly marginalized from the dominant sociopolitical positions of power in their society, sought to redefine preexisting conceptions of gendered spaces, roles, and opportunities. This resulted in rebellious ogaranya and oke-nwami enactments.

My research assistant, Uduma Uka, described Madam Chief Otuwe Agwu as his female grandfather. Agwu had married Uduma Uka's grandmother from Umuahia, a patrilineal Igbo society, around 1930. According to elder Ndukwe Otta, "because Agwu paid the bride-price, thereby fulfilling the customary obligations to make the woman a wife, all the children that woman begot belonged to her [Agwu] and her matrilineage."[63] Born in Ohafia around 1885, Agwu was the first daughter of her parents and, as such, in line to become matriarch of her matrilineage. She had married a husband around 1905 but did not have a child. This meant that upon her death, there would be nobody to raise an ududu monument in her honor and thus enshrine her as an ancestral matriarch of her matrilineage. Without ududu, she would not be a powerful spiritual force after death, she would not be ministered to and fed by any descendants, and she would have no legacy—in effect, she would not be a powerful Ohafia matriarch. Agwu married a wife to remedy this.[64] Because Agwu and her husband belonged to different matrilineages, Agwu's wife, as well as her wife's children, belonged to Agwu's matrilineage. Thus, Agwu's husband had no claims over the children from Agwu's wife.

Amadiume noted that the practice of oke-nwami was a mechanism through which women acquired wealth (human and material) and formal political authority.[65] Achebe argues that for the singular Igbo woman-king Ahebi Ugbabe, the adoption, kidnapping, and marriage of men's wives in colonial northern Igboland was part of a complex process whereby she constructed a powerful and mythical image, controlling women who provided sexual services to male visitors in her court.[66] Both scholars pinpoint superordinate power as central to the gender and sexuality politics of oke-nwami. Because oke-nwami performed superordinate power by appropriating other women's bodies, indigenous Ohafia women critically described wives of oke-nwami as slaves of the matrilineage. But such wives were not in fact slaves; rather, they enjoyed privileged status as nwannediya (husband's sisters).[67] "Slaves of the matrilineage" alludes to the greater expense of marrying a wife from a patrilineal Igbo society, as well as the utility of such wives in saving a dwindling matrilineage through the procreation of daughters.[68] Ohafia is exceptional in the region. Anthropologist Simon Ottenberg observed that in neighboring Afikpo, which possessed a double-descent system, "there was no device of bringing an outside female into the descent group as a fictional relative to produce children for a dying matrilineage."[69]

The related case of Uzo Kamalu, a wealthy trader from Okon Ohafia, sheds more light on practices of oke-nwami. Kamalu had two sons but no daughters, which posed a threat to the continuation of her Umueze matrilineage. Thus, around 1890 she married two wives and purchased a female slave, who produced female descendants that sustained the Umueze matrilineage.[70] Kamalu's story shows that there was a distinction between female wives and female slaves. Both categories of "adopted" women were used to expand lineages, but female slaves were subject to greater physical labor requisition, and social marginality. Yet marriage and slavery capture the centrality of daughters, as opposed to sons, in perpetuating matrilineages. Moreover, they attest that oke-nwami were motivated to marry wives not just because they desired to perform ogaranya masculinity. Reproducing daughters ensured their status as matriarchs of their matrilineages and ensured that their matrilineage continued. In this case, ogaranya was the consequence, not the inspiration, for women's social mobility. Thus, McCall concludes that Ohafia possessed a latent system of practices that enabled women to perform femininity and masculinity simultaneously.[71]

In her effort to fulfill Ohafia-Igbo hegemonic femininity (i.e., become a matrilineage matriarch), Agwu had first to acquire wealth, and this resulted in various gender transformations. After the second smallpox epidemic (1918–20), when some dibias were embracing Christianity, Agwu purchased membership in the dibia guild.[72] Because the dibia guild was a masculine institution, monopolized by men, the few women who became dibia were socially perceived as masculine. In an expression of

Agwu's initiation into the dibia guild, which was an expensive endeavor, the Ohafia say that "she performed masculine bravado."[73]

As part of her performance of dibia, she undertook a medicine pilgrimage (*ije ogwu*), which was the spiritual voyage of the dibia to a distant and unknown community, where "he" must prove "his" expertise and gain popularity. Between 1850 and 1900, ije ogwu was proof of dibia bravery, because the high incidence of slaving and headhunting rendered the roads unsafe for travel. Dibias who fulfilled ije ogwu thereby dramatically showed their power and immunity to physical harm.[74] The relative peace and security ensured by British colonialism, as well as improved means of transportation, helped Agwu fulfill this objective in 1920, in Port Harcourt. Between 1901 and 1940, Bende was Ohafia's administrative headquarters under Owerri Province, and Port Harcourt served as the province's major city.[75]

Agwu's choice of Port Harcourt, and her ability to quickly establish a reputation as "the sun that brings light to the world" (*anyanwu n'enye ihe*) in a urban colonial environment characterized by stifling colonial and missionary campaigns against dibia practices (which colonial officials and missionaries viewed as barbaric), bespoke the effectiveness of her healing methods, and her triumph over modern medicine.[76] According to Ndukwe Otta, in this period when most dibia could not cure yaws and gonorrhea, Agwu healed patients of these ailments, and particularly excelled in enabling barren women to become pregnant.[77] Agwu's reputation as the "impregnator of women" carried both sexually and gender-transgressive connotations.

Through her dibia practice, Agwu accumulated significant wealth and took steps to fulfill two more gender transformations, namely ogaranya and oke-nwami. First, she returned home to Ohafia and became one of the first women to independently purchase a plot of land in the society, where she built a modern four-bedroom house with zinc-iron roofing. Thus, she equated herself with a few distinguished men in her community who had attained ogaranya masculinity through gender-biased missionary education and colonial wage labor. This, according to Mama Docas Kalu and Mary Ezera, was why she was referred to as "chief." Second, in order to have children of her own—sons who would establish a patrilineage in her name and daughters who would immortalize her as a matriarch—Agwu married a wife.

Agwu symbolized what John and Jean Comaroff called a "revolution of values and practices" in consumption, aesthetics, architecture, and domesticity. However, unlike the Comaroff's "right-minded, right-bearing, propertied Twanas, untangled from the primitive webs of relations and recast into a modern personhood," women like Agwu flourished in the messy interstice of traditional economies and modern materialism, without converting to Christianity.[78] Her rectangular, corrugated iron–roofed, four-bedroom house differed remarkably from the surrounding round, mud-and-thatch-roofed houses in her community, constituting a reengineering of gendered domestic social space. Traditionally, the head of the compound, usually male, established his house, comprising one bedroom and a reception hall, at the end of the compound, while the single-room houses of his wives, his sons and their wives, and other dependents surrounded him. The husband visited a wife in her house for coitus or other forms of intimacy. In contrast, Agwu, Agwu's wife, and Agwu's husband each had a room in Agwu's house in Ohafia, and Agwu had a voice in choosing her wife's male sperm donor. Moreover, Agwu was called "madam" because she maintained a secondary residence in Port Harcourt city, until she died in 1976, and styled herself like matrons—with aesthetics of sleek long hair, ball gowns, and high-heel shoes. Upon each annual visit to Ohafia, she brought home gifts of imported clothes and food items, which dramatized her modernity. Hence, she came to be known as "the female grand-visitor" (*obia nwami*).[79] Agwu represents individualized female resistance to emerging male hegemony under British colonial rule and the Scottish missionary regime.

Whereas Agwu performed gender transformations in the process of fulfilling Ohafia ideals of femininity, Unyang Uka actively sought manhood. Born around 1865, Uka was an icon of Ohafia women's performance of ogaranya at the beginning of the twentieth century. Her father, Uka Afijo, was renowned for performing warrior masculinity (ikperikpeogu) between 1850 and 1890. When fighting in a war, he would cut human heads and capture slaves, whom he sold to Aro merchant middlemen or disposed of in the slave markets at Itu, Assan, and Calabar.[80] In commemoration of his bravery in warfare, he was hailed Okpodu. According to his great-granddaughter Tessy Uzoma, "Okpodu was an individual that often single-handedly conquered a village and razed it to the ground with fire."[81] Another of his great-granddaughters,

Grace Emehe, said, "Nna Afijo Okpodu's reputation influenced Unyang Uka so much that she started behaving like a man."[82] Uka's mother was Nne Agbaeze. She was a wealthy farmer and trader, and was said to be a generous philanthropist who often feasted her community.[83] Uka had an elder brother, Johnson Emehe, and a younger sister, Afo Uka. Emehe was "pampered by his mother, and became a Presbyterian minister around 1917."[84] Uka, on the other hand, behaved like a man and assisted her father in his slave-trade ventures in the 1890s.[85] She married a husband, Nna Agwu, around 1885, and they had a daughter, Unyang Agwu. Tessy Uzoma stated:

> Because [Uka] behaved like a man, she named the daughter after herself. After her father passed away, she started purchasing slaves. She would sell most of her male slaves and distribute most of her female slaves as wives to her maternal male cousins and relatives. She also married a lot of wives herself and distributed them. So, if you come to our village, Amangwu, today, you will find half the village is descendants of Unyang Uka and her wives.... Our matrilineage is Ibe-Obobi of Umuaka. Umuaka is the largest matrilineage in Ohafia and it has seven lineal houses. Our lineal house is Ibe-Obobi, and we are the head of Umuaka matrilineage.... Unyang Uka was a major reason why Ibe-Obobi grew into the largest lineal house in Ohafia. She married many wives and distributed them to her male matrikin across Ohafia. Men that did not have money to afford wives came to her and she gave them wives. All those children belonged to her and the Ibe-Obobi matrilineage.... That is how she started behaving like a man. She was a husband of many wives and father of many children.[86]

Did Unyang Uka merely reproduce patriarchy? On the contrary, within the Ohafia sociosexual system, female wives and slaves and their male sperm donors were useful in proliferating Unyang Uka's ogaranya dominion over male and female bodies. She demonstrated that ogaranya entailed the social legitimation of economic and political power. She reflected Uchendu's description of ogaranya as an individual who commanded prestige and obedience because she "helped others to get up."[87] In effect, she performed a socially hegemonic masculinity by redistributing resources to her community. Therefore, nobody challenged her superiority.

After her father passed away, Uka took over the slaving business, and on one of her trips to Opobo around 1895, she met the renowned Ohafia ex-slave Kalu Ezelu, who furnished her with loads of coral beads.[88] It is indeed a remarkable coincidence that the paths of Kalu and Uka crossed, because they both became the most important icons of the changing politics of ogaranya masculinity in Ohafia at the turn of the twentieth century. Uka began to trade in coral beads and slaves, and by 1905, she had developed a prosperous trade between the slave port of Opobo and the hinterland market of Bende.[89] She also established a widespread reputation as a wealthy moneylender who always took her debtors to the Native Court at Bende. All my respondents stated that Uka was business savvy, and it was never her practice to settle disputes with people through palavers. She always took people to court, and she came to be feared as a troublemaker.[90]

It is not clear when Uka's first husband, Nna Agwu, passed away. But sometime before 1922 (when Ugoaha Udonsi Ibe, Uka's granddaughter, was born), Uka married Mr. Cobham, then the *kotuma* (clerk of the Native Court, or CNC) of Bende. Jones informs us that the Bende Native Court was established around 1907, and by 1911, it was handling about 4,162 civil cases annually.[91] At the center of the court was the clerk, who recorded cases, kept a roster of warrant chiefs sitting on the bench, and documented court judgments on which appeals were based.[92] Kotuma were corrupt individuals who often manipulated court information to the advantage of preferred litigants. After 1914, when indirect rule came into effect, the British district commissioner ceased to attend court sittings, and the CNC became a de facto district commissioner.[93] The CNC was salaried at £4 monthly by 1911, and for many miles around, he was regarded as a governor.[94] Uka was older than Cobham, and their marriage enhanced her respectability as a formidable ogaranya.[95] This marriage enabled Uka to expand her moneylending beyond Ohafia to Bende, where she lived with Cobham until 1925. Her marriage to Cobham ensured that her debtors always paid their loans. Otherwise, she arrested them and locked them up in the Bende court prison—an ordeal that emasculated Igbo men, who had no experience with prisons until colonial rule. Public flogging and imprisonment were mechanisms that British colonial officials employed

Female Dissident Sexualities ⌒ 177

to denigrate Igbo male elders as "boys," shore up their own image as superior and more powerful male figures, and construct their hegemony over local rulers. Such practices reinforced "British colonialism's paternalistic machismo" and translated colonial paternal idioms into workable policies.[96] Uka deployed this hegemonic colonial masculinity against Ohafia senior masculinities, whose lack of access to wealth constituted a severe vulnerability. To evade arrest, her male debtors often ran away from the village whenever she returned.[97]

Female husband, female father, giver of wives to men, peopler of Ibe-Obobi matrilineage, female kotuma, wealthy merchant of slaves and coral beads, renowned moneylender, the bank of Igbo people, and imprisoner of men, Unyang Uka was famed for her performance of ogaranya masculinity in the first three decades of the twentieth century. Every December, she made a voyage from Bende to Ohafia. Like British colonial officers of her time, and like Kalu, Unyang Uka was always carried by young men on a hammock. According to Tessy Uzoma:

> Six men carried her in a hammock from Bende to Ohafia. Upon reaching Ohafia, the male age-grades of the first village would carry her to the boundary of the next village, and it would continue like that until she reached her own village, Amangwu. They carried her over hills and streams. . . . The men did not rest until they reached another village. . . . Whenever she came home, she had an entourage of male slaves carrying her several metal trunk boxes filled with European goods and money. She traded some of the goods and gave out many as gifts to her people. Upon her arrival, the ikoro [war drum] would start beating, and people would be shouting, "Our great daughter has returned!" Because of her ogaranya performance, she was no longer considered a woman. So the ikoro was always sounded for her, and they dressed her head in okpu agu [leopard cap of bravery]. She was always wearing okpu agu; that is why she is remembered as Unyang Okpu Agu [the Leopard Cap Female Chief]. Instead of wearing a headdress like other women, she wore the okpu agu, with eagle fathers attached to it. Leopard cap and eagle feathers were reserved for men who cut a head in battle. Her status in the community earned her that honor.[98]

According to the male elders of Ekeluogo patrilineage in Amangwu, Unyang Uka built a modern house with a zinc roof in Port Harcourt in the late 1920s, and was one of the people that provided major funding for the building of St. Mary's Catholic Church in that colonial city in the 1950s. Her house in Port Harcourt was a rallying ground, rest house, and home away from home for all Ohafia persons that visited the city.[99] Tessy Uzoma added:

> If you went to Port Harcourt, you must visit Unyang Okpu Agu's house at No. 96 Agri Road. Students, government workers, and traders from Ohafia stayed at her house. . . . I visited her in the late 1950s. . . . She died at 94 years old. Throughout the period I knew her, I never saw her tie a wrapper, like other women did.[100]

It was through these performances that Unyang Uka, according to Tessy Uzoma, "transformed herself into a man."[101] Her habitual honorific cross-dressing perpetuated that image. As a rule, the ikoro was never sounded for women in Ohafia, except for the few that accomplished warrior masculinity.[102] Ohafia material-culture practices were evidently transformed at the turn of the twentieth century because the constructions of masculinity through ogaranya performance were changing. For such individuals as Unyang Uka, Chief Kalu Awa Kalu stated that "even though [they] did not cut a head with a machete, [they] had actually cut a head, one that was visible and materialistic [i.e., wealth]."[103] Unyang Uka's wealth symbolized the head she had cut to attain masculinity. In commemoration of her unprecedented wealth, Unyang Uka was nicknamed Unyang Pon-Pon (Female Chief of British Pounds). The logic was that she dealt not in cumbersome local currencies or shillings, but in British pounds sterling.[104]

⌒

This chapter argues that Atlanticization in the second half of the nineteenth century and the first two decades of the twentieth century linked changes in gender constructions to changes in gendered power. Building upon the gender inequalities of legitimate trade, the colonial- and missionary-derived hegemony of the emergent ogaranya masculinities between the 1890s and 1920 usurped the sociopolitical authority of male and female traditional institutions. Hence, ogaranya translated itself into political power. The chapter has conceptualized African agency in self-making and social change as a gendered struggle for power because the historical processes of social mobility and the opportunities to attain sociopolitical power in Igboland varied for men and women. The institutions that produced Presbyterian masculinities also sought to fashion subordinate "good Christian wives." African female converts worked out an uneasy accommodation with European missionaries to produce a new social class of matrons, who redefined Presbyterian notions of education and domesticity.

The majority of Igbo women did not convert to Christianity, however, and lacked access to Western education, leadership in Christian churches, or employment within the formal colonial economy. These women, who refused to become "good Christian wives," exhibited individual resistance to the patchwork of European and African patriarchies that emerged between 1900 and 1930. The case studies of Otuwe Agwu and Unyang Uka represent the most remarkable examples among a larger group. They attest that women invaded traditional male spaces and were able to utilize these opportunities to perform ogaranya masculinity like contemporaneous warrant chiefs, court clerks, district officers, and Christian elders performing "Presbyterian masculinity." Moreover, their gender transformations expanded the institutional hegemony of ogaranya masculinity to include postcolonial, anti-Christian, and illicit economic practices, which defied colonial-era social engineering. Hence, ogaranya masculinity was a product of the struggle between colonists and resisters, men and women, and formal structures and fringe economies.

The chapter reconciles the gendered impact of colonial rule with the transformative agency of African men and women. Beyond colonial archives, attention to oral sources, family histories, and changing cultural practices shows that oke-nwami and ogaranya were dialectical social processes through which Igbo women endured and mediated the structural effects of colonialism. Uncoupling masculinity from maleness and patriarchy shows that women were innovators of novel forms of masculinity under colonial rule. Through the examination of gender- and sexual-identity politics, the chapter also demonstrates that Ohafia women undermined the strict Victorian gender binaries propagated through colonial and missionary institutions. As a result, the early twentieth century was characterized by fluid and hybrid gender regimes, ideologies, and practices that were reinforced and elided by women's social-mobility politics and gender transformations. Ogaranya masculinity offers a lens into this period of rapid social change, when the categories "man" and "woman" evinced malleable meanings.

Conclusion

IN OCTOBER 1931, British district officer Biddulph transferred a chieftaincy succession dispute between Kalu Idika of Ebem and Eme Ado of Ebem, which had been brought to his bench at the Bende Provincial Court, to the Ohafia council of chiefs.[1] The Ohafia council weighed the testimonies and "found out that the Plaintiff and the Defendant are [relatives]. They should continue the position of Ezeogo [male king] in rotation." Kalu Idika and Eme Ado were ogaranya men of slave descent, who sought to use colonial institutions to advance their political aspirations in the early twentieth century. Each litigant sought to legitimize his claim to ruling rights by reconstructing his genealogical descent through a complex line of matrilineage matriarchs, all the way to the female founder of Ebem town, a woman named Chiasara. Each party also sought to define the other as a descendant of a female slave-wife or resident-stranger, adopted at some point by the foundation matrilineage. Their accounts and the testimonies of their witnesses constitute practical uses of lineages. They show that although British colonial rule had dismissed female traditional political institutions and legitimized male ones, male political rulers still derived legitimacy to govern by successfully tracing their descent from founding female ancestors, even amid colonial patriarchy. Each of the litigants sought to establish that he was the custodian and minister of the ududu matrilineage ancestor pots, which served as evidence of his claims to ruling rights. The testimonies reveal a historical dual-sex sociopolitical system predicated on several things: bilateral kinship reckoning; the durability of matrifocal principles sustained by the gendered uses of kinship; a long tradition of ogaranya masculinities using slave girls and slave-wives to establish new households and repopulate dwindling matrilineages; and the fact that matrilineages occasionally called on slave lineages they had absorbed to provide rulership, when there were no freeborn adults available from the rightful matrilineage.

The four lineage traditions invoked in this 1931 court case were retrospections of Ohafia-Igbo Atlanticization. The first three traditions respectively recalled that Chiasara's female descendants including Kamalu Agara, Agaraukwu Ugwueze, and Ukoji Idika "bought slave-wives" from Arochukwu and Ibibioland during the eighteenth and nineteenth centuries. They used some of these acquired female slaves as funerary goods to deify their deceased matriarchs, and incorporated most of the enslaved women as wives, who expanded the population of the Ekuke Echi matrilineage. The plaintiff argued that the defendant was a descendant of one of these slave-wives, and as such did not have autochthonous right to the office of the male king. In turn, the defendant argued that the plaintiff's mother, Anyafu, was a resident stranger adopted by the Ekuke Echi matrilineage. Thus, both litigants were incorporated into the Ekuke Echi matrilineage through captive and adopted female ancestresses. The defendant further argued that his male ancestors such as Ukpola Ezema had purchased full incorporation into the Ekuke Echi matrilineage. They had fulfilled a tradition in which female-slave ownership constituted ufiem performance, and had further used their wealth-in-slaves to buy "the right of being Ezeogo." The defendant's ancestral merchant-warriors, who had descended from slave-wives and later acquired wealth-in-slaves, redistributed their wealth from captive supply to matrilineage members and incorporated female captives within their matrilineages, in order to expand the lineage, build social capital, and legitimize political claims. Thus, argued the defendant, because his male ancestors had occupied the office of "male king" and because he was "in possession of their farming lands and raffia palm plantations," which established him as both "Mben" (descendant of Ohafia ancestors) citizen and ogaranya, he had a rightful claim to rule.

The critical role of enslaved women in matrilineage reproduction and expansion, as well as constructions of gendered political power evident in this court case, reinforce the argument that enslaved women's reproductive lives defined social domestic slavery systems in the Bight of Biafra. The uses of enslaved women for the deification of matrilineage ancestresses paralleled the uses of boy captives for the deification of patrilineage merchant-warriors. They capture the rise in violent domestic uses of slaves during the nineteenth century, which are best understood as repercussions of the Atlantic slave trade, because they reflect the competition among lineages and individuals to showcase their wealth and status, at a time when the regional expansion of domestic slavery underpinned expanding legitimate commerce and exacerbated social marginality. Rather than male slaves, however, female slaves were the most common form of wealth, easily convertible into alternative forms of political power. There is a striking similarity between Ukpola Ezema (ca. 1810–1880), Udensi Ekea (ca. 1820–1890), and Kalu Uwaoma (ca. 1865–1968) in terms of how they used slave-wives to propagate their ogaranya masculinity and consolidate their economic and political power. They represent how wealth increasingly attenuated the importance of descent in shifting practices of political power. They show that during the nineteenth and early twentieth century, formerly enslaved persons, and the descendants of slaves and resident-strangers (as opposed to those of freeborn people), provided much of the male political leadership in several Ohafia-Igbo communities. Thus, they evince how entrenched that inverse or revolutionary class formation was, which enabled ex-slaves like Kalu Ezelu Uwaoma and slave descendants like Eme Ado and Okoro Idika to contest political authority in the late nineteenth and early twentieth century. As this book has shown, postabolition mercantilism, Christianity, and the British institution of warrant chieftaincy proliferated this process throughout the Biafran region. Hence, in the nineteenth and twentieth centuries, African slaves achieved freedom and social reintegration by mobilizing kinship, as well as by exploiting the opportunities presented by legitimate trade and colonialism. In so doing, slaves, those on the margins of society, played a major role in redefining dominant conceptions of ufiem.

In demonstrating how ogaranya masculinity and lineage reproduction came to be tied to the redistribution of female slaves, the court case helps us better understand why women like Unyang Uka, Uzo Kamalu, and Otuwe Agwu turned to similar practices of redistributing slave-wives in the early twentieth century to leverage political power. Simultaneously, they were reenacting the legacies of precolonial oke-nwami such as Kamalu Agara and Ukoji Idika and behaving like contemporary colonialist male ogaranya persons in their community in order to gain social prestige. Because female slaves could easily be integrated into matrilineages as uterine sisters, unlike free wives and male slaves, enslaved women predominated Ohafia slaveholding. The court case of Kalu Idika vs. Eme Ado thus chronicles how men and women participated in social practices of hegemonic masculinities based on both the local understandings of kinship and the shifting Atlantic economies of slavery and colonialism. The pre-1850 oke-nwami status of Kamalu Agara and Ukoji Idika does not appear to have amounted to a gender transformation and dissident sexuality, because of the prevailing dual-sex sociopolitical institutional context. This contrasts with the post-1850 performances of Unyang Uka, Uzo Kamalu, and Otuwe Agwu, which stood against an emerging sociopolitical order that fostered wealthy, Christian, and colonialist male breadwinners. Thus, it was the changing sociopolitical contexts that defined the meanings of men and women's social mobility practices. As female husbands *and* female slave-owners, Uzo Kamalu and Unyang Uka ranked with Naomi of Oguta, Omu Okwei of Ossomari, and female king Ahebi Ugbabe. Their coercive mobilization of labor facilitated the postabolition expansion of Biafran slavery and reconciled the "legitimate trade" productive economy, centered around female-slave labor, with the redistributive imperatives of kinship. This use of labor guaranteed them social ascendancy, particularly the hegemonic masculinity of ogaranya.

Elsewhere in sub-Saharan Africa, powerful female slave-owners were not necessarily celebrated as female masculinities. The regions of Senegal, Dahomey, Gold Coast, and Benguela show an earlier history of African women as large-scale slave owners, well before the nineteenth century, when such women became noticeable in the Bight of Biafra. The *kpojitos* (queen mothers) of Dahomey, *donas* of Benguela, *cassare* wives of the Gold Coast, and *signares* of Saint Louis and Gorée (as well as their descendant *métis*) were also African female slave-owners. They exploited their access to coastal trading networks, and their position as royalty and as Euro-African cultural intermediaries, to amass large numbers of male and female slaves, who worked as plantation laborers, traders, porters, domestics, and prostitutes in the seventeenth and eighteenth centuries. These women used slavery to consolidate their power and prestige by assembling a large number of dependents in their households. Their slavery-based wealth accumulation fostered hegemonic femininities and mitigated the prevalence of patriarchy in their distinct communities. In the Gold Coast, Senegal, and Benguela, these female slave-owners further shaped Euro-African creole cultures, but the end of the Atlantic slave trade meant a decline in their power. Slaveholding had increased their social statuses, expanded their personal networks with European and African elites, generated surplus wealth for them, and was virtually the only means by which they gained command of male labor for economic activities such as trade.[2] Such large-scale slave ownership by women did not occur in the Bight of Biafra until the nineteenth century. In the Bight of Biafra, Atlantic slavery enabled men to monopolize slave production and distribution. The expansion of productive economies following the end of the Atlantic slave trade and the rise of legitimate trade afforded a few Biafran women unprecedented opportunities to acquire slaves. Such women socially articulated their slave ownership as ogaranya masculinity performance, by investing their wealth-in-people and wealth-in-commodities into lineage expansion. Such women rose in an environment where emerging patriarchal institutions were undermining dual-sex systems.

Emergent Masculinities generates important implications for West African history. The first has to do with sources and methodology. The colonial archive speaks eloquently of slavery in contrast to prevailing silences in indigenous sources. Unlike the documented court case, for example, which exposes how matrilineages masked slave descent, the Ohafia privilege nonverbal forms of "speaking about the past" through their rituals and material culture practices. For instance, every year, the Ohafia dibia community holds a three-day festival (*umerogwu*) celebrating the historic role of dibias in fortifying warriors before they went to war. It begins with young initiates (*nde apupa*) raiding the surrounding forests with wooden machetes to "cut heads of plantains," in pantomime of historic headhunting and slave-raiding expeditions. This is followed by the second-grade dibias (*atule abali*) known as "spirit combatants" (*ughara mmonwu*) blessing the land and commemorating patterns of patrilineage settlement and descent. Afterward, the first-grade dibias (*aja abali*) stage a grand display of dibia paraphernalia. Lastly, every patrilineage pays a gift-homage (*ibia abia nsi*) to the dibias in their community. There are multiple historical discourses of slavery and colonialism within this dibia festival, which capture the transformative uses of local institutions that characterized Atlanticization. Dibias healed citizens and the body politic, reproduced slaving warriors, and served as a network of slave redistribution. The dibia institution became a basis of local resistance and adaptation to Christian-missionary evangelism, a means of self-emancipation and social ascendancy for male slaves, and a mechanism through which women performed oke-nwami and ogaranya. The dibia institution captures how African traditions underpinned local participation in dynamic Atlantic economies. Both the court case and the dibia institution exemplify the multiplicity of written, oral, and performative discourses that have generated *Emergent Masculinities*. These varied sources enable us to write the histories of subalterns, including women and slaves, and overcome the limitations of structuralist gender analyses of sociopolitical change. They evince the need for historical and anthropological perspectives in understanding the histories of Atlantic Age West Africa.

Second, this book contributes to the revisionist scholarship on historical memory and ethnicity as gendered practices in Africa.[3] Gender-distinctive kinship practices have shaped Ohafia-Igbo ethnic differentiation in the Bight of Biafra region. Both men and women historically reproduced and used matrilineages and patrilineages; but in historical practice and memorialization traditions, women privilege the matrilineage, and men the patrilineage, in advancing internal gendered perceptions of ethnicity. The lineage traditions advanced in "Kalu Idika vs. Eme Ado" evince the lingering salience of kinship—even as Ohafia participated in Atlantic slavery and adapted to colonialism. The role of the matrilineage in the incorporation of slaves, the masking of slave origins, and the rapid sociopolitical mobility of slaves distinguished Ohafia from neighboring patrilineal Igbo societies, which have demonstrated a prominent legacy of marginalizing slave descendants.[4] Even so, there was a region-wide masculinization of power that undermined matrilineage systems and reinforced patrilineage kinship systems. The resilience of Ohafia matrilineal kinship reckoning is especially significant because Atlantic slavery had bolstered the sociopolitical importance of patrilineages. As a result of these parallel processes, by the late nineteenth century, Ohafia had transitioned from a distinctly matrilineal society to a "double unilineal descent" society. Hence, I have argued that lineages, which defined Ohafia-Igbo ethnic identification, were dynamic gendered practices. As the major basis for the organization of male warriors and secret societies, patrilineages fostered masculinist social visions of Ohafia as a land of noble warriors, memorializing the era of the Atlantic slave trade as a heroic age of manliness and preserving a male-dominated history of ufiem accomplishment. Against this background, resilient matrilineage kinship reckoning, combined with female narratives and social practices expressing autonomous political and economic power, counterposits the Ohafia-Igbo as a complex dual-sex Igbo society. Such matrifocal narratives premise the matrilineage as the source of women's dominance in the agro-based economy. They contrast Ohafia-Igbo women's right to own land with patrilineal Igbo women's lack of land-owning rights, and emphasize Ohafia-Igbo women's ability to easily negotiate marriage and matrilineal kinship in a multiethnic frontier. This means that the cultural work of imagining and articulating a shared sense of Ohafia-Igbo consciousness predated European colonialism and Christian missionary evangelism, even though these factors later shaped it. As Allen and Barbara Isaacman point out in their seminal work on the Chikunda of South-Central Africa, it was through gendering practices of "work, status, and power," as well as "dress, language, rituals, and institutions," that Africans configured "fluid" ethnic identities, redefining "themselves in response to changing realities" of slavery, emancipation, mercantilism, and colonialism.[5]

Third, by demonstrating how ufiem social ascendancy combined with intraregional differences in lineage-based kinship practices to transform the hinterland organization of the Biafran Atlantic slave trade and regional domestic slavery in the eighteenth and nineteenth centuries, this book reconciles somewhat the long-standing disciplinary bifurcation in anthropological and historical conceptualizations of "African kinship slavery." Leading anthropologists Suzanne Miers and Igor Kopytoff conceived the structure of African kinship as a benign and stable instrument of assimilating slaves into lineages, and perceived an essential distinction between African kinship slavery and the forms of African domestic slavery that emerged during the era of the Atlantic slave trade. On the other hand, historians such as Walter Rodney, John Thornton, and Paul Lovejoy have tended to emphasize the marginality of kinship reckoning to the violent forms of mercantilist and state-reproductive slavery systems in Africa before and during the Atlantic slave trade. In their view, extreme violence, natal alienation, commercialization (or commodification) of captive populations, and a slave mode of production that benefitted elites and reproduced state structures underpinned the transformative rise of the Atlantic slave trade.[6] There is consequently a notion that in decentralized or small-scale African societies, stable and benign social kinship slavery prevailed, and in centralized African societies of the Sahel, Upper Guinea Coast, and Central Africa, a chattel slavery system prevailed. Frederick Cooper, Jonathan Glassman, and Martin Klein have mediated these disparities by emphasizing that the struggles between masters and slaves socially reproduced the varying local meanings of slavery within Africa.[7] *Emergent Masculinities* shows that although the brutal and alienating racial slavery in the Americas differed significantly from the incorporative social kinship slavery systems in West Africa, the toll of Atlantic slave production and the consolidation of raw material production for Atlantic markets made Biafra's domestic slavery unprecedentedly violent. The book contributes to the scholarship that challenges the predatory-state thesis by emphasizing the complex age-grade structures, regional alliances, and gender and kinship ideologies that underpinned so-called decentralized Ohafia-Igbo agency in violent military slave production. It shows that rather than being marginal to or distinctive from the political economy of the Atlantic slave trade, kinship practices defined Biafra's external and domestic slavery systems. Through the gender-constitutive politics of social ascendancy, real and fictive kinship practices defined the gender dynamics of Biafra's internal frontiers of slaving, the regional organization of the slave trade, the generation of captives and alienation of market slaves, and the internal uses of enslaved persons. In turn, these processes shaped the region's dual-sex sociopolitical systems and conceptions of hegemonic femininity and masculinity.

Fourth, *Emergent Masculinities* has shown that the Atlantic slave trade, postabolition mercantilism, and British colonialism engineered a departure from a pre-1850 period of female sociopolitical and economic superiority in Ohafia-Igbo society. Primarily, this entailed an initial gendered contestation over the parameters and institutional mechanisms of Ohafia dual-sex sociopolitical systems, and eventually the marginalization of the dual-sex systems in favor of androcentric political and economic structures. A regional historiography further affirms that the masculinization of sociopolitical power was a principal mechanism through which West Africans indigenized cross-Atlantic political economies. Therefore, the sociopolitical histories of modern West African societies are most meaningful when gender is placed at the heart of an African-centered Atlantic framework that emphasizes continuities over the *longue durée* and historicizes male power rather than assuming immemorial patriarchy. Moreover, a cross-Atlantic perspective of West African gender transformation shows that Africans who never crossed the Atlantic were nonetheless materially Atlanticized in the everyday theater of gendered social differentiation, that the realities of the homeland shaped the lives of the enslaved diaspora, and that for both migrating and homeland populations, the experience of the Atlantic was gendered. To make sense of the cultural mutation that birthed the Black Atlantic, one must understand West African dynamics of slave production, particularly the role of gender in the political economy of slaving. The dynamic structure of the Atlantic slave trade, as well as its material culture, reshaped gender identities in West Africa in turn. Postabolition legitimate commerce, Christianization, and colonialism consolidated these processes. West African "Atlantic experiences" were manifest in gender-distinctive sociopolitical practices and embodied by individuals who evinced their identities through shifting gender-identity performances. Such Igbo individuals readjusted their daily livelihood practices between 1750 and 1920, signifying what it meant to be masculine or feminine through female-dominated labor regimes of agrarian production and kinship incorporation; female- and child-focused enslavement practices; and male-dominated long-distance commodity trading, Christian conversion, and colonial collaboration. To differing degrees, both men and women participated in these production mechanisms, redefining dual-sex systems, transforming gender roles, and reinventing dynamic notions of gender and sexuality. Because these historical processes were mutually constitutive, it would be partial to talk about colonialism without slavery and its legacy. Furthermore, these successive Atlantic political economies became fused with preexisting sociopolitical institutions and cultural practices. Therefore, any history of West African individual- and social-identity formation cannot begin with a twentieth-century or protocolonialism ethnographic baseline.

Lastly, the thesis of Atlanticization as a gendering process emphasizes a mutual process: African cultural and economic institutions were used to generate networks, patterns, bodies, and materials of cross-Atlantic exchanges, and African sociopolitical institutions and gender ideologies were transformed as a consequence of domesticating cross-Atlantic materials, markets, and capitalist ideologies through individualized social ascendancy. A prominent image of this Atlantic dialogue is the centrality of Igbo and Eboe women in the patriarchal slavery systems of both Biafra and Jamaica during the late eighteenth and early nineteenth centuries. Another enduring image of this Atlantic *articulation* is the duality that came to define diverse forms of hegemonic masculinity, including merchant-warrior ufiem, slave-owning oke-nwami, and male and female ogaranya: they reconciled capitalist individualistic accumulation with corporate redistribution, in order to gain social legitimacy. They performed their emergent masculinities by translating brutal individual successes into social welfare, transforming and gendering existing institutions in the process. They were not unlike past heroic warriors, who returned with head trophies and danced before the war drums to dramatize the centrality of bravery to community survival in a bellicose frontier, while also amassing the social capital to marginalize and subjugate nonwarriors; and they call to mind those matrifocal practices that underpinned violent slaving but also enabled mutual adaptation within a border zone. In providing microhistories of how the cultural practices and knowledge systems of inland and intracoastal African peoples defined Atlantic modes of production, exchange, consumption, and identity formation, *Emergent Masculinities* contributes to the reorientation of Atlantic history as a sum of its diverse regional currents.

APPENDIX
Lineage Charts

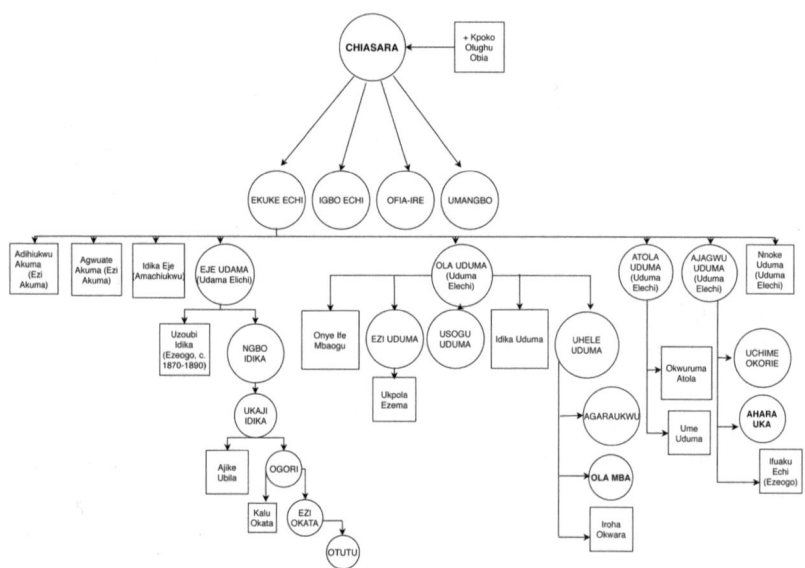

FIGURE A.1. Chiasara matrilineage

192

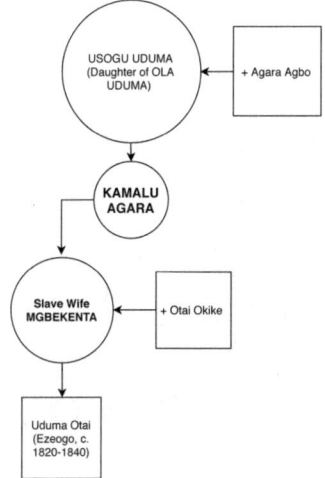

FIGURE A.2. Slave lineage integration I

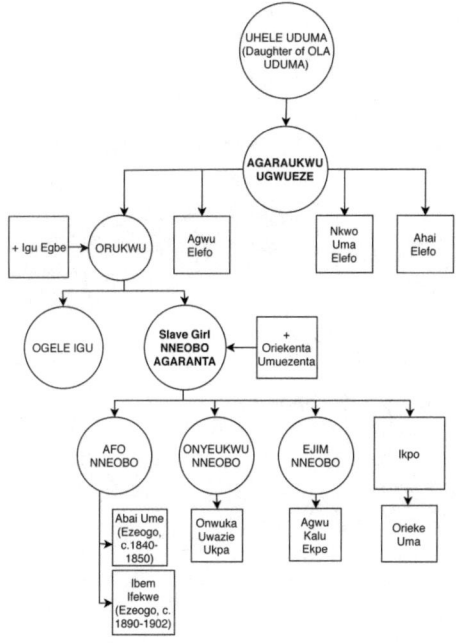

FIGURE A.3. Slave lineage integration II

Lineage Charts ⇌ 193

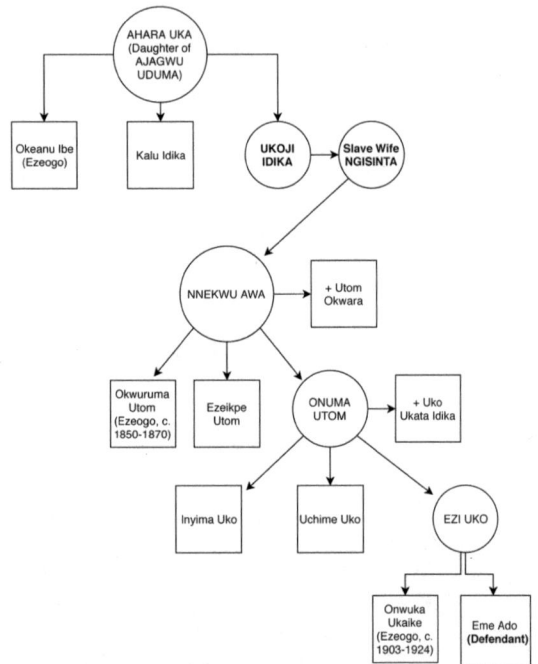

FIGURE A.4. Slave lineage integration III

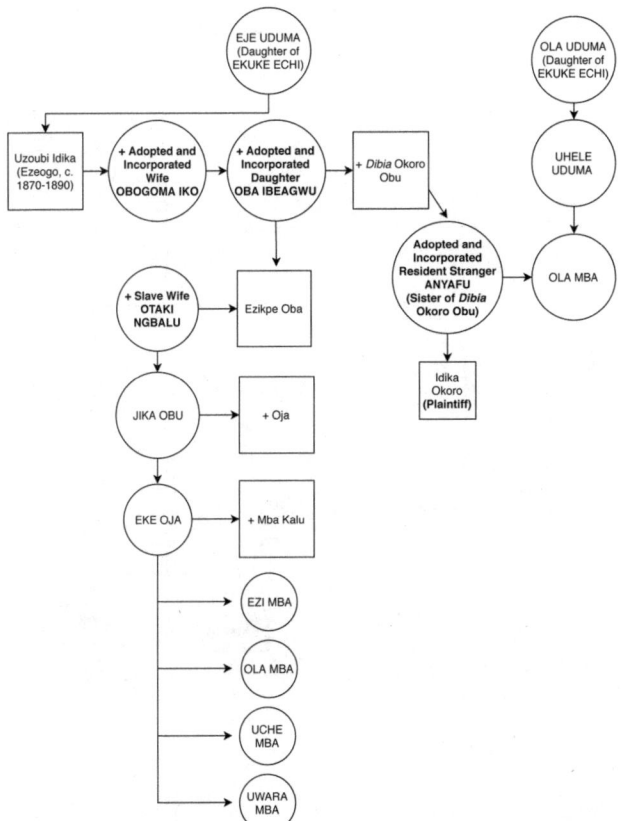

FIGURE A.5. Integration of resident strangers

Lineage Charts

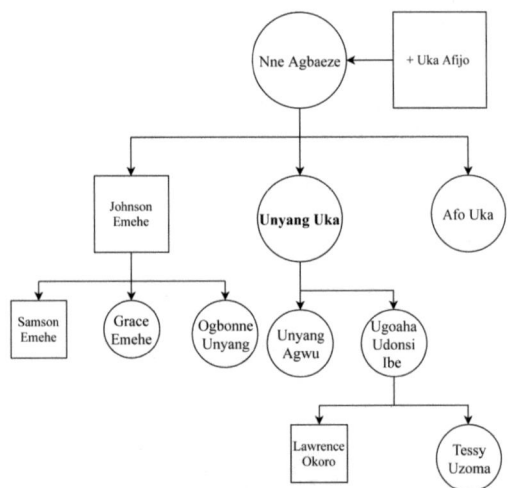

FIGURE A.6. Unyang Uka

Glossary

abu aha	war songs
Akan	male secret society
akpan/umuaka	male court
dibia	medicine men/diviners/spirit mediums
Egbo	patrilineage deity
Ekpe	male secret society
ezie-nwami	female ruler/female king
ezie-nwami ikwu	matriarch of the matrilineage
ezie-ogo	male ruler/male king
Fijoku	yam deity within patrilineage compound
iba mba	warrior's boast
ibiri ikoro	to dance before the ikoro in performance of ufiem accomplishment
ibo ezi	women's collective strike, boycott, and mass desertion of their homes in protest
ichu aja izu Orie	women's ritual inauguration of cultivation
igba nnunu	to kill a hummingbird, and thereby qualify for admission into male age-grades
igbu ishi	to cut a "head," signified ufiem accomplishment
igwa nnu	social performance of the masculinity of yam wealth

ihiwe ududu	to deify a deceased matriarch or ufiem-accomplished individual
ije akpaka	women's ritual sanction of male warfare
ike nwami	to take possession of a woman
ikom	adult male
ikoro	war drum
ikpirikpe ndi inyom	female court
ikpo mgbogho	women's social ostracization and "sitting on a man"
Ikwan	god of war
ikwu	matrilineage
ino nhiha	to undergo first post-menstrual seclusion, and thereby attain adult female status
idoru nna	to deify an ufiem-accomplished individual postmortem
inyom	adult female
iri aha	war dance
ite-odo	secret society of elite warriors
iyi ose	women's ritual purification and social reincorporation of ikpo mgbogho victims
jooji	British-imported Manchester textile
Kamalu	war deity within patrilineage compound
mgbe ichin	olden days
ndi ichin	male and female elders
ndi ikike	warriors
obi	a patriarch's living room
Obon	male secret society
obu	patrilineage meeting house

ochi-udo-eje-ogu	he-that-went-to-war-with-a-rope
ogaranya	wealth masculinity
ogbusua	first among peers to cut a "head"
oke-nwami	female husband
okerenkwa	vivacious warrior's dance accompanying idoru nna
Okonko	male secret society
okpodu	one who single-handedly destroyed a town with fire
Onu-Agba	patrilineage deity
Orie	goddess
osu	spiritual slave
ududu	sex-differentiated ancestral pot monuments
Uduma	goddess of fertility
ufiem	hegemonic masculinity
ujo	degendered male, weak male, coward, victim of ufiem-accomplished peers
uke	age-grade system
uluenta/ulote	boys' living quarters
umerogwu	social performance of spiritual and physical immunity by dibia
umudi	patrilineage
uzo iyi	women-led virginity testing and land purification rite
mgbe ochichi Nna Kalu	in the time of the warrant chieftaincy of Kalu Ezelu (1911–27)
mgbe ogarelu abuo	in the time of the second smallpox epidemic (1918–19)
mgbe ogarelu mbu	in the time of the first smallpox epidemic (1890s)
mgbe uke Emeago	in the time of Emeago Age Grade (1918–1920s)

uso Asaga	in the time of Asaga Exodus (during the 1905–7 Bende hinterland expedition)
uso Lama	in the time of the cattle exodus (c. 1909)

Notes

INTRODUCTION

1. Diana Paton and Pamela Scully, "Introduction: Gender and Slave Emancipation in Comparative Perspective," in *Gender and Slave Emancipation in the Atlantic World*, ed. Diana Paton and Pamela Scully (Durham, NC: Duke University Press, 2005), 4; Michael Zeuske, "Sidney Mintz: Work, Creolization, Atlanticization," *Review* (Fernand Braudel Center) 34, no. 4 (2011): 423–28; Neil L. Norman, "An Archaeology of West African Atlanticization: Regional Analysis of the Huedan Palace Districts and Countryside (Benin), 1650–1727," *African Diaspora Archaeology Newsletter* 12, no. 2 (2009): 27.

2. Also, see Emily Lynn Osborn, *Our New Husbands Are Here: Households, Gender, and Politics in a West African State from the Slave Trade to Colonial Rule* (Athens: Ohio University Press, 2011), 74–91; G. Ugo Nwokeji, *The Slave Trade and Culture in the Bight of Biafra: An African Society in the Atlantic World* (Cambridge: Cambridge University Press, 2010), 73, 79, 178–79; John Oriji, *Political Organization in Nigeria since the Late Stone Age: A History of the Igbo People* (New York: Palgrave Macmillan, 2011), 142–45; Patrick Manning, *Slavery and African Life: Occidental, Oriental, and African Slave Trades* (Cambridge: Cambridge University Press, 1990); Richard L. Roberts, *Warriors, Merchants, and Slaves: The State and the Economy in the Middle Niger Valley, 1700–1914* (Stanford: Stanford University Press, 1987); Raphael Chijoke Njoku, "'Ogaranya' (Wealthy Men) in Late Nineteenth Century Igboland: Chief Igwebe Odum of Arondizuogu, c. 1860–1940," *African Economic History*, no. 36 (2008): 27–52.

3. Pierre Bourdieu, *Outline of a Theory of Practice* (Cambridge: Cambridge University Press, 1977), 79; Pierre Bourdieu and Alan C. M. Ross, *The Algerians* (Boston: Beacon, 1962), 111. Describing a situation when an idiom has gained a life of its own and become a superstructure, Bourdieu defines *habitus* as unconscious practices of social reproduction, continually shaped by individuals' social encounters and agency and sustained through symbolic representation. Habitus denotes "a system of choices which no one makes." Also, see Paulla Ebron, "Constituting Subjects through Performative Acts," in

Africa after Gender?, ed. Catherine Cole, Takyiwaa Manuh, and Stephan F. Miescher (Bloomington: Indiana University Press, 2007), 171–87.

4. Ndubueze L. Mbah, "Matriliny, Masculinity, and Contested Gendered Definitions of Ethnic Identity and Power in Nineteenth-Century Southeastern Nigeria," in *Gendering Ethnicity in African Women's Lives*, ed. Jan Bender Shetler (Madison: University of Wisconsin Press, 2015), 233–64.

5. Toby Green, *The Rise of the Trans-Atlantic Slave Trade in Western Africa, 1300–1589* (Cambridge: Cambridge University Press, 2012), 13, 21.

6. For the original formulation, see David Armitage, "Three Concepts of Atlantic History" in *The British Atlantic World, 1500–1800*, ed. David Armitage and Michael J. Braddock (New York: Palgrave Macmillan, 2002), 11–27. For a circum-Atlantic example see James Sweet, *Domingos Álvares, African Healing, and the Intellectual History of the Atlantic World* (Chapel Hill: University of North Carolina Press, 2011), 1–8. For transatlantic examples, see Roquinaldo Ferreira, *Cross-Cultural Exchange in the Atlantic World: Angola and Brazil during the Era of the Slave Trade* (New York: Cambridge University Press, 2012); Walter Hawthorne, *From Africa to Brazil: Culture, Identity, and an Atlantic Slave Trade, 1600–1830* (New York: Cambridge University Press, 2010); Judith Carney, *Black Rice: The African Origins of Rice Cultivation in the Americas* (Cambridge, MA: Harvard University Press, 2001). For cis-Atlantic examples see Robin Law, *Ouidah: The Social History of a West African Slaving Port, 1727–1892* (Oxford: James Currey, 2004); Mariana P. Candido, *An African Slaving Port and the Atlantic World: Benguela and Its Hinterland* (Cambridge: Cambridge University Press, 2013); Nwokeji, *Slave Trade and Culture*; Kristin Mann, *Slavery and the Birth of an African City: Lagos, 1760–1900* (Bloomington: Indiana University Press, 2007). Some scholars have expanded the cultural approach to Atlantic histories to comparative surveys of the broad cultures of the Atlantic basins of Europe, Africa, and America. See John K. Thornton, *A Cultural History of the Atlantic World, 1250–1820* (New York: Cambridge University Press, 2012); Robert S. DuPlessis, *The Material Atlantic: Clothing, Commerce, and Colonization in the Atlantic World, 1650–1800* (Cambridge: Cambridge University Press, 2016).

7. According to Sandra Greene, for example, the Anlo of the Gold Coast region embraced the Atlantic slave trade because the acquisition of numerous female slaves was a principal adaptive mechanism that prosperous Anlo households used as their society's patrilineal inheritance system transformed to matrilineal following Akwamu conquest in the eighteenth century. Sandra E. Greene, *Gender, Ethnicity, and Social Change on the Upper Slave Coast: A History of the Anlo-Ewe* (Portsmouth, NH: Heinemann, 1996), 20–47.

8. Nwokeji, *Slave Trade and Culture*, 9–11, 114, 159.

9. Walter Hawthorne, *Planting Rice and Harvesting Slaves: Transformations along the Guinea-Bissau Coast, 1400–1900* (Portsmouth, NH: Heinemann, 2003), 141.

10. Candido, *An African Slaving Port*, 320.

11. Judith Van Allen, "'Sitting on a Man': Colonialism and the Lost Political Institutions of Igbo Women," *Canadian Journal of African Studies* 6, no. 2 (1972): 165–78; Kamene Okonjo, "The Dual Sex Political System in Operation: Igbo Women and Community Politics in Midwestern Nigeria," in *Women in Africa: Studies in Social and Economic Change*, ed. Nancy Hafkin and Edna Bay (Stanford: Stanford University Press, 1976), 46–56. Other scholars show that some Igbo women dominated local economies until the colonial period. See Chima Korieh, "The Invisible Farmer? Women, Gender, and Colonial Agricultural Policy in the Igbo Region of Nigeria, c. 1913–1954," *African Economic History*, no. 29 (2001): 117–62; Adiele E. Afigbo, "Women in Nigerian History," in *Women in Nigerian Economy*, ed. Martin O. Ijere (Enugu: Acena, 1991), 35–36; Gloria Chuku, "From Petty Traders to International Merchants: A Historical Account of Three Igbo Women of Nigeria in Trade and Commerce, 1886–1970," *African Economic History*, no. 27 (1999): 1–22; Gloria Chuku, "Women in the Economy of Igboland, 1900–1970: A Survey," *African Economic History*, no. 23 (1995): 37–50; Felicia I. Ekejiuba, "Omu Okwei, the Merchant Queen of Ossomari: A Biographical Sketch," *Journal of the Historical Society of Nigeria* 3, no. 4 (1967): 633–46; Nwando Achebe, *Farmers, Traders, Warriors and Kings: Female Power and Authority in Northern Igboland, 1900–1960* (Portsmouth, NH: Heinemann, 2005), 109–60, 178.

12. Oriji, *Political Organization*, 13–20.

13. Nwokeji, *Slave Trade and Culture*, 84.

14. The Atlantic slave trade funneled African labor to the Americas for the generation of cash crops for European manufactures. So-called legitimate trade entailed the abolition of the international slave trade and the conscious promotion of domestic slavery in West Africa to generate cash crops for European industries. Colonialism, or "effective occupation," signaled a hands-on European coercive supervision of African labor regimes in addition to taxation.

15. J. F. A. Ajayi, "The Continuity of African Institutions under Colonialism," in *Emerging Themes of African History*, ed. T. O. Ranger (Dar es Salaam: East African Publishing House, 1968), 194.

16. Osborn, *Our New Husbands Are Here*, 185.

17. Osborn, 49–112. Because men dominated households, they also dominated the state that emerged from households.

18. The export of enslaved persons from Akwamu-dominated ports to the markets of the Americas assumed growing importance in the 1690s, its value being roughly equivalent to the export value of gold and ivory. Slave export continued to increase steadily into the 1720s. Akwamu slaving and imperial expansion forced refugees into Anlo and placed considerable pressure on arable land. Therefore, from the seventeenth century, Anlo men exploited the slave trade and, later, British colonialism to impose successive limits on the rights of women to marry, participate in political decision-making processes, farm

and inherit land, and participate in the fishing industry. Anlo Atlanticization epitomized women as lineage property (wives), concubines, and slave-wives. Greene, *Gender, Ethnicity, and Social Change*, 5–6, 16, 48–78, 79–107, 136–80. Also, Kwameh Anthony Appiah, and Henry Louis Gates Jr., eds., *Encyclopedia of Africa* (Oxford: Oxford University Press, 2010), 78; Ivor Wilks, *Akwamu 1640–1750: A Study of the Rise and Fall of a West African Empire* (Trondheim: Norwegian University of Science and Technology, Department of History, 2001).

19. Edna G. Bay, *Wives of the Leopard: Gender, Politics, and Culture in the Kingdom of Dahomey* (Charlottesville: University of Virginia Press, 1998).

20. For such existing scholarship, see Robin Horton, "From Fishing Village to City-State: A Social History of New Calabar," in Douglas and Kaberry, *Man in Africa*; Ivor Wilks, "Land, Labour, Capital and the Forest Kingdom of Asante: A Model of Early Change," in Friendman and Rowland, *The Evolution of Social Systems*; Jane Guyer, "Household and Community in African Studies," *African Studies Review*, 24, no. 2/3 (1981): 87–138; Jeff Guy, "Gender Oppression in Southern Africa's Precapitalist Societies," in *Women and Gender in Southern Africa to 1945*, ed. Cherryl Walker (Claremont, South Africa: David Philip, 1990); Elizabeth Schmidt, *Peasants, Traders and Wives: Shona Women in the History of Zimbabwe, 1870–1939* (Portsmouth, NH: Heinemann, 1992); Nakanyinke Musisi, "Women, 'Elite Polygyny,' and Buganda State Formation," *Signs* 16, no. 4 (1991): 757–86; T. C. McCaskie, "State and Society, Marriage and Adultery: Some Considerations towards a Social History of Pre-Colonial Asante," *Journal of African History* 22, no. 4 (1981): 477–94; Simi Afonja, "Changing Modes of Production and the Sexual Division of Labor among the Yoruba," *Signs* 7, no. 2 (Winter 1981): 299–313; Simi Afonja, "Land Control: A Critical Factor in Yoruba Gender Stratification," in *Women and Class in Africa*, ed. Claire Robertson and Iris Berger (New York: Holmes and Meier, 1986), 78–91; Edward A. Alpers, "State, Merchant Capital and Gender Relations in Southern Mozambique to the End of the 19th Century: Some Tentative Hypotheses," *African Economic History*, no. 13 (1984): 23–55; Edward A. Alpers, "'Ordinary Household Chores': Ritual and Power in a 19th-Century Swahili Women's Spirit Possession Cult," *International Journal of African Historical Studies* 17, no. 4 (1984): 677–702; Elizabeth Eldredge, "Women in Production: The Economic Role of Women in Nineteenth-Century Lesotho," *Signs* 16, no. 4 (Summer 1991): 707–31.

21. See Achebe, *Farmers*; Nwando Achebe, *The Female King of Colonial Nigeria: Ahebi Ugbabe* (Bloomington: Indiana University Press, 2011); Stephan F. Miescher, *Making Men in Ghana* (Bloomington: Indiana University Press, 2005).

22. Lisa A. Lindsay and Stephan F. Miescher, eds., *Men and Masculinities in Modern Africa* (Portsmouth, NH: Heinemann, 2003); Robert Morrell and Lahoucine Ouzgane, eds., *African Masculinities: Men in Africa from the Late Nineteenth Century to the Present* (New York: Palgrave Macmillan, 2005).

Robert Morrell and Lahoucine Ouzgane observed that much of African feminist scholarship had come to deal with gender but ignored men, such that while a great deal of attention was given to womanhood and motherhood, there was no equivalent discussion of manhood and fatherhood. Luise White and Meredith McKittrick examine male domesticity and fatherhood in East Africa and Southern Africa: Luise White, afterword to *Men and Masculinities*, ed. Lindsay and Miescher, 177–89; Meredith McKittrick, "Forsaking Their Fathers? Colonialism, Christianity, and Coming of Age in Ovamboland, Northern Namibia," in Lindsay and Miescher, *Men and Masculinities*, 33–47.

23. Ifi Amadiume, *Male Daughters, Female Husbands: Gender and Sex in an African Society* (London: Zed Books, 1989). Amadiume forced West African gender studies to examine the historical processes through which women and men's gender identities came to be constituted in the precolonial period. Her emphasis on shifts in gender regimes is also evident in Gracia Clark's and Barbara Cooper's social histories of how West African women of Kumasi and Maradi, respectively, responded to the cumulative social changes of the Atlantic Age. In both cases, women mobilized precolonial lineage-based sociopolitical institutions to monopolize spaces of economic production, pursue gender-based resource accumulation, and challenge colonial patriarchal structures. See Gracia Clark, *Onions Are My Husband: Survival and Accumulation by West African Market Women* (Chicago: University of Chicago Press, 1994); Barbara Cooper, *Marriage in Maradi: Gender and Culture in a Hausa Society in Niger, 1900–1989* (Portsmouth, NH: Heinemann, 1997). Furthermore, *Male Daughters and Female Husbands* inspired the study of West African female masculinities of the twentieth century. See Nwando Achebe, "'And She Became a Man': King Ahebi Ugbabe in the History of Enugu-Ezike, Northern Igboland, 1880–1948," in Lindsay and Miescher, *Men and Masculinities*, 52–68; Ndubueze L. Mbah, "Female Masculinities, Dissident Sexuality, and the Material Politics of Gender in Early Twentieth-Century Igboland," *Journal of Women's History* 29, no. 4 (Winter 2017): 35–60.

24. Robert Morrell, "Of Boys and Men: Masculinity and Gender in Southern Africa," *Journal of Southern African Studies* 24, no. 4 (1998): 605.

25. For the evolution of this concept, see Victor Uchendu, *The Igbo of Southeastern Nigeria* (New York: Holt, Rinehart, and Winston, 1965), 14; John McCall, "Portrait of a Brave Woman," *American Anthropologist* 98, no. 1 (1996): 127–36; Miescher, *Making Men in Ghana*, 8–13.

26. Sean Stilwell, *Slavery and Slaving in African History* (Cambridge: Cambridge University Press, 2014), 64.

27. Martin Klein, "Slavery and the Early State in Africa," *Social Evolution and History* 8, no. 1 (2009): 171–72.

28. Joseph C. Miller, *Way of Death: Merchant Capitalism and the Angolan Slave Trade, 1730–1830* (Madison: University of Wisconsin Press, 1988), 47–48.

29. Stilwell, *Slavery and Slaving in African History*, 67.

30. Joseph C. Miller, "Domiciled and Dominated: Slaving as a History of Women," in *Women and Slavery*, ed. Gwyn Campbell, Suzanne Miers, and Joseph C. Miller, vol. 2, *The Modern Atlantic* (Athens: Ohio University Press, 2008), 287–88; Moses Finley, "Slavery," in *International Encyclopedia of the Social Sciences*, ed. David L. Sills and Robert K. Merton (New York: Macmillan, 1968), 14:307–13. Elsewhere, in the case of Sokoto royal slavery, Stilwell argues that African slaves were not always socially isolated and kinless outsiders but rather were able to construct family networks and take advantage of court politics to contest the terms of their subjugation as well as gain access to and redefine the political and social system of the dominant aristocratic culture. Sean Stilwell, *Paradoxes of Power: The Kano "Mamluks" and Male Royal Slavery in the Sokoto Caliphate, 1804–1903* (Portsmouth, NH: Heinemann, 2004). For a similar argument, see Jonathan Glassman, *Feasts and Riot: Revelry, Rebellion, and Popular Consciousness on the Swahili Coast, 1865–1888* (Portsmouth, NH: Heinemann, 1995); Jonathan Glassman, "The Bondsman's New Clothes: The Contradictory Consciousness of Slave Resistance on the Swahili Coast," *Journal of African History* 32, no. 2 (1991): 277–312.

31. Stilwell, *Slavery and Slaving in African History*, 49.

32. For *marabouts* see Assan Sarr, *Islam, Power, and Dependency in the Gambia River Basin: The Politics of Land Control, 1790–1940* (New York: University of Rochester Press, 2016). For Biafran merchants see Ekejiuba, "Omu Okwei, the Merchant Queen of Ossomari." For Gold Coast slave owners see Sandra E. Greene, *Slave Owners of West Africa: Decision Making in the Age of Abolition* (Bloomington: Indiana University Press, 2017). For Saro evangelists see J. D. Y. Peel, *Religious Encounter and the Making of the Yoruba* (Bloomington: Indiana University Press, 2003). For Yoruba male breadwinners see Lisa Lindsay, *Working With Gender: Wage Labor and Social Change in Southwestern Nigeria* (Portsmouth, NH: Heinemann, 2003); Lisa A. Lindsay, "Money, Marriage, and Masculinity on the Colonial Nigerian Railway," in Lindsay and Miescher, *Men and Masculinities*, 138–55. For Presbyterian masculinities see Stephan Miescher, "The Making of Presbyterian Teachers: Masculinities and Programs of Education in Colonial Ghana," in Lindsay and Miescher, *Men and Masculinities*, 89–108. For warrant chiefs and the female king, respectively, see Adiele E. Afigbo, *The Warrant Chiefs: Indirect Rule in Southeastern Nigeria* (London: Longman, 1972); and Achebe, *Female King*.

33. Stilwell, *Slavery and Slaving in African History*, 53, 55.

34. Van Allen, "'Sitting on a Man,'" 165–71; Amadiume, *Male Daughters, Female Husbands*, 15–28. An early affirmation of an Igbo gender-complementary or dual-sex sociopolitical system came from Rev. J. C. Taylor's 1865 journal on the Niger Expedition. See Samuel A. Crowther and Christopher J. Taylor, *The Gospel on the Banks of the Niger: Journals and Notices of the Native Missionaries accompanying the Niger Expedition of*

1857–1859 (London: Dawsons, 1868), 266. Later, in the first historical study of Igbo women, following the Igbo Women's War of 1929, Sylvia Leith-Ross observed that Igbo women were "economically and politically . . . the equal of the men" and "because of their economic importance both as mothers, farm cultivators, and traders, [they] have rather more power than is generally thought." See Sylvia Leith-Ross, *African Women: A Study of the Ibo of Nigeria* (London: Faber and Faber, 1938), 21.

35. It was in this sense that Victor Turner argued that Ndembu men of Zambia transformed hunting into a highly masculinized political economy, in order to leverage the inequalities inherent in matrilineal descent and women's socioeconomic control. See Victor Turner, *Schism and Continuity in an African Society: A Study of Ndembu Village Life* (London: Manchester University Press, 1957), 230, 242–43. The cultural template of masculinization of sociopolitical institutions in order to leverage women's sociopolitical salience shaped the ways that Ohafia-Igbo male society adapted to the economic and political opportunities presented by the slave trade, legitimate commerce, Christianity, and British colonialism.

36. The cultural and institutional foundations, regional adaptations, and demographic impact of Ohafia military slaving reinforce the literature critical of the predatory state thesis. See Walter Rodney, "African Slavery and Other Forms of Social Oppression on the Upper Guinea Coast in the Context of the Atlantic Slave-Trade," *Journal of African History* 7, no. 3 (1966): 434; Walter Rodney, *A History of the Upper Guinea Coast, 1545 to 1800* (Oxford: Oxford University Press), 109; Jack Goody, *Tradition, Technology, and the State in Africa* (Oxford: Oxford University Press, 1971); Philip Curtin, *Economic Change in Precolonial Africa: Senegambia in the Era of the Slave Trade* (Madison: University of Wisconsin Press, 1975); Joseph P. Smaldone, *Warfare in the Sokoto Caliphate: Historical and Sociological Perspectives* (Cambridge: Cambridge University Press, 1977); I. A. Akinjogbin, *Dahomey and Its Neighbors, 1708–1818* (Cambridge: Cambridge University Press, 1977); J. D. Fage, "Slavery and the Slave Trade in the Context of West African History," *Journal of African History* 10, no. 3 (1969): 393–404; J. D. Fage, "African Societies and the Atlantic Slave Trade," *Past and Present*, no. 125 (1989): 106–11; A. A. Boahen, "New Trends and Processes in Africa in the Nineteenth Century," in *General History of Africa*, ed. J. F. Ade Ajayi, vol. 6, *Africa in the Nineteenth Century until 1880s* (Oxford: Heinemann International, 1989), 40–63; Patrick Manning, *Slavery and African Life: Occidental, Oriental, and African Slave Trades* (Cambridge: Cambridge University Press, 1990); B. Barry, *Senegambia and the Atlantic Slave Trade* (Cambridge: Cambridge University Press, 1998), 107; Paul Lovejoy, *Transformations in Slavery: A History of Slavery in Africa*, 2nd. ed. (Cambridge: Cambridge University Press, 2000), xv, 68–69, 84–65, 103–4, 126–28, 148, 182–84, 188–89; John K. Thornton, *Africa and Africans in the Making of the Atlantic World, 1400–1680* (Cambridge: Cambridge University Press, 1992); Martin Klein, "The

Impact of the Atlantic Slave Trade on the Societies of the Western Sudan," *Journal of African History* 42, no. 1 (2001): 234–35, 237–39; Rosalind Shaw, *Memories of the Slave Trade: Ritual and the Historical Imagination in Sierra Leone* (Chicago: University of Chicago Press, 2002), 207, 213–16. For challenges to the predatory state thesis, see Richard L. Roberts, "Production and Reproduction of Warrior States: Segu Bambara and Segu Tokolor, c. 1712–1890," *International Journal of African Historical Studies* 13, no. 3 (1980): 393; Robert Baum, *Shrines of the Slave Trade: Diola Religion and Society in Precolonial Senegambia* (New York: Oxford University Press, 1999), 111, 123–24; Andrew Hubbell, "A View of the Slave Trade from the Margin: Souroudougou in the Late Nineteenth-Century Slave Trade of the Niger Bend," *Journal of African History* 42, no. 1 (2001): 32; Walter Hawthorne, *Planting Rice and Harvesting Slaves: Transformations along the Guinea-Bissau Coast, 1400–1900* (Portsmouth, NH: Heinemann, 2003); Martin Klein, "The Atlantic Slave Trade and Decentralized Societies," *Journal of African History* 42, no. 1 (2001): 49–65.

37. G. Ugo Nwokeji, "African Conceptions of Gender and the Slave Traffic," *William and Mary Quarterly* 58, no. 1 (January 2001): 53–65; Elizabeth Donnan, *Documents Illustrative of the History of the Slave Trade to America*, vol. 4, *The Border Colonies and the Southern Colonies* (1935; repr., New York: Octagon Books, 1969), 176–234; Walter Minchinton, Celia King, and Peter Waite, eds., *Virginia Slave-Trade Statistics, 1698–1775* (Richmond: Virginia State Library, 1985); Philip Curtin, *The Atlantic Slave Trade: A Census* (Madison: University of Wisconsin Press, 1969), 156–58; A. Kulikoff, *Tobacco and Slaves: The Development of Southern Cultures in the Chesapeake, 1680–1800* (Chapel Hill: University of North Carolina Press, 1986), 320–22; Michael Gomez, *Exchanging Our Country Marks: The Transformation of African Identities in the Colonial and Antebellum South* (Chapel Hill: University of North Carolina Press, 1998), 115; Douglas B. Chambers, "The Significance of Igbo in the Bight of Biafra Slave-Trade: A Rejoinder to Northrup's 'Myth Igbo,'" *Slavery and Abolition* 23, no. 1 (2002): 104.

38. Sasha Turner, *Contested Bodies: Pregnancy, Childrearing, and Slavery in Jamaica* (Philadelphia: University of Pennsylvania Press, 2017); Michael Mullin, *Africa in America: Slave Acculturation and Resistance in the American South and the British Caribbean* (Urbana: University of Illinois Press, 1992), 26; Nwokeji, *Slave Trade and Culture*, 47–49.

39. Jennifer Morgan, *Laboring Women: Reproduction and Gender in New World Slavery* (Philadelphia: University of Pennsylvania Press, 2004), 6.

40. Gwendolyn Hall, *Slavery and African Ethnicities in the Americas: Restoring the Links* (Chapel Hill: University of North Carolina Press, 2005), 141–43.

41. Hugh Crow, *Memoirs of the Late Captain Hugh Crow of Liverpool* [. . .] (Liverpool: Longman, Rees, Orme, Brown, and Green, 1830), 197–99.

42. Douglas B. Chambers, *Murder at Montpelier: Igbo Africans in Virginia* (Jackson: University Press of Mississippi, 2005), 3–71; Michael Gomez, "A Quality of Anguish: The Igbo Response to Enslavement in the Americas," in *Trans-Atlantic Dimensions of Ethnicity in the African Diaspora*, ed. Paul E. Lovejoy and David V. Trotman (New York: Continuum, 2003), 84; Douglas B. Chambers, "Tracing Igbo into the African Diaspora," in *Identity in the Shadow of Slavery: The Black Atlantic*, ed. Paul Lovejoy (New York: Continuum, 2000), 55–66; Damian A. Pargas, "Slave Crucibles: Interstate Migrants and Social Assimilation in the Antebellum South," *Slavery and Abolition* 36, no. 1 (2015): 26–39.

43. See Douglas B. Chambers, "'My Own Nation': Igbo Exiles in the Diaspora," in *Routes to Slavery: Direction, Ethnicity and Mortality in the Atlantic Slave Trade*, ed. David Eltis and David Richardson (London: Frank Cass, 1997), 73–75; Michael Mullin, "Laura Smalligan's Jonkonu, a Jamaican Slave Dance: Contesting the African in African-American," *Slavery and Abolition* 35, no. 1 (2015): 146; Laura M. Smalligan, "An Effigy for the Enslaved: Jonkonnu in Jamaica and Ballisario's *Sketches of Character*," *Slavery and Abolition* 32, no. 4 (2011): 561–81.

44. Turner, *Contested Bodies*, 61–62.

45. Marianne C. Ferme, *The Underneath of Things: Violence, History, and the Everyday in Sierra Leone* (Berkeley: University of California Press, 2001), 6, 18–19, 165, 226.

46. Some of the precolonial traditions and sociopolitical systems were documented by colonial anthropological reports and appear in other secondary literature. Some scholars share the opinion of G. I. Jones that traditions referring to the distant past "cannot help us. They are no substitute for history and are best regarded as a system in which [a] very limited number of items are manipulated to explain or justify existing institutions and social groups." Adiele Afigbo has shown that the implication of this viewpoint for historians working among segmentary societies would be "complete paralysis." He suggested that instead, one should not ask questions of oral traditions that they cannot answer. See G. I. Jones, *The Trading States of the Oil Rivers* (Oxford: Oxford University Press, 1963), 24; Adiele E. Afigbo, "Oral Tradition and the History of Segmentary Societies," *History in Africa*, no. 12 (1985): 3–9.

47. For an example, see Green, *The Rise of the Trans-Atlantic Slave Trade*, 31–68.

48. Ezie-nwami Ucha Oji Iwe and her cabinet, interview by author, Elu Village, October 25, 2011.

49. Jan Vansina, *Oral Tradition as History* (Madison: University of Wisconsin Press, 1985), 40.

50. Janice Boddy, *Wombs and Alien Spirits: Women, Men, and the Zar Cult in Northern Sudan* (Madison: University of Wisconsin Press, 1989), 4–5.

51. Male elders of Umu-Anya, Ndi Imaga Patrilineage, interview by author, Elu Village, August 14, 2011.

52. This work of cultural adaptation and transformation through practice is what Franz Boas called the "genius of the people." See F. Boas, "Fieldwork for the British Association, 1888–1897," in *The Shaping of American Anthropology, 1833-1911: A Franz Boas Reader*, ed. G. W. Stocking Jr. (1899; repr., Chicago: University of Chicago Press, 1974), 97. Also, see L. L. Langness, *The Study of Culture* (Novato, CA: Chandler and Sharp, 2005), 22; Claude Lévi-Strauss, *Structural Anthropology* (New York: Basic Books, 1976), 2:4; Adam Kuper, *Anthropology and Anthropologists: The Modern British School* (London: Routledge, 1996), 47–48; A. R. Radcliffe-Brown, *A Natural Science of Society* (Chicago: University of Chicago Press, 1957), 45, 55. Similarly, Frederick Cooper, "Conflict and Connection: Rethinking Colonial African History," *American Historical Review* 99, no. 5 (December 1994): 1535, 1544, has observed that African individuals were remaking the meanings of institutions even as they used them.

53. Nnenna E. Obuba, *The History and Culture of Ohafia, covering from about 1432 to 2008: Collated Oral Tradition* (Ohafia, Nigeria: Lintdsons, 2008), 50.

54. Against this background, the commemorative ritual of uzo iyi assumes a greater significance: it reinforces the matrilineage as an essential historic corporate group, battling the pressures of modern individualistic capitalist accumulation and masculinist political power.

55. Chukwuma Azuonye, "The Narrative War Songs of the Ohafia Igbo: A Critical Analysis of Their Characteristic Features in Relation to their Social Functions" (PhD thesis, University of London, 1979); John C. McCall, *Dancing Histories: Heuristic Ethnography with the Ohafia Igbo* (Ann Arbor: University of Michigan Press, 2000).

56. D. T. Niane, *Sundiata: An Epic of Old Mali*, rev. ed. (Harlow, Eng.: Pearson, 2006); Azuonye, "Narrative War Songs," 55–73.

57. Broadly speaking, West African indigenous knowledge systems represent historical chronology in terms of "event systems" such as "the period of migration and settlement," "the period of the Atlantic slave trade," "the period of legitimate trade," and "the period of Christianization and colonialism" as opposed to Western-oriented time-specific dates. Ohafia traditions follow this trend (accounting for environmental, political, and sociological changes).

58. Azuonye, "Narrative War Songs," 93, 101–6.

59. Azuonye, 50–52. Also, Philip O. Nsugbe, *Ohaffia: A Matrilineal Igbo People* (Oxford: Oxford University Press, 1974), 34. They argue that the Ohafia narrative war songs were the principal channel through which Ohafia cultural traditions and ideals of personal success and veneration of heroic ancestors were transmitted to younger generations, inspiring them to emulate the example of their forebears. Through constant performance, the war songs became philosophical traditions and expressions of Ohafia identity and history.

60. In the tradition of Egbele, which chronicles how the woman Nne Ugoenyi invented the war songs, the heroic deeds of her son Egbele, on which

the war songs were founded, included these: "He killed and chopped off the head of a young man, and he captured one man and slung him across his shoulders. He carried him thus, proudly, proudly, and returned to Ebem [Ohafia]." See "Text 42: Egbele B1," in Azuonye, "Narrative War Songs," 490–94.

61. Azuonye, "Narrative War Songs," 81. Tradition singers begin with personifying lyrical lament, and the audience responds in chorus. Having thus introduced the heroic subject, they invoke him as a mythological character by singing his praise names and summarizing his heroic deeds. This heroic poetry interrupts the middle of the narrative and concludes the narrative. The repetitive epithet helps create a magnified picture of the hero. The main narrative delineates the outlines of the story using a formulaic motif of fable. Namely, there is a problem of common concern; the community rallies their resources to solve it; after repeated efforts, they fail; but at the nadir of hope, help comes from an unexpected source; and the problem is solved. This formulaic narrative is applied to incidents of communal defense, as well as military slaving.

62. Ohafia warriors organized as raiding bands as opposed to large-scale military operations, and warriors violated heroic codes of honor by slaving within kinship zones, engaging in slave raids as Aro mercenaries in exchange for Atlantic commodities, and conducting kidnapping raids.

63. Izuogu's mother originated from Elu Ohafia, and members of a matrilineage fulfilled the role of father and protector to the children of matrilineage daughters. Izuogu was a very ugly man of Aro patrilineage descent. While he was passing through Ora en route to his maternal home in Elu Ohafia, Ora people taunted Izuogu. When he arrived in Elu, he narrated his humiliation. To avenge the insult of their son, Elu summoned Ohafia warriors and ravaged the Ora community. In this tradition, the Ora are represented as leopards, which Ohafia warriors slew and bequeathed their skins to the kings of Aro to use as a symbol of their power.

64. Similarly, the tradition of Ogbaka Okorie justifies Ohafia military raids against Igbo and Ibibio communities as vengeance because these communities threatened the well-being of Ohafia traditional institutions, epitomized in the war dancers themselves. See "Text 50: Ogbaka Okorie," in Azuonye, "Narrative War Songs," 85, 507–9.

65. One tradition singer, six warrior-dancers, and three musicians performing with three pairs of elephant ribs, one long drum, and a "talking" antelope horn accompany the leader carrying the human skulls. Preparatory battle songs accompany the scene of warriors proceeding to the village square with their war weapons; operational battle songs complement dramatizations of actual battles; celebratory battle songs inaugurate the warriors' return to the village war drum before which war trophies (human heads and slaves) are presented; and invocative war songs accompany postbattle purification ceremonies. See Azuonye, "Narrative War Songs," 65–67, 70. Ritualistic in tone and

characterized by praise-naming, invocating ancestors, and exorcising cowardice, the invocative war songs are like the Zulu praise poems or the Akan royal poetry. See Leroy Vail and Landeg White, eds. *Power and the Praise Poem: Southern African Voices in History* (Charlottesville: University of Virginia Press, 1991); Kwesi Yankah, *Speaking for the Chief: Akyeame and the Politics of Akan Royal Oratory* (Bloomington: Indiana University Press, 1995).

66. Because present-day manifestations of ufiem are synced with historical precedents in the war dance, the past and present become interpermeable, experience is structured, and history is reconstituted. Through the war dance, writes McCall, "men link their sense of personhood, masculinity, and their somatic knowledge of themselves with a continuum of experience that extends beyond individuals to encompass a corpus of ancestral knowledge." Chukwuma Azuonye, "The Heroic Age of the Ohafia Igbo," *Genève-Afrique* 28, no. 1 (1990): 23; McCall, *Dancing Histories*, 63 (quote), 73–75.

67. I examine Foreign Office (FO) 84, Slave Trade and General Correspondence before 1906, Bight of Biafra (Files 775, 816, 858, 886, 920, 950, 975, 1001, 1030, 1061, 1087, 1117, 1278, 1377, 1634, 1659–61, 1701–2, 1749, 1750, 1881, 1882, 1940, 1941, 2020, 2109–11, 2194); FO881, Confidential Prints; FO541, Confidential Print, Slave Trade Abolition; and FO2, General Correspondence before 1906, Niger Coast Protectorate. See bibliography. For analyses of Ohafia intercoastal trade, see Ogbu U. Kalu, "The River Highway: Christianizing the Igbo," in *A Century and Half of Presbyterian Witness in Nigeria, 1846–1996*, ed. Ogbu U. Kalu (Lagos: Ida-Ivory Press, 1996), 50; Onwuka Njoku, *Inter-Village Trade in Ohafia, 1900–1979* (Nsukka: University of Nigeria, 1981), 11; Onwuka Njoku, *Ohafia: A Heroic Igbo Society* (Ohafia, Nigeria: Whytam, 2000), 47–52; Azuonye, "Narrative War Songs"; Azuonye, "The Heroic Age," 9; Nsugbe, *Ohaffia*, 1–20; John N. Oriji, *Traditions of Igbo Origin: A Study of Pre-colonial Population Movements in Africa*, rev. ed. (New York: Peter Lang, 1994), 32.

68. See Crowther and Taylor, *Gospel on the Banks of the Niger*; "Journal of the Calabar Mission of the United Presbyterian Church, kept by the Reverend Hope M Waddell," 1846–1856, Foreign Mission Records of the Scottish Presbyterian Churches, MSSS.7739–43, MS.8953, National Library of Scotland (NLS); Crowther to Baylis, October 5, 1903, G8/A/0, Church Missionary Society (CMS) Archives; "Church of Scotland Mission Abiriba," UMDIV 3/1/98, Nigerian National Archives Enugu (NAE); "Southern Nigeria Dispatches No. 238. Conf. Report, 24/5/1905," ESO 1/13, Nigerian National Archives Ibadan (NAI); "Calabar Mission Council Minutes," Items 84, 153 of October 23, 1913, and 186 of May 7, 1914, Presbynig 1/1/6, NAE; CMS, *Letters from the Front: Being a Selection from the Annual Letters from the Missions* (London: CMS, 1912), 25–42; "Niger Mission Minutes and Reports of Executive Committee, February 1929," CMS Archives; John Thornton, "European Documents and African History," in *Writing African History*, ed.

John Edward Philips (New York: University of Rochester Press, 2005), 260, 272; Toyin Falola, "Mission and Colonial Documents," in Philips, *Writing African History*, 278–79.

69. I examine "Collins Elizabeth Stewart, Wife of Robert, Missionary in Calabar, nee Glen, Letters to, 1900–1916," United Presbyterian Church (UPC), No. 26, MS.7715, NLS; "Collins Robert, Missionary in Calabar, Letters to, 1898–1929," UPC, NLS; "Copies of Out-going Letters from Mission Committee to Collins," UPC, Acc.7548/A13-14, NLS; "Copies of Out-going Letters from Mission Committee to Mincher," UPC, Acc.7548/D44, NLS; "Minutes Relating to Calabar, Robert Collins and Mincher, United Free Church of Scotland," UPC, Dep.298/127-137, NLS; "Calabar Correspondence and Papers, 1913–1945," UPC, Acc.7548/D44, NLS; "Minutes relating to Calabar, Robert Collins and Mincher, the Church of Scotland," UPC, Dep.298/157-167, NLS; "Journals of News on Women's Missions, 1904–1926," UPC, Shelfmark Q.124, NLS; "Journals of Woman's Work in the Church," UPC, Shelfmark Q.124, NLS; *Missionary Record of the United Free Church of Scotland*, nos. 1–164 (January 1901–August 1914), UPC, NLS; *Record of the Home and Foreign Mission Work of the United Free Church of Scotland*, new ser., no. 165 (September 1914–April 1928), UPC, NLS; *Record of the United Free Church of Scotland*, May 1928–September 1929, UPC, NLS; *Record of the Church of Scotland*, October 1929–December 1929, UPC, NLS; "Foreign Mission Records of the Church of Scotland Since 1929 with some earlier records (Outgoing Letters, 1–186, and Files Relating to Mission Fields, 1938–1964)," UPC. Acc. 7548, NLS; and "Scottish Missionary Journals, 1850–1950: Church of Scotland (1–10), United Presbyterian Church (11–15), and Free Church of Scotland (16–23)," UPC. Acc. 7548, NLS. Geoffrey Johnston, *Of God and Maxim Guns* (Ontario: Wilfrid Laurier University Press, 1988), 197, 221–39.

70. Percy Amaury Talbot, *In the Shadow of the Bush* (London: Heinemann, 1912); Percy Amaury Talbot, *Life in Southern Nigeria* (London: Macmillan, 1923); Percy Amaury Talbot, *The Peoples of Southern Nigeria*, vol. 3, *Ethnology* (London: Oxford University Press, 1926); Northcote Thomas, *Anthropological Report on the Ibo-Speaking Peoples of Nigeria*, 4 vols. (London: Harrison, 1913–14); G. T. Basden, *Among the Ibos of Nigeria* (1921; repr., London: Frank Cass, 1966); G.T. Basden, *Niger Ibos* (1938; repr., London: Frank Cass, 1966); C. K. Meek, *Law and Authority in a Nigerian Tribe: A Study in Indirect Rule* (1937; repr., London: Oxford University Press, 1950).

71. For instance, Northcote Thomas's anthropological survey of Igboland began in the Awka region. He did not see eye to eye with various British officials, particularly Mr. Sproston, the district commissioner famed for his extensive knowledge of the Awka region. British National Archives (BNA), Colonial Office Correspondences (CO) 520/105, Dispatch No. 493, August 23, 1911; and CO 520/115, Dispatch No. 398, May 1912.

72. Kalu, "The River Highway: Christianizing the Igbo," 69. For a critical evaluation of British district officer C. J. Mayne's Intelligence Report on Ohafia, see chapter 1.

73. I examine BNA CO444, 520, 591, 592, 583, 445, and 554; G. I. Jones, ed., *Annual Reports of Bende Division, South Eastern Nigeria, 1905–1912* (Cambridge: Cambridge University Press, 1986), which contains Major W. A. C. Cockburn, "Annual Report on Bende District for the Year Ended 31st December, 1910," and F. Hives, "Intelligence Report: Bende-Onitsha Hinterland Expedition, 1905"; "Annual Reports on Owerri Province, 1918–1934," CSE 12/1, NAE; "Secret Societies," MINLOC 17/1, NAE; "Okonko Secret Society," AD/495/B49, Arodist 1/1/7, NAE; "Okonko Club: Activity of," RIVPROF 8/8/443, NAE; "Ukekwe Society and Okonko: Proclamation as Unlawful," UMDIV 3/1/656, NAE; "Assessment Reports on Bende Division, 1919–1926," CSO 26/3-97, NAI; L. T. Chubb, "Assessment Reports: Bende Division, 1927–1929," CSO 26/3, ABADIST 8/11/2, File OW 342/27, ABADIST 8/11/2; C. J. Mayne, "Intelligence Report on the Ohafia Clan, 1934," CSO 26/3/29196, NAI; H. F. Matthews, "Intelligence Report on the Aro Clan, Arochukwu District, Calabar Province, 1927," Anthropologists Papers on Aro Origin, Discussion and the Basis of the Widespread Aro Influence, ARODIV 20/1/15, NAE; I. R. Heslop, "Intelligence Report on the Nkalu Clan, Orlu District, Okigwi Division, Owerri Province," CSE 1/85/6197A, NAE; J. G. C. Allen, "Intelligence Report on the Ngwa Clan, Vol. 1, 1993," E7021, NAE; "Native Court Records," UMDIV 7/1/70-100, NAE; "Annual Report Bende District, 1909," Calprof 14/4/951, NAE; "Palm Produce Development," C22/1927, ABADIST 2/1/11, NAE; "Bende District—Selection of H.Q. for," UMDIV 7/1/84, NAE; "Owerri Province Annual Report, 1931," CSE 12/1/332, NAE; "Report on Political and Social Organization in the Owerri Division," ABADIST 14/1/267, NAE; "Annual Report Owerri Province, 1932," SCE 12/1/334, File EP1308A, NAE; K. A. B. Cochrane, "Handing Over Note to H.M. Llyod," OW 7045, NAE; "Arochukwu-Bende-Afikpo Road, 1921," UMPROF 5/1/90, NAE. For Ohafia in the Aro Expedition and Christian Missionaries in the Cross-River region, see Calprof 4/10/31, C/40/21; Calprof 5/16/46; Calprof 5/8/97, C145/7; Calprof 5/8/228, C277/18; Calprof 14/756; Calprof 5/14/85; and Calprof 5/16/46, NAE. Also see Donald A. MacAlister, "The Aro Country, Southern Nigeria," *Scottish Geographical Magazine*, no. 18 (December 1902): 631–37.

74. Paul Thompson, *The Voice of the Past: Oral History* (Oxford: Oxford University Press, 1978), 100 (for quote), 1–64, 165–85; David Henige, "Oral Tradition as a Means of Reconstructing the Past," in Philips, *Writing African History*, 169. Also, see Felix Ekechi, "An African View of the Legendary Vansina," in *Paths toward the Past: African Historical Essays in Honor of Jan Vansina*, ed. Robert Harms et al. (Atlanta: African Studies Association, 1994), 1–9; Jan Vansina, *Oral Tradition as History* (Madison: University of Wisconsin Press, 1985), 27, 63–66.

75. Luise White, Stephan Miescher, and David William Cohen, eds., *African Words, African Voices: Critical Practices in Oral History* (Bloomington: Indiana University Press, 2001) 2–10, 15–19; Luise White, *Speaking with Vampires: Rumor and History in Colonial Africa* (Berkeley: University of California Press, 2000). For a more critical view of oral histories, see Vansina, *Oral Tradition as History*, 186–201.

76. Ruth Finnegan, *Oral Literature in Africa* (Oxford: Oxford University Press, 1970), 2–3: Barbara Cooper, "Oral Sources and the Challenge of African History," in Philips, *Writing African History*, 202–7.

77. See Ralph A. Austen, "The Slave Trade as History and Memory: Confrontations of Slaving Voyage Documents and Communal Traditions," *William and Mary Quarterly* 58, no. 1 (January 2001): 229–44; Donald R. Wright, "Requiem for the Use of Oral Tradition to Reconstruct the Precolonial History of the Lower Gambia," *History in Africa*, no. 18 (1991): 401–2; Martin Klein, "Studying the History of Those Who Would Rather Forget: Oral History and the Experience of Slavery," *History in Africa*, no. 16 (1989): 209–17; Anne C. Bailey, *African Voices of the Atlantic Slave Trade: Beyond the Silence and the Shame* (Boston: Beacon, 2005); Ferme, *Underneath of Things*; Shaw, *Memories of the Slave Trade*.

78. Christopher Ehret, "Writing African History from Linguistic Evidence," in Philips, *Writing African History*, 86–111.

79. Fallou Ngom, "Lexical Borrowings as Pathways to Senegal's Past and Present," in *Africanizing Knowledge: African Studies across the Disciplines*, ed. Toyin Falola and Christian Jennings (New Brunswick, NJ: Transaction, 2002), 125.

80. Ebiegberi J. Alagoa, "An African Philosophy of History in the Oral Tradition," in Harms et al., *Paths toward the Past*, 15–24.

81. Susan K. McIntosh, "Archaeology and the Reconstruction of the African Past," in Philips, *Writing African History*, 54–58, 79.

82. Nwando Achebe and Bridget Teboh, "Dialoguing Women," in Cole, Manuh, and Miescher, *Africa after Gender?*, 63–81; Takyiwaa Manuh, "Doing Gender Work in Ghana," in *Africa after Gender*, 131; Eileen Boris, "Gender after Africa!," in *Africa after Gender*, 191–204; Paulla Ebron, "Constituting Subjects through Performative Acts," in *Africa after Gender*, 171–87.

CHAPTER 1: GENDERED KINSHIP, CA. 1480–1850

1. Victor Turner, *Schism and Continuity in an African Society: A Study of Ndembu Village Life* (London: Manchester University Press, 1957), 230–43. Also see Kings M. Phiri, "Some Changes in the Matrilineal Family System among the Chewa of Malawi since the Nineteenth Century," *Journal of African History* 24, no. 2 (1983): 261. For a parallel example of a patrilineal society, in which male warriors devalued and effeminized agriculture in order to elevate the masculinity of the warrior-hunter, see Allen F. Isaacman and Barbara S. Isaacman, *Slavery and Beyond: The Making of Men and Chikunda*

Ethnic Identities in the Unstable World of South-Central Africa, 1750–1920 (Portsmouth, NH: Heinemann, 2004), 1–31.

2. See Robert Sutherland Rattray, *Ashanti* (Oxford: Clarendon Press, 1923), 237–38; Jean Davison, *Gender, Lineage, and Ethnicity in Southern Africa* (Boulder: Westview, 1997).

3. See David Schneider and Kathleen Gough, eds. *Matrilineal Kinship* (Berkeley: University of California Press, 1962), xv, 652, 668; Mary Douglas and Phyllis Kaberry, eds. *Man in Africa* (New York: Anchor Books, 1969), 123–37; Elizabeth Colson, *Marriage and the Family among the Plateau Tonga of Northern Rhodesia* (Oxford: Manchester University Press, 1958), 346–47. For a contrast view, see T.O. Beidelman, *The Matrilineal Peoples of Eastern Tanzania* (London: International African Institute, 1967); Saul Mahir, "Matrilineal Inheritance and Post-colonial Prosperity in Southern Bobo Country," *Man*, n.s., 27, no. 2 (June 1992): 346; Igor Kopytoff, "Matrilineality, Residence, and Residential Zones," *American Ethnologist* 4, no. 3 (1997): 539–58.

4. See Pauline Peters, "Introduction: Revisiting the Puzzle of Matriliny in South-Central Africa," *Critique of Anthropology* 17, no. 2 (1997): 126–34; Chet Lancaster, *The Goba of the Zambezi: Sex Roles, Economics and Change* (Norman: University of Oklahoma Press, 1981); Ladislov Holy, *Strategies and Norms in a Changing Matrilineal Society: Descent, Succession, and Inheritance among the Toka of Zambia* (London: Cambridge University Press, 1986); Francesca Declich, "'Gendered Narratives,' History, and Identity: Two Centuries along the Juba River among the Zigula and Shanbara," *History in Africa*, no. 22 (1995): 93–122; Boddy, *Wombs and Alien Spirits*, 26–27, 35, 82–84, 232–34, 241–42.

5. Wyatt MacGaffey, "Lineage Structure, Marriage, and the Family amongst the Central Bantu," *Journal of African History* 24, no. 2 (1983): 173–97.

6. See Pauline Peters, "Against the Odds: Matriliny, Land and Gender in the Shire Highland of Malawi," *Critique of Anthropology* 17, no. 2 (1997): 189–210; Kate Crehan, "Of Chickens and Guinea Fowl: Living Matriliny in North-Western Zambia in the 1980s," *Critique of Anthropology* 17, no. 2 (June 1997): 211–13; Margot Lovett, "From Sisters to Wives and 'Slaves': Redefining Matriliny and the Lives of Lakeside Tonga Women, 1888–1955," *Critique of Anthropology* 17, no. 2 (1997): 171–84; Cynthia Brantley, "Through Ngoni Eyes: Margaret Read's Matrilineal Interpretations from Nyasaland," *Critique of Anthropology* 17, no. 2 (1997): 147–64.

7. However, the new scholarship departed from the structural-functionalist paradigm reluctantly. See Karla Poewe, "Matriliny and Capitalism: The Development of Incipient Classes in Luapula, Zambia," *Dialectical Anthropology* 3, no. 4 (November 1978): 331–47; Karla Poewe, "Religion, Matriliny, and Change: Jehovah's Witnesses and Seventh-Day Adventists in Luapula, Zambia," *American Ethnologist* 5, no. 2 (May 1978): 303–21; Karla

Poewe, *Matrilineal Ideology: Male- Female Dynamics in Luapala, Zambia* (London: Academic Press, 1981).

8. Mayne, "Intelligence Report," 11–12, CSO 26/3/29196, NAI; Njoku, *Ohafia*, 2–9; Nsugbe, *Ohaffia*, 11–18; Isichei, *History of the Igbo People*, 51–52; Nnenna E. Obuba, *The History and Culture of Ohafia, covering from about 1432 to 2008: Collated Oral Tradition* (Ebem Ohafia, Nigeria: Lintdsons, 2008), 2–5; Cyril Daryll Forde and G. I. Jones, *The Ibo and Ibibio-Speaking Peoples of South-Eastern Nigeria* (London: International African Institute, 1950), 53–56; Kenneth O. Dike, *Trade and Politics in the Niger Delta, 1830–1885: An Introduction to the Economic and Political History of Nigeria* (Oxford: Clarendon Press, 1966), 24; John N. Oriji, *Traditions of Igbo Origin: A Study of Pre-colonial Population Movements in Africa*, rev. ed. (New York: Peter Lang, 1994), 149–51; Nkparom C. Ejituwu, *A History of Obolo (Andoni) in the Niger Delta* (Oron: Mason, 1991), 28–29; Jones, *Annual Reports*, 1, 63–64.

9. Jones, *Annual Reports*, 1; Nsugbe, *Ohaffia*, 35, 116–18; Kenneth O. Dike and Felicia Ekejiuba, "The Aro State: A Case Study of State Formation in Southeastern Nigeria," *Journal of African Studies* 5, no. 3 (1978): 273; Rosemary Harris, "The Influence of Ecological Factors and External Relations on the Mbembe Tribes of South-East Nigeria," *Africa* 32, no. 1 (1962): 43–47; Obuba, *History and Culture*, 8.

10. Forde and Jones, *Ibo and Ibibio*, 52; Adiele E. Afigbo, *Ropes of Sand: Studies in Igbo Culture and History* (Ibadan, Nigeria: University Press, 1981), 229–30; G. I. Jones, *The Trading States of the Oil Rivers* (Oxford: Oxford University Press, 1963), 134; Felicia Ekejiuba, "The Aro System of Trade in the Nineteenth Century," *Ikenga: Journal of African Studies* 1, no. 1 (January 1972): 13–34; David Northrup, *Trade without Rulers: Pre-colonial Economic Development in South-Eastern Nigeria* (Oxford: Clarendon Press, 1978), 35; Nwokeji, *Slave Trade and Culture*, 26, 31–32.

11. A. J. H. Latham, *Old Calabar, 1600–1891: The Impact of the International Economy upon a Traditional Society* (Oxford: Clarendon Press, 1973), 9–10; Kalada Hart, *Report of the Enquiry into the Dispute over the Obongship of Calabar* (Enugu, Nigeria: Enugu Government Printer, 1964), 10–17; Johnston, *Of God and Maxim Guns*, 11–12.

12. Azuonye, "Heroic Age," 13.

13. John McCall, *Dancing Histories: Heuristic Ethnography with the Ohafia Igbo* (Ann Arbor: University of Michigan Press, 2000), 74.

14. Nsugbe, *Ohaffia*, 27–28, 56; Azuonye, "Heroic Age," 13–23; Njoku, *Ohafia*, 68, 87; Harris, "Influence," 46–47; Monday Abasiatti, *Akwa Ibom and Cross River States: The Land, the People and Their Culture* (Calabar, Nigeria: Wusen Press, 1987), 55; Nna Agbai Ndukwe, interview by author, August 10, 2010, Elu Village, Ohafia; Arunsi Kalu, interview by author, August 15, 2011, Amangwu Village, Ohafia; Also see "Africa, West Coast, 1890," 348–59, FO84/2020, BNA; "Southern Nigeria Protectorate Original Correspondence, 1903," 18–20, 44–54, 173–87, 263–65, CO520/20, BNA.

15. Njoku, *Ohafia*, 68–72, 84; Azuonye, "Heroic Age," 9–14; Nsugbe, *Ohaffia*, 13–15; Arthur Glyn Leonard, "Notes of a Journey to Bende," *Journal of the Manchester Geographical Society*, no. 14 (1898): 196–97.

16. Chieka Ifemesia, *Traditional Humane Living among the Igbo: An Historical Perspective* (Enugu, Nigera: Fourth Dimension Publishers, 1979), 76–80; Nsugbe, *Ohaffia*, 51; Njoku, *Ohafia*, 68.

17. M. M. Green, *Ibo Village Affairs* (London: Frank Cass, 1947), 25; Nsugbe, *Ohaffia*, 58, 69; Forde and Jones, *Ibo and Ibibio*, 52; Njoku, *Ohafia*, 26, 59; Afigbo, *Ropes*, 22; Uma O. Eleazu, "Traditional Institutions and Modernization," *Ohafia Review*, no. 1 (April 1981): 9; Victor C. Uchendu, *The Igbo of Southeast Nigeria* (New York: Holt, Rinehart, and Winston, 1965), 84; C.K. Meek, *Law and Authority in a Nigerian Tribe: A Study in Indirect Rule* (1937; repr., London: Oxford University Press, 1950), 198.

18. Njoku, *Ohafia*, 68.

19. Ikpirikpe Ndi Inyom of Akanu, interview by author, November 3, 2011; Nde Ichin (Elders) of Amuma Village, interview by author, November 26, 2011; Kevin Ukiro, interview by author, Asaga Village, August 10, 2010; Ikenga Ibe, interview by author, Amuma Village, November 26, 2011; Torti Kalu, interview by author, Amuma Village, November 26, 2011; Docas Kalu and Mary Ezera, interview by author, Elu Village, August 10, 2010; Nmia Nnaya Agbai, interview by author, Elu Village, August 18, 2011; Ezie-Nwami Oji Iwe and her cabinet, interview by author, Elu Village, October 25, 2011; Nnenna Obuba, interview by author, Amaekpu, August 15, 2011; Ndukwe Otta and Uduma Uka, interview by author, Ebem Village, August 14, 2011; Ezie-ogo Mecha Ukpai Akanu, interview by author, Amangwu Village, August 18, 2011.

20. Simon Ottenberg, *Double Descent in an African Society: The Afikpo Village-Group* (Seattle: University of Washington Press, 1968), 140–41.

21. Forde and Jones, *Ibo and Ibibio*, 10; G. T. Basden, *Niger Ibos* (1938; repr., London: Frank Cass, 1966), 268; Mayne, "Intelligence Report," 39, CSO 26/3/29196, NAI; David Iyam, *The Broken Hoe: Cultural Reconfiguration in Biase Southeast Nigeria* (Chicago: University of Chicago Press, 1995), 29–32.

22. Nsugbe, *Ohaffia*, 18–20, 112–118.

23. Onwuka Njoku, *Inter-village Trade in Ohafia, 1900–1979* (Nsukka: University of Nigeria, 1981), 29.

24. Mayne, "Intelligence Report," 39, CSO 26/3/29196, NAI; Nsugbe, *Ohaffia*, 87.

25. Azuonye, "Heroic Age," 18; Nsugbe, *Ohaffia*, 21.

26. Nsugbe, *Ohaffia*, 16–20, 112–18; Njoku, *Ohafia*, 15; Chukwuma Azuonye, "The Narrative War Songs of the Ohafia Igbo: A Critical Analysis of their Characteristic Features in Relation to the Social Functions" (PhD thesis, University of London, 1979), 22; Mayne, "Intelligence Report," 18–29, 47, CSO 26/3/29196, NAI; Obuba, *History and Culture*, 4.

27. Eze Onuoha Uma, *Guidance and Destiny: My Life and Thought*; *Autobiography of His Royal Highness, Eze Elder Onuoha Uma, Udumeze of Isiama Ohafia* (Ohafia, Nigeria: Eze Onuoha Uma, 2002), 2.

28. McCall, *Dancing*, 83; Mayne, "Intelligence Report," 41–44, CSO 26/3/29196, NAI; Nnenna Emeri and Mmia Nnaya Bassey, in interview of Ikpirikpe Ndi Inyom of Akanu Village; Kalu Awa Kalu, interview by author, Ufiele Village, October 27, 2011; Olua Iro Kalu, interview by author, Ebem Village, August 3, 2010; Elders of Umu-Anya Patrilineage, Ndi Imaga Compound, interview by author, Elu Village, August 14, 2011; Nnaya Agbai, interview by author, Elu Village, August 18, 2011; Docas Kalu and Mary Ezera, interview; Emea O. Arua, "Yam Ceremonies and the Values of Ohafia Culture," *Africa: Journal of the International African Institute* 51, no. 2 (April 1981): 695; Northrup, *Trade*, 116; Nsugbe, *Ohaffia*, 21; Njoku, *Inter-village Trade*, 12–13.

29. N. Uka, "A Note on the 'Abam' Warriors of Igbo Land," *Ikenga: Journal of African Studies* 1, no. 2 (1972): 78; Arua, "Yam Ceremonies," 695; Nsugbe, *Ohaffia*, 27–28.

30. Nsugbe, *Ohaffia*, 37.

31. Jean Barbot, *A Description of the Coast of North and South Guinea* (London: A. and J. Churchill, 1732), 377; S. A. Agboola, "Introduction and Spread of Cassava in Western Nigeria," *Nigerian Journal of Economic and Social Studies* 10, no. 3 (1968): 369; W. O. Jones, "Manioc: An Example of Innovation in African Economics," *Economic Development and Cultural Change* 5, no. 2 (January 1957): 98; Don C. Ohadike, "The Influenza Pandemic of 1918–1919 and the Spread of Cassava Cultivation on the Lower Niger: A Study in Historical Linkages," *Journal of African History* 22, no. 3 (July 1981): 379.

32. Basden, *Among the Ibos*, 150.

33. Njoku, *Ohafia*, 37.

34. Mayne, "Intelligence Report," 6, 15, CSO 26/3/29196, NAI; L. T. Chubb, "Assessment Reports: Bende Division, 1927–1929," 2–6, 20–23, OW 342/27, ABADIST 8/11/2, NAE; Njoku, *Inter-village Trade*, 12–13; Amadiume, *Male Daughters*, 30.

35. Nsugbe, *Ohaffia*, 122; Olua Iro Kalu, interview; Kevin Ukiro, interview; Agbai Ndukwe, interview; Arunsi Kalu, interview; Eke Emetu Kalu, interview by author, Obu Ndi Anaga, August, 11, 2010; Emeh Okonkwo, interview by author, Ebem Village, August 3, 2010.

36. Nsugbe, *Ohaffia*, 62.

37. Arua, "Yam Ceremonies," 701; Torti Kalu, interview by author, Amuma Village, November 26, 2011; Anaso Awalekwa, interview by author, Ndea-Nku, November 17, 2011; Uduma Nnochin Ogbuagu, interview by author, Amuke Village, November 24, 2011.

38. Arua, "Yam Ceremonies," 701; Oriji, *Traditions*, 6; Nwokeji, "African Conceptions," 59–60.

39. Eke Kalu, "An Ibo Autobiography: The Autobiography of Mr. Eke Kalu, Ohaffia's Well-Honored Son," *Nigerian Field* 7, no. 4 (October 1938): 158–70; Leonard, "Notes," 196–97; Nsugbe, *Ohaffia*, 14; Nkoku, *Ohafia*, 43.

40. Nsugbe, *Ohaffia*, 69.

41. Basden, *Among the Ibos*, 145.

42. Azuonye, "Heroic Age," 9, 13–14; Njoku, *Ohafia*, 40, 72.

43. When a child killed his first wild animal, he was said to have cut a head and was celebrated. Obuba, *History and Culture*, 22; Ogbuka Ogbuka Abaa, interview by author, Isiugwu Village, December 10, 2011; Kalu Ibem, in interview of Nde Ichin of Amuma Village.

44. Ijeoma Onyeani, interview by author, Isiugwu, December 10, 2011; Ezie-ogo Godwin Nwankwo Uko and his cabinet members, interview by author, Amankwu Village, October 25, 2011; Nwabueze Kalu, interview by author, Isiugwu, December 10, 2011.

45. Basden, *Among the Ibos*, 144; Njoku, *Ohafia*, 40.

46. David Eltis, *The Rise of African Slavery in the Americas* (New York: Cambridge University Press, 2000), 300; "Africa: Slave Trade, West Coast, 1885," 298–300, FO84/1701, BNA; "Africa (Slave Trade), West Coast, 1888," 35–37, FO84/1882, BNA; "Africa (Slave Trade), West Coast, 1889," 353–61, FO84/1941, BNA. Precision arms came in the colonial period.

47. Leonard, "Notes," 196–97; Kalu, "Ibo," 159–62; Nsugbe, *Ohaffia*, 14.

48. Elizabeth Isichei, *The Ibo and the Europeans: The Genesis of a Relationship—to 1906* (New York: St. Martin's, 1973), 52.

49. Ijeoma Onyeani, interview.

50. Udensi Ekea, interview by author, Okon Village, August 4, 2010; Kalu Uko, interview by author, Okon Village, September 20, 2011; Uche Dimgba, oral interview by author, September 22, 2011; Obasi Kama, interview by author, Okon Village, September 26, 2011.

51. Northrup, *Trade*, 208–19; Njoku, *Ohafia*, 50; Mecha Ukpai Akanu, interview; Ogbuka Ogbuka Abaa, interview; Torti Kalu, interview; Agbai Ndukwe, interview; Eke Emetu Kalu, interview. The market was a female domain.

52. Godwin Nwankwo Uko, interview; Agbai Ndukwe, interview; Olua Iro Kalu, interview; Ndukwe Otta and Uduma Uka, oral conversation with author, Asaga Village, September 16, 2011; Jones, *Annual Reports*, 37. This is a contrast to the notion that Ohafia male preoccupation with warfare precluded Ohafia entirely from pre-colonial Biafran inter-regional trade. See Northrup, *Trade*, 116; Azuonye, "Heroic Age," 9; Elizabeth Isichei, *Igbo Worlds: An Anthology of Oral Histories and Historical Descriptions* (Philadelphia: Institute for the Study of Human Issues, 1978), 132.

53. Mayne, "Intelligence Report," 15, CSO 26/3/29196, NAI; Jones, *Annual Reports*, 33; Kalu, "Ibo Autobiography," 164; Njoku, *Inter-village Trade*, 22–27; Ikpo Chukwu Ndukwe, interview by author, Ndi Ado, 6 April 2012; Ikpirikpe Ndi Inyom Akanu, interview by author; Docas Kalu and Mary

Ezera, interview by author; Nnaya Agbai, interview; *Ezie-nwami* Ucha Oji Iwe of Elu and Cabinet, interview by author, 25 October 2011; *Ezie-nwami* Ogbonne Kalu, interview by author, Uduma Ukwu Ohafia, 17 November 2011; Tessy Uzoma Odum, interview by author, Ebem Ohafia, 5 September 2011: Godwin Nwankwo Uko, interview by author; *Ezie-ogo* Anaso Awalekwa of Ndea-Nku and Cabinet, interview by author, 17 November 2011.

54. Mayne, "Intelligence Report," 39, CSO 26/3/29196, NAI; Nsugbe, *Ohaffia*, 75; Obuba, *History and Culture*, 49–51.

55. Ifi Amadiume, *Male Daughters, Female Husbands: Gender and Sex in an African Society* (London: Zed Books, 1989), 31–33; Achebe, *Farmers*, 206–15.

56. Nsugbe, *Ohaffia*, 72–78.

57. Mayne, "Intelligence Report," 42, CSO 26/3/29196, NAI; Nsugbe, 86, 89–92.

58. Mayne, 43.

59. Nsugbe, *Ohaffia*, 82; Workshop on Widowhood Practices, *Widowhood Practices in Imo State: Proceedings of the Better Life Program for Rural Women Workshop* (Owerri, Nigeria: Government Printer, 1989); Felix Ekechi, *Tradition and Transformation in Eastern Nigeria: A Sociopolitical History of Owerri and its Hinterland, 1902–1947* (Ohio: Kent State University Press, 1989); Chima Jacob Korieh, "Widowhood among the Igbo of Eastern Nigeria" (MA thesis, University of Bergen, Norway, June 1996).

60. Mayne, "Intelligence Report," 44, CSO 26/3/29196, NAI; Obuba, *History and Culture*, 55. This would change from the 1850s.

61. Uchendu, *Igbo*, 13; Obuba, *History and Culture*, 49.

62. Basden, *Among the Ibos*, 76–77; Korieh, "Widowhood," 14–25; Mayne, "Intelligence Report," 47–48, CSO 26/3/29196, NAI; Nnenna Emeri and Mmia Nnaya Bassey, in interview of Ikpirikpe Ndi Inyom of Akanu Village.

63. Ikpirikpe Ndi Inyom of Akanu Village, interview; Chief K. K. Owen, interview by author, Elu Village, August 12, 2010; Arunsi Kalu, interview; Olua Iro Kalu, interview.

64. Njoku, *Ohafia*, 26.

65. Nsugbe, *Ohaffia*, 83.

66. See chapter 5 for case studies. Also, Nwokeji, "African Conceptions," 58; Ndukwe Otta and Uduma Uka, interview; Tessy Uzoma Odum, interview by author, Ebem Village, September 5, 2011.

67. Obuba, *History and Culture*, 51; Njoku, *Ohafia*, 26; Kevin Ukiro, interview; Nnaya Agbai, interview; Orie Emeh and Grace Ojieke, interview by author, Elu Village, August 18, 2011.

68. Ottenberg, *Double Descent*, 141.

69. Ogbonne Kalu, interview by author, Uduma Ukwu Village, November 17, 2011; Ucha Oji Iwe, interview; Docas Kalu and Mary Ezera, interview; Ikpirikpe Ndi Inyom of Akanu Village, interview; Kalu Awa Kalu,

interview; Agbai Ndukwe, interview; Arunsi Kalu, interview; Eke Emetu Kalu, interview; Emeh Okonkwo, interview; Olua Iro Kalu, interview; Mecha Ukpai Akanu, interview; Mayne, "Intelligence Report," 23, CSO 26/3/29196, NAI; Njoku, *Ohafia*, 68.

70. Nsugbe, *Ohaffia*, 73–99; Peters, "Introduction," 127–34; Sally Falk Moore, *Anthropology and Africa: Changing Perspectives on a Changing Scene* (Charlottesville: University of Virginia Press, 1994), 8–15; Schneider and Gough, *Matrilineal Kinship*, vii-23.

71. Amadiume, *Male Daughters*, 99.

72. Uchendu, *Igbo*, 11–12.

73. N. Uka, "A Note," 78; Mayne, "Intelligence Report," 44–45, CSO 26/3/29196, NAI; Azuonye, "Heroic Age," 23; Nsugbe, *Ohaffia*, 103–8; Ottenberg, *Double Descent*, 193–98; Ogbonne Kalu, interview; Ndukwe Otta and Uduma Uka, interview; Mecha Ukpai Akanu, interview; Udensi Ekea, interview; Arunsi Kalu, interview; Eke Emetu Kalu, interview; Emeh Okonkwo, interview; Agbai Ndukwe, interview; Ikenga Ibe, interview; Oluka Mba, interview by author, Nde-Ibe Village, November 3, 2011.

74. Obuba, *History and Culture*, 50; Nsugbe, *Ohaffia*, 93–109; Onwuka Njoku, oral conversation with the author, University of Nigeria, Nsukka, July 12, 2010. Ohafia female leadership of the matrilineage differed from that of neighboring Afikpo, where a male priest and male elders controlled the matrilineage shrines. See Ottenberg, *Double Descent*, 94–141; 204.

75. Amadiume, *Male Daughters*, 174.

76. Nsugbe, *Ohaffia*, 111.

77. Mayne, "Intelligence Report," 46, CSO 26/3/29196, NAI; Nsugbe, *Ohaffia*, 22; Arua, "Yam Ceremonies," 698; Udensi Ekea, interview; Ndukwe Otta and Uduma Uka, interview; Olua Iro Kalu, interview; Kevin Ukiro, interview; Mba Odo Okereke, interview by author, Akanu Village, October 26, 2011; Emeh Okonkwo, interview.

78. Nsugbe, *Ohaffia*, 94; Njoku, *Ohafia*, 26, 68; Eke Emetu, interview.

79. Nnenna Emeri, in interview of Ikpirikpe Ndi Inyom of Akanu Village.

80. Njoku, *Ohafia*, 17–22; Nsugbe, *Ohaffia*, 58–71; Uduma O. Uduma, *The People of Ohafia Ezema* (Calabar, Nigeria: Arinson, 2007), 97–101; E. E. Nkata, "The Role of Women in Development," *Ikoro* 2, no. 2 (1976): 35–36; Ogbeyalu Nchonwa, "The Role of Women in Development," *Ohafia Review*, no. 1 (April 1981): 7–9; A. I. Udensi, "Elevating the Ohafia Woman," *Ikoro* 3, no. 3 (1998): 40–44; Grace U. Kalu, "Women in Social and Economic Change in Ohafia, 1945–1990" (MA thesis, University of Nigeria, Nsukka, 2005), 1, 36.

81. Basden, *Niger Ibos*, 203; Basden, *Among the Ibos*, 88–96; Azuonye, "Heroic Age," 23–29; Caroline Ifeka-Moller, "Female Militancy and Colonial Revolt: The Women's War of 1929, Eastern Nigeria," in Ardener, *Perceiving Women*, 132–35; Phoebe Ottenberg, "The Changing Economic Position of Women among the Afikpo Ibo," in *Continuity and Change in African*

Cultures, eds. W. T. Bascom and M. J. Herskovits (Chicago: University of Chicago Press, 1959), 205–23; Susan Martin, "Gender and Innovation: Farming, Cooking and Palm Processing in the Ngwa Region, South-Eastern Nigeria, 1900–1930," *Journal of African History* 25, no. 4 (1984): 411–27.

82. Age-grade-derived political leadership has been misrepresented as exclusively male. See Nsugbe, *Ohaffia*, 59–70; Amadiume, *Male Daughters*, 173–74; Azuonye, "Heroic Age," 21–22.

83. Mayne, "Intelligence Report," 46, CSO 26/3/29196, NAI.

84. Mayne, 52.

85. Jones, *Annual Reports*, 68–88.

86. See Ruth Finnegan, *Oral Literature in Africa* (Oxford: Oxford University Press, 1970), 2–3; Barbara Cooper, "Oral Sources and the Challenge of African History," in Philips, *Writing African History*, 202–7; Jan Vansina, *Oral Tradition as History* (Madison: University of Wisconsin Press, 1985), 40.

87. Afigbo, *Ropes*, 22; Forde and Jones, *Ibo and Ibibio*, 52; Njoku, *Ohafia*, 26, 59; Azuonye, "Heroic Age," 21–23; Nsugbe, *Ohaffia*; 58–59.

88. Njoku, *Ohafia*, 26.

89. Uchendu, *Igbo*, 84.

90. Njoku, *Ohafia*, 26; Nsugbe, *Ohaffia*, 58; Agbai Ndukwe, interview; Arunsi Kalu, interview.

91. Uduma, *People*, 54; Uka, "A Note," 77; Meek, *Law*, 198; Njoku, *Ohafia*, 27; Robert S. Rattray, *Ashanti Law and Constitution* (Oxford: Clarendon Press, 1929), 11–13.

92. Docas Kalu and Mary Ezera, interview; Nnaya Agbai, interview; Ikpirikpe Ndi Inyom of Akanu Village, interview; Arunsi Kalu, interview; Orie Emeh and Grace Ojieke, interview; Udensi Ekea, interview. First menstruation was articulated as "cutting a head" and celebrated with slaughtering an antelope. It was accompanied by rigorous safeguard of chastity.

93. Arunsi Kalu, interview; Ikpirikpe Ndi Inyom of Akanu Village, interview; Orie Emeh and Grace Ojieke, interview; Docas Kalu and Mary Ezera, interview.

94. Njoku, *Ohafia*, 28; Azuonye, "Heroic Age," 18–22; Nsugbe, *Ohaffia*, 58–59; Onwuka E. Oti, *The Age Grade System and Otomu Ceremony in Ohafia* (Aba, Nigeria: EMS Corporate, 2007), 11. This *ifiwe uke* entailed competitive completion of a community project to become *uke ji ogo*.

95. Oti, *Age Grade*, 14–19; Azuonye, "Heroic Age," 22; Orie Emeh and Grace Ojieke, interview; Ogbonne Kalu, interview; Docas Kalu and Mary Ezera, interview; Ucha Oji Iwe, interview; Uduma Nnochin Ogbuagu, interview; Udensi Ekea, interview.

96. Oti, *Age Grade*, 12.

97. Njoku, *Ohafia*, 28.

98. Mayne, "Intelligence Report," 41–44, CSO 26/3/29196, NAI; Arua, "Yam Ceremonies," 695; Nsugbe, *Ohaffia*, 24; Njoku, *Ohafia*, 24, 37–38;

Uma, *Guidance and Destiny*, 2; Arunsi Kalu, interview; Nnenna Emeri and Mmia Nnaya Bassey, in interview of Ikpirikpe Ndi Inyom of Akanu Village; Kalu Awa Kalu, interview.

99. Docas Kalu and Mary Ezera, interview; Nnaya Agbai, interview; Ikpirikpe Ndi Inyom of Akanu Village, interview; Orie Emeh and Grace Ojieke, interview; Olua Iro Kalu, interview; Kevin Ukiro, interview; K. K. Owen, interview; Udensi Ekea, interview.

100. Azuonye, "Heroic Age," 22.

101. Mayne, "Intelligence Report," 46, CSO 26/3/29196, NAI; Njoku, *Ohafia*, 28; Meek, *Law and Authority*, 200.

102. Ezie-ogo Okorie Kalu, interview by author, Isiugwu Village, December 10, 2011; Elders of Umu-Anya Patrilineage, interview; Mecha Ukpai Akanu, interview; Anaso Awalekwa, interview; Ezie-ogo Vasco Iro, interview by author, Nkwebi Village, November 17, 2011; Ezie-ogo Kalu Awa, interview by author, Ibina (Ihenta) Village, December 12, 2011; Nde Ichin of Amuma Village, interview; Godwin Nwankwo Uko, interview; Mba Odo Okereke, interview; Njoku, *Ohafia*, 21–23; Uchendu, *Igbo*, 41–42.

103. Mayne, "Intelligence Report," 8, 12–13, CSO 26/3/29196, NAI.

104. Mayne, 31.

105. Njoku, *Ohafia*, 22.

106. Nsugbe, *Ohaffia*, 61; Njoku, 22; Meek, *Law and Authority*, 199.

107. Uduma Nnochin Ogbuagu, interview; Oluka Mba, interview; Nde Ichin of Amuma Village, interview; Ndukwe Otta and Uduma Uka, interview.

108. Nsugbe, *Ohaffia*, 69.

109. Mayne, "Intelligence Report," 13, 16, 21, CSO 26/3/29196, NAI.

110. Azuonye, "Heroic Age," 19.

111. Nsugbe, *Ohaffia*, 95–101; Mayne, "Intelligence Report," 20, CSO 26/3/29196, NAI; Okorie Kalu, interview; Mecha Ukpai Akanu, interview; Anaso Awalekwa, interview; Vasco Iro, interview; Kalu Awa, interview; Nde Ichin of Amuma Village, interview; Godwin Nwankwo Uko, interview; Mba Odo Okereke, interview.

112. Njoku, *Ohafia*, 25.

113. Nsugbe, *Ohaffia*, 68.

114. Nina Mba, *Nigerian Women Mobilized: Women's Political Activity in Southern Nigeria, 1900–1965* (Berkeley: Institute of International Studies, University of California, 1982), 29.

115. Ifeka-Moller, "Female Militancy," 134.

116. Annie M. D. Lebeuf, "The Role of Women in the Political Organization of African Societies," in *Women of Tropical Africa*, ed. Denise Paulme (Berkeley: University of California Press, 1960), 109–13.

117. Kamene Okonjo, "The Dual Sex Political System in Operation: Igbo Women and Community Politics in Midwest Nigeria," in Hafkin and Bay, *Women in Africa*, 47–48; Amadiume, *Male Daughters*, 59–67; Achebe, *Farmers*, 164–71.

118. In patrilineal Igbo societies, "wives" remained essential outsiders; daughters, in alliance with their fathers and brothers, often identified themselves with male interests. See Mba, *Nigerian Women*, 62; Amadiume, *Male Daughters*, 67.

119. Amadiume, *Male Daughters*, 174.

120. Ogbonne Kalu, interview; Ucha Oji Iwe, interview; Ikpirikpe Ndi Inyom of Akanu Village, interview; Mecha Ukpai Akanu, interview by author; Anaso Awalekwa, interview; Kalu Awa, interview; Godwin Nwankwo Uko, interview.

121. Uche Kalu Ebi, in interview of Ucha Oji Iwe and her cabinet.

122. Basden, *Niger Ibos*, 209–10.

123. Mayne, "Intelligence Report," 46, CSO 26/3/29196, NAI.

124. Achebe, *Female King*, 2.

125. Nsugbe, *Ohaffia*, 68.

126. Njoku, *Ohafia*, 24; Ikpirikpe Ndi Inyom of Akanu, interview by author; Elders of Nde Odo Patrilineage, interview by author, Akanu Ohafia, 2 November 2011.

127. Ezie-nwami Mmia Abali, interview by author, Eziafor Village, December 17, 2011; Ucha Oji Iwe, interview; Ogbonne Kalu, interview; Ikpirikpe Ndi Inyom of Akanu Village, interview; Orie Emeh and Grace Ojieke, interview.

128. Nnenna Emeri, in interview of Ikipirikpe Ndi Inyom of Akanu Village; Ucha Oji Iwe, interview; Ogbonne Kalu, interview.

129. Mmia Abali, interview; Nne Agwu Ukpai, in group interview of Ikpirikpe Ndi Inyom of Akanu Village; Ucha Oji Iwe, interview; Ogbonne Kalu, interview.

130. Njoku, *Ohafia*, 25.

131. Comfort Ukoha, in interview of Ikpirikpe Ndi Inyom of Akanu Village.

132. Mayne, "Intelligence Report," 32, CSO 26/3/29196, NAI. Also see Olaudah Equiano, *The Interesting Narrative of the Life of Olaudah Quiano, or Gustavus Vassa, the African, Written by Himself*, ed. Werner Sollors (New York: Norton, 2001), 21.

133. Nwokeji, *Slave Trade and Culture*, 135. It seems that the discriminatory enslavement of men for adultery was most common in matrilineal societies. The other known example is from the Ashanti of the Gold Coast. See House of Commons, Parliament, Great Britain, "Report of the Lords of the Committee of Council Appointed for the Consideration of All Matters Relating to Trade and Foreign Plantations, 1789," 60–61, Eighteenth Century Collections Online database.

134. Nsugbe, *Ohaffia*, 68.

135. Njoku, *Ohafia*, 24. Also see Amadiume, *Male Daughters*, 65.

136. Mba, *Nigerian Women*, 29; Amadiume, *Male Daughters*, 67; M. M. Green, *Ibo Village Affairs, Chiefly with Reference to the Village of Umueke*

Agbaja, 2nd ed. (London: Frank Cass, 1964), 196–214; Jack Harris, "The Position of Women in a Nigerian Society," *Transactions of the New York Academy of Sciences*, 2nd ser., 2, no. 5 (March 1940): 141–48.

137. Eke Emetu Kalu, interview; Emeh Okonkwo, interview; Kalu Awa Kalu, interview; Ucha Oji Iwe, interview; Nnaya Agbai, interview; Ikpirikpe Ndi Inyom of Akanu Village, interview.

138. Mary Ezera, interview by author, Eben Village, August 3, 2010; Ucha Oji Iwe, interview; Olua Iro Kalu, interview; Mmia Abali, interview; Kevin Ukiro, interview; Arunsi Kalu, interview; Ogbonne Kalu, interview.

139. Mayne, "Intelligence Report," 41–44, CSO 26/3/29196, NAI; Nsugbe, *Ohaffia*, 68; Arunsi Kalu, interview; Olua Iro Kalu, interview; Tessy Uzoma Odum, interview; Nwannediya Mmonwu-Oti, interview by author, Ndi Owom, Okon Village, August 5, 2010; Orie Emeh and Grace Ojieke, interview; Docas Kalu and Mary Ezera, interview; Nnaya Agbai, interview; Mmia Abali, interview; Ucha Oji Iwe, interview.

140. Ifeka-Moller, "Female Militancy," 132–35; Mba, *Nigerian Women*, viii.

141. Achebe, *Farmers*, 67.

142. Georges Balandier, *Political Anthropology* (London: Penguin, 1970), 36.

143. Nnenna Uma Eke, interview by author, Akanu Village, November 3, 2011.

144. Uduma Nnochin Ogbuagu, interview; Ezie-ogo Ukonu Okoro Ekere of Eziafor Ohafia, interview by author, Eziafor Village, December 17, 2011; Ezie-ogo Okpan Ncheghe of Ndi-Orie-Eke Ohafia, interview by author, Ndi-Orie-Eke Village, December 15, 2011.

145. See Achebe, *Farmers*, 177.

146. Nnenna Emeri, in interview of Ikpirikpe Ndi Inyom of Akanu Village; Ogbonne Kalu, interview; Mmia Abali, interview.

147. Mayne, "Intelligence Report," 23–24, CSO 26/3/29196, NAI.

148. Van Allen, "'Sitting on a Man'"; Shirley Ardener, "Sexual Insult and Female Militancy," in Ardener, *Perceiving Women*, 29–53.

149. Njoku, *Ohafia*, 25.

150. Ikediya Okenu, interview by author, Elu Village, November 12, 2011; Ogbonne Kalu, interview; Nnaya Agbai, interview; Docas Kalu and Mary Ezera, interview.

151. Mayne, "Intelligence Report," 31, CSO 26/3/29196, NAI.

152. Ikpirikpe Ndi Inyom of Akanu Village, interview. For similar rituals, see Van Allen, "'Sitting on a Man,'" 175; Audrey Wipper, "Riot and Rebellion among African Women: Three Examples of Women's Political Clout," in O'Barr, *Perspectives on Power*, 62–65; Ifeka-Moller, "Female Militancy," 132; Achebe, *Farmers*, 176.

153. Richard Werbner, *Tears of the Dead: The Social Biography of an African Family* (Washington, DC: Smithsonian Institution, 1996), 4.

154. Julie Livingstone, *Debility and the Moral Imagination in Botswana* (Bloomington: Indiana University Press, 2005), 1–6; Turner, *Schism and Continuity*, 161–69.

155. Dibia Chikezie Emeri, in interview of Elders of Nde Odo Patrilineage, Akanu Village, November 2, 2011; Dibia Uduma Uchendu, interview by author, Akanu Village, November 2, 2011; Nwannediya Mmonwu-Oti; Nnaya Agbai, interview; Ogbonne Kalu, interview; Orie Emeh and Grace Ojieke, interview; Arunsi Kalu, interview; Mmia Abali, interview; Dibia Azueke Kalu of Nde Idika Okoro, interview by author, Okon Village, September 22, 2011.

156. Nwannediya Mmonwu-Oti, interview; Olua Iro Kalu; interview; Chikezie Emeri, in interview of Elders of Ndo Odo Patrilineage; Arunsi Kalu, interview.

157. Nnenna Obuba, interview; Nnaya Agbai, interview; Orie Emeh and Grace Ojieke, interview; Arunsi Kalu, interview; Chikezie Emeri, in interview of Elders of Ndo Odo Patrilineage; Uduma Uchendu, interview; Kalu Davidson Oki, interview by author, Okon Village, August 5, 2010; K. K. Owen, interview; Obuba, *History and Culture*, 16–20.

158. Arunsi Kalu, interview; Agbai Ndukwe, interview; Karen F. Flint, *Healing Traditions: African Medicine, Cultural Exchange, and Competition in South Africa, 1820–1948* (Athens: Ohio University Press, 2008), 37–89; Livingston, *Debility*, 64–106.

159. John C. Wood, *When Men Are Women: Manhood among Gabra Nomads of East Africa* (Madison: University of Wisconsin Press, 1999), 3–9.

160. Ogbonne Kalu, interview; Nnenna Emeri and Nnaya Bassey, in interview of Ikpirikpe Ndi Inyom of Akanu Village; Arunsi Kalu, interview; Nnenna Uma Eke, interview; Uduma Nnochin Ogbuagu, interview.

161. Nnenna Emeri, in interview of Ikipirikpe Ndi Inyom of Akanu Village.

162. Ikpirikpe Ndi Inyom of Akanu, interview; Kalu Awa, interview; Vasco Iro, interview; Nnaya Agbai, interview; Orie Emeh and Grace Ojieke, interview.

163. Mayne, "Intelligence Report," 32, CSO 26/3/29196, NAI.

164. Njoku, *Ohaffia*, 82.

165. Kalu Awa Kalu, interview; Kalu Davidson Oki, interview; Uduma Nnochin Ogbuagu, interview; Agbai Ndukwe, interview; Azuonye, "Narrative War Songs," 62–64; McCall, *Dancing*, 4–6.

166. Azuonye, "Narrative War Songs," 132.

167. Azuonye, 315–20, 412–463; Kalu Davidson Oki, interview; Ndukwe Otta and Uduma Uka, interview.

168. Azuonye, "Narrative War Songs," 436, 443, 454.

169. Kalu Davidson Oki, interview.

170. I. R. Heslop, "Intelligence Report on the Nkalu Clan, Orlu District, Okigwi Division, Owerri Province," CSE 1/85/6197A, NAE; Obuba, *History and Culture*, 4.

171. Azuonye, "Narrative War Songs," 407–8.

CHAPTER 2: MILITARY SLAVING, CA. 1650–1890

1. Njoku, *Ohafia: A Heroic Igbo Society* (Nigeria: Whytam Press, 2000).
2. Philip O. Nsugbe, *Ohaffia: A Matrilineal Ibo People* (Oxford: Oxford University Press, 1974).
3. Azuonye, "Narrative War Songs," 17.
4. Northrup, *Trade*, 119.
5. Mayne, "Intelligence Report," 50–51, CSO 26/3/29196, NAI; Njoku, *Ohafia*, 50–51.
6. See "Text 17: Elibe Aja," in Azunonye, "Narrative War Songs," 398; and "Texts 27, 28, 29, 32, and 33: Nne Mgbeafo," in Azunonye, "Narrative War Songs," 412–63.
7. Nwokeji, *Slave Trade and Culture*, 33–34.
8. Oriji, *Political Organization*, 118.
9. Nwokeji, *Slave Trade and Culture*, 33–36.
10. Agbai Ndukwe, interview.
11. See for example, Kwesi Yankah, *Speaking for the Chief: Akyeame and the Politics of Akan Royal Oratory* (Bloomington: Indiana University Press, 1995), 95; Afigbo, *Ropes*, 241–42; Adiele Afigbo, *Igbo Enwe Eze: Beyond Onwumechili and Onwuejeogwu* (Nigeria: Whytem, 2001), 1–29; Uchendu, *Igbo*, 41–42, 90–92; Amadiume, *Male Daughters*, 119–23; Achebe, *Farmers*, 171–73, 206–15; Raphael C. Njoku, *African Cultural Values: Igbo Political Leadership in Colonial Nigeria, 1900–1966* (New York: Routledge, 2006), 19–21; McCall, "Atlantic Slave Trade," 71–76; Dorothy L. Hodgson, "'Once Intrepid Warriors': Modernity and the Production of Maasai Masculinities," *Ethnology* 38, no. 2 (Spring 1999): 121–50; Andrea Cornwall, "To Be a Man Is More Than a Day's Work: Shifting Ideals of Masculinity in Ado-Odo, Southwestern Nigeria," in Lindsay and Miescher, *Men and Masculinities in Modern Africa*, 230–48; McKittrick, "Forsaking Their Fathers?" 33–51; Lindsay, "Money," 138–55.
12. Njoku, *Ohafia*, 56–57.
13. For a summary of this criticism, see Isichei, *History*, 82; Njoku, *Ohafia*, 71.
14. Olua Iro Kalu, interview.
15. K. K. Owen, interview.
16. Kalu Davidson Oki, interview.
17. For a full account of this narrative, see chapter 3.
18. "Southern Nigeria Original Correspondence, May–August, 1901," 510–14, CO520/8, BNA; Oriji, "Slave Trade," 111; Njoku, *Ohafia*, 90; Udensi Ekea, interview; Vasco Iro, interview; Kalu Awa, interview; Nde Ichin of Amuma Village, interview; Godwin Nwankwo Uko, interview.
19. Klein, "Impact," 238.
20. Roberts, "Production," 398, 400, 419.
21. Kalu Awa Kalu, interview.
22. McCall, *Dancing*, 73.

23. *Jooji* refers to George V (1865–1936), king of England and emperor of India.

24. Robert S. DuPlessis, *The Material Atlantic: Clothing, Commerce, and Colonization in the Atlantic World, 1650–1800* (Cambridge: Cambridge University Press, 2016), 19–22.

25. Oriji, *Political Organization*, 119; Njoku, *Ohafia*, 63–65; Uka, "A Note," 78; McCall, *Dancing*, 68, 80; Arua, "Yam Ceremonies," 695; Azuonye, "Heroic Age," 15; Agbai Ndukwe, interview; Arunsi Kalu, interview; Eke Emetu Kalu, interview; Emeh Okonkwo, interview; K. K. Owen, interview.

26. Northrup, *Trade*, 119; Nsugbe, *Ohaffia*, 79; Azuonye, "Heroic Age," 14; Njoku, *Ohafia*, 72.

27. "Colonial Office: Southern Nigeria Protectorate Original Correspondence, 1899–1911," 212–31, CO520/107, BNA.

28. Nsugbe, *Ohaffia*, 12–15; Kevin Ukiro, interview; Arunsi Kalu, interview; Chief Priest Idika Aso of Obu Nkwa Shrine, interview by the author, Asaga Village, August 12, 2010; Chief Priest Onwuka Kalu Agwu of Obu Ndi Idika, interview by the author, Ebem Village, August 3, 2010; Nwando Achebe, "When Deities Marry: Indigenous 'Slave' Systems Expanding and Metamorphosing in the Igbo Hinterland," in *African Systems of Slavery*, ed. Jay Spaulding and Stephanie Beswick (Trenton, NJ: Africa World Press, 2010), 105–33.

29. Northrup, *Trade*, 119–21, 142; Richard O. Igwebe, *The Original History of Arondizuogu from 1635 to 1960* (Aba, Nigeria: International Press, 1962), 86–87; Ekejiuba, "Aro System of Trade," 18–19; Njoku, *Ohafia*, 69–72, 84; Leonard, "Notes," 196–97; Nsugbe, *Ohaffia*, 13–15, 27–32; Isichei, *History*, 82. The major four-day fairs visited by Ohafia were Bende, Itu, and Uburu.

30. Nwokeji, *Slave Trade and Culture*, 68.

31. Northrup, *Trade*, 119–21; Njoku, *Ohafia*, 69; Igwebe, *Arondizuogu*, 86–87.

32. Jones, *Annual Reports*, 4–6.

33. Northrup, *Trade*, 137, 142.

34. Nwokeji, *Slave Trade and Culture*, 179.

35. Oriji, *Political Organization*, 119.

36. Azuonye, "Narrative War Songs," 15.

37. Njoku, *Ohafia*, 70; Oriji, *Political Organization*, 119; Agbai Ndukwe, interview; Udensi Ekea, interview.

38. Azuonye, "Narrative War Songs," 32.

39. According to this tradition, Izuogu, the founder of Arondizuogu, had a mother from Elu Ohafia. Izuogu was a very ugly man. While he was passing though Ora en route to Ohafia, Izuogu was taunted by the people for his ugliness. When he arrived Elu, he narrated his humiliation, and to avenge the insult on their son-in-law, Elu summoned warriors and ravaged Ora community. Beyond its truism, this narrative serves to substantiate Izuogu's Ohafia

maternal descent and provide a moral justification for the massacre and enslavement of Ora people.

40. Nwokeji, *Slave Trade and Culture*, 69–72.

41. Nwokeji, 35–40, 45–52, 58, 125.

42. Uka, "A Note," 79; Udensi Ekea, interview; Olua Iro Kalu, interview; Kevin Ukiro, interview; Ndukwe Otta and Uduma Uka, interview; Agbai Ndukwe, interview; Arunsi Kalu, interview; Eke Emetu Kalu, interview; Emeh Okonkwo, interview; Kalu Awa Kalu, interview; K. K. Owen, interview.

43. For the tradition of Elibe Aja, see Azuonye, "Narrative War Songs," 398–404.

44. Godwin Nwankwo Uko, interview; Oluka Mba, interview; Vasco Iro, interview; Mecha Ukpai Akanu, interview; Kalu Awa Kalu, interview; Ogbuka Ogbuka Abaa, interview; Torti Kalu, interview; Ikenga Ibe, in interview of Nde Ichin of Amuma Village; Idika Aso, interview; Njoku, *Ohafia*, 29–30; Obuba, *History and Culture*, 27.

45. Baum, *Shrines of the Slave Trade*, 111, 123–24; Hawthorne, *Planting Rice*.

46. Oriji, *Political Organization*, 131; Isichei, *History*, 82–85; Njoku, *Ohafia*, 66.

47. Azuonye, "Narrative War Songs," 119.

48. Northrup, *Trade*, 119.

49. Kalu Davidson Oki, interview. This view is affirmed by interviews with Godwin Nwankwo Uko, Oluka Mba, Vasco Iro, Mecha Ukpai Akanu, Kalu Awa Kalu, Ogbuka Ogbuka Abaa, Torti Kalu, Ikenga Ibe, and Idika Aso.

50. U. U. Uche writes, "It was considered both demeaning and inhuman to bring back the head of a female after a battle. . . . One did not join the club of the brave with a female or infant trophy." Njoku concurs, "One could not, therefore, become ufiem by bringing home the head of a female, worst still the head of a child." U. U. Uche, "Change and Law in Ohafia," *Ohafia Review*, no. 1 (April 1981): 8; Njoku, *Ohafia*, 63.

51. Njoku, *Ohafia*, 89; Isichei, *History*, 84–85; Richard N. Henderson, *The King in Every Man: Evolutionary Trends in Onitsha Society and Culture* (New Haven: Yale University Press, 1972), 498–501; A. O. Arua, *A Short History of Ohafia* (Enugu, Nigeria: Omnibus Press, 1951), 11; Oriji, *Political Organization*, 126–29.

52. Oriji, *Political Organization*, 121–24.

53. Achebe, "When Deities Marry," 105–33.

54. Isichei, *History*, 84–85; Henderson, *King*, 498–501; Arua, *History of Ohafia*, 11.

55. Oriji, *Political Organization*, 129.

56. Njoku, *Ohafia*, 89–90; Isichei, *History*, 85.

57. Ohafia carried out raids mostly in Awka, Nnewi, Onitsha, Awkuzu, Nteje, Aguleri, Okija, Ezinnachi, Ndi Nnadata, Ozubulu, Ihiala, Enugu Ukwu, Nsugbe, Obosi, Urualla, Uli, Ugwu Ele, Mkpa, Ukwa, and Isingu in

central Igboland; Agwu, Igbariam, Ngwo, Agbaja, Umuagu, Umuogima, Ora, Okigwe, Ihuala, Okam, Isiagu, Nike, Isi Ngwo, and Okpanku in Enugu; Opi, Ukehe, Eror, and Ukpati in Nsukka; Ndienu, Nneato, Arondizuogu, Isuochi, Igbere, and Ohuhu in southern Igboland; Umuajuju, Ohia-Ukwu, Obegu, Ihube, Isuogu, and Akara Isu in Imo River valley; and Ibesikpo, Ikorokpan Nwan, Mmin, Umuerem, Ekwero, Ugep, Nkpo Ukwa, Owo, Ete, Mgbom, Nden, and Ntan in the Cross River. Oriji, *Political Organization*, 118–30; John Oriji, "Slave Trade, Warfare and Aro Expansion in the Igbo Hinterland," *Genève-Afrique* 24, no. 2 (1986): 107–14; Isichei, *History*, 82–85; Jones, *Annual Reports*, 4; Njoku, *Ohafia*, 84–85; Henderson, *King*, 502; Nwokeji, "African Conceptions," 53–54; G. Ugo Nwokeji, "The Atlantic Slave Trade and Population Density: A Historical Demography of the Biafran Hinterland," *Canadian Journal of African Studies* 34, no. 3 (2000): 617–26. In contrast, the riverine and dense forest region of Osomari, Aboh, Akwete, Azumini, and Ahoada rendered western Igboland inaccessible and discouraged Ohafia raids.

58. Such reprisal attacks continued into the late nineteenth century. See report of Afikpo reprisal by British Commissioner of Cross River Division, Richard Morrisey. "Colonial Office: Southern Nigeria Protectorate Original Correspondence, 1903," 6–10, CO520/18, BNA.

59. Arunsi Kalu, interview; Eke Emetu Kalu, interview; Emeh Okonkwo, interview; Kalu Awa Kalu, interview; Igwebe, *History of Arondizuogu*, 86–91; Njoku, *Ohafia*, 90–91; Arua, *History of Ohafia*, 11.

60. Charles Partridge, *Cross River Natives* (London: Hutchinson, 1905), 70–75; Basden, *Among the Ibos*, 37, 208–9; Basden, *Niger Ibos*, 377–88; Talbot, *Peoples of Southern Nigeria*, 184; Nsugbe, *Ohaffia*, 13, 27–28; Oriji, "Slave Trade," 107–14; Jones, *Annual Reports*, 6–7.

61. Nwokeji, *Slave Trade and Culture*, 178–79.

62. Paul Obiani, "The Stigmatization of the Descendants of Slaves in Igboland," in Brown and Lovejoy, *Repercussions of the Atlantic Slave Trade*, 321–28.

63. Uka, "A Note," 79; Udensi Ekea, interview; Olua Iro Kalu, interview; Kevin Ukiro, interview; Ndukwe Otta and Uduma Uka, interview; Agbai Ndukwe, interview; Arunsi Kalu, interview; Eke Emetu Kalu, interview; Emeh Okonkwo, interview; Kalu Awa Kalu, interview; K. K. Owen, interview.

64. Paul Lovejoy, *Transformations in Slavery: A History of Slavery in Africa*, 2nd ed. (Cambridge: Cambridge University Press, 2000), 68–69, 84–86, 103–4, 126–28, 148, 182–84, 188–89.

65. Oriji, *Political Organization*, 126–29.

66. Oriji, 132–33.

67. Nwokeji, *Slave Trade and Culture*, 37–38.

68. Nwokeji, 118–19, 126, 129.

69. Elizabeth Isichei, *A History of African Societies to 1870* (Cambridge: Cambridge University Press, 1977), 45–47; Oriji, *Political Organization*, 134.

70. House of Commons, "Report of the Lords, 1789," 49, Eighteenth Century Collections Online.

71. Nwokeji, *Slave Trade and Culture*, 123–28.

72. Olatunji Ojo, "Child Slaves in Pre-colonial Nigeria, c.1725–1860," *Slavery and Abolition* 33, no. 3 (2012): 421.

73. Equiano, *Olaudah Equiano*, 32.

74. Nwokeji, *Slave Trade and Culture*, 129–30, 133–43.

75. House of Commons, Parliament, Great Britain, "Abridgement of the Minutes of the Evidence, Taken Before a Committee of the Whole House, to whom it was Referred to Consider of the Slave Trade, 1790," 228, Eighteenth Century Collections Online database.

76. House of Commons, "Report of the Lords, 1789," 50, Eighteenth Century Collections Online.

77. Nwokeji, *Slave Trade and Culture*, 77–79.

78. Oluka Mba, interview; Chief Kalu Ukariwe, interview by the author, Akanu Village, November 6, 2011; Torti Kalu, interview; Anaso Awalekwa, interview; Uduma Nnochin Ogbuagu, interview; Njoku, *Ohafia*, 48–49.

79. McCall, *Dancing*, 81; Mayne, "Intelligence Report," 45–46, CSO 26/3/29196, NAI; Nwokeji, *Slave Trade and Culture*, 77–79.

80. Ifemesia, *Traditional Humane Living*, 45.

81. "Okonko Club: Activity of," RIV PROF. 8/8/433, NAE. Both men and women were admitted upon payment of £20.

82. Oriji, *Political Organization*, 115–17.

83. J. G. C. Allen, "Intelligence Report on the Ngwa Clan, Vol. 1, 1933," 41, E7021, NAE.

84. Ottenberg, *Double Descent*, 147.

85. Njoku, *Ohafia*, 30.

86. "Southern Nigeria Original Correspondence, 1911," 220, CO520/107, BNA; Njoku, *Ohafia*, 49; Jones, *Annual Reports*, 33.

87. Mayne, "Intelligence Report," 45–46, CSO 26/3/29196, NAI.

88. Nwokeji, *Slave Trade and Culture*, 140.

89. "Okonko Club: Activity of," RIV PROF. 8/8/433, NAE; Ifemesia, *Traditional Humane Living*, 93–94; Chieka Ifemesia, *Southern Nigeria in the Nineteenth Century: An Introductory Analysis* (New York: NOK, 1978), 43–46; Patrick Nwosu, "The Age of Cultural Hybridisation: A Case Study of Okonko Society vis-à-vis Christianity in Igboland," *Anthropologist* 12, no. 3 (2010): 163; Dike, *Trade and Politics*, 155–59; G. I. Jones, "The Political Organization of Old Calabar," in Forde, *Efik Traders of Old Calabar*, 148–57; Kannan K. Nair, *Politics and Society in South Eastern Nigeria, 1841–1906* (London: Frank Cass, 1972), 48–55; Latham, *Old Calabar*, 34–41, 75–79, 91–96; Danial O. Offiong, *Continuity and Change in Some Traditional Societies of Nigeria* (Zaria, Nigeria: Ahmadu Bello University Press, 1998), 92; Victoria O. Ibewuike, *African Women and Religious Change: A Study of the Western Igbo of Nigeria; With a Special*

Focus on Asaba Town (Uppsala: Victoria O. Ibewuike, 2006), 45; Leonard, "Notes," 197.

90. Onuora Nzekwe, "Omo Ukwu Temple," *Nigeria Magazine*, no. 81 (June 1964): 124; Njoku, *Ohafia*, 87; Obuba, *History*, 379; Olua Iro Kalu, interview; Kevin Ukiro, interview; Egbe Okafor, interview with author, Asaga Village, August 12, 2010; Idika Aso, interview; Elder Ukpai Onum Ndukwe, interview with author, Asaga Village, April 13 and May 15, 2012.

91. Oriji, "Slave Trade," 109–11.

92. Njoku, *Ohafia*, 63; Ikenga Ibe, interview; Oluka Mba, interview; Kalu Awa Kalu, interview; K. K. Owen, interview; Kalu Davidson Oki, interview; Agbai Ndukwe, interview; Arunsi Kalu, interview; Eke Emetu Kalu, interview.

93. Chief Egbe Abba Iro, interview with author, Oboro Village, November 17, 2011.

94. Emeh Okonkwo, interview; Olua Iro Kalu, interview; Kevin Ukiro, interview; Ndukwe Otta and Uduma Uka, interview; Arua, *Short History of Ohafia*, 11; Isichei, *History*, 85; Igwebe, *Arondizuogu*, 91.

95. Mayne, "Intelligence Report," 46, CSO 26/3/29196, NAI.

96. Ndukwe Otta and Uduma Uka, interview.

97. Agbai Ndukwe, interievw.

98. Ndukwe Otta and Uduma Uka, interview.

99. Njoku, *Ohafia*, 64.

100. Ndukwe Otta and Uduma Uka, interview.

101. Nsugbe, *Ohaffia*, 49–51. See Mayne, "Intelligence Report," 4, CSO 26/3/29196, NAI; and Azuonye, "Heroic Age," 21.

102. Njoku, *Ohafia*, 81; Azuonye, "Heroic Age," 19; G. I. Jones, "Ohaffia Obu Houses," *Nigerian Field* 6, no. 4 (1937): 170–71; Basden, *Among the Ibos*, 246; Ezie-ogo Ugbu Uduma, interview by author, Ihenta (Ibina) Village, November 11, 2011; Elders of Nde Odo Compound, interview by the author, Akanu Ohafia, November 2, 2011; Agbai Ndukwe, interview; Nnenna Obuba, interview.

103. G. I. Jones, "Ohaffia Obu Houses," 169; Ogbonne Kalu, interview; Mecha Ukpai Akanu, interview; Udensi Ekea, interview; Vasco Iro, interview; Kalu Awa, interview; Idika Aso, interview; Kevin Ukiro, interview; Onwuka Kalu Agwu, interview; Eke Emetu Kalu, interview; Obuba, *History and Culture*, 26; Ottenberg, *Double Descent*, 93, 192–93.

104. Ikenga Ibe, interview; Oluka Mba, interview.

105. Mayne, "Intelligence Report," 44, CSO 26/3/29196, NAI.

106. Jones, *Annual Reports*, 4.

107. United Free Church of Scotland, "The Recent Expedition against the Aros," *Missionary Record of the United Free Church of Scotland*, no. 1-164 (1902): 453.

108. Frank Ashcroft, "Report on Calabar Mission: Tour of the Calabar Mission Districts, July to August 1921," 28, West Africa, MS.7796, NLS.

109. Partridge, *Cross River Natives*, 70; Leonard, "Notes," 190–201; Basden, *Niger Ibos*, 126, 195; Basden, *Among the Ibos*, 37–38.

110. Leonard, "Notes," 196.

111. Basden, *Among the Ibos*, 37–38.

112. Njoku, *Ohafia*, 82.

113. "Southern Nigeria Protectorate Original Correspondence, May–August, 1901," 717–22, CO520/8, BNA; Jan Buchanan to Robert Collins, September 26, 1901, MS.7672, Foreign No. 16, United Free Church of Scotland (UFC), NLS.

114. Chubb, "Assessment Reports," 19, OW 342/27, ABADIST 8/11/2, NAE; Johnston, *Of God and Maxim Guns*, 26.

115. For this British view of Asaga, documented as "Patrol up the Cross River: Enyong Creek to Obubra Hill" and "Field Operations, October 1904 to June 1905," see "Southern Nigeria Original Correspondence, June to August, 1905," 387–425, 526–28, CO520/31, BNA.

116. Luise White, *Speaking with Vampires: Rumor and History in Colonial Africa* (Berkeley: University of California Press, 2000), 4, 18, 44–45, 50–54, 58, 91, 98–102, 114.

117. Sweet, *Domingos Álvares*, 10–12.

118. This was similar to okonko burial practices in the Bight of Biafra. See "Okonko Club: Activity of," 37–40, RIV PROF. 8/8/433, NAE.

119. Ndukwe Otta and Uduma Uka, interview.

120. Njoku, *Ohafia*, 64.

121. Mayne, "Intelligence Report," 45, CSO 26/3/29196, NAI. The Gold Coast had similar burial practices. See Erik Seeman, *Death in the New World*, 21.

122. "Southern Nigeria Protectorate Original Correspondence, June–August, 1906," 170–84, CO520/36, BNA; Partridge, *Cross River Natives*, 72; Nsugbe, *Ohaffia*, 108.

123. Njoku, *Ohafia*, 64.

124. Uka, "Note," 78.

125. Ndukwe Otta, interview.

126. Uchendu, *Igbo*, 16.

127. Chinua Achebe, *Things Fall Apart* (London: Heinemann, 1958), 6.

128. Azuonye, "Heroic Age," 23.

129. David Eltis, quoted in Toby Green, *The Rise of the Trans-Atlantic Slave Trade in Western Africa, 1300–1589* (Cambridge: Cambridge University Press, 2012), 9.

130. S. Behrendt, A. J. H. Latham, and D. Northrup, *Diary of Antera Duke, an Eighteenth-Century African Slave Trader* (Oxford: Oxford University Press, 2010), 29; Isichei, *Igbo Worlds*, 144.

131. Azuonye, "Heroic Age," 14; Obuba, *History*, 26–27; "Southern Nigeria Protectorate Original Correspondence, May–August, 1901," 570–74, CO520/8, BNA; "Southern Nigeria Protectorate Original Correspondence, 1906," 170–84, CO520/36, BNA; Partridge, *Cross River Natives*, 72.

132. "Southern Nigeria Protectorate Original Correspondence, May–August, 1901," 573–74, CO520/8, BNA.

133. "Southern Nigeria Protectorate Original Correspondence, June–August, 1906," 170–84, CO520/36, BNA; Adiele E. Afigbo, *The Abolition of the Slave Trade in Southeastern Nigeria, 1885–1950* (New York: University of Rochester Press, 2006), 42.

134. McCall, "Atlantic Slave Trade," 75–76; Isichei, *History*, 104; Njoku, *African Cultural Values*, 19; Njoku, *Ohafia*, 64; "Africa (Slave Trade), West Coast, 1890," 348–51, FO84/2020, BNA; Udensi Ekea, interview; Kalu Awa and Ikenga Ibe, interviewed as part of group interview of Nde Ichin of Amuma by author, November 26, 2011; Oluka Mba, interview, November 3, 2011.

135. Mayne, "Intelligence Report," 44, CSO 26/3/29196, NAI; Chubb, "Assessment Reports," 6, OW 342/27, ABADIST 8/11/2, NAE; Jones, *Annual Reports*, 36; Njoku, *Inter-village Trade*, 29; Isichei, *History*, 85; Achebe, *Farmers*, 75; Nakanyinke Musisi, "Women, 'Elite Polygyny,' and Buganda State Formation," *Signs* 16, no. 4 (1991): 757–86.

136. Igor Kopytoff and Suzanne Miers, "Introduction: 'African Slavery' as an Institution of Marginality," in Miers and Kopytoff, *Slavery in Africa*, 76; John K. Thornton, "Sexual Demography: The Impact of the Slave Trade on Family Structure," in Robertson and Klein, *Women and Slavery in Africa*, 39–40; Spaulding and Beswick, *African Systems of Slavery*; Brown and Lovejoy, *Repercussions*.

137. Jones, "Ohaffia Obu Houses," 170; Njoku, *Ohafia*, 42; Idika Aso, interview; Kevin Ukiro, interview; Arunsi Kalu, interview.

138. Uchendu, *Igbo*, 89; Uchendu, "Slaves and Slavery," 130.

139. Achebe, "When Deities Marry," 105–33.

CHAPTER 3: GENDERED SLAVERY IN THE BIGHT OF BIAFRA, CA. 1750–1890

1. "Estimates," Trans-Atlantic Slave Trade Database, accessed February 2017, http://slavevoyages.org/assessment/estimates. Of the 600,248 captives embarked from the Bight of Biafra for the British Caribbean, 508,636 disembarked. Of the 257,438 captives embarked from Biafra for Jamaica, 220,990 disembarked.

2. Carolyn Brown and Paul Lovejoy, "The Bight of Biafra and Slavery," in Brown and Lovejoy, *Repercussions of the Atlantic Slave Trade*, 6.

3. Philip Morgan, "The Cultural Implications of the Atlantic Slave Trade: African Regional Origins, American Destinations and New World Developments," *Slavery and Abolition* 18, no. 1 (2008): 122.

4. Lorand J. Matory, *Black Atlantic Religion: Tradition, Transnationalism, and Matriarchy in the Afro-Brazilian Candomblé* (Princeton: Princeton University Press, 2005), 1–36.

5. Diana Paton, "Enslaved Women and Slavery before and after 1807," History in Focus, Institute of Historical Research, accessed February 2017, https://www.history.ac.uk/ihr/Focus/Slavery/articles/paton.html.

6. See Trevor Burnard, "Evaluating Gender in Early Jamaica, 1674–1784," *History of the Family* 12, no. 2 (2007): 81–91; David V. Trotman, "Africanizing and Creolizing the Plantation Frontier of Trinidad, 1787–1838," in Lovejoy and Trotman, *Trans-Atlantic Dimensions of Ethnicity in the African Diaspora*, 218–39.

7. Paton and Scully, "Introduction: Gender and Slave Emancipation," 4.

8. Nwokeji, *Slave Trade*, 144, 148.

9. Nwokeji, 162–70. Nwokeji writes, "Kolanut reverence among the Igbo partly accounted for the virtual absence of the trans-Saharan trade in the Bight of Biafra's forest region, which would have absorbed many female captives that ended up in the Americas."

10. Nwokeji, *Slave Trade*, 149. In support of the female marginality argument, the question has been posed, "If the economic role of women was so great, why was a higher proportion of females sent into the trade from [the Bight of Biafra] than from elsewhere in Atlantic Africa?" The notion of Igbo male supremacy in agriculture is predicated on the yam argument. Although yam may have been the favorite food of Igbo people, was designated the king of crops by androcentric colonial anthropologists, and served as a basis of male sociopolitical differentiation through title-taking rites, it did not overtly determine the demography of Biafra's slave production and slave use. Contrary to common assumption, the yam was not a staple food. The cassava, which became a staple in the nineteenth century, was cultivated primarily by women. The yam crop is fragile, and although it required exacting labor, extensive acreage, and enormous soil nutrients, it yielded relatively little. The Igbo fixation on yam defied economic rationality. Women's subsistence production of root crops and vegetables enabled men to cultivate yams as a niche cultural-prestige crop. And women's laborious weeding during eight months of the year ensured the survival of the yam crop. Thus, the notion that "women did not primarily work yam and were not acknowledged as important in its production" overlooks the centrality of women's direct labor to yam production, as well as their indirect labor through the provision of food staples that ensured yam's marginal prestige. It also oversimplifies the complexity of local and external factors that shaped Biafra's slave supply. One should perhaps rather ask, If the economic role of men was so great, why was a greater proportion of males than females sent into the transatlantic slave trade from the Bight of Biafra?

11. Nwokeji, *Slave Trade*, 153; Nwokeji, "African Conceptions," 50, 56, 62–64. The female marginality thesis further suggests that in seventeenth-century Kongo, enslaved women cost the same as men because such women were critical to domestic production and polygyny, in contrast to Biafra, where enslaved women were valued less than men. This informs

Nwokeji's conclusion that "Biafra slavery did not rest on women . . . female slavery for domestic purposes was marginal." See Nwokeji, *Slave Trade*, 154. The central idea here is that African regions where women constituted the majority of the enslaved population were also areas where women performed the bulk of agrarian labor and were valued as doing so. Domestic slavery in those regions centered on women. However, using Portuguese testimonials from the Kongo to allude to Biafra-Igbo women's marginality to agricultural production, and thus to domestic slavery, is misleading. If we are to rely on European observers to understand how the comparative cost of male and female slaves reflected their labor and economic value and defined their relative importance to domestic slavery, we ought then to look at the reports of British slave traders in the Bight of Biafra—not those of the Portuguese in the Kongo. Biafra was similar to the Kongo, in terms of women performing the bulk of the agricultural labor and being valued for that.

12. Amadiume, *Male Daughters*, 29–38; Felix Ekechi, "Gender and Economic Power: The Case of Igbo Market Women in Southeastern Nigeria," in *African Market Women and Economic Power: The Role of Women in African Economic Development*, ed. B. House-Midamba and F. K. Ekechi (Westport, CT: Greenwood Press, 1995), 41–57; Adiele E. Afigbo, "Women in Nigerian History," in *Women in Nigerian Economy*, ed. Martin O. Ijere (Enugu, Nigeria: Acena, 1991), 35–36; Gloria Chuku, "From Petty Traders to International Merchants: A Historical Account of Three Igbo Women of Nigeria in Trade and Commerce, 1886–1970," *African Economic History*, no. 27 (1999): 1–22; Felicia Ekejiuba, "Omu Okwei, the Merchant Queen of Ossomari: A Biographical Sketch," *Journal of the Historical Society of Nigeria* 3, no. 4 (1967): 633–46; Achebe, *Farmers*, 109–60.

13. Audrey Smedley, *Women Creating Patrilyny: Gender and Environment in West Africa* (Walnut Creek, CA: AltaMira, 2004), 1–3. Even Nwokeji provides strong contradictory evidence of the centrality of women to Aro lineage, wealth, and territorial expansion (*mmuba*).

14. House of Commons, "Report of the Lords, 1789," 60, Eighteenth Century Collections Online.

15. House of Commons, 61–62.

16. Nwokeji, *Slave Trade*, 177.

17. "Minutes of the Evidence Taken before the Select Committee, House of Commons and Lords," 123–24, ZHC 1/84, cited in Audra Diptee, *From Africa to Jamaica: The Making of an Atlantic Slave Society, 1775–1807* (Gainesville: University Press of Florida, 2010), 50.

18. Diptee, *From Africa to Jamaica*, 50.

19. Diptee, 45–48.

20. Gwyn Campbell, Suzanne Miers, and Joseph C. Miller, "Strategies of Women and Constraints of Enslavement in the Modern Americas," in Campbell, Miers, and Miller, *The Modern Atlantic*, 9.

21. Claire Robertson and Marsha Robinson, "Re-modeling Slavery as if Women Mattered," in Campbell, Miers, and Miller, *The Modern Atlantic*, 264.

22. Henrice Altink, "Deviant and Dangerous: Proslavery Representations of Jamaican Slave Women's Sexuality, ca. 1780–1834," in *Women and Slavery: The Modern Atlantic*, 209–30.

23. The severe privatization of human property that distinguished chattel slavery in Jamaica did not define Biafra's kinship slavery. Therefore, a mere comparison is fraught with disparities in the relative significance of race, labor regimes, and social alienation. For instance, in Jamaica, enslaved African women's sexuality became critical to both planters' and abolitionists' debates about deleterious sexual deviance, which defined Jamaican slave society between 1780 and 1834. Proslavery writers constructed African bondswomen as threatening deviants from the Victorian model of female sexual passivity, and enslaved African women's sexuality provided a basis for post-1820s antiabolitionism discourse. Interracial sex, in fact white male sexual abuse of African women, proved fundamental to the maintenance of plantation slavery. Perhaps the most forceful picture is found in Thomas Thistlewood's account of his savage use of his female slaves for sexual gratification, and sadistically forcing slaves to ingest feces. Trevor Burnard sums this up as physical torment and psychological distress. See Trevor G. Burnard, *Mastery, Tyranny, and Desire: Thomas Thistlewood and His Slaves in the Anglo-Jamaican World* (Chapel Hill: University of North Carolina Press, 2004), 178–79. Heather Vermeulen has recently emphasized the necessity of naming Thistlewood a serial rapist. See Heather V. Vermeulen, "Thomas Thistlewood's Libidnal Linnaean Project: Slavery, Ecology, and Knowledge Production," *Small Axe* 22, no. 1 (2018): 18–38. Even after abolition, in the 1840s, displaced white elite anxieties about the dangers of freedom resulted in the "manufacture" and prosecution of African sexual deviance, which facilitated the abandonment of postemancipation reform. See Jonathan Dalby, "'Such a Mass of Disgusting and Revolting Cases': Moral Panic and the 'Discovery' of Sexual Deviance in Post-emancipation Jamaica (1835–1855)," *Slavery and Abolition* 36, no. 1 (2015): 136–59. The presence of reproductive black female slaves in the Americas and the consequent white reaction to their reproductive capacities and offspring defined notions of race and racism. Scientific discourse, European popular culture, slaveholding classes' elaboration of the ideal of white womanhood, and abolitionists' rhetoric converged to define black femininity as pathological. See Diana Paton and Pamela Scully, introduction to Paton and Scully, *Gender and Slave Emancipation in the Atlantic World*, 20. Such racialized and sexualized female degradation in the service of slavery did not occur in the Bight of Biafra.

24. Provenance for captives transported to Jamaica, 1776–1808: Bight of Biafra (43.1 percent), Gold Coast (23.8 percent), West-Central Africa (18.6 percent), Bight of Benin (6.2 percent), Sierra Leone (6.6 percent), and other (1.7 percent). Of the estimated 411,884 embarked, 370,670

disembarked in Jamaica. "Estimates," Trans-Atlantic Slave Trade Database, accessed February 2017, http://slavevoyages.org/assessment/estimates; Diptee, *From Africa to Jamaica*, 47, 118, 139, estimates 98,032 and 177,529 for Gold Coast and Biafra embarkations.

25. Lucille M. Mair, *A Historical Study of Women in Jamaica, 1655–1844* (Kingston: University of the West Indies Press, 2006), xiv.

26. Northrup, "Igbo and Myth Igbo," 3–4; Morgan, "Cultural Implication," 130–39.

27. Douglass B. Chambers, *Murder at Montpelier: Igbo Africans in Virginia* (Jackson: University Press of Mississippi, 2005), 3–71; Douglass Chambers, "Ethnicity and the Diaspora: The Slave Trade and the Creation of African 'Nations' in the Americas," *Slavery and Abolition* 22, no. 3 (2001): 25–39; Chambers, "Significance," 101–20; Michael Mullin, "Laura Smalligan's *Jonkonu, a Jamaican Slave Dance*: Contesting the African in African-American," *Slavery and Abolition* 35, no. 1 (2015): 142; Sweet, *Domingos Álvares*, 1–8. These debates feed into an older conversation about how African *culture* was reproduced in the Americas, from Melville Herkovists's survivalist "Africanism" and Franklin Frazier's counternotion that "the Negro was stripped of his social heritage," to bifurcated schools of thought, which posit that the reconstitution of African identities in the New World required either collective group consciousness and "additivity" or transnational individualism. Such conversations also concerned whether creolization was a unidirectional or dialectical process. For this historiography, see Melville Herskovits, *The Myth of the Negro Past* (1941; repr., Boston: Beacon, 1958); Sidney Wilfred Mintz and Richard Price, *The Birth of African-American Culture: An Anthropological Perspective* (Boston: Beacon, 1976); John Thornton, *Africa and Africans in the Making of the Atlantic World, 1400–1680* (Cambridge: Cambridge University Press, 1998); James H. Sweet, *Recreating Africa: Culture, Kinship, and Religion in the African-Portuguese World, 1441–1770* (Chapel Hill: University of North Carolina Press, 2003); Carney, *Black Rice*; J. Lorand Matory, *Black Atlantic Religion: Tradition, Transnationalism, and Matriarchy in the Afro-Brazilian Candomblé* (Princeton: Princeton University Press, 2005).

28. Crow, *Memoirs of the Late Captain Hugh Crow of Liverpool*, 198–201, 226–33.

29. Johann Jakob Bossard, Arnold R. Highfield and Vladimir Barac, eds. *C. G. A. Oldendorp's History of the Mission of the Evangelical Brethren on the Caribbean Islands of St. Thomas, St. Croix, and St. John* (Ann Arbor: Karoma, 1987), 167–85.

30. Morgan, *Laboring Women*, 7, 107.

31. Kalu Davidson Oki, interview.

32. Kopytoff and Miers, "Introduction," 14, 67.

33. This is critical of the tendency in African slavery literature to equate marriage/polygyny with slavery. Igbo slave owners made a distinction between female slaves and wives.

34. Victor C. Uchendu, "Slaves and Slavery in Igboland, Nigeria," in Miers and Kopytoff, *Slavery in Africa*, 125.

35. Claire C. Robertson and Martin A. Klein, "Women's Importance in African Slave Systems," in Robertson and Klein, *Women and Slavery in Africa*, 6–15.

36. Uchendu, "Slaves," 121–32.

37. Biafra's seventeenth-century 51:49 (or 55:45) and eighteenth-century 44:56 export ratio of female to male slaves was inverted in other parts of coastal Africa, such as Upper Guinea with a ratio of 25:75. Ojo, "Child Slaves," 418; Nwokeji, *Slave Trade and Culture*, 171–72.

38. Morgan, "Cultural Implications," 125–27.

39. Diptee, *From Africa to Jamaica*, 84.

40. Burnard, "Evaluating Gender in Early Jamaica," 81–91.

41. House of Commons, "Report of the Lords, 1789," 47–49, Eighteenth Century Collections Online.

42. Crow, *Memoirs of the Late Captain Hugh Crow of Liverpool*, 228. They specify, the "Africans become domestic slaves, or are sold to Europeans, by losing their liberty in war, resigning it in famine, or forfeiting it by insolvency, or the crimes of murder, adultery, or sorcery," as well as "hunt[ing]" for captives in a bid to exchange them for European supplies.

43. House of Commons, "Report of the Lords, 1789," 48–49; House of Commons, "Abridgement of the Minutes, 1790," 20, Eighteenth Century Collections Online.

44. House of Commons, "Abridgement of the Minutes, 1790," 15.

45. House of Commons, 16.

46. House of Commons, 229–30.

47. William Blake to James Rogers, October 1790, Chancery Records, C107/12, BNA. For other examples, see William Dinely to James Rogers, September 1791, Chancery Records, C107/5, BNA; Robert Peake to James Rogers, undated, Chancery Records, C107/6, BNA.

48. House of Commons, "Report of the Lords, 1789," 120; House of Commons, "Abridgement of the Minutes, 1790," 15–22, Eighteenth Century Collections Online.

49. House of Commons, "Report of the Lords, 1789," 116.

50. House of Commons, 116.

51. House of Commons, "Abridgement of the Minutes, 1790," 244.

52. Hugh Crow identifies "Eboes" and "Breches," "Brasses," "Quaws," "Appas," and "Otams."

53. William Blake to James Rogers, October 1790, Chancery Records, C107/12, BNA. For other examples, see William Dinely to James Rogers, September 1791, Chancery Records, C107/5, BNA; Robert Peake to James Rogers, undated, Chancery Records, C107/6, BNA.

54. Diptee, *From Africa to Jamaica*, 44, 74–7. The surgeon on the *African Queen*, thirty crew members, and one-third of the 330 captives died in the

Atlantic crossing. In total 169 captives died; 202 captives survived, including 65 men, 74 women, 5 adolescents, and 58 children.

55. Diptee, *From Africa to Jamaica*, 60

56. Nwokeji, *Slave Trade and Culture*, 45–50.

57. For these debates, see Chambers, *Murder at Montpelier*, 3–71; Douglass B. Chambers, "'My Own Nation': Igbo Exiles in the Diaspora," in *Routes to Slavery: Direction, Ethnicity and Mortality in the Atlantic Slave Trade*, ed. David Eltis and David Richardson (London: Frank Cass, 1997), 73–75; Northrup, "Igbo and Myth Igbo," 3–4; Morgan, "Cultural Implication," 130–39; Mullin, "Laura Smalligan's *Jonkonu*," 146.

58. Nwokeji, "Slave Trade and Population Density," 616–55; Diptee, *From Africa to Jamaica*, 60.

59. Northrup, "Igbo and Myth Igbo," 1–20; Chambers, "Significance," 101–20; Chambers, "Tracing Igbo."

60. Morgan, "Cultural Implications," 122–45; Walter Rucker, *Gold Coast Diasporas: Identity, Culture, and Power* (Bloomington: Indiana University Press, 2015), 6–8, 14.

61. Diptee, *From Africa to Jamaica*, 25–30.

62. The Bight of Biafra, especially the port of Bonny, had one of the highest daily average number of captives loaded on a vessel, as well as the fastest rate of filling ships with captives during the second half of the eighteenth century, when ships spent on average 109 days in the region compared to 203.6 days in Sierra Leone, 215.9 in Windward Coast, 137.4 in Gold Coast, 145 in the Bight of Benin, 162.3 in West-Central Africa, and 126.8 in Southeast Africa. Nwokeji, *Slave Trade and Culture*, 37–40; Diptee, *From Africa to Jamaica*, 61.

63. Simon Newman et al., "The West African Ethnicity of the Enslaved in Jamaica," *Slavery and Abolition* 34, no. 3 (2012): 377–79.

64. Diptee, *From Africa to Jamaica*, 53.

65. Morgan, "Cultural Implications," 127–28.

66. Newman et al., "West African Ethnicity," 397–89; Mair, *Historical Study of Women*, 33; Turner, *Contested Bodies*, 253.

67. Intensive surveillance and intervention characterized Jamaican planters' pro-natalist policies. See Paton, "Enslaved Women and Slavery"; Higman, *Slave Populations*, 349–54; Morrissey, *Slave Women*, 126–30; Morgan, "Slave Women," 29–30; Ward, *British West Indian Slavery*, 166–70; Barbara Bush, "Hard Labor: Women, Childbirth, and Resistance in British Caribbean Slave Societies," in *More Than Chattel: Black Women and Slavery in the Americas*, ed. David Barry Gasper and Darlene Clark Hine (Bloomington: Indiana University Press, 1996), 193–217; Laurence Brown and Tara Innis, "Slave Women, Family Strategies, and the Transition to Freedom in Barbados, 1834–41," in Campbell, Miers, and Miller, *The Modern Atlantic*, 172–85.

68. House of Commons, "Abridgement of the Minutes, 1790," 129, Eighteenth Century Collections Online.

69. Turner, *Contested Bodies*, 59–63, 66.

70. Uchendu, "Slaves," 129.

71. Udensi Ekea, interview; Dibia Kalu Ekea of Nde Edem, interview by author, Okon Village, September 24, 2011; Dibia Agwu Arua, interview by author, Okon Village, August 4, 2010; Dibia Akirika, interview by author, Okon Village, September 26, 2011.

72. Njoku, *Ohafia*, 44–45.

73. Robin Law, "Ethnicity and the Slave Trade: 'Lucumi' and 'Nago' as Ethnonyms in West Africa," *History in Africa*, no. 24 (1997): 205–19, identifies the "Nago" as a New World and West African ethnonym for Yoruba and Fon slaves embarked from Dahomey and Whydah.

74. Diptee, *From Africa to Jamaica*, 92.

75. At this point, he had spent a whole year as the only white person and overseer, living among a slave community of forty-two (twenty-four males, eighteen females) at a livestock pen (Vineyard Pen at Sweet River), where the slaves schooled him in Jamaican flora and fauna and African medicine, cuisine, and music, and he carried on a year-long sexual affair with an "Ebo" slave girl, Marina.

76. Burnard writes, "In the third quarter of the eighteenth century, when Thistlewood was active in the slave market, the Bight of Biafra and the Gold Coast accounted for 63 percent of Africans imported into Jamaica, with just over 30 percent coming from the Bight of Benin, the Windward Coast, and west-central Africa." Burnard, *Mastery, Tyranny, and Desire*, 16.

77. These are chronicled in Douglass Hall, *In Miserable Slavery: Thomas Thistlewood in Jamaica, 1750–86* (Mona, Jamaica: University of the West Indies Press, 1999), chapters 1 and 2. Also see Burnard, *Mastery, Tyranny, and Desire*, 1–35.

78. Jerome Handler, "Custom and Law: The Status of Enslaved Africans in Seventeenth-Century Barbados," *Slavery and Abolition* 37, no. 2 (2016): 233–55.

79. Uchendu, "Slaves," 128; Kopytoff and Miers, "Introduction," 7–14; Nwokeji, *Slave Trade*, 73.

80. For instance, Nwokeji asserts, "Fieldwork among the Aro supports the argument that female slavery was marginal in the region," because when a man acquired a female slave, the relationship invariably changed to that of husband and wife. It was not "practical" to keep women as slaves because "the Aro believed that women were difficult, their mobility was minimal," and "a woman could not establish a lineage." Nwokeji, *Slave Trade*, 157. Certainly, a major basis of Biafra's domestic social slavery was kinship incorporation and lineage expansion. The features that popularized female slavery in the Bight of Biafra—women's easy incorporation as wives—have been erroneously portrayed as a hindrance to the enslavement of women.

81. These traditions are also documented in "Case No. 31/31, Transferred from the Provincial Court Bende 29.9.31, Chief Kalu Idika of Ebem vs. Eme Ado of Ebem," 1–32, NAE.

82. Mbah, "Matriliny, Masculinity, and Contested Gendered Definitions," 249–50.

83. Nwokeji, *Slave Trade*, 170–73. Nwokeji interprets the increased volume of girl captives as a reflection of the "short-term need for women in the Bight of Biafra in the nineteenth century."

84. Morgan, "Cultural Implications," 126–27; Nwokeji, "African Conceptions," 49, 52–53.

85. "Southern Nigeria Protectorate Original Correspondence, May–August, 1901," 570–74, CO520/8, BNA; Paul Lovejoy and David Richardson, "Competing Markets for Male and Female Slaves: Prices in the Interior of West Africa, 1750–1850," *International Journal of African Historical Studies* 28, no. 2 (1995): 261–93. The matrifocal conceptions of Ohafia-Igbo citizenship, the position of women as premier food producers and breadwinners, and the sociocultural value that matrilineages placed on women for lineage reproduction and property expansion rendered females a needed strategic resource within Ohafia.

86. Anaso Awalekwa, interview; Udensi Ekea, interview; Mecha Ukpai Akanu, interview; Arunsi Kalu, interview; Kevin Ukiro, interview; Docas Kalu, interview; Agbai Ndukwe, interview; Mayne, "Intelligence Report," 45–48, CSO 26/3/29196, NAI; Kalu, "Ibo Autobiography," 166–67; Arua, "Yam Ceremonies," 695; Njoku, *Ohafia*, 62–68; McCall, *Dancing*, 83; Catherine Coquery-Vidrovitch, *African Women: A Modern History* (Boulder: Westview, 1997), 11.

87. Mayne, "Intelligence Report," 58–59, CSO 26/3/29196, NAI; Arunsi Kalu, interview; Oluka Mba, interview by the author; Kalu Awa Kalu, interview; Ndukwe Otta and Uduma Uka, interview; K. K. Owen, interview; Olua Iro Kalu, interview.

88. Oriji, *Political Organization in Nigeria*, 141.

89. Diptee, *From Africa to Jamaica*, 103–4; Burnard, *Mastery, Tyranny, and Desire*, 217; Hall, *In Miserable Slavery*, 142, 179, 191–92, 217. Sasha Turner similarly writes that Taylor and other planters often complained about enslaved women's nocturnal wanderings; Turner suggests that they were ways women claimed control over bodily pleasures. See Turner, *Contested Bodies*, 63.

90. Paton, "Enslaved Women and Slavery." Paton concludes that enslaved women's experiences of pregnancy, birth, and motherhood was marked by ill health and death, pain, and grief. And the everyday loss of children was a prominent trauma of slavery.

91. Herbert Klein and Stanley Engerman, "Fertility Differentials between Slaves in the United States and the British West Indies: A Note on Lactation Practices and Their Possible Implications," *William and Mary Quarterly* 35, no. 2 (April 1978): 358, 368; Jerome Handler and Robert Corruccini, "Weaning among West Indian Slaves: Historical and Bioanthropological Evidence from Barbados," *William and Mary Quarterly* 43, no. 1 (January

1986): 111–17; Lucille Mathurin, "The Arrivals of Black Women," *Jamaica Journal* 9, no. 2/3 (1975): 4. Often malnourished, enslaved women also extended lactation because they found it difficult to secure reliable sources of other food for their infants. Lengthy lactation aggravated the rigors of overwork, leaving mothers in a constant state of nutritional deprivation. To shore up deficient thiamine, enslaved African women consumed baked clay, which planters blamed as the cause of women's amenorrhea (cessation of menstruation). See Morgan, "Slave Women and Reproduction in Jamaica," 32, 38.

92. Pregnant slaves were subjected to excessive stooping, they carried heavy weights, and they toiled under unceasing compulsion until six weeks before birth. Four to six weeks after delivery they returned to the "second gang" so long as they continued to breastfeed. By the nineteenth century, it had become standard practice to lay pregnant women facedown over a hole dug in the ground to receive their bulging belly and then to flog them on the back. White overseers and bookkeepers "kicked black women in the belly from one end of Jamaica to the other." Such severe physical punishments resulted in prolapsed uterus, urinary inconsistency, premature labor, and miscarriage. Indeed, harsh material circumstances including poor nutrition, strenuous work, overseers' brutality, and infectious diseases further inhibited enslaved women's reproduction. Kenneth Morgan, "Slave Women and Reproduction in Jamaica, ca. 1776–1834," in *Women and Slavery: The Modern Atlantic*, 27–45.

93. Douglass B. Chambers, "'My Own Nation': Igbo Exiles in the Diaspora," in *Routes to Slavery: Direction, Ethnicity and Mortality in the Atlantic Slave Trade*, ed. David Eltis and David Richardson (London: Frank Cass, 1997), 73–75; Morgan, *Laboring Women*, 114. "Dirt eating" was especially associated with "Ebo" suicidal tendencies. See Diptee, *From Africa to Jamaica*, 90. Historian Kenneth Morgan observed that African slaves practiced extended birth spacing more than creoles, which may lend some credence to the possibility that Igbo women slaves in Jamaica continued (in some form) the homeland practice of a two-year postpartum taboo against the resumption of intercourse during the nursing of infants. As an illustration, Oldendorp writes that "among the Ibo" slaves in the Caribbean, "a sacrifice is made by the priest for a woman in childbed six weeks after her delivery since she is considered unclean up to that point and hence is visited only by her closest relatives." Bossard, Highfield, and Barac, *C. G. A. Oldendorp's History*, 194. This postpartum sacrifice, combined with extended lactation, facilitated extended birth spacing.

94. Jerome Handler and Kenneth Bilby, "On the Early Use and Origin of the Term 'Obeah' in Barbados and the Anglophone Caribbean," *Slavery and Abolition* 22, no. 2 (2001): 87–100. See Crow, *Memoirs of the Late Captain Hugh Crow of Liverpool*, 226–27, for reference to "Oboe doctors, or Dibbeah" from the Biafran port of Bonny destined to Jamaica. In contrast, in Ohafia, abortion was a heinous crime regulated by the ikpirikpe female court.

95. Verene A. Shepherd, "'Petticoat Rebellion'? The Black Woman's Body and Voice in the Struggle for Freedom in Colonial Jamaica," in *In the Shadow of the Plantation: Caribbean History and Legacy*, ed. Alvin O. Thompson (Kingston: Ian Randle, 2002), 24.

96. Orlando Patterson, *Slavery and Social Death: A Comparative Study* (Cambridge, MA: Harvard University Press, 1982), 133; Stella Dadzie, "Searching for the Invisible Woman: Slavery and Resistance in Jamaica," *Race and Class* 32, no. 2 (October 1990): 21–38.

97. Klein and Engerman, "Fertility," 357–74; Handler and Corruccini, "Weaning," 111–17.

98. This interpretation differs from Diana Paton's argument that their persistent flight and "suicidal tendencies" reflected "a desire to transform those aspects of pronatalism from which they benefited into rights." Paton, "Enslaved Women and Slavery."

99. Audra A. Diptee, "Atlantic Connections: An African Cohort in the Making of a Slave Society, Jamaica 1775–1807" (PhD thesis, University of Toronto, 2006), 33, 38–40, 66; Diptee, *From Africa to Jamaica*, 54. Little has been done on the content of this Africanization.

100. Burnard, *Mastery, Tyranny, and Desire*, 15–18. Burnard argues, "Africans failed to thrive [in Jamaica] due to poor diet, debilitating work regimes, and brutal treatment." This necessitated incessant captive importation, mostly from the Bight of Biafra, resulting in "a slave population that remained between 75 and 80 percent African," as well as "a rapid Africanization or re-Africanization of slave culture." Also, "The clear evidence of extensive Africanization in Jamaica and the failure of effective white settlement greatly alarmed contemporary commentators."

101. Afigbo, *Ropes*, 241–42.

102. David Northrup, "The Compatibility of the Slave and Palm Oil Trades in the Bight of Biafra," *Journal of African History* 17, no. 3 (1976): 353–64. I provide ancillary evidence for this in chapter 4, where I further examine coastal and hinterland polygyny and female slavery practices.

103. Oriji, *Political Organization*, 140–41. This was akin to 1670s Jamaica, where large landholdings dedicated to intensive sugar production based on a highly capitalized labor system made survival of the small to medium farmer precarious, resulting in white depopulation and expansion of African slave labor. See Mair, *Historical Study of Women*, 30.

104. Oriji, *Political Organization*, 142–45.

105. Nwokeji, *Slave Trade*, 73, 94.

106. Nwokeji, 173–74.

107. Gloria Chuku, *Igbo Women and Economic Transformation in Southeastern Nigeria, 1900–1960* (New York: Routledge, 2005), 181–82.

108. Ekejiuba, "Omu Okwei," 633–46.

109. Robertson and Robinson, "Re-modeling Slavery," 260.

110. Jones, *Annual Reports*, 70; Mayne, "Intelligence Report," 50, CSO 26/3/29196, NAI; "Southern Nigeria Protectorate Original Correspondence, May–August, 1901," 574, CO520/8, BNA.

111. Isichei, *History*, 29–30; Ojo, "Child Slaves," 422–27.

112. The negotiation of rights-in-land through kinship networks was gendered. Men gained access to farming land through women—mothers (descent) and wives (marriage)—whereas women qualified for individual land allocation by attaining adult femininity signified through marriage. Ohafia women inherited and bequeathed land to descendants in contrast to patrilineal Igbo societies where women could not own land. This system had guaranteed women economic autonomy, and ensured their breadwinner status. Mayne, "Intelligence Report," 41–43, CSO 26/3/29196, NAI; Uchendu, *Igbo*, 86; Obuba, *History*, 49–56; Nsugbe, *Ohaffia*, 89; M. M. Green, *Land Tenure in an Ibo Village in South-Eastern Nigeria* (London: LSEPS, 1941), 13; L. T. Chubb, *Ibo Land Tenure* (Ibadan, Nigeria: Ibadan University Press, 1961); Uchendu, *Igbo*, 87; Udensi Ekea, interview; K. K. Owen, interview; Nmia Nnaya Agbai, interview; Kevin Ukiro, interview; Ikpirikpe Ndi Inyom of Akanu Village, interview; Elders of Umu-Anya Patrilineage, Ndi Imaga Compound, interview; Mecha Ukpai Akanu, interview; Arunsi Kalu, interview.

113. Mayne, "Intelligence Report," 41–42, CSO 26/3/29196, NAI.

114. Njoku, *Ohafia*, 38; Nsugbe, *Ohaffia*, 90. By the twentieth century, with the growth of a colonial market economy, individual land purchase became commonplace.

115. Nsugbe, *Ohaffia*, 122; Ottenberg, *Double Descent*, 199–200; Obuba, *History*, 54, 58; A. K. Uche, *Customs and Practices in Ohaffia* (Aba, Nigeria: A. K. Uche, 1960), 39–40; Udensi Ekea, interview; Ogbuka Abaa, interview; Mecha Ukpai, interview; Eke Emetu Kalu, interview; Emeh Okonkwo, interview; Kalu Awa Kalu, interview; Kevin Ukiro, interview; K. K. Owen, interview.

116. Arunsi Kalu, interview.

117. Olua Iro Kalu, interview.

118. McKittrick, "Forsaking Their Fathers?," 33–40.

119. Mayne, "Intelligence Report," 47, CSO 26/3/29196, NAI.

120. Ekechi, *Tradition*, 145–46; Njoku, *African Cultural Values*, 19–21; McCall, "Atlantic Slave Trade," 71–76; Afigbo, *Ropes*, 241–42.

121. Mecha Ukpai, interview; Godwin Nwankwo Uko, interview; Anaso Awalekwa, interview.

CHAPTER 4: GENDERED EMANCIPATION, CA. 1860–1940

1. Paton and Scully, introduction to *Gender and Slave Emancipation*, 1–34.

2. Robertson and Klein, "Women's Importance," 15.

3. Taiwo Adetunji Osinubi, "Chinua Achebe and the Uptakes of African Slaveries," *Research in African Literatures* 40, no. 4 (2009): 25–46.

4. Isichei, *Ibo*, 52; Felix Ekechi, "Colonialism and Christianity in West Africa: The Igbo Case, 1900–1915," *Journal of African History* 12, no. 1 (1971): 103–15; Don Ohadike, "The Decline of Slavery among the Igbo," in *The End of Slavery in Africa*, ed. Suzanne Miers and Richard Roberts (Madison: University of Wisconsin Press, 1988), 443–57; Gibril R. Cole, *The Krio of West Africa: Islam, Culture, Creolization and Colonialism in the Nineteenth Century* (Athens: Ohio University Press, 2013); Ibrahim K. Sundiata, *From Slavery to Neoslavery: The Bight of Biafra and Fernando Po in the Era of Abolition, 1827–1930* (Madison: University of Wisconsin Press, 1996); Adiele Afigbo, "The Warrant Chief System in Eastern Nigeria: Direct or Indirect Rule?," *Journal of the Historical Society of Nigeria* 3, no. 4 (June 1967): 683–700.

5. Amadiume, *Male Daughters*, 119–23; Mba, *Nigerian Women*, 37–89.

6. Achebe, *Female King*.

7. Ohadike, "Decline," 451; Oriji, *Political Organization*, 139–59; Mann, *Slavery and the Birth of an African City*, 12–16, similarly argues that Lagos's oligarchic "big men and women" broke down when they lost control of trade, labor, and credit, while slaves saw increasing capitalist opportunities.

8. McKittrick, "Forsaking," 33–51; Gregory Mann, "Old Soldiers, Young Men: Masculinity, Islam, and Military Veterans in Late 1950s Soudan Français (Mali)," in Lindsay and Miescher, *Men and Masculinities in Modern Africa*, 69–86.

9. Paul Obiani, "The Stigmatization of the Descendants of Slaves in Igboland," in Brown and Lovejoy, *Repercussions*, 321–28; Trevor Getz, *Slavery and Reform in West Africa: Toward Emancipation in Nineteenth-Century Senegal and the Gold Coast* (Athens: Ohio University Press, 2010); James F. Searing, *West African Slavery and Atlantic Commerce: The Senegal River Valley, 1700–1860* (Cambridge: Cambridge University Press, 2003); P. Haenger, *Slaves and Slave Holders on the Gold Coast: Towards an Understanding of Social Bondage in West Africa* (Basel: P. Schlettwein, 2000); Martin Klein, *Slavery and Colonial Rule in French West Africa* (Cambridge: Cambridge University Press, 1998); Alice L. Conklin, *A Mission to Civilize: The Republican Idea of Empire in France and West Africa, 1895–1930* (Stanford: Stanford University Press, 1997); G. McSheffrey, "Slavery, Indentured Servitude, Legitimate Trade, and the Impact of Abolition in the Gold Coast, 1874–1910," *Journal of African History* 24, no. 3 (1983): 349–68.

10. Raphael C. Njoku, "'Ogaranya' (Wealthy Men) in Late Nineteenth Century Igboland: Chief Igwebe Odum of Arondizuogu, c. 1860–1940," *African Economic History*, no. 36 (2008): 27–52.

11. Miers and Roberts, *End of Slavery*, 38; Robertson and Klein, *Women and Slavery in Africa*.

12. Claire Robertson, "Post-proclamation Slavery in Accra: A Female Affair?," in Robertson and Klein, *Women and Slavery in Africa*, 220–45.

13. Trevor Getz and Liz Clarke, *Abina and the Important Men: A Graphic History* (New York: Oxford University Press, 2016).

14. Martin Klein and Richard Roberts, "Gender and Emancipation in French West Africa," in *Gender and Slave Emancipation*, 162–80.

15. Paton and Scully, introduction to *Gender and Slave Emancipation*, 26.

16. S. Peabody, "Negresse, Mulatresse, Citoyenne: Gender and Emancipation in the Caribbean," in Paton and Scully, *Gender and Slave Emancipation*, 56–78.

17. Klein and Roberts, "Gender and Emancipation in French West Africa," 162–80; Christopher Leslie Brown and Philip D. Morgan, eds., *Arming Slaves: From Classical Times to the Modern Age* (New Haven: Yale University Press, 2006); J. G. Landers and B. M. Robinson, eds., *Slaves, Subjects, and Subversives: Blacks in Colonial Latin America* (Albuquerque: University of New Mexico Press, 2006).

18. Christopher Leslie Brown, "The Arming of Slaves in Comparative Perspective," in Brown and Morgan, *Arming Slaves*, 330–53.

19. Lovejoy, *Transformations*, 258–69; John Thornton, "Armed Slaves and Political Authority in Africa in the Era of the Slave Trade, 1450–1800" in Brown and Morgan, *Arming Slaves*, 79–94; Allen F. Isaacman and Derek Peterson, "Making the Chikunda: Military Slavery and Ethnicity in Southern Africa," in Brown and Morgan, *Arming Slaves*, 95–119.

20. Osinubi, "Chinua Achebe," 25.

21. Ohadike, "Decline," 451.

22. Judith Butler, *Gender Trouble: Feminism and the Subversion of Identity* (New York: Routledge, 1990), 7.

23. Kalu, "Ibo Autobiography," 158–70.

24. Sandra E. Greene, *West African Narratives of Slavery: Texts from Late Nineteenth- and Early Twentieth-Century Ghana* (Bloomington: Indiana University Press, 2011), 4–7; Marcia Wright, *Strategies of Slaves and Women: Life-Stories from East/Central Africa* (New York: Lilian Barber, 1993); Haenger, *Slaves*, 181–91; Edward Alpers, "The Story of Swema: Female Vulnerability in Nineteenth-Century East Africa," in Robertson and Klein, *Women and Slavery in Africa*, 185–219.

25. Kalu, "Ibo Autobiography," 161.

26. Miescher, *Making Men in Ghana*, 2, 48, 58, 80, 138, 150, 199; "Southern Nigeria Protectorate Original Correspondence, April–May 1913," CO520/124, BNA; Johnston, *Of God and Maxim Guns*, 84, 221–33; Kalu, "Ibo Autobiography," 166–67; Geoffrey Johnston, "Ohafia 1911–40: A Study in Church Developments in Eastern Nigeria," *Bulletin of the Society for African Church History* 2, no. 2 (1966): 148.

27. Joyce Lowe, "A Brief History of the Nigerian Field Society, 1930–2001," *Nigerian Field*, no. 66 (2001): 147–63.

28. Mberi Ndukwe, "From Slavery to the Order of British Empire: A Biography of Chief Eke Kalu Uwaoma of Ohafia" (BA thesis, University of Nigeria Nsukka, October 1998), 59–60; Udensi Ekea, interview, August 4, 2010; Agbai Ndukwe, interview; Arunsi Kalu, interview; Olua Iro Kalu, interview; Kevin Ukiro, interview, August 10, 2010. It has not been possible to substantiate the claim of British knighthood in colonial archives, but several of Kalu's family relatives insisted in oral interviews that he received this honor.

29. Amadiume, *Male Daughters*, 55–57; Lisa Lindsay, "'No Need . . . to Think of Home'? Masculinity and Domestic Life on the Nigerian Railway, c. 1940–61," *Journal of African History* 39, no. 3 (1998): 439–66; Michael Twaddle, *Kakungulu and the Creation of Uganda, 1868–1928* (Athens: Ohio University Press, 1993); John Illife, *Africans: The History of a Continent* (Cambridge: Cambridge University Press, 1995), 94.

30. Ferme, *Underneath of Things*, 6, 18–19, 165, 226; Bailey, *African Voices*, 160.

31. Akuma-Kalu Njoku, "Before the Middle Passage: Igbo Slave Journeys to Old Calabar and Bonny," in Brown and Lovejoy, *Repercussions*, 67.

32. John Milton Cooper, "Conception, Conversation, and Comparison: My Experiences as a Biographer," in *Writing Biography: Historians and Their Craft*, ed. L. E. Ambrosius (Lincoln: University of Nebraska Press, 2004), 83–87.

33. Kalu, "Ibo Autobiography," 158.

34. Ojo, "Child Slaves," 422.

35. Ohadike, "Decline," 455.

36. Ojo, "Child Slaves," 423–24.

37. Njoku, *Inter-village Trade*, 30; Ikenga Ibe, interview; Kalu Awa, interview; Anaso Awalekwa, interview; Ogbuka Ogbuka Abaa, interview by author, Isiuwgu, December 10, 2011.

38. Kalu, "Ibo Autobiography," 159. The speech form evident in this quote suggests that Kalu was dictating his story to an amanuensis, or that he was writing in a familiar oral narrative genre.

39. "The Horrors of Fetish Worship," *Daily Telegraph Supplement*, June 24, 1899.

40. "Slave Trade: Bight of Biafra (Consular), January–December 1855," 211, FO84/975, BNA; "Slave Trade: West Coast of Africa, Bight of Biafra, January–December 1856," 68–72, 163, 169, 306–307, 312–316, FO84/1001, BNA; "Dispatches, 10 August–30 September 1916," 49–54, CO583/48, BNA; Latham, *Old Calabar*, 106; Cole, *Krio of West Africa*, 21–37; Sundiata, *From Slavery to Neoslavery*, 23, 68–73.

41. Roberts and Miers, "The End of Slavery in Africa," in Miers and Roberts, *End of Slavery*, 33–38.

42. Uchendu, *Igbo*, 81; Davidson Kalu Oki, interview; Kalu Uko, interview, September 20, 2011; Elders of Nde Nbila Compound, group interview

by author, Okon, September 15, 2011; Elders of Nde Oka Compound, group interview by author, Okon Village, September 14, 2011.

43. Jones, *Annual Reports*, 4–5; "Nigeria Original Correspondence, October–November, 1916," CO583/49, BNA.

44. Three times the contemporary local market value of male slaves. "Southern Nigeria Protectorate Original Correspondence, May–August, 1901," 570–74, CO520/8, BNA.

45. Kalu, "Ibo Autobiography," 160–62.

46. "Southern Nigeria Original Correspondence, May–August, 1901," 570–74, CO520/8, BNA; Anaso Awalekwa, interview; Udensi Ekea, interview; Mecha Ukpai, interview; Arunsi Kalu, interview; Kevin Ukiro, interview.

47. Randy Sparks, *The Two Princes of Calabar: An Eighteenth-Century Atlantic Odyssey* (Cambridge, MA: Harvard University Press, 2004), 54–58.

48. "Slave Trade: West Coast of Africa, Bight of Biafra, January–December 1856," 312–13, FO84/1001, BNA; Daniel Offiong, "The Status of Slaves in Igbo and Ibibio of Nigeria," *Phylon* 46, no. 1 (1985): 55.

49. Arthur Glyn Leonard, "Notes of a Journey to Bende," *Journal of the Manchester Geographical Society*, no. 14 (1898): 196–97; Torti Kalu, interview; Kalu Ibem, interview by author, Amuma, November 26, 2011; Godwin Nwankwo Uko, interview by author, Amankwu, October 25, 2011; Nwabueze Kalu, interview.

50. "Southern Nigeria Original Correspondence, May–August, 1901," 574, CO520/8, BNA; Arunsi Kalu, interview; Oluka Mba, interview; Kalu Awa, interview; Idika Aso, interview; Udensi Ekea, interview. Elite polygyny and concubinage rose dramatically between 1880 and 1920. Jones, *Annual Reports*, 70; Musisi, "'Elite Polygyny,'" 757–86; Nwokeji, "African Conceptions," 65; Mayne, "Intelligence Report," 50–59, CSO 26/3/29196, NAI.

51. Kalu, "Ibo Autobiography," 162.

52. Chubb, "Assessment Reports," 58–59, OW 342/27, ABADIST 8/11/2, NAE; Njoku, *Inter-village Trade*, 28; Ndukwe, "From Slavery," 31.

53. Kalu, "Ibo Autobiography," 163–64; J. C. Anene, *Southern Nigeria in Transition, 1885–1906* (Cambridge: Cambridge University Press, 1966), 231.

54. Kalu, "Ibo Autobiography," 160–62; Njoku, *Ohafia*, 71.

55. Jones, *Annual Reports*, 8–9; Kalu, "Ibo Autobiography," 164; Johnston, *Of God and Maxim Guns*, 35; "Southern Nigeria Protectorate Original Correspondence, June–August, 1905," 387–528, CO520/31, BNA; "The Recent Expedition against the Aros," *Missionary Record of the United Free Church of Scotland*, no. 1-164 (1902): 453, UFC, NLS; Donald A. MacAlister, "The Aro Country, Southern Nigeria," *Scottish Geographical Magazine*, no. 18 (1902): 634.

56. "Southern Nigeria Original Correspondence, May–August, 1901," 717–22, CO520/8, BNA; Jan Buchanan to Robert Collins, September 26, 1901, Foreign No. 16, MS.7672, UFC, NLS; "The Recent Expedition against

the Aros," 453, UFC, NLS; Johnston, *Of God and Maxim Guns*, 26; Johnston, "Ohafia 1911–40," 139–43; Jones, *Annual Reports*, 48; O. Kalu, "The River Highway: Christianizing the Igbo," in Kalu, *Presbyterian Whiteness*, 55.

57. Chubb, "Assessment Reports," 6, OW 342/27, ABADIST 8/11/2, NAE; Jones, *Annual Reports*, 36; Njoku, *Inter-village Trade*, 29; Uduma Nnochin Ogbuagu, interview; Ezie Uka Uduma Uka, interview by author, Akanu-Ukwu, November 6, 2011.

58. Kalu, "Ibo Autobiography," 164.

59. Olua Iro Kalu, interview; Agbai Ndukwe, interview; Njoku, *Ohafia*, 96–97.

60. Afigbo, *Warrant Chiefs*, 6–7, 37, 80; Obaro Ikime, "Reconstructing Indirect Rule: The Nigerian Example," *Journal of the Historical Society of Nigeria* 4, no. 3 (1968): 421–38; Isaac M. Okonjo, *British Administration in Nigeria, 1900–1950: A Nigerian View* (New York: NOK, 1974); Jones, *Annual Reports*, 27, 59–61; Njoku, *Ohafia*, 104.

61. W. A. C. Cockburn, "Annual Report on Bende District for the Year Ended 31st December, 1910," in Jones, *Annual Reports*, 68–84; Kalu, "Ibo Autobiography," 164–65; Kalu, "River Highway," 70–71; Jones, *Annual Reports*, 88. Vincent extorted foods, livestock, and money from the people, routinely sexually harassed girls and married women, and subjected men to public flogging and imprisonment.

62. Johnston, "Ohafia 1911–40," 140; Njoku, *Ohafia*, 113.

63. Cockburn, "Annual Report," 68–84; Njoku, *Ohafia*, 106.

64. Kalu, "Ibo Autobiography," 165.

65. Jones, *Annual Reports*, 50.

66. Johnston, *Of God and Maxim Guns*, 42–43; Kalu, "River Highway," 70–71; Udensi Ekea, interview; Agbai Ndukwe, interview; Kalu Awa, interview.

67. Robert Collins to Mr. Ashcroft, April 8, 1921, 70–71; Robert Collins to Mr. Ashcroft, November 24, 1924, 76; Robert Collins to Mr. Ashcroft, August 5, 1925, 148, MS.7793, UPC, West Africa, NLS.

68. Valentine to Collins, August 10 and December 31, 1910, 179, 357, Foreign No. 21, MS.7676, UFC, NLS; Johnston, "Ohafia 1911–40," 140; Elder Agwu Kalu, interview by author, Amaekpu, May 18, 2012; Kalu, "River Highway," 71.

69. Robert Collins to Mr. Ashcroft, July 14 and 17, 1920, 29–32; Robert Collins to Mr. Ashcroft, September 28, 1920, 39–40; Robert Collins to Mr. Ashcroft, September 16, 1921, 98–99; Robert Collins to Mr. Ashcroft, February 21, 1925, 106, MS.7793, UPC, West Africa, NLS; K. K. Owen, interview; Agwu Kalu, interview; Udensi Ekea, interview; Agbai Ndukwe, interview; Johnston, "Ohafia 1911–40," 144; Ndukwe, "From Slavery," 34–35, 59–60; Kalu, "Ibo Autobiography," 166.

70. Jones, *Annual Reports*, 54.

71. John Watts, *A True Relation of the Inhuman and Unparalleled Actions and Barbarous Murders of Negroes or Moors Committed on Three English-Men*

in Old Calabar in Guinny (London: Printed for Thomas Passinger and Benjamin Hurlock, 1672).

72. G. Williams, *History of the Liverpool Privateers and Letters of Marque with an Account of the Liverpool Slave Trade* (1897; repr., New York: August M. Kelley, 1966), 582; John Adams, *Remarks on the Country Extending from Cape Palmas to the River Congo* (London: Whittaker, 1823), 144; G. A. Roberston, *Notes on Africa: Particularly Those Parts Which Are Situated between Cape Verde and the River Congo* (London: Sherwood, Neely, and Jones, 1819), 1313; Sparks, *Two Princes*, 11, 24.

73. Antera Duke, "The Diary of Antera Duke, an Efik Slave-Trading Chief of the Eighteenth Century," in *Efik Traders of Old Calabar*, ed. Cyril Daryll Forde (London: Published for the International African Institute by Oxford University Press, 1956), 1–38. Coastal ogaranya masculinities consolidated their power by marrying the daughters of fellow leading traders through expensive gift-giving. Antera Duke gifted Eyo Willy Honesty's daughter 1,496 rods, cloth, gunpowder, and iron, and he witnessed various male suitors bringing his own sister's daughter gifts of cloths. Such bridal gifts enabled elite women to begin independent trading. Elite men also sponsored the initiation of their girl-wives (child-brides) into womanhood. Thus, Duke paid a smith "1 rod, 5 yams, and a jar of palm oil" to fashion copper bracelets for his girl-wife's legs, and provided her with her "first" cloth to signal her new womanhood. Through such commoditized acquisition of wives, coastal elite male traders consolidated their wealth-in-people and wealth-in-commodities, which signified ogaranya masculinity.

74. Edward Bold, *The Merchants' and Mariners' African Guide: Containing an Accurate Description of the Coast, Bays, Harbours, and Adjacent Islands of West Africa* (1819; repr., Salem: Cushing and Appleton, 1823); James Holman, *Travels in Madeira, Sierra Leone, Teneriffe, St. Jago, Cape Coast, Fernando Po, Princes Island, Etc. Etc.*, 2nd ed. (Leicester Square: George Routledge, 1840); Donald C. Simmons, ed., *Holman's Voyage to Old Calabar* (Calabar, Nigeria: American Association for African Research, 1959), 1–28; Richard Francis Burton, *Wanderings in West Africa from Liverpool to Fernando Po* (London: Tinsley Brothers, 1863), 277, 292; Crow, *Memoirs*, 7–10, 235, 275; Hope Masterton Waddell, *Twenty-Nine Years in the West Indies and Central Africa: A Review of Missionary Work and Adventure, 1829–1858*, 2nd ed. (1863; repr., London: Frank Cass, 1970), 242; Hugh Goldie, *Calabar and Its Mission* (Edinburgh: Oliphant, Anderson, and Ferrier, 1890); Northrup, *Trade without Rulers*, 22–25. Lovejoy and Richardson concur that mastering the "commercial conventions of European merchants" and conspicuous consumption was cardinal to gendered and class-based social ascendancy in Old Calabar. See Paul E. Lovejoy and David Richardson, "Trust, Pawnship, and Atlantic History: The Institutional Foundations of the Old Calabar Slave Trade," *American Historical Review* 104, no. 2 (April 1999): 342.

75. Crow, *Memoirs*, 196, 235. In Bonny, during the late eighteenth and early nineteenth centuries, men achieved greater status as they married more wives. Because it was a "municipal regulation" that a husband should provide a separate house for each wife he married, men with many wives had larger compounds than other men. According to Burton, *Wanderings*, 292, the wives of Bonny's elite men "pass their time in making nets, hats, fishing-lines, and little mats" as well as "selling food commodities in the market," and "those who are trusted by their husbands are put in charge of the villages on the banks of the river." At Old Calabar, Antera Duke's diary entry of March 21, 1786, shows that polygyny was important because wives supervised elite men's farming estates. Crow, *Memoirs*, 274, noted that Duke Ephraim of Old Calabar had more than two hundred wives and each had her own house. All his wives' houses were surrounded by a mud wall "within which no one ha[d] access without his especial permission." According to Waddell, *Twenty-Nine Years*, 249, Duke Ephraim's contemporary, King Eyo, had a compound in the nineteenth century that consisted of "eight or nine court-yards, surrounded by low thatched buildings and opening into one another. These were for his wives, principal and secondary."

76. Macgregor Laird and R.A.K. Oldfield, *Narrative of an Expedition into the Interior of Africa by the River Niger, in the Steam-Vessel Quorra and Alburkah in 1832, 1833, and 1834*, vol. 1 (London: Richard Bentley, 1837), 88, 165–66, 413–14.

77. Missionary Record of the United Presbyterian Church, November 1886, NLS. Slessor operated at Old Calabar, Unwana, Akunakuna, Okoyong, Umon, Arochukwu, Itu, Ikotobong, Use, Ikpe, and Odoro Ikpe.

78. Chubb, "Assessment Reports," OW 342/27, ABADIST 8/11/2, NAE.

79. Johnston, "Ohafia 1911–40," 144; Agbai Ndukwe, interview; Ogbuka Ogbuka Abaa, interview.

80. Johnston, "Ohafia 1911–40," 143; Ndukwe, "From Slavery," 35; Kalu, "Ibo Autobiography," 166–67.

81. Jones, *Annual Reports*, 26.

82. Kalu, "Ibo Autobiography," 166.

83. Kalu, 166; Njoku, *Inter-village Trade*, 30.

84. Kalu, "Ibo Autobiography," 164; Agbai Ndukwe, interview; K. K. Owen, interview.

85. Ndukwe, "From Slavery," 40–41; Njoku, *Ohafia*, 118; K. K. Owen, interview.

86. Kalu, "Ibo Autobiography," 166; Ndukwe, "From Slavery," 41; K. K. Owen, interview.

87. Johnston, "Ohafia 1911–40," 144; Kalu, "Ibo Autobiography," 166; Ndukwe, "From Slavery," 49–50; Njoku, *Ohafia*, 117; Agbai Ndukwe, interview.

88. Kalu, "Ibo Autobiography," 162.

89. Kalu, 164.

90. Jones, *Annual Reports*, 27; Ndukwe, "From Slavery," 23; Interview with Godwin Uko.

91. Hives, "Intelligence Report," 62–67.

92. Cockburn, "Annual Report," 75.

93. Interviews with Godwin Nwankwo Uko, Agbai Ndukwe, Kalu Awa, Udensi Ekea, Ikenga Ibe, and Oluka Mba.

94. Isichei, *History*, 105.

95. Mayne, "Intelligence Report," 68, CSO 26/3/29196, NAI.

96. Mayne, 13.

97. Njoku, *Ohafia*, 103.

98. Mayne, "Intelligence Report," 68–69, CSO 26/3/29196, NAI.

99. Chubb, "Assessment Reports," 17, OW 342/27, ABADIST 8/11/2, NAE.

100. "Introduction of Direct Taxation in Southern Provinces, 1928," CO583/159/12, BNA; Mayne, "Intelligence Report," 69, CSO 26/3/29196, NAI; Chubb, "Assessment Reports," Minute No. 69/1927.

101. Chubb, "Assessment Repots," 6, OW 342/27, ABADIST 8/11/2, NAE.

102. Chubb, 8.

103. K. A. B. Cochrane, "Handing Over Note to H.M. Llyod," OW 7045, NAE; Johnston, "Ohafia 1911–40," 142; Njoku, *Ohafia*, 101.

104. H. F. Matthews, "Intelligence Report on the Aro Clan, Arochukwu District, Calabar Province, 1927," 13–14, 26, Anthropologists Papers on Aro Origin, Discussion and the Basis of the Widespread Aro Influence, ARODIV 20/1/15, NAE.

105. Matthews, 1.

106. Mayne, "Intelligence Report," 69, CSO 26/3/29196, NAI.

107. Njoku, *Ohafia*, 117.

108. Kalu, "Ibo Autobiography," 166.

109. Chubb, "Assessment," 7–17; Kalu, "Ibo Autobiography," 166; Ndukwe, "From Slavery," 61–64; Uche Anya Elekwa, in group interview with elders of Umu-Anya patrilineage, Ndi Imaga compound, Elu Village, August 14, 2011; Agbai Ndukwe, interview.

110. Kalu, "Ibo Autobiography," 166–167; Ndukwe, "From Slavery," 63; Uche Anya Elekwa, in group interview; Agbai Ndukwe, interview; Johnston, "Ohafia 1911–40," 148.

111. Kalu, "Ibo Autobiography," 167.

112. Lindsay and Miescher, introduction to *Men and Masculinities*, 6.

113. Mann, "Old Soldiers," 69–86.

114. Kalu, "Ibo Autobiography," 164–167.

115. "Arochukwu-Bende-Afikpo Road, 1921," UMPROF 5/1/90, NAE; Kalu, "Ibo Autobiography," 168–69.

116. Peter Nnate Eke Kalu, interview by author, Elu Ohafia, July 23, 2014.

117. Kalu, "Ibo Autobiography," 167–170.
118. Uchendu, *Igbo*, 14.
119. Kalu, "Ibo Autobiography," 168.
120. Udensi Ekea, interview; Kalu Awa, interview; Godwin Nwankwo Uko, interview; Anaso Awalekwa, interview; Ogbuka Ogbuka Abaa, interview; Uche Anya Elekwa, interview by author, Elu Village, August 14, 2010; Agbai Ndukwe, interview; Ucha Oji Iwe, interview; Kalu, "Ibo Autobiography," 168.
121. Kalu, "Ibo Autobiography," 170.
122. Matory, *Black Atlantic Religion*, 149; Glassman, "Bondsman's New Clothes," 280–84.
123. For contrary views, see Thornton, *Africa and Africans*, 274–300; Walter Hawthorne, "'Being Now, as It Were, One Family:' Shipmate Bonding on the Slave Vessel *Emilia*, in Rio de Janeiro and throughout the Atlantic World," *Luso-Brazilian Review* 45, no. 1 (2008): 53–77; Sweet, *Recreating Africa*, 20.

CHAPTER 5: REVOLUTIONARY MASCULINITIES, CA. 1850–1940

1. *Oke-nwami* means "masculine woman" and "female husband." *Oke* translates into "male" and *nwami* means "woman." Secondly, the verb *ike*, "to possess," is personalized as *oke*, which means "possessor," hence "possessor of woman" or "female husband." Recall that the practice of male warriors taking women captive as productive and reproductive resources was known as ike nwami. Thus, in the early twentieth century, women who achieved ogaranya status exploited that practice by acquiring wives; hence, they became known as oke-nwami, women possessors.
2. Idika Aso, interview.
3. Jones, "Ohaffia Obu Houses," 170–71.
4. Laird and Oldfield, *Narrative*, 1:160, 1:242.
5. Laird and Oldfield, 1:242, 1:384, 1:392, 2:25, 2:324
6. W. B. Baikie, *Narrative of an Exploring Voyage* (1856; repr., London: Frank Cass, 1966), 49, 263.
7. Ekechi, "Colonialism and Christianity," 103–15.
8. Afigbo, "Women," 35–36; Chuku, "Petty Traders," 1–22; Achebe, *Farmers*, 110–54.
9. Van Allen, "'Sitting on a Man,'" 172–80.
10. For revisionist critiques see Lorelle Semley, *Mother Is Gold, Father Is Glass: Gender and Colonialism in a Yoruba Town* (Bloomington: Indiana University Press, 2011); Oyeronke Oyewunmi, "Visualizing the Body: Western Theories and African Subjects," in *African Gender Studies: A Reader*, ed. Oyeronke Oyewunmi (New York: Palgrave Macmillan, 2005), 3–21; Edna G. Bay, *Wives of the Leopard: Gender, Politics, and Culture in the Kingdom of Dahomey* (Charlottesville: University of Virginia Press, 1998); Amadiume, *Male Daughters*, 15–28; Morrell and Ouzgane, *African Masculinities*, 1–7;

Morrell, "Of Boys and Men," 605. For assumptions of entrenched patriarchy see Van Allen, "'Sitting on a Man,'" 165–71; Mba, *Nigerian Women Mobilized*, 27, 29, 37, 62; Lebeuf, "Role of Women," 109–13; Ifeka-Moller, "Female Militancy," 134.

11. Cooper, *Marriage in Maradi*; Clark, *Onions Are My Husband*; Greene, *Gender, Ethnicity, and Social Change*; Davison, *Gender, Lineage, and Ethnicity*; Achebe, *Farmers*, 53–224.

12. Miescher, "Making of Presbyterian Teachers," 89–108.

13. McCall, "Portrait of a Brave Woman," 127–36.

14. Numerous Ohafia women performed igwa nnu, particularly in Ebem in the early twentieth century. Madame Aru Otta purchased the services of several women to cultivate large tracts of land with yams, such that her yam barns "surpassed and overshadowed" those of her husband, who was the most senior and accomplished male member of the nnu society.

15. Theodore Jun Yoo, "The Biography of Ch'oe Yŏng-suk and the Politics of Gender in Colonial Korea," *Journal of Women's History* 21, no. 4 (2009): 161–63.

16. Penny Russell, "Life's Illusions: The 'Art' of Critical Biography," *Journal of Women's History* 21, no. 4 (2009): 154.

17. HRH Engr. Dr. A. A. Ubobi, interview by author, Amangwu Ohafia, June 23, 2015.

18. Docas Kalu and Mary Ezera, interview; Ndukwe Otta and Uduma Uka, interview.

19. Ann Stoler and Frederick Cooper, "Between Metropole and Colony: Rethinking a Research Agenda," in *Tensions of Empire, Colonial Cultures in a Bourgeois World*, ed. Frederick Cooper and Ann Stoler (Berkeley: University of California Press, 1997), 1–37; Jane Burbank and Frederick Cooper, *Empire in World History: Power and the Politics of Difference* (Princeton: Princeton University Press, 2010), 3–8; A. McClintock, *Imperial Leather: Race, Gender and Sexuality in the Colonial Contest* (London: Routledge, 1995).

20. David Halperin, "Is There a History of Sexuality?," in *The Lesbian and Gay Studies Reader*, ed. Henry Abelove, Michele Barale, and David Halperin (London: Routledge, 1993), 420.

21. Kristin Mann, *Marrying Well: Marriage, Status and Social Change among the Educated Elite in Colonial Lagos* (Cambridge: Cambridge University Press, 1985).

22. Henriette Gunkel, "Through the Postcolonial Eyes: Images of Gender and Female Sexuality in Contemporary South Africa," *Journal of Lesbian Studies* 13, no. 1 (2009): 80.

23. Halperin, "Is There a History of Sexuality?," 420.

24. Wives of oke-nwami remind us of the women of the Niger River Doma community, who "select any man they choose, and give him up when they get tired of him." Baikie, *Narrative*, 114.

25. Michel Foucault, *The History of Sexuality*, vol. 1, *An Introduction* (New York: Vintage Books, 1978), 11–47.

26. "Southern Nigeria Protectorate Original Correspondence, May–August, 1901," 717–22, CO520/8, BNA; "The Recent Expedition against the Aros," *Missionary Record of the United Free Church of Scotland* (1902): 453, UFC, NLS; Johnston, *Of God and Maxim Guns*, 26–39; Johnston, "Ohafia 1911–40," 139–43; Jones, *Annual Reports*, 48; Kalu, "River Highway," 55.

27. "Southern Nigeria Protectorate Original Correspondence, September 14–November 18, 1907," 293–304, CO520/49, BNA; "Nigeria Original Correspondence; Reports on Education Departments of Northern and Southern Provinces and Colony, 1927," CO583/162/13, BNA; Jones, *Annual Reports*, 48; Johnston, *Of God and Maxim Guns*, 48–57, 136; Kalu, "River Highway," 62.

28. Njoku, *Ohafia*, 96–116; Jones, *Annual Reports*, 36; Hives, "Intelligence Report," 62–67; Chubb, "Assessment Reports: Bende Division, 1927–1929," in Jones, *Annual Reports*, 58–59; Johnston, "Ohafia 1911–40," 142–43; Ukpai Onum Ndukwe, interview, April 13, 2012.

29. Johnston, *Of God and Maxim Guns*, 10–27; Njoku, *Ohafia*, 111; Johnston, "Ohafia 1911–40," 142.

30. Robert Collins to Mr. Ashcroft, May 7, 1920, 17; Robert Collins to Mr. Livingstone, November 10, 1920, 41–42, MS.7793, UPC, West Africa, NLS; Johnston, "Ohafia 1911–40," 142–23; UFC, West Africa, MS. 7793, Robert Collins to Mr. Ashcroft, April 28, 1919, 563, MS.7793, UPC, West Africa, NLS; E. E. Ecoma, "Binding the Wounds: Presbyterians and the Health of the Nation," in Kalu, *Century and a Half of Presbyterian Witness*, 179; Isichei, *Igbo Worlds*, 231–32.

31. Johnston, "Ohafia 1911–40," 146.

32. Ikpo Kalu Ukoha, interview, Ebem Village, May 19, 2012; Margaret Eke Anya, interview by author, Amaekpu Ohafia, May 18, 2012; Ukpai Onum Ndukwe, interview, April 13, 2012; Njoku, *Ohafia*, 118–19; Ogbu Kalu and Ogun Kalu, "The Battle of the Gods: Christianization of Cross River Igboland, 1903–1950," *Journal of the Historical Society of Nigeria* 10, no. 1 (1979): 15; Johnston, "Ohafia 1911–40," 146; Kalu, "River Highway," 71.

33. Margaret Eke Anya, interview; Uche Anya Elekwa, in group interview with elders of Umu-Anya patrilineage, Ndi-Inaga compound, Elu Village, August 14, 2011; Agbai Ndukwe, interview; Agwu Kalu, interview; Ukpai Onum Ndukwe, interview, April 13, 2012; K. K. Oyeoku, interview by author, Ebem Village, August 2, 2010; I. Ukoha, interview by author, Ebem Village, October 27, 2011.

34. Njoku, *Ohafia*, 119. Such teachers turned ministers include Onuoha Kalu, Otisi Agwu Otisi, N. A. Udu, U. Ikenga, O. A. Olugu, and Ikpo Anya.

35. Johnston, "Ohafia 1911–40," 147.

36. Uche Anya Elekwa, in group interview; Agbai Ndukwe, interview; Agwu Kalu, interview.

37. Mayne, "Intelligence Report," 49, CSO 26/3/29196, NAI; *Missionary Record of the United Free Church of Scotland*, Shelfmark U.402 (1908), 21–23, NLS; *Missionary Record of the United Free Church of Scotland*, Shelfmark U.402 (1913), 19–21, NLS; Nsugbe, *Ohaffia*, 123; Njoku, *Ohafia*, 117–20; I. Ukoha, interview; Ukapi Onum Ndukwe, interview; Orie Emeh and Grace Ojieke, interview; Docas Kalu and Mary Ezera, interview; Kevin Ukiro, interview; Arunsi Kalu, interview.

38. Njoku, *Ohafia*, 118; Ukpai Onum Ndukwe, interview; Agwu Kalu, interview.

39. Agwu Kalu, interview.

40. Johnston, *Of God and Maxim Guns*, 84; Agwu Kalu, interview; Ukpai Onum Ndukwe, interview.

41. Johnston, *Of God and Maxim Guns*, 84.

42. Mayne, "Intelligence Report," 70, CSO 26/3/29196, NAI; Johnston, "Ohafia 1911–40," 145–48; Kalu, "Ibo Autobiography," 166–67.

43. Johnston, "Ohafia 1911–40," 146–49.

44. Njoku, *Ohafia*, 112; Nsugbe, *Ohaffia*, 121–36.

45. Njoku, *Inter-village Trade*, 29; Chubb, "Assessment Reports," 58–59.

46. Mayne, "Intelligence Report," 69, CSO 26/3/29196, NAI.

47. Interviews with Ogbonne Kalu; Orie Emeh and Grace Ojieke; Ucha Oji Iwe; Ikpirikpe Ndi Inyom of Akanu; and Nmia Nnaya Agbai.

48. Ndukwe Otta and Uduma Uka, interview; Olua Iro Kalu, interview.

49. McCall, *Dancing*, 83; Mayne, "Intelligence Report," 41–44, CSO 26/3/29196, NAI; Arua, "Yam Ceremonies," 695; Nsugbe, *Ohaffia*, 21; Njoku, *Ohafia*, 37.

50. Ukapi Onum Ndukwe, interview. Also Agwu Kalu, interview; Ucha Oji Iwe, interview; Uduma Nnochin Ogbuagu, interview; Robert Collins to Mr. Ashcroft, September 16, 1921, 98–99, MS.7793, UPC, West Africa, NLS.

51. "Nigeria Original Correspondence; Reports on Education Departments of Northern Provinces, Southern Provinces and Colony, 1928," 7, CO583/166/6, BNA.

52. Jones, *Annual Reports*, 47–51; "Nigeria Original Correspondence, 8 February–March, 1917," 151–52, 160, CO583/56, BNA; Ukpai Onum Ndukwe, interview; K. K. Oyeoku, interview.

53. Johnston, *Of God and Maxim Guns*, 109; "Southern Nigeria Protectorate Original Correspondence, May–August, 1901," 297–313, 321–30, CO520/8, BNA.

54. Johnston, *Of God and Maxim Guns*, 113–20.

55. Johnston, "Ohafia 1911–40," 148.

56. Vasco U. Iro, interview.

57. Interviews with Ukpai Onum Ndukwe, K. K. Oyeoku, Margaret Eke Anya, and Agwu Kalu.

58. "Reports on Education Departments of Northern Provinces, Southern Provinces and Colony, 1928," 47–48, CO583/166/6, BNA; Johnston, *Of God and Maxim Guns*, 227–30.

59. Mayne, "Intelligence Report," 49, CSO 26/3/29196, NAI; Margaret Eke Anya, interview; Johnston, "Ohafia 1911–40," 145.

60. Ukpai Onum Ndukwe, interview.

61. Interviews with Margaret Eke Anya, Agwu Kalu, Ukpai Onum Ndukwe, and K. K. Oyeoku.

62. Orie Emeh and Grace Ojieke, interview; Docas Kalu and Mary Ezera, interview; Margaret Eke Anya, interview; Johnston, *Of God and Maxim Guns*, 228–31.

63. Ndukwe Otta and Uduma Uka, interview.

64. Docas Kalu and Mary Ezera, interview; Ndukwe Otta and Uduma Uka, interview, September 16, 2011.

65. Amadiume, *Male Daughters*, 123–32.

66. Achebe, *The Female King*, 209–11.

67. Obuba, *History and Culture of Ohafia*, 51; Njoku, *Ohafia*, 26; Nwannediya Mmonwu-Oti, interview; Nmia Nnaya Agbai, interview; Orie Emeh and Grace Ojieke, interview; Arunsi Kalu, interview; Ikpirikpe Ndi Inyom of Akanu, interview.

68. Nwannediya Mmonwu-Oti, interview; Nmia Agbai, interview; Orie Emeh and Grace Ojieke, interview; Udensi Ekea, interview, August 4, 2010; Obuba, *History*, 51.

69. Ottenberg, *Double Descent*, 141.

70. Davidson Kalu Oki, interview.

71. McCall, "Portrait of a Brave Woman," 130–34.

72. Ndukwe Otta and Uduma Uka, interview, September 16, 2011.

73. Docas Kalu and Mary Ezera, interview; Ndukwe Otta and Uduma Uka, interview.

74. Njoku, *Ohafia*, 45.

75. Jones, *Annual Reports*, 12.

76. Robert Collins to Mr. Livingstone, November 10,1920, 41–42, MS.7793, UPC, West Africa, NLS.

77. Ndukwe Otta and Uduma Uka, interview.

78. Comaroff and Comaroff, *Of Revelation*, 2:48, 2:236–39, 2:408.

79. Ndukwe Otta and Uduma Uka, interview; Docas Kalu and Mary Ezera, interview.

80. Grace Emehe, interview.

81. Tessy Uzoma Odum, interview by author, Amangwu Ohafia, September 5, 2011.

82. Grace Emehe, interview.

83. Tessy Uzoma Odum, interview.

84. Grace Emehe, interview.
85. Tessy Uzoma Odum, interview.
86. Tessy Uzoma Odum, interview.
87. Uchendu, *Igbo*, 14.
88. Tessy Uzoma Odum, interview; Grace Emehe, interview; Kalu, "Ibo Autobiography," 169.
89. The date is "the time of Uso Asaga," the exodus of Asaga Village, during the Bende-Onitsha hinterland expedition of 1905–7. Tessy Uzoma Odum, interview; Grace Emehe, interview.
90. Hon. Kingsley, interview by author, Ebem Ohafia, September 3, 2011; E. I. Udensi, interview by author, Ebem Village, September 5, 2011; Tessy Uzoma Odum, interview; Grace Emehe, interview.
91. Jones, *Annual Reports*, 27.
92. Jones, 28, 60; Njoku, *Ohafia*, 104.
93. Njoku, *Ohafia*, 104.
94. Jones, *Annual Reports*, 61.
95. Interviews with E. I. Udensi, Tessy Uzoma Odum, and Grace Emehe.
96. "Southern Nigeria Correspondence No. 40212," 102, 260–92, CO502/37, PRO 969, BNA; Moses E. Ochonu, *Colonial Meltdown: Northern Nigeria in the Great Depression* (Athens: Ohio University Press, 2009), 26.
97. Male elders of Ekeluogo patrilineage, interview by author, Amangwu Ohafia, June 23, 2015.
98. Tessy Uzoma Odum, interview Odum.
99. Male elders of Ekeluogo patrilineage, interview by author, Amangwu Ohafia, June 23, 2015.
100. Tessy Uzoma Odum, interview.
101. Tessy Uzoma Odum, interview.
102. Azuonye, "Heroic Age," 9–20.
103. Kalu Awa Kalu, interview.
104. Kingsley, interview; E. I. Udensi, interview.

CONCLUSION

1. "Case No. 31/31, Transferred from the Provincial Court Bende 29.9.31, Chief Kalu Idika of Ebem vs. Eme Ado of Ebem," 1–32, NAE. According to the plaintiff Kalu Idika, around 1890, a member of his matrilineage named Ukpa Uma Orie committed murder, so his relatives went on customary propitiatory exile. Kalu Idika was a child when his matrilineage fled. His granduncle, Uzoubi Idika, was the ezie-ogo. By the time Kalu Idika and his family returned, "Ibem Ifekwe was made Ezeogo." Kalu Idika's family challenged Ibem Ifekwe's usurpation of the office. In the ensuing dispute, the British district officer determined that because Kalu Idika's family had fled Ebem, Ibem Ifekwe should continue to serve as ezie-ogo. The Ohafia council of ezie-ogo also agreed that since Ibem Ifekwe had already been installed as ezie-ogo, his

position could not then be revoked. They concluded that after Ibem Ifekwe had ruled, Kalu Idika should succeed him. However, when Ibem Ifekwe died, his cousin Onwuka Ukaike assumed the office. Onwuka Ukaike argued that Kalu Idika was still too young to rule. He said that "he was looking after the position for [Kalu Idika]" and "that [Kalu Idika] would succeed to it when [he] grew up." Kalu Idika and Onwuka Ukaike signed a written agreement to that effect, which was sealed with gift exchanges. Onwuka Ukaike's agnatic kin were displeased that he gave up the office. In the ensuing dispute, Ebem patrilineages resolved that Kalu Idika should succeed as ezie-ogo. A new agreement stipulated that Okoro Idika (Ibem Ifekwe's nephew) would succeed Kalu Idika, and Eme Ado (Onwuka Ukaike's nephew) would succeed Okoro Idika. Onwuka Ukaike was displeased that Ibem Ifekwe's lineage preceded his in the new arrangement. So his nephew Eme Ado seized the akpan drums, the instruments of political enforcement for the office of the ezie-ogo. Kalu Idika then sued Eme Ado.

2. Bonafice I. Obichere, "Women and Slavery in the Kingdom of Dahomey," *Revue française d'histoire d'outre-mer* 65, no. 238 (1978): 5–20; Bay, *Wives of the Leopard*, 5–27, 72–88, 315; George E. Brooks, Jr., "The *Signares* of Saint-Louis and Gorée: Women Entrepreneurs in Eighteenth-Century Senegal," in Hafkin and Bay, *Women in Africa*, 19–44; Hilary Jones, *The Métis of Senegal: Urban Life and Politics in French West Africa* (Bloomington: Indiana University Press, 2013), 11–14, 34–50; Adam Jones, "Female Slave-Owners on the Gold Coast: Just a Matter of Money?," in *Slave Cultures and the Cultures of Slavery*, ed. Stephan Palmié (Knoxville: University of Tennessee Press, 1995), 100–110; Kwabena Adu-Boahen, "A Worthwhile Possession: A Reading of Women's Valuation of Slaveholding in the 1875 Gold Coast Ladies' Anti-abolition Petition," *Itinerario* 33, no. 3 (November 2009): 95–112; Pernille Ipsen, *Daughters of the Trade: Atlantic Slavers and Interracial Marriage on the Gold Coast* (Philadelphia: University of Pennsylvania Press, 2015), 7–31, 235; Candido, *An African Slaving Port*, 129–37.

3. Especially, see Shetler, *Gendering Ethnicity*.

4. See Obiani, "Stigmatization of the Descendants," 321–28.

5. Isaacman and Isaacman, *Slavery and Beyond*, 324–27.

6. Miers and Kopytoff, *Slavery in Africa*; Claude Meillassoux, *The Anthropology of Slavery: The Womb of Iron and Gold* (1986; repr., Chicago: University of Chicago Press, 1992); Walter Rodney, "African Slavery and Other Forms of Social Oppression on the Upper Guinea Coast in the Context of the Atlantic Slave-Trade," *Journal of African History* 7, no. 3 (1966): 431–43; Thornton, *Africa and Africans*; Lovejoy, *Transformations in Slavery*.

7. Frederick Cooper, "The Problem of Slavery in African Studies," *Journal of African History* 20, no. 1 (1979): 103–25; Klein, *Slavery and Colonial Rule*; Glassman, "Bondsman's New Clothes," 277–312.

Bibliography

PRIMARY SOURCES

NIGERIAN NATIONAL ARCHIVES ENUGU (NAE)

ABADIST 14/1/267. "Report on Political and Social Organization in the Owerri Division."
AD/495/B49 Arodist 1/1/7. "Okonko Secret Society."
ARODIV 20/1/15. H. F. Matthews. "Intelligence Report on the Aro Clan, Arochukwu District, Calabar Province, 1927." Anthropologists Papers on Aro Origin, Discussion and the Basis of the Widespread Aro Influence.
Calprof. 14/4/951. "Annual Report Bende District, 1909."
Calprof 4/10/31. C40/21; Calprof 5/16/46; Calprof. 5/8/97. C145/7; Calprof. 5/8/228. C277/18; Calprof. 14/756; Calprof. 5/14/85; Calprof. 5/16/46. "Dispatches: Aro Expedition."
CSE 1/85/6197A. I. R. Heslop. "Intelligence Report on the Nkalu Clan, Orlu District, Okigwi Division, Owerri Province."
CSE 12/1. "Annual Reports on Owerri Province, 1918–1934."
CSE 12/1/332. "Owerri Prof. Annual Report, 1931."
CSE 12/1/334. File EP1308A. "Annual Report Owerri Province, 1932."
C22/1927. ABADIST 2/1/11. "Palm Produce Development."
E7021. J. G. C. Allen. "Intelligence Report on the Ngwa Clan, Vol. 1, 1933."
ESO 1/13. Southern Nigeria Despatches No. 238: Conf. Report, 24/5/1905.
MINLOC 17/1: "Secret Societies."
OW 342/27, ABADIST 8/11/2. L. T. Chubb. "Assessment Reports: Bende Division, 1927–1929."
OW 7045. K. A. B. Cochrane. "Handing Over Note to H.M. Llyod."
Presbynig 1/1/6. Calabar Mission Council Minutes, 84, 153 of October 23, 1913, and 186 of May 7, 1914.
RIV PROF. 8/8/433. "Okonko Club: Activity of."
UMDIV 3/1/98. "Church of Scotland Mission Abiriba."
UMDIV 3/1/656. "Ukekwe Society and Okonko: Proclamation as Unlawful."
UMDIV 7/1/70-100. "Native Court Records."
UMDIV 7/1/84. "Bende District - Selection of H.Q. for."
UMPROF 5/1/90. "Arochukwu-Bende-Afikpo Road, 1921."

NIGERIAN NATIONAL ARCHIVES IBADAN (NAI)

CSO 26/3/29196. C. J. Mayne, "Intelligence Report on the Ohafia Clan, 1934."

CSO 26/3-97. "Assessment Reports on Bende Division, 1919–1926."

NATIONAL LIBRARY OF SCOTLAND (CHURCH OF SCOTLAND MISSION ARCHIVES), EDINBURGH

Acc. 7548. Foreign Mission Records of the Church of Scotland Since 1929 with some earlier records (Outgoing Letters, 1–186, and Files Relating to Mission Fields, 1938–1964).

Acc. 7548/ A13–14. "Copies of Out-going Letters from Mission Committee to Collins."

Acc. 7548/D44. "Copies of Out-going Letters from Mission Committee to Mincher."

Acc. 7548/D44. "Calabar Correspondence and Papers, 1913–1945."

Church of Scotland, Dep.298/157-167. "Minutes Relating to Calabar, Robert Collins and Mincher."

Journals of News on Women's Missions, 1904–1926, Shelfmark Q.124.

Journals of Woman's Work in the Church, Shelfmark Q.124.

Missionary Record of the United Free Church of Scotland, no. 1 (January 1901)

Missionary Record of the United Free Church of Scotland, Shelfmark U.402 (1906).

Missionary Record of the United Free Church of Scotland, Shelfmark U.402 (1908).

Missionary Record of the United Free Church of Scotland, Shelfmark U.402 (1913).

Missionary Record of the United Presbyterian Church, November 1886.

MS.7796. Frank Ashcroft. "Report on Calabar Mission: Tour of the Calabar Mission Districts, July to August 1921."

Record of the Home and Foreign Mission Work of the United Free Church of Scotland, new ser., no. 165 (September 1914–April 1928).

Record of the United Free Church of Scotland, May 1928–September 1929.

Record of the Church of Scotland, October 1929–December 1929.

Scottish Missionary Journals, 1850–1950: Church of Scotland (1–10), United Presbyterian Church (11–15), and Free Church of Scotland (16–23).

United Free Church of Scotland, "The Recent Expedition against the Aros." *Missionary Record of the United Free Church of Scotland*, no. 1–164 (1902).

United Free Church of Scotland, Dep.298/127–37. "Minutes Relating to Calabar, Robert Collins and Mincher."

United Free Church of Scotland, Foreign No. 21, MS.7676. "Letters from Valentine to Collins, December 1910."

United Presbyterian Church, No. 26, MS.7715. "Collins Elizabeth Stewart, Wife of Robert, Missionary in Calabar, nee Glen; Letters to, 1900–1916."

United Presbyterian Church, "Collins Robert, Missionary in Calabar, Letters to, 1898–1929."

United Presbyterian Church, West Africa, MSSS.7793–95. "Collins Robert, Missionary in Calabar, Letters of, 1898–1933."

Waddell, Hope Masterton. "Journal of the Old Calabar Mission (1846–58)," United Presbyterian Church Papers, National Library of Scotland, MSSS. 7739–7743 and 8953.

BRITISH NATIONAL ARCHIVES (BNA), KEW GARDENS, LONDON

CO444/2. "Niger Coast Protectorate Original Correspondence, August–October, 1899."

CO520/8. "Southern Nigeria Protectorate Original Correspondence, May–August, 1901."

CO520/16. "Southern Nigeria Protectorate Original Correspondence, November–December, 1902."

CO520/20. "Southern Nigeria Protectorate Original Correspondence, August–October, 1903."

CO520/26. "Southern Nigeria Protectorate Original Correspondence, October–December, 1904."

CO520/31. "Southern Nigeria Protectorate Original Correspondence, June–August, 1905."

CO520/36. "Southern Nigeria Protectorate Original Correspondence, June–August, 1906."

CO520/38. "Southern Nigeria Protectorate Original Correspondence, December 1906."

CO520/47. "Southern Nigeria Protectorate Original Correspondence, June 12–July 22, 1907."

CO520/49. "Southern Nigeria Protectorate Original Correspondence, September–November 1907."

CO520/105. Dispatch No. 493, August 23, 1911.

CO520/107. "Southern Nigeria Protectorate Original Correspondence, October 9–November 30, 1911."

CO520/115. Dispatch No. 398, May 1912.

CO520/123. "Southern Nigeria Protectorate Original Correspondence, March 1913."

CO520/124. "Southern Nigeria Protectorate Original Correspondence, April–May 1913."

CO520/126. "Southern Nigeria Protectorate Original Correspondence, July 1913."

CO583/8. "Southern Nigeria Protectorate Original Correspondence, December 1913."

CO583/12. "Southern Nigeria Protectorate Original Correspondence, April 1914."

CO583/30. "Southern Nigeria Protectorate Original Correspondence, February 1915."
CO583/34. "Nigeria Original Correspondence; Dispatches, 16 June–31 July, 1915."
CO583/48. "Dispatches, August 10–September 30, 1916."
CO583/49. "Nigeria Original Correspondence, October–November, 1916."
CO583/56. "Nigeria Original Correspondence, February 8–March, 1917."
CO583/162/13. "Nigeria Original Correspondence; Reports on Education Departments of Northern and Southern Provinces and Colony, 1927."
CO583/166/6. "Nigeria Original Correspondence; Reports on Education Departments of Northern Provinces, Southern Provinces and Colony, 1928."
CO583/159/12. "Nigeria Original Correspondence; Introduction of Direct Taxation in Southern Provinces, 1928."

Foreign Office

FO2. General Correspondence before 1906, Niger Coast Protectorate.
FO84. Slave Trade and General Correspondence before 1906, Bight of Biafra.
FO84/775. "Slave Trade: Africa (West Coast) Consular, January–December 1849."
FO84/816. "Slave Trade: Africa, West Coast (Consular), January–December 1850."
FO84/858. "Slave Trade: Africa, West Coast (Consular), January–December 1851."
FO84/920. "Slave Trade: West Coast of Africa (Consular); January–December 1853."
FO84/950. "Slave Trade: West Coast of Africa (Consular); January–December 1854."
FO84/975. "Slave Trade: Bight of Biafra (Consular), January–December 1855."
FO84/1001. "Slave Trade: West Coast of Africa, Bight of Biafra, January–December 1856."
FO84/1030. "Slave Trade: Bight of Biafra, January–December 1857."
FO84/1061. "Slave Trade: Bight of Biafra, Bight of Benin, January–December 1858."
FO84/1087. "Slave Trade: Bight of Biafra, January–December 1859."
FO84/1701–2. "Africa: Slave Trade, West Coast, 1885."
FO84/1750. "Africa (Slave Trade) West Coast, January–December 1886."
FO84/1881. "Africa, West Coast, 1888."
FO84/1882. "Africa (Slave Trade), West Coast, 1888."
FO84/2019. "Africa (Slave Trade) West Coast, 1890."
FO84/1941. "Africa (Slave Trade), West Coast, 1889."
FO84/2020. "Africa (Slave Trade), West Coast, 1890."
FO541. Confidential Print, Slave Trade Abolition.
FO881. Confidential Prints.

EIGHTEENTH-CENTURY COLLECTIONS ONLINE

House of Commons, Parliament, Great Britain. "Abridgement of the Minutes of the Evidence, Taken Before a Committee of the Whole House, to whom it was Referred to Consider of the Slave Trade, 1790." http://research.lib.buffalo.edu/eighteenth-century-collection-online.

——. "Report of the Lords of the Committee of Council Appointed for the Consideration of All Matters Relating to Trade and Foreign Plantations, 1789." http://research.lib.buffalo.edu/eighteenth-century-collection-online.

PUBLISHED PRIMARY SOURCES

Adams, John. *Remarks on the Country Extending from Cape Palmas to the River Congo*. London: Whittaker, 1823.

Baikie, W. B. *Narrative of an Exploring Voyage*. 1856. Reprint, London: Frank Cass, 1966.

Barbot, Jean. *A Description of the Coast of North and South Guinea*. London: A. and J. Churchill, 1732.

Basden, G. T. *Among the Ibos of Nigeria*. 1921. Reprint, London: Frank Cass, 1966.

——. *Niger Ibos*. 1938. Reprint, London: Frank Cass, 1966.

Bold, Edward. *The Merchants' and Mariners' African Guide: Containing an Accurate Description of the Coast, Bays, Harbours, and Adjacent Islands of West Africa*. 1819. Reprint, Salem: Cushing and Appleton, 1823.

Bossard, Johann Jakob, Arnold R. Highfield, and Vladimir Barac, eds. *C. G. A. Oldendorp's History of the Mission of the Evangelical Brethren on the Caribbean Islands of St. Thomas, St. Croix, and St. John*. Ann Arbor: Karoma, 1987.

Burton, Richard Francis. *Wanderings in West Africa from Liverpool to Fernando Po*. London: Tinsley Brothers, 1863.

Cockburn, W. A. C. "Annual Report on Bende District for the Year Ended 31st December, 1910." In Jones, *Annual Reports of Bende Division*, 68–84.

Crow, Hugh. *Memoirs of the Late Captain Hugh Crow of Liverpool Comprising a Narrative of His Life, together with Descriptive Sketches of the Western Coast of Africa; Particularly of Bonny; the Manners and Customs of the Inhabitants, the Production of the Soil, and the Trade of the Country; to Which Are Added Anecdotes and Observations Illustrative of the Negro Character; Comprised Chiefly of His Own Manuscripts, with Authentic Additions from Recent Voyages and Approved Authors*. Liverpool: Longman, Rees, Orme, Brown, and Green, 1830.

Crowther, Samuel A., and Christopher J. Taylor. *The Gospel on the Banks of the Niger: Journals and Notices of the Native Missionaries accompanying the Niger Expedition of 1857–1859*. London: Dawsons, 1868.

Donnan, Elizabeth. *The Border Colonies and the Southern Colonies*. Vol. 4 of *Documents Illustrative of the History of the Slave Trade to America*. 1935. Reprint, New York: Octagon Books, 1969.

Duke, Antera. "The Diary of Antera Duke, an Efik Slave-Trading Chief of the Eighteenth Century." In *Efik Traders of Old Calabar*, edited by Cyril Daryll Forde, 1–38. London: Published for the International African Institute by Oxford University Press, 1956.

Equiano, Olaudah. *The Interesting Narrative of the Life of Olaudah Equiano, or Gustavus Vassa, the African, Written by Himself*. Edited by Werner Sollors. New York: Norton, 2001.

Goldie, Hugh. *Calabar and Its Mission*. Edinburgh: Oliphant, Anderson, and Ferrier, 1890.

Hall, Douglass. *In Miserable Slavery: Thomas Thistlewood in Jamaica, 1750–86*. Mona, Jamaica: University of the West Indies Press, 1999.

Hives, F. "Intelligence Report: Bende-Onitsha Hinterland Expedition, 1905." In Jones, *Annual Reports of Bende Division*, 62–67.

Holman, James. *Travels in Madeira, Sierra Leone, Teneriffe, St. Jago, Cape Coast, Fernando Po, Princes Island, Etc. Etc*. 2nd ed. Leicester Square: George Routledge, 1840.

Jones, G. I., ed. *Annual Reports of Bende Division, South Eastern Nigeria, 1905–1912*. Cambridge: University of Cambridge Press, 1986.

Kalu, Eke. "An Ibo Autobiography: The Autobiography of Mr. Eke Kalu, Ohaffia's Well-Honored Son." *Nigerian Field* 7, no. 4 (October 1938): 158–70.

Laird, Macgregor, and R. A. K. Oldfield. *Narrative of an Expedition into the Interior of Africa by the River Niger, in the Steam-Vessel Quorra and Alburkah in 1832, 1833, and 1834*. 2 vols. London: Richard Bentley, 1837.

Leonard, Arthur Glyn. "Notes of a Journey to Bende." *Journal of the Manchester Geographical Society*, no. 14 (1898): 196–97.

MacAlister, Donald A. "The Aro Country, Southern Nigeria." *Scottish Geographical Magazine*, no. 18 (December 1902): 631–37.

Minchinton, Walter, Celia King, and Peter Waite, eds. *Virginia Slave-Trade Statistics, 1698–1775*. Richmond: Virginia State Library, 1985.

Partridge, Charles. *Cross River Natives*. London: Hutchinson, 1905.

Roberston, G. A. *Notes on Africa; Particularly those Parts which are Situated between Cape Verde and the River Congo*. London: Sherwood, Neely, and Jones, 1819.

Talbot, Percy Amaury. *In the Shadow of the Bush*. London: Heinemann, 1912.

———. *Life in Southern Nigeria*. London: Macmillan, 1923.

———. *The Peoples of Southern Nigeria: A Sketch of Their History, Ethnology, and Languages with an Account of the 1921 Census*. Vol. 3, *Ethnology*. London: Oxford University Press, 1926.

Thomas, Northcote W. *Anthropological Report on the Ibo-Speaking Peoples of Nigeria*. 4 vols. London: Harrison, 1913–14.

———. *Twenty-Nine Years in the West Indies and Central Africa*. 2nd ed. 1863. Reprint, London: Frank Cass, 1970.

Watts, John. *A True Relation of the Inhuman and Unparalleled Actions and Barbarous Murders of Negroes or Moors Committed on Three English-Men in Old Calabar in Guinny.* London: Printed for Thomas Passinger and Benjamin Hurlock, 1672.

Williams, G. *History of the Liverpool Privateers and Letters of Marque with an Account of the Liverpool Slave Trade.* 1897. Reprint, New York: August M. Kelley, 1966.

SELECT INTERVIEWS AND PERSONAL COMMUNICATION

Abaa, Ogbuka Ogbuka. Oral interview by author. Nde Oji Compound, Isiugwu Village. December 10, 2011.

Abali, Mmia, ezie-nwami of Eziafor Village. Oral interview by author. Digital voice recording. Eziafor Village. December 17, 2011.

Agbai, Nmia Nnaya. Oral interview by author. Digital voice recording. Elu Village. August 18, 2011.

Agwu, Agwu Ojo, chief. Oral interview by author. Video recording. Okon Village. September 22, 2011.

Agwu, Ibem Kalu, nna, carpenter, and sculptor (erected the statue of heroic ancestor Olumba Ezi Akuma at Amuma Village). Oral interview by author. Handwritten notes. Uduma Awoke Village. October 25, 2011.

Agwu, Onwuka Kalu, chief. Oral interview by author. Digital voice recording. Obu Nde Idika, Ebem. August 3, 2010.

Akanu, Mecha Ukpai, ezie-ogo, the Uduma Anaga Second of Amangwu Village. Oral interview by author. Digital voice recording. Amangwu Village. August 18, 2011.

Akirika, dibia. Oral interview by author. Digital voice recording. Nde Edem Compound, Okon. September 26, 2011.

Anya, Margaret Eke. Oral interview by author. Digital voice recording. Amaekpu. May 18, 2012.

Anya, O. K., ezie-ogo, of Ufiele. Oral interview by author. Digital voice recording. Ufiele Village. August 21, 2010.

Arua, Agwu, dibia. Oral interview by author. Digital voice recording. Okon Village. August 4, 2010.

Aso, Idika, chief priest, of Obu Nkwa. Oral interview by author. Digital voice recording. Obu Nkwa Shrine, Asaga Village. August 12, 2010.

Awa, Kalu, ezie-ogo, of Ibina (Ihenta). Oral interview by author. Digital voice recording. Ibina (Ihenta) Village. December 12, 2011.

Awalekwa, Anaso, ezie-ogo, of Ndea-Nku; and members of the Men's Court. Group Interview by author. Digital voice recording. November 17, 2011.
    Kalu, Arua, chief, of Nde Ole Compound. Oldest man in Ndea-Nku. (98 years, Uke Lucky)
    Otuu, Agwu, chief, of Ndea Lekwa Compound. Ezie umuaka society. (70 years, Uke Okpetemba)

Lekwa, Egwuonwu, chief. (65 years, Uke Ugwumba)

Bassey, George, chief. Oral interview by author. Digital voice recording. Ebem Village. May 2, 2012

Dimgba, Ndukwe Uche, dibia. Oral interview by author. Digital voice recording. Okon Village. September 22, 2011.

Ebebe, Uko, dibia. Oral interview by author. Handwritten notes. Okon Village. September 14, 2011.

Eke, Kalu, dibia. Oral interview by author. Video recording, Nde Idika Okoro, Okon Village. September 22, 2011.

Eke, Orie Udo. Oral interview by author. Digital voice recording. Asaga Village. April 30, 2012.

Ekea, Kalu, dibia. Oral interview by author. Digital voice recording. Nde Ekea Compound, Okon. September 24, 2011.

Ekea, Udensi, chief. Oral interview by author. Digital voice recording. Ndi Ekea Compound, Okon Village. August 4 and 5, 2010.

Ekere, Ukonu Okoro, ezie-ogo, of Eziafor Village. Oral interview by author. Digital voice recording. Eziafor Village. December 17, 2011.

Elders of Nde Nbila Compound. Group Interview by author. Digital voice recording. Okon. September 15, 2011.

Elders of Nde Odo Patrilineage, Akanu Village. Group interview by author. Digital voice recording. Akanu Village. November 2, 2011.

    Akuma, Kalu, nna, of Nde Odo Patrilineage, Akanu Village. (82 years/Amashiri)

    Emeri, Chikezie, dibia, of Nde Odo Patrilineage, Akanu Village. (60 years/Akajiaku)

    Idika, Alhaji, nna, of Nde Odo Patrilineage, Akanu Village (56 years/Egwu-Ano)

    Idika, John O., nna, of Nde Odo Patrilineage, Akanu Village (74 years/Bianko)

    Uduma Uchendu, dibia, of Nde Odo Patrilineage, Akanu Village (82 years/Mba-Ishiagu)

    Uma, Uma Ukariwe, nna, of Nde Odo Patrilineage, Akanu Village (74 years/Bianko)

Elders of Nde Oka Compound. Group interview by author. Digital voice recording. Okon Village. September 14–15, 2011.

Elekwa, Uche Anya. Oral interview by author. Digital voice recording. Elu Village. August 14, 2010.

Eme, Agwu K., chief. Oral interview by author. Digital voice recording. Nde Ukike, Elu Village. August 15, 2010.

Emeh, Orie, and Grace Ojieke, chief. Oral interview by author. Digital voice recording. Ebem Village. August 11, 2010.

Emehe, Grace, niece of Unyang Uka, daughter of Johnson Emehe. Oral interview by author. Digital voice recording. Amangwu Village. September 10, 2011.

Ezera, Mary. Oral interview by author. Digital voice recording. Ebem Ohafia. August 3, 2010.
Ibe, Okoro Ekeanya, chief. Oral interview by author. Digital voice recording. Nde Edem, Okon. September 26, 2011.
Ibe, Ikenga, chief. Oral interview by author. Digital voice recording. Amuma Village. November 26, 2011.
Igwe, M. A. Oral interview by author. Digital voice recording. Amaekpu. August 16, 2010.
Igwe Oji, self-styled traditional prime minister of Akanu Village. Oral interview by author. Digital voice recording. Akanu Village. November 2, 2011.
Ijeoma, Oji, chief, security for Akanu Village's *Ikpirikpe* drum. Oral interview by author. Digital voice recording. Akanu Village. November 3, 2011.
Ikpirikpe Ndi Inyom of Akanu Village. Group interview by author. Akanu Village. November 3, 2011.
    Bassey, Mmia Nnaya, of Nde Odo Compound. (45 years, Uke Akumba ["Ohu Ali"])
    Emeri, Nnenna, of Nde Odo Compound. (52 years, Uke Anyafumba)
    Kalu, Eunice. Ezi Ndea Mba of Ibina-Ukwu Compound. (53 years, Uke Ugwumba)
    Kalu, Lovina. Nde Alulu of Amafor Compound. (53 years, Uke Ugwumba)
    Ukoha, Comfort. Ezi Nde Okoro of Ekeluogo Compound. (60 years, Uke Okezie)
    Ukpai, Nne Agwu. Nde Okoro of Ekeluogo Compound. (53 years, Uke Ugwumba)
Imaga, Kalu, chief. Oral interview by author. Digital voice recording. Nde Edem, Okon Village. September 26, 2011.
Imaga, U. E., ezie-ogo, of Elu Village. Oral interview by author. Digital voice recording. August 15, 2010.
Iro, A. N. (JP), chief. Oral interview by author. Digital voice recording. Ekeluogo, Akanu. November 4, 2011.
Iro, Egbe Abba, chief. Oral interview by author. Digital voice recording. Oboro Village. November 17, 2011.
Iro, Vasco U., ezie-ogo, of Nkwebi Village, Ohafia; in council with elders of Nkwebi Village. Group interview by author. Digital voice recording. Obu-Nta Kwebi. November 17, 2011.
    Agwu, Azu, chief, of Nde Echem Compound. (82 years, Uke Amasiri)
    Agwu, Ndukwe Kalu, chief, of Nde Ibe Compound. (82 years, Uke Amasiri)
    Amadi, Kalu, chief, of Nde Ibe Compound. (88 years, Uke Ejindu)
    Amogu, Agwu Kalu, chief, of Nde Agu Compound. (82 years, Uke Amasiri)
    Eke, Ike, chief, of Nde Ufere Compound. (88 years, Uke Ejindu)
    Eke, Ota, chief, of Eziukwu Compound. Council speaker. (88 years, Uke Ejindu)

Ekpe, Josiah Onum, elder, of Eziukwu Compound. (70 years, Uke Ekwueme)
Iwe, Ezema O., chief, of Nde Ibe Compound. (77 years, Uke Okezie)
Ojo, Agwu, chief, of Nde Agu Compound. (91 years, Uke Onyiwa)
Okike, Igwe, chief, of Nde Okoro. (68 years, Uke Emeago)
Onuma, Ojike, chief, of Nde Echem Compound. Court messenger. (60 years, Ugwumba)
Elders of Umu Mkpara Awa (four men).
Members of Nkwebi Autonomous Development Union (five men).

Iwe, Ucha Oji, ezie-nwami, of Elu Village; and her cabinet. Group interview by author. Digital voice recording. Elu Village. October 25, 2011.
Ebi, Uche Kalu, of Nde Aja Compound.
Ezichi, Nne Ucha, of Nde Imaga Compound.
Kalu, Celina, of Nde Anaga Compound.
Kalu, Nne Grace, of Nde Kalu Compound.
Kalu, Nne Mary, of Nde Imaga Compound.
Ochonu, Nne, of Nde Aja Compound.
Okenu, Ikediya, of Nde Uka Ibe Compound.
Opele, Unyang, of Nde Imaga Compound.

Justman, Uduma, chief. Oral interview by author. Handwritten notes. Ebem Village. August 2, 2010.

Kakarere (Oyibo), dibia. Oral interview by author. Video recording. Okon Village. September 22, 2011.

Kalu, Adanneya. Oral interview by author. Digital voice recording. Uduma Ukwu Village. November 17, 2011.

Kalu, Agwu, elder. Oral interview by author. Digital voice recording. Amaekpu Village. May 18, 2012.

Kalu, Arunsi. Oral interview by author. Digital voice recording. Amangwu Village. August 15, 2011.

Kalu, Azueke, dibia. Oral interview by author. Digital voice recording. Nde Idika Okoro, Okon. September 22, 2011.

Kalu, Docas, and Mary Ezera. Group interview by author. Digital voice recording. Elu. August 10, 2010

Kalu, Eke Emetu, chief. Oral interview by author. Digital voice recording. Obu Ndi Anaga. August 11, 2010.

Kalu, Kalu Awa, chief, ezie-agba (second in command to ezie-ogo) of Ufiele. Oral interview by author. Digital voice recording. Ufiele Village. October 27, 2011.

Kalu, Nwabueze. Oral interview by author. Digital voice recording. Isiugwu. December 10, 2011.

Kalu, Ogbonne Kalu, ezie-nwami. Oral interview by author. Digital voice recording. Nde Uba Patrilineage of Nde Okorocha Compound, Uduma Ukwu Village. November 17, 2011.

Kalu, Okorie, ezie-ogo, of Isiugwu. Oral interview by author. Digital voice recording. Isiugwu. December 10, 2011.
Kalu, Olua Iro, chief. Oral interview by author. Handwritten notes. Ebem Village. August 3, 2010.
Kalu, Onu Idika. Oral interview by author. Handwritten notes. Okagwe Village. August 25, 2011.
Kalu, Torti, chief. Oral interview by author. Digital voice recording. Amuma Village. November 26, 2011.
Kalu, Ugoenyi. Oral interview by author. Digital voice recording. Nde Unua Nnechi, Elu. August 18, 2010.
Kalu, Uka. Oral interview by author. Handwritten notes. University of Nigeria, Nsukka. July 29, 2010.
Kama, Obasi, chief. Oral interview by author. Digital voice recording. Nde Edem Compound, Okon. September 26, 2011.
Kingsley, Hon., Peoples Democratic Party Chairman of Ohafia Local Government Area. Oral interview by author. Digital voice recording. Ebem Village, September 3, 2011.
Male elders of Umu-Anya Patrilineage, Ndi Imaga Compound, Elu Ohafia. Group interview by author. Digital voice recording. Elu Village. August 14, 2011.
  Anya, Idika-Uma, chief. (85 years, Uke Ugwumba)
  Anya, Ofor-Okoro. Served as interpreter for the elders. (50 years)
  Elekwa, Awa Anya, chief. (75 years, Uke Azummini)
  Elekwa, Uche Anya, chief. Head of Umu-Anya, fulfills rite of isuyi nzu isi in Elu. (86 years, Uke Obimba)
  Three others.
Mba, Agba, chief. Oral interview by author. Digital voice recording. Amafor, Akanu. November 4, 2011.
Mba, Oluka, chief. Oral interview by author. Digital voice recording. Nde-Ibe Village. October 27 and November 3, 2011.
Members of the Men's Court of Amangwu Village. Group Interview by author. Digital voice recording. Amangwu Village. August 18, 2011.
Mmonwu-Oti, Nwannediya. Oral interview by author. Digital voice recording. Ndi Owom, Okon. August 5, 2010.
Ncheghe, Okpan, ezie-ogo, of Ndi-Orie-Eke Village. Oral interview by author. Digital voice recording. Ndi-Orie-Eke Village. December 15, 2011.
Nde Ichin (Elders) of Amuma Village. Group interview by author. Digital voice recording. Amuma Village. November 26, 2011.
  Awa, Kalu, nna, of Nde Torti Compound, Amuma Village.
  Ibe, Ikenga, chief, of Nde Torti Compound, Amuma Village.
  Ibem, Kalu, chief, of Nde Ibe-Anya Compound, Amuma Village.
  Kalu, Nsi, of Nde Okpo Compound, Amuma Village.
  Kalu, Torti, chief, of Nde Torti Compound, Amuma Village.

Okoro, Okoro, of Nde Torti, Amuma Village.
Ten Elders of Akpan, Amuma Village.
Nde Ichin (Elders) of Nde Edem Compound. Group interview by author. Digital voice recording. Okon. September 26, 2011
   Ibe, Okoro Ekeanya, chief, of Nde Edem Compound. (75 years/Akajiaku)
   Imaga, Kalu, chief, ezie ezi of Nde Edem Compound. (87 years/Oka-Omee)
   Kama, Obasi, chief, of Nde Edem Compound.
   Obuba, Okoro, chief, of Nde Edem Compound. (50 years/Enyimba)
   Oka, Imagha, chief, of Nde Edem Compound
   Oka, Moses Enwere, dibia, of Nde Edem Compound. (50 years)
   Torti, Imaga, chief, of Nde Edem Compound. (95 years/Anyafumba)
   Uma, Eke, dibia, of Nde Edem Compound. (75 years/Akajiaku)
Ndukwe, Agbai, nna. Oral interview by author. Digital voice recording. Elu Ohafia. August 10, 2010.
Ndukwe, Echeme, dibia. Oral interview by author. Digital voice recording. Nde Ukike, Elu. August 18, 2011.
Ndukwe, Ikpo C., chief, secretary of Ebem's male court. Oral interview by author. Digital voice recording. Nde Ado Compound, Ebem Ohafia. August 3, 2010, April 6, and May 2, 2012.
Ndukwe, reverend doctor. Oral interview by author. Handwritten notes. Presbyterian Church Manse, Elu. August 20, 2011.
Ndukwe, Ukpai Onum, elder. Oral interview by author. Digital voice recording. Asaga Village. April 13 and May 15, 2012.
Njoku, Onwuka, professor. Oral conversation with author. University of Nigeria, Nsukka. July 12, 2010.
Njoku, Onwuka, professor. Phone conversation with author. Lansing, Michigan, to Enugu, Nigeria. March 22, 2013.
Nwankwo, Oyidiya Ukpai. Oral interview by author. Digital voice recording. Nde Agwu, Elu. August 18, 2010.
Nwojo, U., ezie-ogo, of Okagwe. Oral interview by author. Digital voice recording. Okagwe Village. August 17, 2010.
Obuba, Nnenna. Oral interview by author. Digital voice recording. Amaekpu. August 15, 2011.
Ocho, Agwunsi, chief, retired teacher. Oral interview by author. Handwritten notes. Okon. September 22, 2011.
Odum, Tessy Uzoma. Oral interview by author. Digital voice recording. Ohafia Local Government Council Office, Ebem Village. September 5, 2011
Ogbuagu, Uduma Nnochin, chief. Oral interview by author. Digital voice recording. Amuke Village. November 24, 2011
Oka, Imagha, chief. Oral interview by author. Digital voice recording. Nde Edem Compound, Okon, September 26, 2011.
Okafor, Egbe, chief. Oral interview by author. Digital voice recording. Asaga Village. August 12, 2010.

Okereke, Mba Odo (Modok), ezie-ogo, of Akanu Village. Oral conversation with author. Akanu Village. October 15, 2011.
——. Oral interview by author. Akanu Village. October 26, 2011.
Okezie, evangelist. Oral interview by author. Handwritten notes. Nde Ufere Compound, Eziafor. November 11, 2011.
Oki, Kalu Davidson. Oral interview by author. Okon Village. August 5, 2010.
Okonkwo, Emeh, chief. Oral interview by author. Digital voice recording. Ebem Village. August 3, 2010
Onuma, Agwu, dibia, provost of Ohafia-Arochukwu Native Herbal Doctors (Ebube Dike) Union. Oral interview by author. Digital voice recording. Ihenta (Ibina). December 12, 2011.
Onwunta, Uma, reverend doctor, former principal clerk of the Presbyterian Church of Nigeria. Oral interview by author. Handwritten notes. Umuahia, Nigeria. August 23, 2011.
Onyeani, Ijeoma. Oral interview by author. Digital voice recording. Isiugwu. December 12, 2011.
Onyeani, Isaac, chief, secretary to the late ezie-ogo of Nde Uduma Ukwu. Oral interview by author. Handwritten notes. Nde Uduma Ukwu Village. November 17, 2011.
Osonwa, Elvis. Oral interview by author. Digital voice recording. Nde Umachi, Akanu. October 29, 2011.
Oti-Mmonwu, Nwadiala. Oral interview by author. Digital voice recording. Ndi Owom, Okon. August 5, 2010.
Otta, Ndukwe. Oral interview by author. Handwritten notes. Ebem Village. August 2, 2010.
Otta, Ndukwe, and Uduma Uka, elder. Group interview by author. Ebem Village. August 14, 2011.
——. Group interview with author. Asaga Village. September 16, 2011.
Owen, K. K., chief. Oral interview by author. Digital voice recording. Elu Village. August 12, 2010.
Oyeoku, K. K., chief. Oral interview by author. Handwritten notes. Ebem Village. August 2, 2010.
Torti, Imaga, chief, of Nde Edem Compound. Oral interview by author. Digital voice recording. Okon. September 26, 2011.
Uchendu, Uduma, dibia. Oral interview by author. Digital voice recording. Akanu Village. November 2, 2011.
Udemele, chief. Oral interview by author. Digital voice recording. Ekeluogo, Akanu. November 4, 2011.
Udensi, E. I. Oral interview by author. Digital voice recording. Ebem Village. September 5, 2011.
Udensi, Kalu, ezie-akpan of Nde-Ibe Village. Oral interview by author. Handwritten notes. Nde-Ibe. October 27, 2011.
Uduma, Enwelu Agwu. Oral interview by author. Handwritten notes. Amaekpu. August 16, 2010.

Uduma, Ugbu, ezie-ogo, of Nde-Amogu Village. Oral interview by author. Digital voice recording. Ihenta (Ibina) Village. November 11, 2011.

Ufere, L. U., chief. Oral interview by author. Digital voice recording. Nde Uduma Ukwu Village. September 15, 2011.

Uka, Uka Uduma, "Okpere Oha 1 of Akanu-Ukwu Autonomous Community." Oral interview by author. Digital voice recording. Akanu Village. November 6, 2011.

Ukariwe, Kalu, chief, of Nde Odo. Oral interview by author. Digital voice recording. Akanu Village. November 6, 2011.

Ukiro, Kevin, chief. Oral interview by author. Digital voice recording. Asaga Village. August 10 and 12, 2010.

Uko, Godwin Nwankwo, ezie-ogo, of Amankwu Village; and his cabinet members. Group Interview by author. Digital voice recording. Amankwu Village. October 25, 2011.

Uko, Kalu, dibia. Oral interview by author. Digital voice recording. Okon Village. September 14, 20, and 26, 2011

Ukoha, I. Oral interview by author. Digital voice recording. Ebem Village. October 27, 2011.

Ukoha, Ikpo Kalu. Oral interview by author. Digital voice recording. Ebem Village. May 19, 2012.

Ukoha, Kalu, ezie-ogo, of Amuma. Oral interview by author. Digital voice recording. Amuma. November 30, 2011.

Uma Eke, Nnenna. Oral interview by author. Akanu Village. November 3, 2011.

Uma, Eke, dibia. Oral interview by author. Digital voice recording. Nde Edem Compound, Okon, September 26, 2011.

Utuma, Olugu, chief. Oral interview by author. Digital voice recording. Nde Imaga, Elu. August 15, 2010.

Video recording of *ije iwa* (massive food production in preparation for the annual dibia festival) by author. Clip AVI-5.AVI. Okon. September 22, 2011.

Video recording of *umerogwu* (magic) performances by author. Clips DSCN 1672, DSCN 1673, and DSCN 1674. Okon Village. September 26, 2011.

SECONDARY SOURCES

Abasiattai, Monday. *Akwa Ibom and Cross River States: The Land, the People and Their Culture*. Calabar, Nigeria: Wusen Press, 1987.

Achebe, Chinua. *Things Fall Apart*. London: Heinemann, 1958.

Achebe, Nwando. "'And She Became a Man': King Ahebi Ugbabe in the History of Enugu-Ezike, Northern Igboland, 1880–1948." In Lindsay and Miescher, *Men and Masculinities in Modern Africa*, 52–68.

———. *Farmers, Traders, Warriors and Kings: Female Power and Authority in Northern Igboland, 1900–1960*. Portsmouth, NH: Heinemann, 2005.

———. *The Female King of Colonial Nigeria: Ahebi Ugbabe*. Bloomington: Indiana University Press, 2011.
———. "Nwando Achebe—Daughter, Wife, and Guest—A Researcher at the Crossroads." *Journal of Women's History* 14, no. 3 (Autumn 2002): 9–31.
———. "When Deities Marry: Indigenous 'Slave' Systems Expanding and Metamorphosing in the Igbo Hinterland." In *African Systems of Slavery*, edited by Jay Spaulding and Stephanie Beswick, 105–33. Trenton, NJ: Africa World Press, 2010.
Achebe, Nwando, and Bridget Teboh. "Dialoguing Women." In Cole, Manuh, and Miescher, *Africa after Gender?*, 63–81.
Afigbo, Adiele E. *The Abolition of the Slave Trade in Southeastern Nigeria, 1885–1950*. New York: University of Rochester Press, 2006.
———. *Igbo Enwe Eze: Beyond Onwumechili and Onwuejeogwu*. Nigeria: Whytem, 2001.
———. "Oral Tradition and the History of Segmentary Societies." *History in Africa*, no. 12 (1985): 1–10.
———. *Ropes of Sand: Studies in Igbo Culture and History*. Ibadan, Nigeria: University Press, 1981. Published in association with Oxford University Press.
———. *The Warrant Chiefs: Indirect Rule in Southeastern Nigeria*. London: Longman, 1972.
———. "The Warrant Chief System in Eastern Nigeria: Direct or Indirect Rule?" *Journal of the Historical Society of Nigeria* 3, no. 4 (June 1967): 683–700.
———. "Women in Nigerian History." In *Women in Nigerian Economy*, ed. Martin O. Ijere, 22–40. Enugu, Nigeria: Acena, 1991.
Afonja, Simi. "Changing Modes of Production and the Sexual Division of Labor among the Yoruba." *Signs* 7, no. 2 (Winter 1981): 299–313.
———. "Land Control: A Critical Factor in Yoruba Gender Stratification." In *Women and Class in Africa*, edited by Claire Robertson and Iris Berger, 78–91. New York: Holmes and Meier, 1986.
Agboola, S. A. "Introduction and Spread of Cassava in Western Nigeria." *Nigerian Journal of Economic and Social Studies* 10, no. 3 (1968): 369–85.
Aguwa, Jude C. *The Agwu Deity in Igbo Religion: A Study of the Patron Spirit of Divination and Medicine in an African Society*. Enugu, Nigeria: Fourth Dimension, 1995.
Agwu, Ebi. *A Short History of the Presbyterian Church of Nigeria in Asaga Ohafia*. Ohafia: Presbyterian Church of Nigeria, 1999.
Ajayi, J. F. A. "The Continuity of African Institutions under Colonialism." In *Emerging Themes of African History*, edited by T. O. Ranger, 189–200. Dar es Salaam: East African Publishing House, 1968.
Akinjogbin, I. A. *Dahomey and Its Neighbors, 1708–1818*. Cambridge: Cambridge University Press, 1977.
Alagoa, Ebiegberi J. "An African Philosophy of History in the Oral Tradition." In Harms et al., *Paths toward the Past*, 15–26.

———. *Jaja of Opobo: The Slave Who Became a King*. London: Longman, 1970.

Alegi, Peter. *Laduma! Soccer, Politics and Society in South Africa*. South Africa: University of KwaZulu-Natal Press, 2004.

Allman, Jean, Susan Geiger, and Nakanyike Musisi. "Women in African Colonial Histories: An Introduction." In *Women in African Colonial Histories*, edited by Jean Allman, Susan Geiger, and Nakanyike Musisi, 1–17. Indianapolis: Indiana University Press, 2002.

Alpers, Edward A. "'Ordinary Household Chores': Ritual and Power in a 19th-Century Swahili Women's Spirit Possession Cult." *International Journal of African Historical Studies* 17, no. 4 (1984): 677–702.

———. "State, Merchant Capital and Gender Relations in Southern Mozambique to the End of the 19th Century: Some Tentative Hypotheses." *African Economic History*, no. 13 (1984): 23–55.

———. "The Story of Swema: Female Vulnerability in Nineteenth-Century East Africa." In Robertson and Klein, *Women and Slavery in Africa*, 185–219.

Altink, Henrice. "Deviant and Dangerous: Proslavery Representations of Jamaican Slave Women's Sexuality, ca. 1780–1834." In Capbell, Miers, and Miller, *The Modern Atlantic*, 209–30.

Amadiume, Ifi. *Male Daughters, Female Husbands: Gender and Sex in an African Society*. London: Zed Books, 1989.

———. *Re-Inventing Africa: Matriarchy, Religion and Culture*. London: Zed Books, 1997.

Anene, J. C. *Southern Nigeria in Transition, 1885–1906*. Cambridge: Cambridge University Press, 1966.

Anyanwu, U. D., and J.C.U. Aguwa, eds. *The Igbo and the Tradition of Politics*. Enugu, Nigeria: Fourth Dimension, 1993.

Appiah, Kwameh Anthony, and Henry Louis Gates Jr., eds. *Encyclopedia of Africa*. Oxford: Oxford University Press, 2010.

Ardener, Shirley, ed. *Perceiving Women*. New York: John Wiley, 1975

———. "Sexual Insult and Female Militancy." In Ardener, *Perceiving Women*, 29–53.

Arinze, Francis. *Sacrifice in Igbo Religion*. Ibadan, Nigeria: Ibadan University Press, 1970.

Armitage, David. "Three Concepts of Atlantic History." In *The British Atlantic World, 1500–1800*, edited by David Armitage and Michael J. Braddock, 11–27. New York: Palgrave Macmillan, 2002.

Arua, A. O. *A Short History of Ohafia*. Enugu, Nigeria: Omnibus Press, 1951.

Arua, Emea O. "Yam Ceremonies and the Values of Ohafia Culture." *Africa: Journal of the International African Institute* 51, no. 2 (April 1981): 694–705.

Attoe, Stella. *A Federation of the Biase People: Origin and Development of Biase Ethnicity, 1750–1950*. Enugu, Nigeria: Harris, 1990.

Austen, Ralph A. "The Slave Trade as History and Memory: Confrontations of Slaving Voyage Documents and Communal Traditions." *William and Mary Quarterly* 58, no. 1 (January 2001): 229–44.

Azuonye, Chukwuma. "The Heroic Age of the Ohafia Igbo." *Genève-Afrique* 28, no. 1 (1990): 15–23.

Bailey, Anne C. *African Voices of the Atlantic Slave Trade: Beyond the Silence and the Shame*. Boston: Beacon, 2005.

Baker, B. "When the Bakassi Boys Came: Eastern Nigeria Confronts Vigilantism." *Journal of Contemporary African Studies*, 20 no. 2 (2002): 223–44.

Balandier, Georges. *Political Anthropology*. London: Penguin, 1970.

Barber, Gillian. "'It's Only Natural!': The Views of Villagers from Chiradzulu District, Southern Malawi on Matrilineal Inheritance and Matrilocal Residence." In *Twentieth Century Malawi: Perspectives on History and Culture*, edited by John McCracken, Timothy J. Lovering, and Fiona Johnson Chalamanda. Stirling: Center of Commonwealth Studies, University of Stirling, 2001.

Barry, B. *Senegambia and the Atlantic Slave Trade*. Cambridge: Cambridge University Press, 1998.

Baum, Robert. *Shrines of the Slave Trade: Diola Religion and Society in Precolonial Senegambia*. New York: Oxford University Press, 1999.

Bay, Edna G. *Wives of the Leopard: Gender, Politics, and Culture in the Kingdom of Dahomey*. Charlottesville: University of Virginia Press, 1998.

Behrendt, S., A. J. H. Latham, and D. Northrup. *Diary of Antera Duke, an Eighteenth-Century African Slave Trader*. Oxford: Oxford University Press, 2010.

Beidelman, T. O. *The Matrilineal Peoples of Eastern Tanzania*. London: International African Institute, 1967.

Bentley, Jerry. "Myths, Wagers, and Some Moral Implications of World History." *Journal of World History* 16, no. 1 (March 2005): 51–82.

Beoku-Betts, Josephine. "Western Perceptions of African Women in the 19th and Early 20th Centuries." In *Readings in Gender in Africa*, edited by Andrea Cornwall. Bloomington: Indiana University Press, 2005.

Berry, Sara. *No Condition Is Permanent: The Social Dynamics of Agrarian Change in Sub-Saharan Africa*. Madison: University of Wisconsin Press, 1993.

Boahen, A. A. "New Trends and Processes in Africa in the Nineteenth Century." In *General History of Africa*, edited by J. F. Ade Ajayi. Vol. 6, *Africa in the Nineteenth Century until 1880s*, 40–63. Oxford: Heinemann International, 1989.

Boddy, Janice. *Wombs and Alien Spirits: Women, Men, and the Zar Cult in Northern Sudan*. Madison: University of Wisconsin Press, 1989.

Boone, Catherine. *Property and Political Order in Africa: Land Rights and the Structure of Politics*. Cambridge: Cambridge University Press, 2014.

Boris, Eileen. "Gender after Africa!" In Cole, Manuh, and Miescher, *Africa after Gender?*, 191–204.

Bourdieu, Pierre. *Outline of a Theory of Practice*. Cambridge: Cambridge University Press, 1977.
Bourdieu, Pierre, and Alan C. M. Ross. *The Algerians*. Boston: Beacon, 1962.
Brantley, Cynthia. "Through Ngoni Eyes: Margaret Read's Matrilineal Interpretations from Nyasaland." *Critique of Anthropology* 17, no. 2 (June 1997): 147–69.
Browitt, Jeff, and Brian Nelson, eds. *Practicing Theory: Pierre Bourdieu and the Field of Cultural Production*. Newark: University of Delaware Press, 2004.
Brown, Carolyn, and Paul Lovejoy, eds. *Repercussions of the Atlantic Slave Trade: The Interior of the Bight of Biafra and the African Diaspora*. Trenton, NJ: African World Press, 2010.
Brown, Christopher Leslie. "The Arming of Slaves in Comparative Perspective." In Brown and Morgan, *Arming Slaves*, 330–53.
Brown, Christopher Leslie, and Philip D. Morgan, eds. *Arming Slaves: From Classical Times to the Modern Age*. New Haven: Yale University Press, 2006.
Brown, Laurence, and Tara Innis. "Slave Women, Family Strategies, and the Transition to Freedom in Barbados, 1834–41." In Campbell, Miers, and Miller, *The Modern Atlantic*, 172–85.
Burbank, Jane, and Frederick Cooper. *Empire in World History: Power and the Politics of Difference*. Princeton: Princeton University Press, 2010.
Burnard, Trevor. "Evaluating Gender in Early Jamaica, 1674–1784." *History of the Family* 12, no. 2 (2007): 81–91.
———. *Mastery, Tyranny, and Desire: Thomas Thistlewood and His Slaves in the Anglo-Jamaican World*. Chapel Hill: University of North Carolina Press, 2004.
Bush, Barbara. "Hard Labor: Women, Childbirth, and Resistance in British Caribbean Slave Societies." In *More Than Chattel: Black Women and Slavery in the Americas*, ed. David Barry Gasper and Darlene Clark Hine, 193–217. Bloomington: Indiana University Press, 1996.
———. *Slave Women in Caribbean Society, 1650–1838*. Kingston: Heinemann Caribbean, 1990.
Butler, Judith. *Gender Trouble: Feminism and the Subversion of Identity*. New York: Routledge, 1990.
Campbell, Gwyn, Suzanne Miers, and Joseph C. Miller, eds. *The Modern Atlantic*. Vol. 2 of *Women and Slavery*. Athens: Ohio University Press, 2008.
———. "Strategies of Women and Constraints of Enslavement in the Modern Americas." In Campbell, Miers, and Miller, *The Modern Atlantic*, 1–25.
Candido, Mariana. *An African Slaving Port and the Atlantic World: Benguela and Its Hinterland*. Cambridge: Cambridge University Press, 2013.
Carney, Judith. *Black Rice: The African Origins of Rice Cultivation in the Americas*. Cambridge, MA: Harvard University Press, 2001.
Chambers, Douglass B. "Ethnicity and the Diaspora: The Slave Trade and the Creation of African 'Nations' in the Americas." *Slavery and Abolition* 22, no. 3 (2001): 25–39.

———. *Murder at Montpelier: Igbo Africans in Virginia*. Jackson: University Press of Mississippi, 2005.

———. "'My Own Nation': Igbo Exiles in the Diaspora." In *Routes to Slavery: Direction, Ethnicity and Mortality in the Atlantic Slave Trade*, edited by David Eltis and David Richardson, 72–97. London: Frank Cass, 1997.

———. "The Significance of Igbo in the Bight of Biafra Slave-Trade: A Rejoinder to Northrup's 'Myth Igbo.'" *Slavery and Abolition* 23, no. 1 (2002): 101–20.

———. "Tracing Igbo into the African Diaspora." In *Identity in the Shadow of Slavery: The Black Atlantic*, edited by Paul Lovejoy, 55–71. New York: Continuum, 2000.

Chubb, L. T. *Ibo Land Tenure*. Ibadan, Nigeria: Ibadan University Press, 1961.

Chuku, Gloria. "From Petty Traders to International Merchants: A Historical Account of Three Igbo Women of Nigeria in Trade and Commerce, 1886–1970." *African Economic History*, no. 27 (1999): 1–22.

———. *Igbo Women and Economic Transformation in Southeastern Nigeria, 1900–1960*. New York: Routledge, 2005.

———. "Women in the Economy of Igboland: A Survey." *African Economic History*, no. 23 (1995): 37–50.

Church Missionary Society. *Letters from the Front: Being a Selection from the Annual Letters from the Missions*. London: Church Missionary Society, 1912.

Clark, Gracia. *Onions Are My Husband: Survival and Accumulation by West African Market Women*. Chicago: University of Chicago Press, 1994.

Cole, Catherine M., Takyiwaa Manuh, and Stephan F. Miescher. *Africa after Gender?* Bloomington: Indiana University Press, 2007.

Cole, Gibril R. *The Krio of West Africa: Islam, Culture, Creolization and Colonialism in the Nineteenth Century*. Athens: Ohio University Press, 2013.

Colson, Elizabeth. *Marriage and the Family among the Plateau Tonga of Northern Rhodesia*. Oxford: Manchester University Press, 1958.

Comaroff, Jean. *Body of Power, Spirit of Resistance: The Culture and History of a South African People*. Chicago: University of Chicago Press, 1985.

Comaroff, John, and Jean Comaroff. *Of Revelation and Revolution*. Vol. 2, *The Dialectics of Modernity on a South African Frontier*. Chicago: University of Chicago Press, 1997.

Conklin, Alice L. *A Mission to Civilize: The Republican Idea of Empire in France and West Africa, 1895–1930*. Stanford: Stanford University Press, 1997.

Connell, Robert W. *Masculinities*. Berkeley: University of California Press, 1995.

———. *Which Way is Up? Essays on Class, Sex and Culture*. Sydney: Allen and Unwin, 1983.

Cookey, S. J. S. "An Igbo Slave Story of the Late Nineteenth Century and Its Implications." *Ikenga: Journal of African Studies* 1, no. 2 (July 1972): 1–9.

———. *King Jaja of the Niger Delta: His Life and Times, 1821–1891.* New York: NOK, 1974.

Cooper, Barbara. *Marriage in Maradi: Gender and Culture in a Hausa Society in Niger, 1900–1989.* Portsmouth, NH: Heinemann, 1997.

———. "Oral Sources and the Challenge of African History." In Philips, *Writing African History*, 191–215.

Cooper, Frederick. "Conflict and Connection: Rethinking Colonial African History." *American Historical Review* 99, no. 5 (December 1994): 1516–45.

Cooper, John Milton. "Conception, Conversation, and Comparison: My Experiences as a Biographer." In *Writing Biography: Historians and Their Craft*, edited by L. E. Ambrosius, 79–102. Lincoln: University of Nebraska Press, 2004.

Coquery-Vidrovitch, Catherine. *African Women: A Modern History.* Boulder: Westview, 1997.

Cornwall, Andrea, ed. *Readings in Gender in Africa.* Bloomington: Indiana University Press, 2005.

———. "To Be a Man Is More Than a Day's Work: Shifting Ideals of Masculinity in Ado-Odo, Southwestern Nigeria." In Lindsay and Miescher, *Men and Masculinities in Modern Africa*, 230–48.

Cornwall, Andrea and Nancy Lindisfanne, eds. *Dislocating Masculinities: Comparative Ethnographies.* London: Routledge, 1994.

Cox, Edward L. *Rekindling the Ancestral Memory: King Ja Ja of Opobo in St. Vincent and Barbados, 1888–1891.* Cave Hill: Department of History, University of the West Indies, 1998.

Crehan, Kate. "Of Chickens and Guinea Fowl: Living Matriliny in North-Western Zambia in the 1980s." *Critique of Anthropology* 17, no. 2 (June 1997): 211–27.

Curtin, Philip. *The Atlantic Slave Trade: A Census.* Madison: University of Wisconsin Press, 1969.

———. *Economic Change in Precolonial Africa: Senegambia in the Era of the Slave Trade.* Madison: University of Wisconsin Press, 1975.

Dadzie, Stella. "Searching for the Invisible Woman: Slavery and Resistance in Jamaica." *Race and Class* 32, no. 2 (October 1990): 21–38.

Dalby, Jonathan. "'Such a Mass of Disgusting and Revolting Cases': Moral Panic and the 'Discovery' of Sexual Deviance in Post-emancipation Jamaica (1835–1855)." *Slavery and Abolition* 36, no. 1 (2015): 136–59.

Davison, Jean. *Gender, Lineage, and Ethnicity in Southern Africa.* Boulder: Westview, 1997.

Declich, Francesca. "'Gendered Narratives,' History, and Identity: Two Centuries along the Juba River among the Zigula and Shanbara." *History in Africa*, no. 22 (January 1995): 93–122.

Dike, Kenneth O. *Trade and Politics in the Niger Delta, 1830–1885: An Introduction to the Economic and Political History of Nigeria.* Oxford: Clarendon Press, 1966.

Dike, Kenneth O., and Felicia I. Ekejiuba. *The Aro of South-Eastern Nigeria, 1650–1980: A Study of Socio-Economic Formation and Transformation in Nigeria.* Ibadan, Nigeria: University Press, 1990.

———. "The Aro State: A Case Study of State Formation in Southeastern Nigeria." *Journal of African Studies* 5, no. 3 (1978): 268–300.

Diptee, Audra. *From Africa to Jamaica: The Making of an Atlantic Slave Society, 1775–1807.* Gainesville: University Press of Florida, 2010.

Donnan, Elizabeth. *Documents Illustrative of the History of the Slave Trade to America.* Vol. 4, *The Border Colonies and the Southern Colonies.* 1935. Reprint, New York: Octagon Books, 1969.

Douglas, Mary. "Is Matriliny Doomed in Africa?" In Douglas and Kaberry, *Man in Africa*, 121–136.

Douglas, Mary, and Phyllis M. Kaberry, eds. *Man in Africa.* New York: Anchor Books, 1969.

Downs, R. E., and S. Reyna, eds. *Land and Society in Contemporary Africa.* London: University Press of New England, 1988.

DuPlessis, Robert S. *The Material Atlantic: Clothing, Commerce, and Colonization in the Atlantic World, 1650–1800.* Cambridge: Cambridge University Press, 2016.

Ebeogu, Afam. "Onomastics and Igbo Tradition of Politics." *African Languages and Cultures* 6, Iss. 2 (1993): 133–46.

Ebron, Paulla. "Constituting Subjects through Performative Acts." In Cole, Manuh, and Miescher, *Africa After Gender?*, 171–87.

Ecoma, E. E. "Binding the Wounds: Presbyterians and the Health of the Nation." In Kalu, *A Century and Half of Presbyterian Witness in Nigeria*, 175–92.

Edwards, Paul, ed. *Equiano's Travels: His Autobiography; The Interesting Narrative of the Life of Olaudah Equiano or Gustavus Vassa the African.* New York: Frederick Praeger, 1967.

Ehret, Christopher. "Writing African History from Linguistic Evidence." In Philips, *Writing African History*, 86–111.

Ejituwu, Nkparom C. *A History of Obolo (Andoni) in the Niger Delta.* Oron: Mason, 1991.

Ekechi, Felix. "An African View of the Legendary Vansina." In Harms et al., *Paths toward the Past*, 1–14.

———. "Colonialism and Christianity in West Africa: The Igbo Case, 1900–1915." *Journal of African History* 12, no. 1 (1971): 103–15.

———. "Gender and Economic Power: The Case of Igbo Market Women in Southeastern Nigeria." In *African Market Women and Economic Power: The Role of Women in African Economic Development*, edited by B. House-Midamba and F. K. Ekechi, 41–57. Westport, CT: Greenwood Press, 1995.

———. *Tradition and Transformation in Eastern Nigeria: A Sociopolitical History of Owerri and its Hinterland, 1902–1947.* Ohio: Kent State University Press, 1989.

Ekejiuba, Felicia. "The Aro System of Trade in the Nineteenth Century." *Ikenga: Journal of African Studies* 1, no. 1 (January 1972): 13–34.

———. "Omu Okwei, the Merchant Queen of Ossomari: A Biographical Sketch." *Journal of the Historical Society of Nigeria* 3, no. 4 (1967): 633–46.

Eldredge, Elizabeth. "Women in Production: The Economic Role of Women in Nineteenth-Century Lesotho." *Signs* 16, no. 4 (Summer 1991): 707–31.

Eleazu, Uma O. "Traditional Institutions and Modernization." *Ohafia Review*, no. 1 (April 1981): 9.

Eltis, David. *The Rise of African Slavery in the Americas*. New York: Cambridge University Press, 2000.

Fage, J. D. "African Societies and the Atlantic Slave Trade." *Past and Present*, no. 125 (1989): 97–115.

———. "Slavery and the Slave Trade in the Context of West African History." *Journal of African History* 10, no. 3 (1969): 393–404.

Fair, Laura. *Pastimes and Politics: Culture, Community and Identity in Post-Abolition Urban Zanzibar, 1890–1945*. Athens: Ohio University Press, 2001.

Falola, Toyin. "Mission and Colonial Documents." In Philips, *Writing African History*, 278–83.

———, ed. *Nigerian History, Politics and Affairs: The Collected Essays of Adiele Afigbo*. Trenton, NJ: Africa World Press, 2005.

Ferme, Mariane C. *The Underneath of Things: Violence, History, and the Everyday in Sierra Leone*. Berkeley: University of California Press, 2001.

Ferreira, Roquinaldo. *Cross-Cultural Exchange in the Atlantic World: Angola and Brazil during the Era of the Slave Trade*. New York: Cambridge University Press, 2012.

Finley, Moses. "Slavery." In *International Encyclopedia of the Social Sciences*, ed. David L. Sills and Robert K. Merton, 14:307–13. New York: Macmillan, 1968.

Finnegan, Ruth. *Oral Literature in Africa*. Oxford: Oxford University Press, 1970.

Flint, Karen E. *Healing Traditions: African Medicine, Cultural Exchange, and Competition in South Africa, 1820–1948*. Athens: Ohio University Press, 2008.

Forde, Cyril Daryll. *Efik Traders of Old Calabar*. London: Oxford University Press, 1956. Published for the International African Institute.

Forde, Cyril Daryll, and G. I. Jones. *The Ibo and Ibibio-Speaking Peoples of South-Eastern Nigeria*. London: International African Institute, 1950.

Fortes, Meyer. "Structure of Unilineal Descent Groups." *American Anthropologist*, no. 55 (1953): 17–41.

Foucault, Michel. *The History of Sexuality*. Vol. 1, *An Introduction*. New York: Vintage Books, 1978.

Friedman, Jonathan, and Michael J. Rowland, eds. *The Evolution of Social Systems*. London: Gerald Duckworth, 1978.

Gailey, H. A. *The Road to Aba*. London: London University Press, 1970.

Gerrits, Trudie. "Infertility and Matrilineality: The Exceptional Case of the Macua of Mozambique." In *Infertility Around the Globe*, edited by Marcia C. Inhorn and Frank van Balen, 233–246. Berkeley: University of California Press, 2002.

Getz, Trevor. *Slavery and Reform in West Africa: Toward Emancipation in Nineteenth-Century Senegal and the Gold Coast*. Athens: Ohio University Press, 2010.

Getz, Trevor, and Liz Clarke. *Abina and the Important Men: A Graphic History*. New York: Oxford University Press, 2016.

Glassman, Jonathan. "The Bondsman's New Clothes: The Contradictory Consciousness of Slave Resistance on the Swahili Coast." *Journal of African History* 32, no. 2 (1991): 277–312.

———. *Feasts and Riot: Revelry, Rebellion, and Popular Consciousness on the Swahili Coast, 1865–1888*. Portsmouth, NH: Heinemann, 1995.

Glazier, Jack. *Land and the Uses of Tradition among the Mbeere of Kenya*. Lanham: University Press of America, 1985.

Gomez, Michael. *Exchanging Our Country Marks: The Transformation of African Identities in the Colonial and Antebellum South*. Chapel Hill: University of North Carolina Press, 1998.

———. "A Quality of Anguish: The Igbo Response to Enslavement in the Americas." In Lovejoy and Trotman, *Trans-Atlantic Dimensions of Ethnicity in the African Diaspora*, 82–95.

Goody, Jack. "The Classification of Double Descent Systems." *Current Anthropology* 2, no. 1 (February 1961): 3–25.

———. *Comparative Studies in Kinship*. Stanford: Stanford University Press, 1969.

———. *Tradition, Technology, and the State in Africa*. Oxford: Oxford University Press, 1971.

Green, M. M. *Ibo Village Affairs*. London: Frank Cass, 1947.

———. *Ibo Village Affairs, Chiefly with Reference to the Village of Umueke Agbaja*. 2nd ed. London: Frank Cass, 1964.

———. *Land Tenure in an Ibo Village in South-Eastern Nigeria*. London: LSEPS, 1941.

Green, Toby. *The Rise of the Trans-Atlantic Slave Trade in Western Africa, 1300–1589*. Cambridge: Cambridge University Press, 2012.

Greene, Sandra E. *Gender, Ethnicity, and Social Change on the Upper Slave Coast: A History of the Anlo-Ewe*. Portsmouth, NH: Heinemann, 1996.

———. *Slave Owners of West Africa: Decision Making in the Age of Abolition*. Bloomington: Indiana University Press, 2017.

———. *West African Narratives of Slavery: Texts from Late Nineteenth- and Early Twentieth-Century Ghana*. Bloomington: Indiana University Press, 2011.

Gunkel, Henriette. "Through the Postcolonial Eyes: Images of Gender and Female Sexuality in Contemporary South Africa." *Journal of Lesbian Studies* 13, no. 1 (2009): 77–87.

Guy, Jeff. "Gender Oppression in Southern Africa's Precapitalist Societies." In *Women and Gender in Southern Africa to 1945*, edited by Cherryl Walker, 33–47. Claremont, South Africa: David Philip, 1990.

Guyer, Jane. "Household and Community in African Studies." *African Studies Review* 24, no. 2/3 (1981): 87–138.

Haenger, P. *Slaves and Slave Holders on the Gold Coast: Towards an Understanding of Social Bondage in West Africa*. Basel: P. Schlettwein, 2000.

Hafkin, Nancy, and Edna G. Bay, eds. *Women in Africa: Studies in Social and Economic Change*. Stanford: Stanford University Press, 1976

Hall, Douglass. *In Miserable Slavery: Thomas Thistlewood in Jamaica, 1750–86*. Mona, Jamaica: University of the West Indies Press, 1999.

Hall, Gwendolyn. *Slavery and African Ethnicities in the Americas: Restoring the Links*. Chapel Hill: University of North Carolina Press, 2005.

Halperin, David. "Is There a History of Sexuality?" In *The Lesbian and Gay Studies Reader*, edited by Henry Abelove, Michele Barale, and David Halperin, 416–431. London: Routledge, 1993.

Hammond, Dorothy, and Alta Jablow. *The Myth of Africa*. New York: Library of Social Science, 2012.

Handler, Jerome. "Custom and Law: The Status of Enslaved Africans in Seventeenth-Century Barbados." *Slavery and Abolition* 37, no. 2 (2016): 233–55.

Handler, Jerome, and Kenneth Bilby. "On the Early Use and Origin of the Term 'Obeah' in Barbados and the Anglophone Caribbean." *Slavery and Abolition* 22, no. 2 (2001): 87–100.

Handler, Jerome, and Robert Corruccini. "Weaning among West Indian Slaves: Historical and Bioanthropological Evidence from Barbados." *William and Mary Quarterly* 43, no. 1 (January 1986): 111–17.

Harms, Robert, Joseph Miller, David Newbury, and Michele Wagner, eds. *Paths toward the Past: African Historical Essays in Honor of Jan Vansina*. Atlanta: African Studies Association, 1994.

Harnischfeger, Johannes. "The Bakassi Boys: Fighting Crime in Nigeria." *Journal of Modern African Studies* 40, no. 1 (March 2003): 23–49.

Harris, Jack S. "The Position of Women in a Nigerian Society." *Transactions of the New York Academy of Sciences*, 2nd ser., 2, no. 5 (March 1940): 141–48.

———. "Some Aspects of the Economics of Sixteen Ibo Individuals." *Africa* 14, no. 6 (April 1944): 302–35.

Harris, Joseph E. *Africans and Their History*. New York: Meridan, 1998.

Harris, Rosemary. "The Influence of Ecological Factors and External Relations on the Mbembe Tribes of South-East Nigeria." *Africa* 32, no. 1 (1962): 38–52.

Hart, Kalada A. *Report of the Enquiry into the Dispute over the Obongship of Calabar.* Enugu, Nigeria: Enugu Government Printer, 1964.

Hawthorne, Walter. "'Being Now, as It Were, One Family': Shipmate Bonding on the Slave Vessel *Emilia*, in Rio de Janeiro and throughout the Atlantic World." *Luso-Brazilian Review* 45, no. 1 (2008): 53–77.

———. *From Africa to Brazil: Culture, Identity, and an Atlantic Slave Trade, 1600–1830.* New York: Cambridge University Press, 2010.

———. *Planting Rice and Harvesting Slaves: Transformations along the Guinea-Bissau Coast, 1400–1900.* Portsmouth, NH: Heinemann, 2003.

Hay, Margaret Jean, and Sharon Stichter, eds. *African Women South of the Sahara.* London: Longman, 1995.

Hearn, Jeff. "Theorizing Men and Men's Theorizing: Varieties of Discursive Practices on Men's Theorizing of Men." *Theory and Society* 27, no. 6 (December 1998): 781–816.

Henderson, Richard N. *The King in Every Man: Evolutionary Trends in Onitsha Society and Culture.* New Haven: Yale University Press, 1972.

Henige, David. "Oral Tradition as a Means of Reconstructing the Past." In Philips, *Writing African History*, 169–90.

Herskovits, Melville. *The Myth of the Negro Past.* 1941. Reprint, Boston: Beacon, 1958.

Higman, B. W. *Slave Populations of the British Caribbean, 1807–1834.* 1984. Reprint, Kingston: University of the West Indies Press, 1995.

Hirschmann, David and Megan Vaughan. "Food Production and Income Generation in a Matrilineal Society: Rural Women in Zomba, Malawi," *Journal of Southern African Studies* 10, no. 1 (October 1983): 86–99.

Hodgson, Dorothy L. "'Once Intrepid Warriors': Modernity and the Production of Maasai Masculinities." *Ethnology* 38, no. 2 (Spring 1999): 121–50.

Holden, Clare Janaki, and Ruth Mace. "Spread of Cattle Led to the Loss of Matrilineal Descent in Africa: A Coevolutionary Analysis." *Proceedings: Biological Sciences* 270, no. 1532 (2003): 2425–433.

Holy, Ladislov. *Strategies and Norms in a Changing Matrilineal Society: Descent, Succession, and Inheritance among the Toka of Zambia.* London: Cambridge University Press, 1986.

Hopkins, Anthony G. "Property Rights and Empire Building: Britain's Annexation of Lagos, 1861." *Journal of Economic History* 40, no. 4 (December 1980): 777–98.

Horton, Robin. "From Fishing Village to City-State: A Social History of New Calabar." In Douglas and Kaberry, *Man in Africa*, 37–58.

Hubbell, Andrew. "A View of the Slave Trade from the Margin: Souroudougou in the Late Nineteenth-Century Slave Trade of the Niger Bend." *Journal of African History* 42, no. 1 (2001): 25–47.

Hunwick, John. "Arabic Sources for African History," In Philips, *Writing African History*, 216–53.

Ibewuike, Victoria O. *African Women and Religious Change: A Study of the Western Igbo of Nigeria; With a Special Focus on Asaba Town*. Uppsala: Victoria O. Ibewuike, 2006.

Ifeka-Moller, Caroline. "Female Militancy and Colonial Revolt: The Women's War of 1929, Eastern Nigeria." In Ardener, *Perceiving Women*, 127–157.

Ifemesia, Chieka. *Southern Nigeria in the Nineteenth Century: An Introductory Analysis*. New York: NOK, 1978.

———. *Traditional Humane Living among the Igbo: An Historical Perspective*. Enugu, Nigeria: Fourth Dimension Publishers, 1979.

Igwegbe, Richard O. *The Original History of the Arondizuogu from 1635 to 1960*. Aba, Nigeria: International Press, 1962.

Ikime, Obaro. "Reconstructing Indirect Rule: The Nigerian Example." *Journal of the Historical Society of Nigeria* 4, no. 3 (1968): 421–38.

Ikpa, Ole U. *The Age Grade System: A Way of Life in Ohafia*. Lagos: 1984.

Illife, John. *Africans: The History of a Continent*. Cambridge: Cambridge University Press, 1995.

Isaacman, Allen F., and Barbara S. Isaacman. *Slavery and Beyond: The Making of Men and Chikunda Ethnic Identities in the Unstable World of South-Central Africa, 1750–1920*. Portsmouth, NH: Heinemann, 2004.

Isaacman, Allen F., and Derek Peterson. "Making the Chikunda: Military Slavery and Ethnicity in Southern Africa." In Brown and Morgan, *Arming Slaves*, 95–119.

Isichei, Elizabeth. *A History of African Societies to 1870*. Cambridge: Cambridge University Press, 1977.

———. *A History of the Igbo People*. London: Macmillan, 1976.

———. *The Ibo and the Europeans: The Genesis of a Relationship—to 1906*. New York: St. Martin's, 1973.

———. *Igbo Worlds: An Anthology of Oral Histories and Historical Descriptions*. Philadelphia: Institute for the Study of Human Issues, 1978.

Iwundu, M. "Naming and Heroism in Igbo Traditional Life." *Journal of Liberal Studies* 4, no. 1/2 (1994): 34-47.

Iyam, David. *The Broken Hoe: Cultural Reconfiguration in Biase Southeastern Nigeria*. Chicago: University of Chicago Press, 1995.

Jaja, E. A. *King Jaja of Opobo (1821–1891): A Sketch History of the Development and Expansion of Opobo*. Lagos: Opobo Action Council, 1977.

Jaja, S. O., E. O. Erim, and Bassey W. Andah, eds. *History and Culture of the Upper Cross River*. Enugu, Nigeria: Harris, 1990.

Jędrej, M. C. "Structural Aspects of a West African Secret Society." *Journal of Anthropological Research* 32, no. 3 (Autumn 1976): 234–45.

Johnston, Geoffrey. *Of God and Maxim Guns: Presbyterianism in Nigeria, 1846–1966*. Ontario: Wilfrid Laurier University Press, 1988.

———. "Ohafia 1911–40: A Study in Church Developments in Eastern Nigeria." *Bulletin of the Society for African Church History*, no. 2 (1966): 139–54.

Jones, G. I. "Ohaffia Obu Houses." *Nigerian Field* 6, no. 4 (1937): 169–71.
———. "The Political Organization of Old Calabar." In Forde, *Efik Traders of Old Calabar*, 148–57.
———. *The Trading States of the Oil Rivers*. Oxford: Oxford University Press, 1963.
Jones, W. O. "Manioc: An Example of Innovation in African Economics." *Economic Development and Cultural Change* 5, no. 2 (January 1957): 97–117.
Jun Yoo, Theodore. "The Biography of Ch'oe Yŏng-suk and the Politics of Gender in Colonial Korea." *Journal of Women's History* 21, no. 4 (2009): 161–63.
Kalu, U. Ogbu and Ogun U. Kalu. "The Battle of the Gods: Christianization of Cross River Igboland, 1903–1950." *Journal of the Historical Society of Nigeria* 10, no. 1 (1979): 1-18.
———, ed. *A Century and Half of Presbyterian Witness in Nigeria, 1846–1996*. Lagos: Ida-Ivory Press, 1996.
———. "The River Highway: Christianizing the Igbo." In Kalu, *A Century and Half of Presbyterian Witness in Nigeria*, 50–95.
Kanogo, Tabitha. *African Womanhood in Colonial Kenya, 1900–1950*. Athens: Ohio University Press, 2005.
Kimmel, Michael, Jeff Hearn, and R. W. Connell, eds. *Handbook of Studies on Men and Masculinities*. London: Sage, 2005.
Klein, Herbert, and Stanley Engerman. "Fertility Differentials between Slaves in the United States and the British West Indies: A Note on Lactation Practices and Their Possible Implications." *William and Mary Quarterly* 35, no. 2 (April 1978): 357–74.
Klein, Martin. "The Atlantic Slave Trade and Decentralized Societies." *Journal of African History* 42, no. 1 (2001): 49–65.
———. "The Impact of the Atlantic Slave Trade on the Societies of the Western Sudan." *Social Science History* 14, no. 2 (Summer 1990): 231–53.
———, ed. *Peasants in Africa: Historical and Contemporary Perspectives*. London: Sage, 1980.
———. *Slavery and Colonial Rule in French West Africa*. Cambridge: Cambridge University Press, 1998.
———. "Slavery and the Early State in Africa." *Social Evolution and History* 8, no. 1 (2009): 168–94.
———. "Studying the History of Those Who Would Rather Forget: Oral History and the Experience of Slavery." *History in Africa*, no. 16 (1989): 209–17.
———. "Women and Slavery in the Western Sudan." In Robertson and Klein, *Women and Slavery in Africa*, 67–92.
Klein, Martin, and Richard Roberts. "Gender and Emancipation in French West Africa." In Paton and Scully, *Gender and Slave Emancipation in the Atlantic World*, 162–80.

Kopytoff, Igor. "Matrilineality, Residence, and Residential Zones." *American Ethnologist* 4, no. 3 (1997): 539–58.

Kopytoff, Igor, and Suzanne Miers. "Introduction: 'African Slavery' as an Institution of Marginality." In Miers and Kopytoff, *Slavery in Africa*, 3–84.

Korieh, Chima Jacob. "The Invisible Farmer? Women, Gender, and Colonial Agricultural Policy in the Igbo Region of Nigeria, c. 1913–1954." *African Economic History*, no. 29 (2001): 117–62.

Kulikoff, A. *Tobacco and Slaves: The Development of Southern Cultures in the Chesapeake, 1680–1800*. Chapel Hill: University of North Carolina Press, 1986.

Kuper, Adam. *Anthropology and Anthropologists: The Modern British School*. New York: Routledge, 1996.

Kyomunhendo, Grace B., and Marjorie K. McIntosh. *Women, Work, and Domestic Virtue in Uganda, 1900–2003*. Athens: Ohio University Press, 2006.

Lancaster, Chet S. "Battle of the Sexes in Zambia: A Reply to Karla Poewe." *American Anthropologist* 81, no. 1 (March 1979): 117–19.

———. "Brideservice, Residence, and Authority among the Goba (N. Shona) of the Zambezi Valley." *Africa* 44, no. 1 (January 1974): 46–64.

———. *The Goba of the Zambezi: Sex Roles, Economics and Change*. Norman: University of Oklahoma Press, 1981.

———. "Women, Horticulture and Society in Sub-Saharan Africa." *American Anthropologist* 78, no. 3 (1976): 539–64.

Landers, J. G., and B. M. Robinson, eds. *Slaves, Subjects, and Subversives: Blacks in Colonial Latin America*. Albuquerque: University of New Mexico Press, 2006.

Langness, L. L. *The Study of Culture*. Novato, CA: Chandler and Sharp, 2005.

Latham, A. J. H. *Old Calabar, 1600–1891: The Impact of the International Economy upon a Traditional Society*. Oxford: Clarendon Press, 1973.

Law, Robin. "Ethnicity and the Slave Trade: 'Lucumi' and 'Nago' as Ethnonyms in West Africa." *History in Africa*, no. 24 (1997): 205–19.

———. *Ouidah: The Social History of a West African Slaving Port, 1727–1892*. Oxford: James Currey, 2004.

Leach, Edmund. *Rethinking Anthropology*. London: University of London Press, 1961.

Lebeuf, Annie M. D. "The Role of Women in the Political Organization of African Societies." In *Women of Tropical Africa*, edited by D. Paulme, 93–119. Berkeley: University of California Press, 1971.

Leith-Ross, Sylvia. *African Women: A Study of the Ibo of Nigeria*. London: Faber and Faber, 1938.

Leonard, Arthur Glyn. *The Lower Niger and Its Tribes*. London: Macmillan, 1906.

Lévi-Strauss, Claude. *Structural Anthropology*. Vol. 2. New York: Basic Books, 1976.

Lindsay, Lisa A. "Money, Marriage, and Masculinity on the Colonial Nigerian Railway." In Lindsay and Miescher, *Men and Masculinities in Modern Africa*, 138–155.

———. "'No Need . . . to Think of Home'? Masculinity and Domestic Life on the Nigerian Railway, c. 1940–61." *Journal of African History* 39, no. 3 (1998): 439–66.

———. *Working with Gender: Wage Labor and Social Change in Southwestern Nigeria*. Portsmouth, NH: Heinemann, 2003.

Lindsay, Lisa A., and Stephan F. Miescher, eds. *Men and Masculinities in Modern Africa*. Portsmouth, NH: Heinemann, 2003.

Livingston, Julie. *Debility and the Moral Imagination in Botswana*. Bloomington: Indiana University Press, 2005.

Lovejoy, Paul, ed. *Identity in the Shadow of Slavery: The Black Atlantic*. New York: Continuum, 2000.

———. *Transformations in Slavery: A History of Slavery in Africa*. 2nd ed. Cambridge: Cambridge University Press, 2000.

Lovejoy, Paul, and David Richardson. "Competing Markets for Male and Female Slaves: Prices in the Interior of West Africa, 1750–1850." *International Journal of African Historical Studies*, no. 28 (1995): 261–93.

———. "Trust, Pawnship, and Atlantic History: The Institutional Foundations of the Old Calabar Slave Trade." *American Historical Review* 104, no. 2 (April 1999): 333–55.

Lovejoy, Paul, and David V. Trotman, eds. *Trans-Atlantic Dimensions of Ethnicity in the African Diaspora*. New York: Continuum, 2003.

Lovett, Margot L. "From Sisters to Wives and 'Slaves': Redefining Matriliny and the Lives of Lakeside Tonga Women, 1888–1955." *Critique of Anthropology* 17, no. 2 (June 1997): 171–87.

Lowe, Joyce. "A Brief History of the Nigerian Field Society, 1930–2001." *Nigerian Field*, no. 66 (2001): 147–63.

Loyal, Steven. *The Sociology of Anthony Giddens*. London: Pluto Press, 2003.

Lyons, Robert, and Chinua Achebe. *Another Africa*. New York: Anchor Books, 1998.

MacGaffey, Wyatt. "Lineage Structure, Marriage, and the Family amongst the Central Bantu." *Journal of African History* 24, no. 2 (April 1983): 173–87.

Mahir, Saul. "Matrilineal Inheritance and Post-colonial Prosperity in Southern Bobo Country." *Man*, n.s., 27, no. 2 (June 1992): 341–62.

Mair, Lucille M. *A Historical Study of Women in Jamaica, 1655–1844*. Kingston: University of the West Indies Press, 2006.

Mandala, Elias C. *Work and Control in a Peasant Economy*. Madison: University of Wisconsin Press, 1990.

Mann, Gregory. "Old Soldiers, Young Men: Masculinity, Islam, and Military Veterans in Late 1950s Soudan Français (Mali)," in Lindsay and Miescher, *Men and Masculinities in Modern Africa*, 69–86.

Mann, Kristin. *Marrying Well: Marriage, Status and Social Change among the Educated Elite in Colonial Lagos*. Cambridge: Cambridge University Press, 1985.

———. *Slavery and the Birth of an African City: Lagos, 1760–1900*. Bloomington: Indiana University Press, 2007.

Manning, Patrick. *Slavery and African Life: Occidental, Oriental, and African Slave Trades*. Cambridge: Cambridge University Press, 1990.

Manuh, Takyiwaa. "Doing Gender Work in Ghana." In Cole, Manuh, and Miescher, *Africa After Gender?*, 125–149.

Martin, Phyllis. *Leisure and Society in Colonial Brazzaville*. Cambridge: Cambridge University Press, 1995.

Martin, Susan. "Gender and Innovation: Farming, Cooking and Palm Processing in the Ngwa Region, South-Eastern Nigeria, 1900–1930." *Journal of African History* 25, no. 4 (1984): 411–27.

Mathurin, Lucille. "The Arrivals of Black Women." *Jamaica Journal* 9, no. 2/3 (1975): 2–7.

Matory, J. Lorand. *Black Atlantic Religion: Tradition, Transnationalism, and Matriarchy in the Afro-Brazilian Candomblé*. Princeton: Princeton University Press, 2005.

Mba, E. I. *Condensed History of Church in the Wild Wood, 1904–1953*. Ohafia, Nigeria: SKA Press, 1973.

Mba, Nina. *Nigerian Women Mobilized: Women's Political Activity in Southern Nigeria, 1900–1965*. Berkeley: Institute of International Studies, University of California, 1982.

Mbah, Ndubueze L. "Female Masculinities, Dissident Sexuality, and the Material Politics of Gender in Early Twentieth-Century Igboland. *Journal of Women's History* 29, no. 4 (Winter 2017): 35–60.

———. "Matriliny, Masculinity and Contested Gendered Definitions of Ethnic Identity and Power in Nineteenth-Century Southeastern Nigeria." In *Gendering Ethnicity in African Women's Lives*, edited by Jan Bender Shetler. Madison: University of Wisconsin Press, 2015.

McCall, Daniel. "Introduction." In Philips, *Writing African History*, 1–24.

McCall, John C. "The Atlantic Slave Trade and the Ohafia Warrior Tradition: Global Forces and Local Histories." In Brown and Lovejoy, *Repercussions of the Atlantic Slave Trade*, 71–78.

———. *Dancing Histories: Heuristic Ethnography with the Ohafia Igbo* (Ann Arbor: University of Michigan Press, 2000).

———. "Dancing the Past: Experiencing Historical Knowledge in Ohafia, Nigeria." *Passages: A Chronicle of the Humanities*, no. 6 (1993): 8–9.

———. "Portrait of a Brave Woman." *American Anthropologist* 98, no. 1 (1996): 127–36.

McCaskie, T. C. "State and Society, Marriage and Adultery: Some Considerations towards a Social History of Pre-colonial Asante." *Journal of African History* 22, no. 4 (1981): 477–94.

McClintock, A. *Imperial Leather: Race, Gender and Sexuality in the Colonial Contest.* London: Routledge, 1995.

McIntosh, Susan K. "Archaeology and the Reconstruction of the African Past." In Philips, *Writing African History*, 51–85.

McKittrick, Meredith. "Forsaking Their Fathers? Colonialism, Christianity, and Coming of Age in Ovamboland, Northern Namibia." In Lindsay and Miescher, *Men and Masculinities in Modern Africa*, 33–47.

McNeill, William. "Mythistory, or Truth, Myth, History, and Historians." *American Historical Review* 91, no. 1 (February 1986): 1–10.

McSheffrey, G. "Slavery, Indentured Servitude, Legitimate Trade, and the Impact of Abolition in the Gold Coast, 1874–1910." *Journal of African History* 24, no. 3 (1983): 349–68.

Meagher, K. "Hijacking Civil Society: The Inside Story of the Bakassi Boys Vigilante Group of South-Eastern Nigeria." *Journal of Modern African Studies* 45, no. 1 (March 2007): 89–115.

Meek, C. K. *Law and Authority in a Nigerian Tribe: A Study in Indirect Rule.* 1937. Reprint, London: Oxford University Press, 1950.

Meillassoux, Claude. "Female Slavery." In Robertson and Klein, *Women and Slavery in Africa*, 49–66.

———. "The Role of Slavery in the Economic and Social History of Sahelo-Sudanic Africa." In *Forced Migration: The Impact of the Export Slave Trade on African Societies*, edited by Joseph E. Inikori, 74–99. New York: Africana, 1982.

Miers, Suzanne, and Igor Kopytoff, eds. *Slavery in Africa: Historical and Anthropological Perspectives.* Madison: University of Wisconsin Press, 1977.

Miers, Suzanne, and Richard Roberts, eds. *The End of Slavery in Africa.* Madison: University of Wisconsin Press, 1988.

Miescher, Stephan. "The Life Histories of Boakye Yiadom: Exploring the Subjectivity and 'Voices' of a Teacher-Catechist in Colonial Ghana." In *African Words, African Voices: Critical Practices in Oral History*, edited by Luise White, Stephan Miescher, and David William Cohen, 162–193. Bloomington: Indiana University Press, 2001.

———. *Making Men in Ghana.* Bloomington: Indiana University Press, 2005.

———. "The Making of Presbyterian Teachers: Masculinities and Programs of Education in Colonial Ghana." In Lindsay and Miescher, *Men and Masculinities*, 89–108.

Miller, Joseph C. "Domiciled and Dominated: Slaving as a History of Women." In Campbell, Miers, and Miller, *The Modern Atlantic*, 284–304.

———. *Way of Death: Merchant Capitalism and the Angolan Slave Trade, 1730–1830.* Madison: University of Wisconsin Press, 1988.

Mintz, Sidney Wilfred, and Richard Price. *The Birth of African-American Culture: An Anthropological Perspective.* Boston: Beacon, 1976.

Mitchell, Clyde J. *The Kalela Dance: Aspects of Social Relationships among Urban Africans in Northern Rhodesia*. Manchester: Manchester University Press, 1956.

———. "Marriage, Matriliny and Social Structure among the Yao of Southern Nyasaland." *International Journal of Comparative Sociology* 3, no. 1 (September 1962): 29–42.

Moore, Henrietta, and Megan Vaughan. *Cutting Down Trees: Gender, Nutrition and Agricultural Change in the Northern Province of Zambia, 1890–1990*. Portsmouth, NH: Heinemann, 1994.

Moore, Sally Falk. *Anthropology and Africa: Changing Perspectives on a Changing Scene*. Charlottesville: University of Virginia Press, 1994.

Morgan, Jennifer L. *Laboring Women: Reproduction and Gender in New World Slavery*. Philadelphia: University of Philadelphia Press, 2004.

Morgan, Kenneth. "Slave Women and Reproduction in Jamaica, ca. 1776–1834." In Campbell, Miers, and Miller, *The Modern Atlantic*, 27–45.

Morgan, Philip. "The Cultural Implications of the Atlantic Slave Trade: African Regional Origins, American Destinations and New World Developments." *Slavery and Abolition* 18, no. 1 (2008): 122–45.

Morrell, Robert, ed. *Changing Men in Southern Africa*. Pietermaritzburg: University of Natal Press, 2001.

———. *From Boys to Gentlemen: Settler Masculinity in Colonial Natal, 1880–1920*. Pretoria: Unisa Press, University of South Africa, 2001.

———. "Of Boys and Men: Masculinity and Gender in Southern Africa." *Journal of Southern African Studies* 24, no. 4 (1998): 605–30.

Morrell, Robert, and Lahoucine Ouzgane, eds. *African Masculinities: Men in Africa from the Late Nineteenth Century to the Present*. New York: Palgrave Macmillan, 2005.

Morrissey, Marietta. *Slave Women in the New World: Gender Stratification in the Caribbean*. Lawrence: University Press of Kansas, 1989.

Mugambi, Helen. "The 'Post-Gender' Question in African Studies." In Cole, Manuh, and Miescher, *Africa after Gender?*, 285–302.

Mullin, Michael. *Africa in America: Slave Acculturation and Resistance in the American South and the British Caribbean*. Urbana: University of Illinois Press, 1992.

———. "Laura Smalligan's *Jonkonu, a Jamaican Slave Dance*: Contesting the African in African-American." *Slavery and Abolition* 35, no. 1 (2015): 142–55.

Murdock, George. *Social Structure*. New York: Macmillan, 1949.

Murray, Stephen O., and Will Roscoe, eds. *Boy-Wives and Female Husbands: Studies in African Homosexualities*. New York: Palgrave, 1998.

Musisi, Nakanyinke. "Women, 'Elite Polygyny,' and Buganda State Formation." *Signs* 16, no. 4 (1991): 757–86.

Nair, Kannan K. *Politics and Society in South Eastern Nigeria, 1841–1906*. London: Frank Cass, 1972.

Nchonwa, Ogbeyalu. "The Role of Women in Development." *Ohafia Review*, no. 1 (April 1981): 7–9.
Ndambuki, Berida, and Claire C. Robertson. *"We Only Come Here to Struggle": Stories from Berida's Life*. Bloomington: Indiana University Press, 2000.
Newell, Stephanie. *The Forger's Tale: The Search for Odeziaku*. Athens: Ohio University Press, 2006.
Newman, Simon P., Michael L. Deason, Yannis P. Pitsiladis, Antonio Salas, and Vincent A. Macaulay. "The West African Ethnicity of the Enslaved in Jamaica." *Slavery and Abolition* 34, no. 3 (2013): 376–400.
Ngom, Fallou. "Lexical Borrowings as Pathways to Senegal's Past and Present." In *Africanizing Knowledge: African Studies across the Disciplines*, edited by Toyin Falola and Christian Jennings, 125–147. New Brunswick, NJ: Transaction, 2002.
Niane, D. T. *Sundiata: An Epic of Old Mali*. Rev. ed. Harlow, Eng.: Pearson, 2006.
Njaka, Elechukwu N. *Igbo Political Culture*. Evanston: Northwestern University Press, 1974.
Njoku, Akuma-Kalu. "Before the Middle Passage: Igbo Slave Journeys to Old Calabar and Bonny." In Brown and Lovejoy, *Repercussions of the Atlantic Slave Trade*, 57–69.
Njoku, Onwuka. *Inter-village Trade in Ohafia, 1900–1979*. Nsukka: University of Nigeria, 1981.
———. *Ohafia: A Heroic Igbo Society*. Ohafia, Nigeria: Whytam, 2000.
Njoku, Raphael Chijoke. *African Cultural Values: Igbo Political Leadership in Colonial Nigeria, 1900–1966*. New York: Routledge, 2006.
———. "'Ogaranya' (Wealthy Men) in Late Nineteenth Century Igboland: Chief Igwebe Odum of Arondizuogu, c. 1860–1940." *African Economic History*, no. 36 (2008): 27–52.
Nkata, E. E. "The Role of Women in Development." *Ikoro* 2, no. 2 (1976): 35–36.
Northrup, David. "The Compatibility of the Slave and Palm Oil Trades in the Bight of Biafra." *Journal of African History* 17, no. 3 (1976): 353–64
———. *Trade without Rulers: Pre-colonial Economic Development in South-Eastern Nigeria*. Oxford: Clarendon Press, 1978.
Nsugbe, Philip O. *Ohaffia: A Matrilineal Ibo People*. Oxford: Oxford University Press, 1974.
Nugent, Stephen. "Editorial." *Critique of Anthropology* 17, no. 2 (June 1997): 123–24.
Nwabara, S. N. *Iboland: A Century of Contact with Britain, 1860–1960*. London: Hodder and Stoughton, 1977.
Nwabueze, Emeka. "The Masquerade as Hero in Igbo Traditional Society." *Frankfurter Afrikanistische Blatter*, no. 1 (1989): 95–107.

Nwachukwu, I. N., O. U. Oteh, C. C. Ugoh, and C. Ochomma. "Buying Attitude of Yam Consumers in Southeastern Nigeria." *Tropicultura* 29, no. 4 (2011): 238–42.

Nwokeji, G. Ugo. "African Conceptions of Gender and the Slave Traffic." *William and Mary Quarterly* 58, no. 1 (January 2001): 47–68.

———. "The Atlantic Slave Trade and Population Density: A Historical Demography of the Biafran Hinterland." *Canadian Journal of African Studies* 34, no. 3 (2000): 616–55.

———. *The Slave Trade and Culture in the Bight of Biafra: An African Society in the Atlantic World*. Cambridge: Cambridge University Press, 2010.

Nwosu, Patrick U. "The Age of Cultural Hybridisation: A Case Study of Okonko Society vis-à-vis Christianity in Igboland." *Anthropologist* 12, no. 3 (2010): 161–65.

———. "The Role of Okonko Society in Preserving Igbo Environment." *Journal of Human Ecology* 31, no. 1 (2010): 59–64.

———. "The Theory and Practice of Secrecy in Okonko and Ogboni Societies." Accessed April 30, 2019. https://www.academia.edu/518980/The_Theory_and_Practice_of_Secrecy_in_Okonko_and_Ogboni_Societies_in_Nigeria.

Nzegwu, Nkiru, "Chasing Shadows: The Misplaced Search for Matriarchy," *Canadian Journal of African Studies* 32, no. 3 (1998): 594–622.

Nzekwu, Onuora. "Omo Ukwu Temple." *Nigeria Magazine*, no. 81 (June 1964): 117–26.

O'Barr, Jean, and Firmin-Sellers, Kathryn. "African Women in Politics." In Hay and Stichter, *African Women South of the Sahara*, 189–212.

———, ed. *Perspectives on Power: Women in Africa, Asia, and Latin America*. Durham, NC: Duke University Center for International Studies, 1982.

Obiani, Paul. "The Stigmatization of the Descendants of Slaves in Igboland." In Brown and Lovejoy, *Repercussions of the Atlantic Slave Trade*, 321–28.

Obuba, Nnenna E. *The History and Culture of Ohafia, covering from about 1432 to 2008: Collated Oral Tradition*. Ebem Ohafia, Nigeria: Lintdsons, 2008.

Ochonu, Moses E. *Colonial Meltdown: Northern Nigeria in the Great Depression*. Athens: Ohio University Press, 2009.

Offiong, Daniel A. *Continuity and Change in Some Traditional Societies of Nigeria*. Zaria, Nigeria: Ahmadu Bello University Press, 1998.

———. "The Status of Slaves in Igbo and Ibibio of Nigeria." *Phylon* 46, no. 1 (1985): 49–57.

Oha, Obododimma. "Praise Names and Power De/constructions in Contemporary Igbo Chiefship." *Culture, Language, and Representation*, no. 7 (2009): 101–16.

Ohadike, Don C. "The Decline of Slavery among the Igbo." In Miers and Roberts, *The End of Slavery in Africa*, 443–57. Madison: University of Wisconsin Press, 1988.

———. "The Influenza Pandemic of 1918–1919 and the Spread of Cassava Cultivation on the Lower Niger: A Study in Historical Linkages." *Journal of African History* 22, no. 3 (July 1981): 379–91.

Ojo, Olatunji. "Child Slaves in Pre-colonial Nigeria, c.1725–1860." *Slavery and Abolition* 33, no. 3 (2012): 417–34.

Okonjo, Isaac M. *British Administration in Nigeria, 1900–1950: A Nigerian View*. New York: NOK, 1974.

Okonjo, Kamene "The Dual Sex Political System in Operation: Igbo Women and Community Politics in Midwestern Nigeria." In Hafkin and Bay, *Women in Africa*, 45–58.

Onor, Sandy O. *The Ejagham Nation in the Cross River Region of Nigeria*. Ibadan, Nigeria: Kraft Books, 1994.

Onyeneke, Augustine O. *The Dead among the Living: Masquerades in Igbo Society*. Nimo, Nigeria: Holy Ghost Congregation, Province of Nigeria, 1987.

Oriji, John N. *Political Organization in Nigeria since the Late Stone Age: A History of the Igbo People*. New York: Palgrave Macmillan, 2011.

———. "Slave Trade, Warfare and Aro Expansion in the Igbo Hinterland." *Genève-Afrique* 24, no. 2 (1986): 101–18.

———. *Traditions of Igbo Origin: A Study of Pre-colonial Population Movements in Africa*. Rev. ed. New York: Peter Lang, 1994.

Osborn, Emily Lynn. *Our New Husbands Are Here: Households, Gender, and Politics in a West African State from the Slave Trade to Colonial Rule*. Athens: Ohio University Press, 2011.

Osinubi, Taiwo Adetunji. "Chinua Achebe and the Uptakes of African Slaveries." *Research in African Literatures* 40, no. 4 (2009): 25–46

Oteieno, Wambui Waiyaki. *Mau Mau's Daughter: A Life History*. Boulder: Lynne Rienner, 1998.

Oti, Onwuka E. *The Age Grade System and Otomu Ceremony in Ohafia*. Aba, Nigeria: EMS Corporate, 2007.

Ottenberg, Phoebe. "The Changing Economic Position of Women among the Afikpo Ibo." In *Continuity and Change in African Cultures*, edited by W. T. Bascom and M. J. Herskovits, 205–23. Chicago: University of Chicago Press, 1959.

Ottenberg, Simon. *Double Descent in an African Society: The Afikpo Village-Group*. Seattle: University of Washington Press, 1968.

Oyewunmi, Oyeronke. *The Invention of Women: Making an African Sense of Western Gender Discourses*. Minneapolis: University of Minnesota Press, 1997.

———. "Visualizing the Body: Western Theories and African Subjects." In *African Gender Studies: A Reader*, edited by Oyeronke Oyewunmi, 3–21. New York: Palgrave Macmillan, 2005.

Pargas, Damian A. "Slave Crucibles: Interstate Migrants and Social Assimilation in the Antebellum South." *Slavery and Abolition* 36, no. 1 (2015): 26–39.

Paton, Diana. "Enslaved Women and Slavery before and after 1807." History in Focus, Institute of Historical Research. Accessed February 2017. https://www.history.ac.uk/ihr/Focus/Slavery/articles/paton.html.

Paton, Diana, and Pamela Scully, eds. *Gender and Slave Emancipation in the Atlantic World*. Durham, NC: Duke University Press, 2005.

Patterson, Orlando. *Slavery and Social Death: A Comparative Study*. Cambridge, MA: Harvard University Press, 1982.

Peabody, S. "Negresse, Mulatresse, Citoyenne: Gender and Emancipation in the Caribbean." In Paton and Scully, *Gender and Slave Emancipation in the Atlantic World*, 56–78.

Peel, J. D. Y. *Religious Encounter and the Making of the Yoruba*. Bloomington: Indiana University Press, 2003.

Perham, Margery. *Native Administration in Nigeria*. London: Oxford University Press, 1937.

Perks, Robert, and Alistair Thomson. *The Oral History Reader*. London: Routledge, 1998.

Perry, Donna L. "Wolof Women, Economic Liberalization, and the Crisis of Masculinity in Rural Senegal." *Ethnology* 44, 3 (Summer 2005): 207–26.

Peters, Pauline E. "Against the Odds: Matriliny, Land and Gender in the Shire Highland of Malawi." *Critique of Anthropology* 17, no. 2 (1997): 189–210.

———. "Introduction: Revisiting the Puzzle of Matriliny in South-Central Africa." *Critique of Anthropology* 17, no. 2 (1997): 125–46.

Philips, John Edward, ed. *Writing African History*. New York: University of Rochester Press, 2005.

Phiri, Kings M. "Some Changes in the Matrilineal Family System among the Chewa of Malawi Since the Nineteenth Century." *Journal of African History* 24, no. 2 (1983): 257–74.

Piot, Charles. "Of Slaves and the Gift: Kabre Sale of Kin During the Era of the Slave Trade." *Journal of African History* 37, 1 (1996): 36–46.

———. *Remotely Global: Village Modernity in West Africa*. Chicago: University of Chicago Press, 1999.

Poewe, Karla. *Matrilineal Ideology: Male-Female Dynamics in Luapala, Zambia*. London: Academic Press, 1981.

———. "Matrilineal Ideology: The Economic Activities of Women in Luapula, Zambia." In *The Versatility of Kinship*, edited by Linda S. Cordell and Stephen Beckerman, 333–58. London: Academic Press, 1980.

———. "Matriliny and Capitalism: The Development of Incipient Classes in Luapula, Zambia." *Dialectical Anthropology* 3, no. 4 (November 1978): 331–47.

———. "Matriliny in the Throes of Change: Kinship, Descent and Marriage in Luapula, Zambia. Part One." *Africa* 48, no. 3 (1978): 205–18.

———. "Matriliny in the Throes of Change: Kinship, Descent and Marriage in Luapula, Zambia. Part Two." *Africa* 48, no. 4 (1978): 353–67.

———. *Religion, Kinship, and Economy in Luapula, Zambia*. New York: Edwin Meller, 1989.
———. "Religion, Matriliny, and Change: Jehovah's Witnesses and Seventh-Day Adventists in Luapula, Zambia." *American Ethnologist* 5, no. 2 (May 1978): 303–21.
Powdermaker, Hortense. *Copper Town: Changing Africa, The Human Situation on the Rhodesian Copperbelt*. New York: Harper and Row, 1962.
Pratten, David, ed. "Perspectives on Vigilantism in Nigeria." Special issue, *Africa* 78, no. 1 (2008).
Radcliffe-Brown, A. R. *A Natural Science of Society*. Chicago: University of Chicago Press, 1957.
Ramphele, Mamphela. *Across Boundaries: The Journey of a South African Woman Leader*. New York: Feminist Press, 1996.
Rattray, Robert Sutherland. *Ashanti*. Oxford: Clarendon Press, 1923.
———. *Ashanti Law and Constitution*. Oxford: Clarendon Press, 1929.
Richards, Audrey. "Some Types of Family Structure amongst the Central Bantu." In *African Systems of Kinship and Marriage*, edited by A. R. Radcliffe-Brown and Daryll Forde, 207–51. London: Oxford University Press, 1950.
Roberts, Christopher. "Making Peace with the Power of Death: Tabwa Matriliny and Memory." *Michigan Quarterly Review* 26, no. 1 (Winter 1987): 163–74.
Roberts, Richard. "Production and Reproduction of Warrior States: Segu Bambara and Segu Tokolor, c. 1712–1890." *International Journal of African Historical Studies* 13, no. 3 (1980): 389–419.
———. *Warriors, Merchants, and Slaves: The State and the Economy in the Middle Niger Valley, 1700–1914*. Stanford: Stanford University Press, 1987.
Roberts, Richard, and Suzanne Miers. "The End of Slavery in Africa." In Miers and Roberts, *The End of Slavery in Africa*, 3–68.
Robertson, Claire C. "Post-proclamation Slavery in Accra: A Female Affair?" In Robertson and Klein, *Women and Slavery in Africa*, 220–45.
Robertson, Claire C., and Martin A. Klein. "Women's Importance in African Slave Systems." In Robertson and Klein, *Women and Slavery in Africa*, 3–25.
———, eds. *Women and Slavery in Africa*. Portsmouth, NH: Heinemann, 1997
Robertson, Claire C., and Marsha Robinson. "Re-modeling Slavery as if Women Mattered." In Campbell, Miers, and Miller, *The Modern Atlantic*, 253–283.
Rodney, Walter. "African Slavery and Other Forms of Social Oppression on the Upper Guinea Coast in the Context of the Atlantic Slave-Trade." *Journal of African History* 7, no. 3 (1966): 431–43.
———. *A History of the Upper Guinea Coast, 1545 to 1800*. Oxford: Oxford University Press, 1971.
Rucker, Walter. *Gold Coast Diasporas: Identity, Culture, and Power*. Bloomington: Indiana University Press, 2015.

Russell, Penny. "Life's Illusions: The 'Art' of Critical Biography." *Journal of Women's History* 21, no. 4 (2009): 152–56.

Sacks, Karen. "An Overview of Women and Power in Africa." In O'Barr, *Perspectives on Power*, 1–10.

Salamone, Frank A. "Hausa Concepts of Masculinity and the 'Yan Dauda." In *African Masculinities: Men in Africa from the Late Nineteenth Century to the Present*, edited by Robert Morrell and Lahoucine Ouzgane, 75–86. New York: Palgrave Macmillan, 2005.

Sarr, Assan. *Islam, Power, and Dependency in the Gambia River Basin: The Politics of Land Control, 1790–1940*. New York: University of Rochester Press, 2016.

Schmidt, Elizabeth. *Peasants, Traders and Wives: Shona Women in the History of Zimbabwe, 1870–1939*. Portsmouth, NH: Heinemann, 1992.

Schneider, David M., and Kathleen Gough, eds. *Matrilineal Kinship*. Berkeley: University of California Press, 1962.

Schoenbrun, David. *A Green Place, A Good Place*. London: Heinemann, 1998.

Searing, James F. *West African Slavery and Atlantic Commerce: The Senegal River Valley, 1700–1860*. Cambridge: Cambridge University Press, 2003.

Semley, Lorelle. *Mother Is Gold, Father Is Glass: Gender and Colonialism in a Yoruba Town*. Bloomington: Indiana University Press, 2011.

Shaw, Rosalind. *Memories of the Slave Trade: Ritual and the Historical Imagination in Sierra Leone*. Chicago: University of Chicago Press, 2002.

Shepherd, Verene A. "'Petticoat Rebellion'? The Black Woman's Body and Voice in the Struggle for Freedom in Colonial Jamaica." In *In the Shadow of the Plantation: Caribbean History and Legacy*, edited by Alvin O. Thompson, 17–39. Kingston: Ian Randle, 2002.

Shetler, Jan Bender, ed. *Gendering Ethnicity in African Women's Lives*. Madison: University of Wisconsin Press, 2015.

Shumway, Rebecca. *The Fante and the Transatlantic Slave Trade*. New York: University of Rochester Press, 2014.

Simmons, Donald C., ed. *Holman's Voyage to Old Calabar*. Calabar, Nigeria: American Association for African Research, 1959.

Smaldone, Joseph P. *Warfare in the Sokoto Caliphate: Historical and Sociological Perspectives*. Cambridge: Cambridge University Press, 1977.

Smalligan, Laura M. "An Effigy for the Enslaved: Jonkonnu in Jamaica and Belisario's *Sketches of Character*." *Slavery and Abolition* 32, no. 4 (2011): 561–81.

Smedley, Audrey. *Women Creating Patriliny: Gender and Environment in West Africa*. Walnut Creek, CA: AltaMira, 2004.

Sparks, Randy J. *The Two Princes of Calabar: An Eighteenth-Century Atlantic Odyssey*. Cambridge, MA: Harvard University Press, 2004.

———. *Where the Negroes Are Masters: An African Port in the Era of the Slave Trade*. Cambridge, MA: Harvard University Press, 2014.

Spaulding, Jay, and Stephanie Beswick, eds. *African Systems of Slavery*. Trenton, NJ: Africa World Press, 2010.

Stilwell, Sean. *Paradoxes of Power: The Kano "Mamluks" and Male Royal Slavery in the Sokoto Caliphate, 1804–1903*. Portsmouth, NH: Heinemann, 2004.

———. *Slavery and Slaving in African History*. Cambridge: Cambridge University Press, 2014.

Stoler, Ann, and Frederick Cooper. "Between Metropole and Colony: Rethinking a Research Agenda." In *Tensions of Empire, Colonial Cultures in a Bourgeois World*, edited by Frederick Cooper and Ann Stoler, 1–37. Berkeley: University of California Press, 1997.

Sundiata, Ibrahim K. *From Slavery to Neoslavery: The Bight of Biafra and Fernando Po in the Era of Abolition, 1827–1930*. Madison: University of Wisconsin Press, 1996.

Sweet, James. *Domingos Álvares, African Healing, and the Intellectual History of the Atlantic World*. Chapel Hill: University of North Carolina Press, 2011.

———. *Recreating Africa: Culture, Kinship, and Religion in the African-Portuguese World, 1441–1770*. Chapel Hill: University of North Carolina Press, 2003.

Tadman, Michael. "The Demographic Costs of Sugar: Debates on Slave Societies and Natural Increase in the Americas." *American Historical Review* 105, no. 5 (2000): 1534–75.

Thompson, Paul. *The Voice of the Past: Oral History*. Oxford: Oxford University Press, 1978.

Thornton, John K. *Africa and Africans in the Making of the Atlantic World, 1400–1680*. Cambridge: Cambridge University Press, 1992.

———. "Armed Slaves and Political Authority in Africa in the Era of the Slave Trade, 1450–1800." In Brown and Morgan, *Arming Slaves*, 79–94.

———. *A Cultural History of the Atlantic World, 1250–1820*. New York: Cambridge University Press, 2012.

———. "European Documents and African History." In Philips, *Writing African History*, 254–72.

———. "Sexual Demography: The Impact of the Slave Trade on Family Structure," In Robertson and Klein, *Women and Slavery in Africa*, 39–48.

Tilley, Louise A. "People's History and Social Science History." *Social Science History* 7, no. 4 (Autumn 1983): 457–74.

Trotman, David V. "Africanizing and Creolizing the Plantation Frontier of Trinidad, 1787–1838." In Lovejoy and Trotman, *Trans-Atlantic Dimensions of Ethnicity in the African Diaspora*, 218–39.

Turner, Sasha. *Contested Bodies: Pregnancy, Childrearing, and Slavery in Jamaica*. Philadelphia: University of Pennsylvania Press, 2017.

Turner, Victor. *Schism and Continuity in an African Society: A Study of Ndembu Village Life*. London: Manchester University Press, 1957.

Twaddle, Michael. *Kakungulu and the Creation of Uganda, 1868–1928.* Athens: Ohio University Press, 1993.

Uche, A. K. *Customs and Practices in Ohaffia.* Aba, Nigeria: A. K. Uche, 1960.

Uche, U. U. "Change and Law in Ohafia." *Ohafia Review,* no. 1 (April 1981): 8.

Uchendu, Victor C. *The Igbo of Southeast Nigeria.* New York: Holt, Rinehart, and Winston, 1965.

———. "Slaves and Slavery in Igboland, Nigeria." In Miers and Kopytoff, *Slavery in Africa,* 121–132.

Udensi, A. I. "Elevating the Ohafia Woman." *Ikoro* 3, no. 3 (1998): 40–44.

Uduma, Uduma O. *The People of Ohafia Ezema.* Calabar, Nigeria: Arinson, 2007.

Uka, N. "A Note on the 'Abam' Warriors of Igbo Land." *Ikenga: Journal of African Studies* 1, no. 2 (1972): 76–82.

Ukiwo, U. "Deus Ex Machina or Frankenstein Monster? The Changing Roles of Bakassi Boys in Eastern Nigeria." *Democracy and Development: A Journal of West African Affairs* 3, no. 1 (2002): 39–51.

Uma, Eze Onuoha. *Factors in Ohafia History.* Ohafia, Nigeria: Eze Onuoha Uma, 1989.

———. *Guidance and Destiny: My Life and Thought; Autobiography of His Royal Highness, Eze Elder Onuoha Uma, Udumeze of Isiama Ohafia.* Ohafia, Nigeria: Eze Onuoha Uma, 2002.

Uriom, Kamalu. *The Adventures of Ancient Ikperikpeogu Warriors.* Owerri, Nigeria: Basich, 1990.

Vail, Leroy, and Landeg White, eds. *Power and the Praise Poem: Southern African Voices in History.* Charlottesville: University of Virginia Press, 1991.

Van Allen, Judith. "'Aba Riots' or Igbo 'Women's War'? Ideology, Stratification, and the Invisibility of Women." In Hafkin and Bay, *Women in Africa,* 59–85.

———. "'Sitting on a Man': Colonialism and the Lost Political Institutions of Igbo Women." *Canadian Journal of African Studies* 6, no. 2 (1972): 165–81.

Vansina, Jan. *Oral Tradition as History.* Madison: University of Wisconsin Press, 1985.

———. *Paths in the Rainforests.* Madison: University of Wisconsin Press, 1990.

Vermeulen, Heather V. "Thomas Thistlewood's Libidinal Linnaean Project: Slavery, Ecology, and Knowledge Production." *Small Axe* 22, no. 1 (2018): 18–38.

Vuyk, Trudeke. *Children of One Womb: Descent, Marriage, and Gender in Central African Societies.* Leiden, Neth.: Centre of Non-Western Studies, Leiden University, 1991.

Waetjen, Thembisa. *Workers and Warriors: Masculinity and the Struggle for Nation in South Africa.* Urbana: University of Illinois Press, 2004.

Ward, J. R. *British West Indian Slavery, 1750–1834: The Process of Amelioration.* Oxford: Clarendon Press, 1988.

Watson-Franke, Maria-Barbara. "Masculinity and the 'Matrilineal Puzzle.'" *Anthropos* 87, no. 4/6 (1992): 475–88.

Werbner, Richard. *Tears of the Dead: The Social Biography of an African Family.* Washington, DC: Smithsonian Institution, 1996.

White, Luise. Afterword to *Men and Masculinities*, ed. Lindsay and Miescher, 177–89.

——. "Separating the Men from the Boys: Constructions of Gender, Sexuality, and Terrorism in Central Kenya, 1939–1959." *International Journal of African Historical Studies* 23, no. 1 (1990): 1–25.

——. *Speaking with Vampires: Rumor and History in Colonial Africa.* Berkeley: University of California Press, 2000.

White, Luise, Stephan Miescher, and David William Cohen, eds. *African Words, African Voices: Critical Practices in Oral History.* Bloomington: Indiana University Press, 2001.

Wilks, Ivor. *Akwamu 1640–1750: A Study of the Rise and Fall of a West African Empire.* Trondheim: Norwegian University of Science and Technology, Department of History, 2001.

——. "Land, Labour, Capital and the Forest Kingdom of Asante: A Model of Early Change." In *The Evolution of Social Systems*, edited by Jonathan Friedman and Michael J. Rowland, 487–534. London: Gerald Duckworth, 1978.

Wipper, Audrey. "Riot and Rebellion among African Women: Three Examples of Women's Political Clout." In O'Barr, *Perspectives on Power*, 50–72.

——. "Women's Voluntary Associations." In Hay and Stichter, *African Women South of the Sahara*, 69–86.

Wood, John Colman. *When Men Are Women: Manhood among Gabra Nomads of East Africa.* Madison: University of Wisconsin Press, 1999.

Workshop on Widowhood Practices. *Widowhood Practices in Imo State: Proceedings of the Better Life Programme for Rural Women Workshop, Multi-Purpose Hall, Owerri, June 6–7.* Owerri, Nigeria: Government Printer, 1989.

Wright, Donald R. "Requiem for the Use of Oral Tradition to Reconstruct the Precolonial History of the Lower Gambia." *History in Africa*, no. 18 (1991): 399–408.

Wright, Marcia. *Strategies of Slaves and Women: Life-Stories from East/Central Africa.* New York: Lilian Barber, 1993.

Yankah, Kwesi. *Speaking for the Chief: Akyeame and the Politics of Akan Royal Oratory.* Bloomington: Indiana University Press, 1995.

Zeuske, M. "Sidney Mintz: Work, Creolization, Atlanticization," *Review* (Fernand Braudel Center) 34, no. 4 (2011): 423–28.

UNPUBLISHED SOURCES

Azuonye, Chukwuma. "The Narrative War Songs of the Ohafia Igbo: A Critical Analysis of Their Characteristic Features in Relation to Their Social

Functions." PhD thesis, University of London, 1979. https://eprints.soas.ac.uk/29523/.
Chima, Agwu D. "The Age Grade System in Traditional Ohafia up to 1935." BA thesis, University of Nigeria Nsukka, October 1996.
Diptee, Audra A. "Atlantic Connections: An African Cohort in the Making of a Slave Society, Jamaica 1775–1807." PhD thesis, University of Toronto, 2006.
Kalu, Agwu, L. N. Chika, and N. O. Nkata. "The Advent of Christianity in Ohafia: An Unpublished Work by Isiama Parish of the Presbyterian Church of Nigeria." 2005.
Kalu, Grace U. "Women in Social and Economic Change in Ohafia, 1945–1990." MA thesis, University of Nigeria Nsukka, 2005.
Kalu, Nwoke C. "Cassava Revolution in Ohafia up to 1990: A Historical Analysis of Economic Change." BA thesis, University of Nigeria Nsukka, July 1991.
Korieh, Chima Jacob. "Widowhood among the Igbo of Eastern Nigeria." MA thesis, University of Bergen, Norway, June 1996.
Ndukwe, Mberi. "From Slavery to the Order of British Empire: A Biography of Chief Eke Kalu Uwaoma of Ohafia." BA thesis, University of Nigeria Nsukka, October 1998.
Norman, Neil L. "An Archaeology of West African Atlanticization: Regional Analysis of the Huedan Palace Districts and Countryside (Benin), 1650–1727." PhD diss., University of Virginia, 2008.
Odimmegwa, Augustine Chukwuemeka. "Widowhood and the Dignity of Womanhood in Igboland: A Pastoral Challenge to the Discipleship of the Roman Catholic Church in Igboland." January 1, 2010.
Oji, Oji K. "A Study of Migrations and Warfare in Ohafia." BA thesis, University of Nigeria Nsukka, 1974.
Uma, Uma O. "Ohafia and Her Neighbors: Intergroup Relations up to 1967." BA thesis, University of Nigeria Nsukka, 1984.

Index

Abina and the Important Men (Getz), 133–34
abortion, 120–21
adultery, 51
Africanists, 6, 28–29
Afro-Atlanticists, 6
age-grades, 34, 45–47
agriculture: commercialized, 99–00; land ownership and, 126; military pursuits and, 55; palm produce, 40, 122–23; women and, 35–37, 40, 55, 97, 122–23; yam cultivation, 36–38, 97, 163
Agwu, Otuwe (oke-nwami), 158–60, 162–63, 172–75
Ahebi Ugbabe (female warrant chief), 131, 154–55, 172
akpan (male court), 13, 45–49; power limits of, 47–49; retirement from, 47
ancestors, 42–43, 89–90; elders as living, 47; governance rights due to, 182–83; spirits of, 90
Anlo-Ewe people, 9
anthropologists, 31–32, 42; colonial, 35, 45
archery, 85
architecture of Ohafia villages, 84–85
Aro people, 63–65, 68–71; British expedition against, 86–87, 144–45, 167; incorporation of slave-wives, 118–19
Atlantic slave trade: big men and, 11; British Parliament committee on, 97–98; commodification of captives in, 105–6; demography of captives in, 105–10; "Ebo/Eboe" (Biafran) slaves and, 99–100, 102–3, 106–13, 116–17, 119–21; female slave-owners and, 185–86; mortality rates in, 106–8; Ohafia military practices and, 62–63,

72–73; socioethnic differentiation of captives in, 102; valuation of slaves in, 98, 108; Virginia and, 15
attire: of colonial elites, 148–49, 160; jooji cloth, 67; of warriors, 67, 178

Balanta people, 7, 72
Batê people, 8
Benguela, 7, 185–86
Bight of Biafra, xvi; British slave trade and, 94; demography of captives from, 15, 76–77, 99, 103; domestic slavery in, 99–00, 117–19, 183–84; female marginality thesis, 96–97; military slaving in, 14–15, 62–65, 68–78, 98–99; settling of, 32–35
big man masculinity, 10–12, 155–56, 160
Bonny, 108–9, 137–39; slave traders from, 105–6
boycotts against men, 21–22, 52–53

cannibalism, 86–87
cassava, 37
children: pawning of, 125–26, 138–39; of slaves, 120–21; slaves, 125–26, 133–34
Christianity: domestication of women and, 18, 161, 164–65, 170; modernity and, 135, 168; Presbyterian masculinity, 165
Church of Scotland Mission (CSM), 86–87, 144–45, 167–70; Kalu Uwaoma and, 150
citizenship: matrilineages and, 41–42, 182–83; women as definers of, 53, 118
clothing. *See* attire
Collins, Robert, 27, 167–69; house of, 146

305

colonial actors: British military, 86–87, 144–45, 167; cannibalism myths and, 86–87; district officers, 153–55; elite Africans and, 147–49, 168, 170–71; emancipation and, 133–34; family structure and, 164; hegemony over local rulers, 178; Kalu Ezelu Uwaoma and, 136, 143–46, 149–54; missionaries, 86–87, 144–46, 161, 167–70; patriarchy and, 3, 7, 154–55, 161, 168; records of, 27–28, 163
confraternities. *See* ite odo secret society; okonko secret society
conspicuous consumption, 147–49
courts: church elders and, 168–69; emancipation and British, 133–34; female, 13, 45–46, 49–54; male, 13, 45–49; Native Courts, 81, 145, 153, 161, 177; okonko, 80–81
creolization, 102, 111–12
Cross River, 32–33
CSM. *See* Church of Scotland Mission

Dahomey, 9, 87–88, 185
deities, 42–43; egbo, 85; sacrificial dedication to, 91–92; ukwuzi and, 82, 91; Uma Ukwu (the Great Uma), 82, 91
dibias (medicine men), 113–15, 173–74, 186–87; Ekea Udensi, 113–14; Kalu Ezelu Uwaoma, 143–44, 151; medicine pilgrimage (ije ogwu) of, 174; ogaranya and, 114–15, 174; social status of, 140, 143–44, 174–75
divorce, 35, 41; Christianity and, 169

education: industrial, 170; missionary, 145, 168–71; Ohafia Girls' School, 171; women and, 161, 170
Ekea Udensi (ogaranya ex-slave), 113–15
ekpe. *See* okonko secret society
elders, 47; church, 168–70
elephants, 38
elites, 8, 147–49, 168, 170–71
emancipation: circumvention of, 126, 133–34; gender differences in, 125, 130–35, 143; of Kalu Ezelu Uwaoma, 134–35; marriage and, 134; slave owners and, 132
enyi nnaya (father's friend), 127–28
Equiano, Olaudah, 78
ese-ike institution, 82. *See also* ite odo secret society
Esulalu Diola people, 72

European fashions, 147–49
Ezelu, Kalu. *See* Uwaoma, Kalu Ezelu
ezie-nwami (female king), 50–52
ezie-ogo (male king), 48–49

fatherhood: matriliny and, 166–67; property practices and, 126–28
femininity, 163–64, 173; Presbyterian, 165

Getz, Trevor, 133–34
Gold Coast: British slave trade and, 94; circumvention of abolition in, 133–34; female slave-owners in, 185–86; gendered emancipation in, 132–33
guns, 39

headhunting, 1–2, 33, 63–66; symbolic, 2–3, 25, 66–67, 159, 179
heritable property, 41, 126–28
historical revisionism, 22, 32, 162
houses, 146–47, 174–75, 179
hunting, 38–39

idioms, 29–30
Igboland. *See* Bight of Biafra; Ohafia
igbu isi (cutting a head), 1–2; changing meanings of, 2–3, 25, 66–67, 159, 179
ije akpaka (ritual declaration of war), 21, 53, 55–56
ike nwami (female captivity), 104, 118–19; ogaranya masculinity and, 123–24
ikoro (war drum), 83–85, 178
ikperikpeogu (warrior masculinity), 62–65, 82–85, 175; captives, ropes, and, 65–66; ite odo and, 82–84
ikpirikpe (female court), 13, 45–46, 49–54; drum, 51; monopoly on domestic markets, 40, 50–51; patrilineal Igbo organizations vs., 49–50; retirement from, 47; ritual declarations of war, 53
ikpo mgbogho (social ostracism), 21–22, 53–54
inheritances, 41, 126–28
interviews, 21–23, 163–64
ite odo secret society, 61, 78, 81–84; burial of members, 88–89; cannibalism myths, 86–87; public performances, 83; ufiem and, 82–83, 89–90

Jamaica: Africanization of, 121; as destination for Biafran captives, 16, 94; disembarkation ratios of slaves in, 110–11; gender and slavery in, 16, 99–01, 105–8, 109–13, 119–21; pregnancy and rebellion in, 119–21; pro-natalism in, 111–12
jooji cloth, as status symbol, 67

Kalu Ezelu Uwaoma. See Uwaoma, Kalu Ezelu
Kalu Oki (tradition singer), 103–4
kidnapping, 71–72, 76, 138; slave raids and, 77–78
kings: ezie-nwami (female), 50–52; ezie-ogo (male), 48–49
kinship practices, 187–88; Christianity and, 164; matrilineal kinship networks, 34–35; military/slaving zones and, 13, 55, 74; oke-nwami and, 165–66; slavery and, 10–11, 100–102, 104–5, 117, 125–28, 182–86, 188–89. See also matrilineages; patrilineages; ukwuzi (protective kinship contracts)

land: ownership, 126; purification rite, 54–55
law enforcement, 48, 51
legitimate trade, 2, 17–18, 122
leopards, 38; caps, 67, 178
lineages. See ancestors; matrilineages; patrilineages

marriage: Christianity and, 170–71, 171–72; to deities, 91–92; emancipation and, 134; endogamous, 50; masculinity and, 127; matrilineages and, 34, 41–42; ujo and, 67, 127
masculinity: biological sex and, 4, 162–63, 180; marriage and, 127; Presbyterian, 165; yams and, 37–38. See also ikperikpeogu (warrior masculinity)); ogaranya (wealth) masculinity; oke-nwami (female husbands); ufiem (hegemonic masculinity)
matrilineages, 16–17, 31–32; citizenship and, 41–42, 182–83; fatherhood and, 166; inheritance of property and, 41, 126–28; kinship networks, 34–36; marriage and, 34, 41–42; matriarchs, 43–44, 166, 172–73; of Ohafia settlers, 23; slaves and continuity of, 42, 92, 117–18, 182–85
matronship, 19, 171; Ohafia women and, 162
Mbgafo, Nne, 58
medicine men. See dibias
military heroism, 64–65
military practices: agrarian production and, 55; Atlantic slave trade and, 72–73; confederacies and, 74; emancipation and, 134; ije akpaka (ritual declaration of war), 21, 53, 55–56; patriliny and, 34, 71; slaving and, 14–15, 62–65, 68–78, 98–99
missionaries, 86–87, 144–46, 161, 167–71; education by, 145, 168–70; records of, 27
mobility, social. See social mobility
morality: Christian, 169; Ohafia women's shaping of, 45, 53, 55

Naomi of Oguta (ogaranya), 124, 125
Native Court system, 81, 145, 153, 161; clerks of, 177
nsibidi secret language, 79
nwannediya (husband's sisters), 42, 55, 166–65; oke-nwami and, 173

obu (patrilineage meeting houses), 85, 159
ogaranya (wealth) masculinity, 2–3; Atlanticization and changes in, 131–32; colonialism and, 144–56; conspicuous consumption and, 147–49, 160; dibias and, 174; female, 124–25, 158–60, 163, 166, 173–79; ike nwami (possessing women) and, 123–24; polygyny and, 147–48; slaves and, 90–91, 114, 131–32, 142–43; wealth redistribution and, 155–56, 176, 178; yams and, 37–38
Ohafia: British occupation of, 145; geography of, 33–34; political system, 49–55; sociosexual system of, 165–66; traditions, 20–25, 186–87 (see also rites and rituals); tradition singers, 23–24; village architecture, 84–85; war songs and war dance, 23–25, 57–58, 71–72, 90
Ohafia Girls' School, 171
oke-nwami (female husbands), 162–63, 165–66, 172–79, 185; wives of, 173
Oki, Kalu (tradition singer), 103–4
okonko secret society, 61, 78–81; origins of, 79; slaves and, 81

Okwei, Omu (ogaranya), 124–25
Olugu, Unyang (ikperikpeogu), 59
Omoukwu shrine, 82, 91
Opobo, 137–40
oral histories and traditions, 20–25, 29–30, 58–59, 71–72
osu (spiritual slaves), 91–92
Otuwe Agwu (oke-nwami), 158–60, 162–63, 172–75

palm produce, 40; women and, 122–23
panyaring, 125, 138–39
patrilineages: Atlantic slave trade and, 187–88; matrilineage property transfer to, 127; meeting houses, 85, 159; military institutions and, 34; of Ohafia settlers, 23
pawnship, 75–76, 125–26, 138–39
pot monuments. See ududu
prisons, 177–78
property practices and slave ownership, 126–28

raids, 33, 63, 68–78, 99; consequences of Ohafia, 75–76; kidnapping and, 15, 77–78
revisionism, historical, 22, 32, 162
rites and rituals: age-grade initiation, 46–47; cleansing (iyi ose), 54; declaration of war (ije akpaka), 21, 53, 55–56; deification of warriors (idoru nna), 89; as historical memorialization, 21–22, 186–87; land purification (idighi omara), 54–55; virginity testing (uzo iyi), 21, 54–55; warrior purification, 57

sacrifices: animal, 57; human, 87–88, 90–91
schools. See education
secret societies: akang and obon, 71; masquerade, 48; okonko, 61, 78–81. See also ite odo secret society
Senegal, 132, 185–86
Senegambia, 7, 72
sexual exploitation, 100, 115–16
sexuality, 165–66; colonial regulation of, 164–65; ikpirikpe (female court) and, 51, 53; oke-nwami as dissident, 172–79, 185
slaves: British subjecthood of ex-slaves, 140; child, 75–76, 125–26, 133–34; coping mechanisms of, 137; debt, 125–26, 138–39; gender inequality among domestic, 121–26; matrilineage continuity and, 42, 92, 117–18, 182–85; okonko and, 81; palm produce and, 122–23; property practices and ownership of, 126–28; punitive enslavement, 51; as reproductive units, 104–5, 113, 118; spiritual, 91–92; ujo vs. male, 93; as wealth, 2, 90, 117; wives and, 23, 173. See also Atlantic slave trade; ike nwami (female captivity); Jamaica
social mobility: Christian missionaries and gendered, 167–71; of hunters, 38–39; ikperikpeogu (warrior masculinity) and, 62, 82–84; of oke-nwami and female ogaranya, 161–66, 172–79; slavery and gendered, 119, 125–26, 130–35, 143. See also Uwaoma, Kalu Ezelu
songs: foreign wives and, 55; ikpo mgbogho (social ostracism) and, 54; war, 23–25, 71–72, 90
spirit mediums. See dibias
strikes by women, 21–22, 52–53

teachers, 168–69; matrons as, 171
trade: Biafran domestic slave, 62–63, 65, 99–00, 117–19; okonko and, 79; palm produce, 123; regional, 26–27, 75; women's empowerment through, 39–40. See also Atlantic slave trade; legitimate trade
traditions. See Ohafia: traditions; rites and rituals
tradition singers, 23–24
trophies: animal, 38; human head, 33, 58, 62
Udensi, Ekea (ogaranya ex-slave), 113–15
ududu (pot monuments), 42–43, 170, 172; male vs. female, 43, 44, 85; for warriors, 89
Uduma festivals, 43–44
ufiem (hegemonic masculinity), 1–5, 57–59; colonialism and, 3, 144–56; fathers, sons, and, 127–28; hunting and, 38–39; ite odo and, 82–83, 89–90; jooji cloth and, 67; in Ohafia vs. other West African societies, 64; purification ritual after attaining, 57; ujo as property of, 142; women and, 4–5, 58–59

Ugbabe, Ahebi (female warrant chief), 131, 154–55, 172
ujo (degendered men), 2; male slaves vs., 93; marriage and, 127; ostracization of, 67–68, 84; as property, 142; as robbers and kidnappers, 71–72; women and, 58–59, 67
Uka, Unyang (oke-nwami), 158–60, 162–63, 175–79
Ukpai, Uma Ukwu (ite odo founder), 81–82
ukwuzi (protective kinship contracts), 69; Aro and Ohafia, 63–65, 68–71, 71; deties and, 82, 91; military/slaving zones and, 55, 74–76; violations of, 72
Unyang Olugu (ikperikpeogu), 59
Uwaoma, Kalu Ezelu, 3, 131–32, 135–47, 149–57; ascendancy to ogaranya, 143–47, 149–56; captivity and escape, 138–43; colonial actors and, 136; public works of, 155–56; Unyang Uka and, 177

vampirism, 87
Virginia, 15
virginity testing, 21, 54–55

war dance, Ohafia, 25, 57–58
war drums, 83–85, 178
warfare. *See* ikperikpeogu (warrior masculinity); military practices
warrant chiefs, 152–53, 161; Ahebi Ugbabe, 131, 154–55; Kalu Ezelu Uwaoma, 149, 151–54; social mobility of, 131, 149
warriors: attire of, 67, 178; boasts of, 82, 84–85; female, 58–59, 62; human heads and, 87–88; ikoro (war drum) and, 84–85; merchant-warriors, 14, 80, 90–91; Ohafia as, 63–65, 70–71; purification ritual of, 57; recruitment of, 71. *See also* ikperikpeogu (warrior masculinity); ite odo secret society; military practices
war-song narratives, 23–25, 71–72; ite odo members and, 90
wealth: land and, 126, 174; ogaranya and redistribution of, 155–56, 176, 178; okonko and, 80–81; okpogho (brass rods) as, 127; in people, 10–11, 90, 117, 123–25, 150; in yams, 37–38. *See also* ogaranya (wealth) masculinity
womb practices, 119–21
women: agriculture and, 35–37, 40, 55, 97; boycotts and strikes by, 52–53; as breadwinners, 35–37, 39–40, 43–44; colonialism and power of, 7, 21; contestation of eroding power, 3, 19; as domestic Biafran slaves, 98–00; palm produce and, 122–23; as reproductive units, 113; ufiem performance of, 4–5, 58–59; ujo and, 58–59

yams, 36–38, 97, 163; masculinity and, 37–38; new yam festivals, 83–84